THE
WAY
THINGS
WORK

THE
WAY
THINGS
WORK

DAVID MACAULAY
WITH
NEIL ARDLEY

DK

LONDON, NEW YORK, MUNICH,
MELBOURNE, AND DELHI

Project Editor David Burnie
Designer Peter Luff
Revised Edition
Senior Editor Sue Leonard
Art Editor Cathy Chesson
Production Kate Oliver

First published in Great Britain in 1988
by Dorling Kindersley Limited, London
80 Strand, London WC2 ORL
A Penguin Company
Reprinted 1989, 1990 (twice), 1991, 1992, 1994, 1995, 1996, 1997
Revised Editions 1998, 2004, 2006, 2010

A CIP catalogue record for this book is available from the British Library

ISBN-13: 978-1-4053-0238-8

Colour reproduction by Colourscan, Singapore
Printed and bound in Hong Kong by Toppan

Discover more at
www.dk.com

CONTENTS

INTRODUCTION

To ANY MACHINE, work is a matter of principle, because everything a machine does is in accordance with a set of principles or scientific laws. To see the way a machine works, you can take the covers off and look inside. But to understand what goes on, you need to get to know the principles that govern its actions. The machines in this and the following parts of *The New Way Things Work* are therefore grouped by their principles rather than by their uses. This produces some interesting neighbours: the plough rubs shoulders with the zipper, for example, and the hydroelectric power station with the dentist's drill. They may look different, be vastly different in scale, and have different purposes, but when seen in terms of principles, they work in the same way.

MACHINERY IN MOTION

Mechanical machines work with parts that move. These parts include levers, gears, belts, wheels, cams, cranks, and springs, and they are often interconnected in complex linkages, some large enough to move mountains and others almost invisible. Their movement can be so fast that it disappears in a blur of spinning axles and whirling gears, or it can be so slow that nothing seems to be moving at all. But whatever their nature, all machines that use mechanical parts are built with the same single aim: to ensure that exactly the right amount of force produces just the right amount of movement precisely where it is needed.

MOVEMENT AND FORCE

Many mechanical machines exist to convert one form of movement into another. This movement may be in a straight line (in which case it is often backward-and-forward, as in the shuttling of a piston-rod) or it may be in a circle. Many machines convert linear movement into circular or rotary movement and vice-versa, often because the power source driving the machine moves in one way and the machine in another. But whether direction is altered or not, the mechanical parts move to change the force applied into one – either larger or smaller – that is appropriate for the task to be tackled. Mechanical machines all deal with forces. In one way they are just like people when it comes to getting them on the move: it always takes some effort. Movement does not simply occur of its own accord, even when you drop something. It needs a driving force – the push of a motor, the pull of muscle or gravity, for example. In a machine, this driving force must then be conveyed to the right place in the right amount. When you squeeze and twist the handles of a can opener, the blade cuts easily through the lid of the can. This device makes light work of something that would otherwise be impossible. It does this not by giving you strength that you do not have, but by converting the force that your wrist produces into the most useful form for the job – in this case, by increasing it – and applying it where it is needed.

HOLDING MATTER TOGETHER

Every object on Earth is held together and in place by three basic kinds of force; virtually all machines make use of only two of them. The first kind of force is gravity, which pulls any two pieces of matter together. Gravity may seem to be a very strong force, but in fact it is by far the weakest of the three. Its effects are noticeable only because it depends on the masses of the two pieces of matter involved, and because one of these pieces of matter – the whole Earth – is enormous. The second force is the electrical force that exists between atoms. This is responsible for electricity, a subject explored in Part 4 of the book. Electrical force binds the atoms that make up all materials, and it holds them together with tremendous strength. Movement in machines is transmitted – unless the parts break – only because the atoms and molecules (groups of atoms) in these parts are held together by electrical force. So all mechanical machines use this force indirectly. In addition, some machines, such as springs and friction devices, use it directly, both to produce movement and to prevent it. The third and strongest force is the nuclear force that binds particles in the nuclei of atoms. This force is released only by machines that produce nuclear power.

THE CONSERVATION OF ENERGY

Underlying the actions of all machines is one principle which encompasses all the others – the conservation of energy. This is not about saving energy, but about what happens to energy when it is used. It holds that you can only get as much energy out of a machine as you put into it in the first place – no more and no less. As a motor or muscles move to supply force to a machine, they give it energy; more force or more movement provides more energy. Movement is a form of energy called kinetic energy. It is produced by converting other forms of energy, such as the potential energy stored in a spring, the heat in a petrol engine, the electric energy in an electric motor, or the chemical energy in muscles. When a machine transmits force and applies it, it can only expend the same amount of energy as that put into it to get things moving. If the force the machine applies is to be greater, then the movement produced must be correspondingly smaller, and vice-versa. Overall, the total energy always remains the same. The principle of conservation of energy governs all actions. Springs may store energy, and friction will convert energy to heat, but when everything is taken into account, no energy is created and none destroyed. If the principle of conservation of energy were to vanish, then nothing would work. If energy were destroyed as machines worked, then, no matter how powerful they might be, they would all slow down and stop. And if the workings of machines created energy, then all machines would get faster and faster in an energy build-up of titanic proportions. Either way, the world would end – with a whimper in one case and a bang in the other. But the principle of conservation of energy holds good and all machines obey. Or nearly all. Nuclear machines are an exception – but that is a story for the second part of this book.

THE INCLINED PLANE

ON CAPTURING A MAMMOTH

In the spring of that year, I was invited to the land of the much sought-after woolly mammoth, a land dotted by the now familiar high wooden towers of the mammoth captors. In ancient times the mammoth had been hunted simply for its meat. But its subsequent usefulness in industry and growing popularity as a pet had brought about the development of a more sophisticated and less terminal means of apprehension.

Each unsuspecting beast was lured to the base of a tower from which a boulder of reasonable dimensions was then dropped from a humanitarian height onto its thick skull. Once stunned, a mammoth could easily be lead to the paddock where an ice pack and fresh swamp grass would quickly overcome hurt feelings and innate distrust.

THE PRINCIPLE OF THE INCLINED PLANE

The laws of physics decree that raising an object, such as a mammoth-stunning boulder, to a particular height requires a certain amount of work. Those same laws also decree that no way can ever be found to reduce that amount. The ramp makes life easier not by altering the amount of work that is needed, but by altering the *way* in which the work is done.

Work has two aspects to it: the effort that you put in, and the distance over which you maintain the effort. If the effort increases, the distance must decrease, and vice versa.

This is easiest to understand by looking at two extremes. Climbing a hill by the steepest route requires the most effort, but the distance that you have to cover is shortest. Climbing up the gentlest slope requires the least effort, but the

distance is greatest. The work you do is the same in either case, and equals the effort (the force you exert) multiplied by the distance over which you maintain the effort.

So what you gain in effort, you pay in distance. This is a basic rule that is obeyed by many mechanical devices, and it is the reason why the ramp works: it reduces the effort needed to raise an object by increasing the distance that it moves.

The ramp is an example of an inclined plane. The principle behind the inclined plane was made use of in ancient times. Ramps enabled the Egyptians to build their pyramids and temples. Since then, the inclined plane has been put to work in a whole host of devices from locks and cutters to ploughs and zippers, as well as in all the many machines that make use of the screw.

While the process was more or less successful, it had a couple of major drawbacks. The biggest problem was that of simply getting a heavy boulder to the right height. This required an almost Herculean effort, and Hercules was not due to be born for several centuries yet. The second problem was that the mammoth, once hit, would invariably crash into the tower, either hurling his captors to the ground, or at least seriously damaging the structure.

After making a few calculations, I informed my hosts that both problems could be solved simultaneously by building earth ramps rather than wooden towers. The inherent sturdiness of the ramp would make it virtually indestructible should a mammoth fall against it. And now, rather than trying to hoist the boulder straight up, it could be rolled gradually to the required height, therefore needing far less effort.

At first, the simplicity of my solution was greeted with understandable scepticism. "What do we do with the towers?" they asked. I made a few more calculations and then suggested commercial and retail development on the lower levels and luxury apartments above.

THE WEDGE

In most of the machines that make use of the inclined plane, it appears in the form of a wedge. A door wedge is a simple application; you push the sharp end of the wedge under the door and it moves in to jam the door open.

The wedge acts as a moving inclined plane. Instead of having an object move up an inclined plane, the plane itself can move to raise the object. As the plane moves a greater distance than the object, it raises the object with a greater force. The door wedge works in this way. As it jams under the door, the wedge raises the door slightly and exerts a strong force on it. The door in turn forces the wedge hard against the floor, and friction (see pp.82-3) with the floor makes the wedge grip the floor so that it holds the door open.

HOW EFFORT AND DISTANCE ARE LINKED

The sloping face of this ramp is twice as long as its vertical face. The effort that is needed to move a load up the sloping face is therefore half that needed to raise it up the vertical face.

HALF EFFORT
FULL EFFORT

SLOPING FACE

VERTICAL FACE

LOCKS AND KEYS

Here's a puzzle not unconnected with locks: how to separate two blocks held together by five two-part pins. The gap in each pin is at a different height. In order to separate the blocks, the pins must be raised so that the gaps line up.

Knowing the principle of the inclined plane, we insert a wedge. It pushes up the pins easily enough, but by the wrong distances.

More thought suggests five wedges — one for each pin. This raises the pins so that the gaps line up, freeing the two halves of the block. However, the wedges themselves are now stuck fast in the lower half.

The key to the puzzle is just that — a key — because the block is a simplified cylinder lock. The serrated edge of the key acts as a series of wedges that raises the pins to free the lock. Because the serrations on the key are double-sided, the key can be removed after use. The springs will then push the pins firmly back into position, closing the lock.

PINS

SPRING

CAM

CYLINDER

BOLT

KEY

BOLT PULLED BACK

KEY TURNED

CYLINDER LOCK

When the door is closed, the spring presses the bolt into the door frame. Inserting the key raises the pins and frees the cylinder. When the key is turned, the cylinder rotates, making the cam draw back the bolt against the spring. When the key is released, the spring pushes back the bolt, rotating the cylinder to its initial position and enabling the key to be withdrawn.

BOLT PIN

BOLT

TUMBLERS

STUMP

SPRING

KEY

2 TURNING THE KEY
The key lifts the tumblers. The bolt pin is freed so that it can move along the slots.

3 KEY HALFWAY
As the key continues to turn, it engages the bolt, moving it outwards.

4 DOOR LOCKED
When the bolt is fully extended, the springs make the tumblers fall back, securing the bolt pin.

1 DOOR OPEN
The springs hold the tumblers down. The bolt pin is held in front of the stump in each tumbler so that the bolt cannot move.

LEVER LOCK

A lever lock works in much the same way as a cylinder lock. The projections on the key align slots in a set of different-sized tumblers so that the bolt can move. The key then turns to slide the bolt in or out.

[13]

CUTTING MACHINES

Nearly all cutting machines make use of the wedge, a form of inclined plane. A wedge-shaped blade converts a forward movement into a parting movement that acts at right angles to the blade.

MOVEMENT DOWNWARDS

MOVEMENT SIDEWAYS

WEDGE-SHAPED BLADES

SCISSORS

Each blade acts as a first-class lever (see p.19). The sharpened edges of the blades form two wedges that cut with great force into a material from opposite directions. As they meet, they part the material sideways.

AXE

An axe is simply a wedge attached to a shaft. The axe's long movement downwards creates a powerful sideways force that splits open the wood.

The axe has another built-in wedge: a sliver of metal is driven into the top of the shaft, and this jams the shaft tightly into the socket in the axe's head.

SERRATED BLADES

MOVEMENT SIDEWAYS

ELECTRIC TRIMMER

An electric trimmer contains two serrated blades driven by a crank mechanism (see pp.48-9). The blades move to and fro over each other. As gaps open between the serrations, stems or hairs enter to be trapped and then sliced as the blades cross. The trimmer's blades act as paired wedges like the blades of scissors.

BLADE SCREEN

CIRCLE OF BLADES

ELECTRIC SHAVER

A shaver contains a fine screen through which hairs protrude as the shaver is slid over the skin. The screen holds the hairs so that cutting blades under the screen can slice through them. Each circle of blades is pressed against the screen by a sprung drive shaft.

THE CAN OPENER

HANDLE

CUTTING WHEEL

HANDLE

SPUR GEARS

A can opener has a sharp-edged cutting blade or wheel that slices into the lid. A toothed wheel fits beneath the lip of the can, and rotates the can so that the cutting wheel is forced into the lid. Two further toothed wheels — one above the other — form a pair of spur gears (see p.37) to transmit the turning force from the handle.

THE PLOUGH

A plough is a wedge that is dragged through the ground either by a draught animal or a tractor. It cuts away the top layer of soil, and then lifts and turns over the layer. In this way, the soil is broken up for planting crops. In addition, vegetation growing in or lying on the soil is buried so that it rots and provides nutrients for the crops. The plough is one of our oldest machines. Wooden ploughs have been in use for about five thousand years, although metal ploughs date back less than two centuries.

THE MAIN PARTS OF A PLOUGH

SIDE VIEW

TOP VIEW

LANDSIDE

COULTER

SHARE

MOULDBOARD

A plough has four main parts, which are all made of steel. The coulter precedes the main body of the plough, which consists of the share, mouldboard and landside. The coulter, share and mould-board all act as wedges, and can exert great force to plough hard and heavy soil.

THE PLOUGHING SEQUENCE

THE COULTER *slices a furrow in the soil.*

The coulter creates a furrow by making a vertical cut in the soil. With animal ploughs, the coulter is a knife-like blade. Tractor-drawn ploughs normally have disc coulters, which are sharp-edged wheels that spin freely as the plough is drawn forwards.

The share follows the coulter, making a horizontal cut and freeing the top layer of soil. Attached to the share is the mouldboard, which lifts and turns the layer. The landside is fixed to the side of the mouldboard and slides along the vertical wall of the furrow. It thrusts the mouldboard outwards to move the layer of soil.

THE SHARE *cuts loose the top layer of soil.*

THE MOULDBOARD *lifts and turns the layer of soil.*

THE ZIP[PER

T he zipper cleverly exploits the principle of the inclined plane to join or separate two rows of interlocking teeth. The zipper's slide contains wedges that turn the little effort with which you pull it into a strong force that opens and closes the fastener. The teeth are designed so that they can only be opened or closed one after the other. Without using the slide, it is practically impossible to free the teeth or make them mesh together.

SLIDE

INSIDE THE SLIDE

UPPER WEDGE

LOWER WEDGES

WEDGES AT WORK

As you open a zipper, the triangular upper wedge in the slide detaches the teeth and forces them apart. On closing, the two lower wedges (which are often the curved sides of the slide) force the teeth back together so that they intermesh. Plastic zippers contain two intermeshing spirals instead of two rows of teeth.

LEVERS

ON WEIGHING A MAMMOTH

*B*efore being shipped to its final destination, a mammoth must be weighed. I was fortunate enough in one village to witness the procedure at first hand. The centre of a tree trunk was placed directly on a boulder. One end of the trunk was then pulled down and the mammoth encouraged to sit on it. No sooner did the beast seem reasonably comfortable than a number of villagers scrambled onto the other end of the trunk. Slowly their end sank and, as it did, the startled mammoth rose into the air. I was told that when the trunk reached a horizontal position, the combined weight of the people would equal that of the mammoth. This seemed reasonable enough.

THE PRINCIPLE OF LEVERS

The tree trunk is acting as a lever, which is simply a bar or rod that tilts on a pivot, or fulcrum. If you apply a force by pushing or pulling on one part of the lever, the lever swings about the fulcrum to produce a useful action at another point. The force that you apply is called the *effort*, and the lever moves at another point to raise a weight or overcome a resistance, both of which are called the *load*.

Where you move a lever is just as important as the amount of effort you apply to it. Less effort can move the same load, provided that it is applied further from the fulcrum; however, the effort has to move a greater distance to shift the load. As with the inclined plane, you gain in force what you pay in distance. Some levers reverse this effect to produce a gain in distance moved at the expense of force.

With levers, the distances moved by the effort and load depend on how far they are from the fulcrum. The principle of levers, which relates the effort and load, states that the effort times its distance from the fulcrum equals the load times its distance from the fulcrum.

FULCRUM IN CENTRE

The effort and load are the same distance from the fulcrum. In this situation, the load and effort are equal, and both move the same distance up or down as the lever balances.

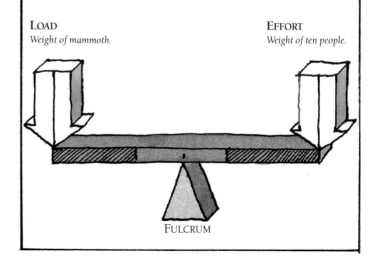

LOAD
Weight of mammoth.

EFFORT
Weight of ten people.

FULCRUM

It was then that I noticed across the square a second equally large mammoth about to be weighed, this time using far fewer people as a counterbalance. As I watched, anticipating disaster, the boulder was rolled closer to what would be the mammoth's end of the tree trunk. Once the mammoth was in place, a mere handful of people climbed onto the other end. To my amazement the tree trunk gently assumed a horizontal position. I was then informed that the length of the tree trunk from the people to the boulder multiplied by their combined weight would equal the length of the trunk from the boulder to the mammoth multiplied by its weight.

I was in the midst of calculations to verify this most unlikely theory when I heard a scream. Apparently, all the villagers had not disembarked from the trunk simultaneously, thereby causing a lad to be dramatically launched. I made a note, thinking that one day this might be useful.

FIRST-CLASS LEVERS

There are three different basic kinds of levers. All the levers on these two pages are first-class levers. First-class levers aren't superior to other-class levers; they are just levers in which the fulcrum is always placed between the effort and the load.

If the fulcrum is placed in the centre — as in the diagram on the left — the effort and load are at the same distance from it and are equal. The weight of the people is the same as the weight of the mammoth.

However, if the people are placed twice as far from the fulcrum as the mammoth — as in the diagram on the right — only half the number of people is needed to raise the mammoth. And if the people were three times as far from the fulcrum than the mammoth, only a third would be needed, and so on, because the lever magnifies the force applied to it.

These mammoth-weighing levers balance in order to measure weight, which is why this kind of weighing machine is called a balance. When the lever comes to rest, the force of the effort balances the force of the load, which is its weight. Many other kinds of levers work to produce movement.

FULCRUM OFF-CENTRE

The effort is twice as far from the fulcrum as the load. Here, the effort moves twice as far as the load, but is only half its amount.

LOAD
Weight of mammoth.

EFFORT
Weight of five people.

FULCRUM

ON MAMMOTH HYGIENE

Early in my researches I discovered that mammoths smell and so unavoidably do their immediate surroundings. I was therefore gratified to observe that in order to minimize any unpleasant odour, the staff of the mammoth paddock train their animals to sit on mats. These they change with some regularity.

Since mammoths often refuse to budge once settled, the keepers have learned how to remove mats while in use. One end of a trimmed tree trunk is carefully slipped under the mammoth. By raising the other end a fair distance the mammoth is lifted just enough to release the foetid fabric.

I found the ease with which the keepers could raise their oversize charges quite astounding. I also noted that wheelbarrows are an invaluable asset during clean-up sessions.

SECOND-CLASS LEVERS

Both the mammoth-lifter and the wheelbarrow are examples of second-class levers. Here, the fulcrum is at one end of the bar or rod and the effort is applied to the other end. The load to be raised or overcome lies between them.

With this kind of lever, the effort is always further from the fulcrum than the load. As a result, the load cannot move as far as the effort, but the force with which it moves is always greater than the effort. The closer the load is to the fulcrum, the more the force is increased, and the easier it becomes to raise the load. A second-class lever always magnifies force but decreases the distance moved.

A wheelbarrow works in the same way as the mammoth-lifter, allowing one to lift and shift a heavy load with the wheel as a fulcrum. Levers can also act to press on objects with great force rather than to lift them. In this case, the load is the resistance that the object makes to the pressing force. Scissors and nutcrackers (see p.22) are first-class and second-class examples. These devices are compound levers, which are pairs of levers hinged at the fulcrum.

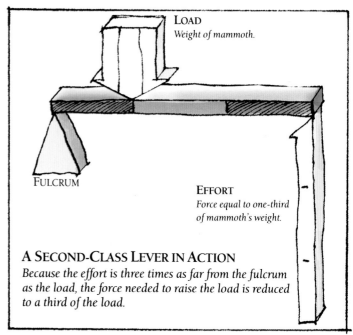

LOAD
Weight of mammoth.

FULCRUM

EFFORT
Force equal to one-third of mammoth's weight.

A SECOND-CLASS LEVER IN ACTION
Because the effort is three times as far from the fulcrum as the load, the force needed to raise the load is reduced to a third of the load.

ON TUSK TRIMMING AND ATTENDANT PROBLEMS

I watched with great curiosity a mammoth that was having its tusks trimmed as a precaution prior to being shipped. The beast was clearly not happy as the workers sawed, chipped and filed away. No sooner had I recalled the old adage that second only to the fury of a woman scorned is the wrath of a

disgruntled mammoth, when suddenly the enraged creature wrapped its trunk around the end of a nearby weighing log and began swinging it from side to side.

I was able to note during the ensuing collapse of the trimming stand that although the mammoth's head pivoted only a short distance, the free end of the log was swinging much further thereby achieving a stunning velocity.

THIRD-CLASS LEVERS

In extending its trunk with that of a tree, the mammoth now has something in common with such innocuous devices as a fishing rod and a pair of tweezers. It has become a giant-sized third-class lever.

Here, the fulcrum is again at one end of the lever but this time the positions of the load and effort are reversed. The load to be raised or overcome is furthest away from the fulcrum, while the effort is applied between the fulcrum and the load. As the load is furthest out, it always moves with less force than the effort, but it travels a proportionately greater distance. A third-class lever therefore always magnifies the distance moved but reduces the force.

The mammoth's neck is the fulcrum, and the end of the log moves a greater distance than the trunk gripping it. The force with which the log strikes the people is less than the effort of the trunk, but still enough to overcome their weight and scatter them far and wide. The end of the log moves faster than the trunk and builds up quite a speed to get the people moving smartly.

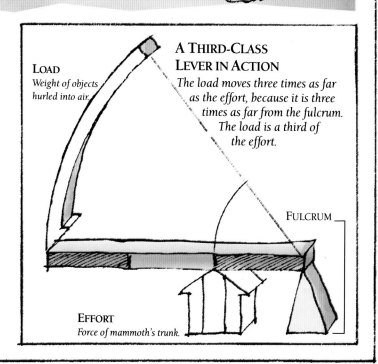

A THIRD-CLASS LEVER IN ACTION
The load moves three times as far as the effort, because it is three times as far from the fulcrum. The load is a third of the effort.

LOAD
Weight of objects hurled into air.

FULCRUM

EFFORT
Force of mammoth's trunk.

LEVERS IN ACTION

*Oh, Lever! How do I use thee?
Why not count the ways?*

FULCRUM   LOAD   EFFORT

FIRST-CLASS LEVERS

BALANCE
The object to be weighed is the load and the weights make up the effort. The two are equal, being at the same distance from the fulcrum.

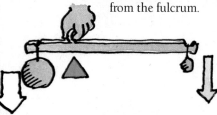

BEAM SCALE
The fulcrum is off-centre, and the weight is moved along the bar until it balances the object being weighed.

NAIL EXTRACTOR

The effort of the hand is magnified to pull out a nail. The load is the resistance of a nail to extraction.

TROLLEY

Tipping the handle of the trolley with a light effort raises a heavy load.

PLIERS

A pair of pliers is a compound lever (a pair of levers hinged at the fulcrum). The load is the resistance of an object to the grip of the pliers.

SCISSORS
A pair of scissors is a compound first-class lever. It produces a strong cutting action very near the hinge. The load is the resistance of the fabric to the cutting blades.

SECOND-CLASS LEVERS

WHEELBARROW
Lifting the handles with a light effort raises a heavy load nearer the wheel.

BOTTLE OPENER
Pushing up the handle overcomes the strong resistance of a bottle cap.

NUTCRACKERS
A pair of nutcrackers is a compound second-class lever. The load is the resistance of a shell to cracking.

THIRD-CLASS LEVERS

HAMMER

A hammer acts as a third-class lever when it is used to drive in a nail. The fulcrum is the wrist, and the load is the resistance of the wood. The hammer head moves faster than the hand to strike the nail.

FISHING ROD

One hand supplies the effort to move the rod, while the other hand acts as the fulcrum. The load is the weight of the fish, which is raised a long distance with a short movement of the hand.

TWEEZERS

A pair of tweezers is a compound third-class lever. The effort exerted by the fingers is reduced at the tweezer tips, so that delicate objects can be gripped. The load is the resistance of the hair.

MULTIPLE LEVERS

EXCAVATOR

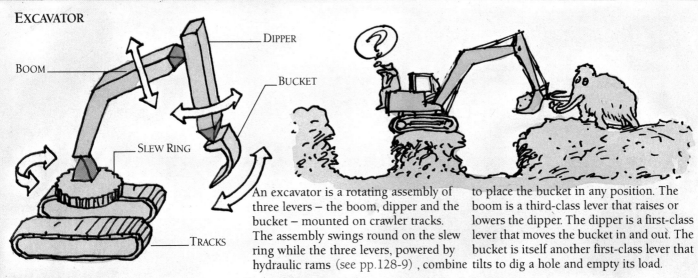

BOOM — DIPPER — BUCKET — SLEW RING — TRACKS

An excavator is a rotating assembly of three levers – the boom, dipper and the bucket – mounted on crawler tracks. The assembly swings round on the slew ring while the three levers, powered by hydraulic rams (see pp.128-9) , combine to place the bucket in any position. The boom is a third-class lever that raises or lowers the dipper. The dipper is a first-class lever that moves the bucket in and out. The bucket is itself another first-class lever that tilts to dig a hole and empty its load.

NAIL CLIPPERS

Nail clippers are a neat combination of two levers that produce a strong cutting action while at the same time being easy to control. The handle is a second-class lever that presses the cutting blades together. It produces a strong effort on the blades, which form a compound third-class lever. The cutting edges move a short distance to overcome the tough resistance of the nail as they slice through it.

FULCRUM OF HANDLE — HANDLE — CUTTING BLADES — FULCRUM OF BLADES

WEIGHING MACHINES

THE ROBERVAL ENIGMA

This simple kitchen balance or scales is based on the Roberval enigma, a linkage of parallel levers devised by the French mathematician Roberval in 1669. This allows the pans to remain horizontal, and also allows objects and weights to be placed at any position in the pans without affecting the accuracy of the scales.

At first sight, this seems to defy the principle of levers – hence the enigma. But their weight acts at the support of each pan, and not at its position on the pan.

A balance is a first-class lever. As the centres of the two pans are the same distance from the central pivot, they balance when the weight on one pan equals that on the other. Balances with suspended pans work in the same way.

It can't be true!

PLATFORM

LEVERS

DIAL

BATHROOM SCALES

For safety, your bathroom scales will barely move as you step onto the platform, no matter how heavy you are. The mechanism inside magnifies this tiny movement considerably, turning the dial sufficiently to register your weight.

A system of third-class levers pivoting on the case beneath the platform transmits its movement to the calibrating plate, which is attached to the powerful main spring. The levers force the plate down, extending the spring by an amount in exact proportion to your weight, one of the key properties of springs (see pp.78-9). The crank – a first-class lever – turns, pulled by another spring attached to the dial mechanism. This contains a rack and pinion gear (see p.37) which turns the dial, showing your weight through a window in the platform.

On stepping off the platform, the main spring retracts. It raises the platform and turns the crank to return the dial to zero.

LEVER 2

CONNECTING BARS

CALIBRATED BAR

CONNECTING BARS

LEVER 3

LEVER 1

WEIGHT

PLATFORM SCALES

Platform scales weigh heavy objects using a combination of third-class and first-class levers in which the load on one lever becomes the effort that moves the next lever. The object to be weighed is placed on the platform, which moves down a very short distance. The calibrated bar with the scale moves up, and the weight is slid along it until all the levers connected to the platform balance. The weight of the object is then read from the scale.

The scales use a total of three levers, all arranged so that they progressively increase the distance moved, shown here by the length of the arrows. In doing this, they reduce the effort that has to be exerted on the calibrated bar to balance the object to be weighed. Through this arrangement, a tiny weight can balance a massive object.

MAIN SPRING
The main spring extends, allowing the dial spring to rotate the crank.

CRANK

DIAL

DIAL SPRING

PINION

RACK

WEIGHT
The weight on the scales presses down the four levers which together pass the force on to the calibrating plate.

CALIBRATING PLATE
When the scales are in use, the calibrating plate is pushed downwards, extending the main spring.

LEVER

GRAND PIANO

Each key of a piano is linked to a complex system of levers called the action. Overall, the levers transmit the movement of the fingertip to the felt-tipped hammer that strikes the taut piano wire and sounds a note. The action magnifies movement so that the hammer moves a greater distance than the player's fingertip. The system of levers is very responsive, allowing the pianist to play quickly and produce a wide range of volume.

THE ACTION IN ACTION

The key raises the wippen, which forces up the jack against the hammer roller and lifts the lever carrying the hammer. The key also raises the damper and immediately *after striking the wire, the hammer drops back, allowing the wire to sound. On releasing the key, the damper drops back onto the wire, cutting off the sound.*

PARTS OF THE ACTION
1 KEY
2 WIPPEN
3 JACK
4 HAMMER ROLLER
5 REPETITION LEVER
6 HAMMER
7 WIRE
8 DAMPER
9 CHECK

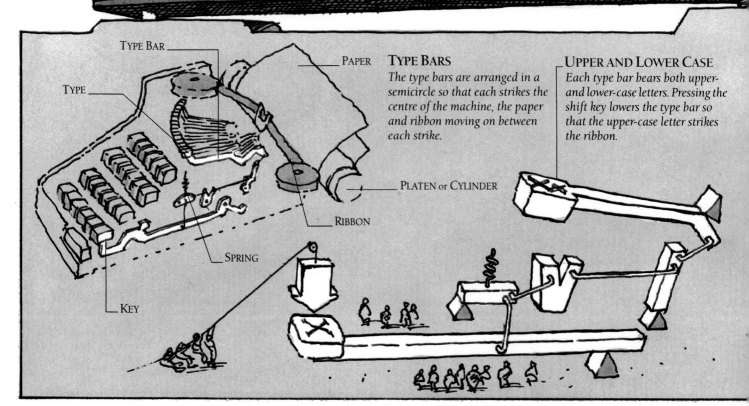

TYPE BARS
The type bars are arranged in a semicircle so that each strikes the centre of the machine, the paper and ribbon moving on between each strike.

UPPER AND LOWER CASE
Each type bar bears both upper- and lower-case letters. Pressing the shift key lowers the type bar so that the upper-case letter strikes the ribbon.

TYPE BAR
PAPER
TYPE
PLATEN or CYLINDER
RIBBON
SPRING
KEY

REPEATING A NOTE

The hammer drops back after striking the wire. If the key is not released, the fall of the hammer is arrested by the check and repetition lever. The hammer is held in this position so that it is ready to strike the wire rapidly if the key is immediately pressed again.

MANUAL TYPEWRITER

Like the piano, the typewriter also contains a system of levers that converts the small movement of a fingertip on a key into a long movement — in this case the movement of the raised type on the end of the type bar. As the typewriter is always played *fortissimo*, a simple system of levers suffices to connect the key to the type. Most manual typewriters use at least five levers between key and type bar.

BICYCLE BRAKE

Just a little effort with the hands can quickly undo all the effort made by the feet in getting a bicycle up to speed. Each brake on a bicycle consists of a set of three levers. This transmits the force with which each hand grips its brake lever to the brake blocks which, in turn, rub against the rims of the wheels. Each handle magnifies the grip force several times. The two arms of each brake press the blocks to the rims, producing sufficient friction (see p.82) to slow and stop the bicycle.

PIVOT

CABLE

BRAKE HANDLE

The handle pulls the cable connecting the handle to the brake. It is a second-class lever. The end of the handle moves a greater distance than the cable, which is pulled with more force than the force exerted by the hand.

ARM

PIVOT

ARM

TYRE

BRAKE ARMS

The cable moves up and pulls the two arms together. One arm is a third-class lever and the other a first-class lever. They transfer the magnified force to the brake blocks.

BRAKE
BLOCK

WHEEL
RIM

HYDRAULIC PLATFORM

CAGE

UPPER BOOM
A ram mounted on the lower boom retracts to pull up the base of the upper boom. This effort raises the end of the upper boom to lift the cage and firefighter into position.

Firefighters may have to tackle a fire in the upper floors of a tall building and possibly rescue people. They use a hydraulic platform that can raise them high in the air. It consists of a cage on the end of a pair of long booms that are hinged together. The vehicle carrying the platform first lowers stabilizers to secure it firmly to the ground. Hydraulic rams (see p.129) then push and pull on the booms, which are both third-class levers. The upper ends move up a greater distance than the rams, so that the booms can be extended to reach the fire or people.

UPPER-BOOM RAM

EXTENDING SECTIONS

EFFORT (PULL OF CABLE)

FULCRUM

ARM (FIRST-CLASS LEVER)

LOAD (RESISTANCE OF RIM)

FULCRUM

ARM (THIRD-CLASS LEVER)

EFFORT (PULL OF CABLE)

LOAD (RESISTANCE OF RIM)

FULCRUM

EFFORT (PULL OF HAND)

LOAD (RESISTANCE OF BOTH RIMS)

HANDLE (SECOND-CLASS LEVER)

LOWER BOOM
A pair of powerful rams pushes up the base of the boom. The lower boom contains several sections that extend to raise the upper boom.

EFFORT

LOAD (WEIGHT OF CAGE)

FULCRUM

LOAD (WEIGHT OF UPPER BOOM AND CAGE)

EFFORT

FULCRUM

STABILIZER RAMS

LOWER-BOOM RAMS

[29]

THE WHEEL AND AXLE

ON THE GROOMING OF MAMMOTHS

*T*he problem with washing a mammoth, assuming that you can get close enough with the water (a point I will address further on), is the length of time it takes for the creature's hair to dry. The problem is greatly aggravated when steady sunshine is unavailable.

Recalling the incident between the mammoth and the tusk trimmers, and particularly the motion of the free end of the log, I invented a mechanical drier. It was composed of feathers secured to the ends of long spokes which radiated from one end of a sturdy shaft. At the other end of the shaft radiated a set of short boards. The entire machine was powered by a continuous line of sprightly workers who leaped one by one from a raised platform onto the projecting boards. Their weight against the boards turned the shaft. Because the spokes at the opposite end of the shaft were considerably longer than the boards, their feathered ends naturally turned much faster thereby producing the steady wind required for speedy drying.

A colleague once suggested I replace manpower with a constant stream of water. I left him in no doubt as to my views on this ludicrous proposal.

*I*n the very same village where I built my first feather drier there began the strange — albeit fashionable — practice of tusk modification. A blindfolded mammoth was drawn up against a fixed post or tree by ropes secured to its tusks. The other ends of the ropes were fastened around the drum of a powerful winch — a most ingenious device. As workers turned the drum with handles which projected from it, they were able to straighten the tusks.

Keeping the tusks straight would of course require frequent visits and have been quite lucrative. However, since the process not only made movement through doors impossible, but also affected a mammoth's breathing, it had to be abandoned.

WHEELS AS LEVERS

While many machines work with parts that move up and down or in and out, most depend on rotary motion. These machines contain wheels, but not only wheels that roll on roads. Just as important are a class of devices known as the wheel and axle, which are used to transmit force. Some of these devices look like wheels with axles, while others do not. However, they all rotate around a fixed point to act as a rotating lever.

The centre of the wheel and axle is the fulcrum of the rotating lever. The wheel is the outer part of the lever, and the axle is the inner part near the centre. In the mammoth drier, the feathers form the wheel and the boards are the axle. In the winch, the drum is the axle and the handles form the wheel.

As the device rotates, the wheel moves a greater distance than the axle but turns with less force. Effort applied to the wheel, as in the winch, causes the axle to turn with a greater force than the wheel. Many machines use the wheel and axle to increase force in this way. Turning the axle, as in the mammoth drier, makes the wheel move at a greater speed than the axle.

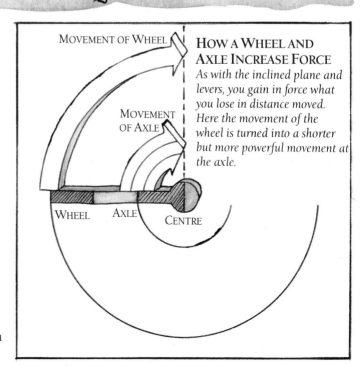

MOVEMENT OF WHEEL

MOVEMENT OF AXLE

WHEEL AXLE CENTRE

HOW A WHEEL AND AXLE INCREASE FORCE

As with the inclined plane and levers, you gain in force what you lose in distance moved. Here the movement of the wheel is turned into a shorter but more powerful movement at the axle.

THE WHEEL AND AXLE AT WORK

SCREWDRIVER

The handle of a screwdriver does more than enable you to hold it. It amplifies the force with which you turn it to drive the screw home.

SARDINE CAN

The key of a sardine can exerts a strong force to pull the metal sealing band away from the can.

STEERING WHEEL

The force of the driver's hands is magnified to turn the shaft, producing sufficient force to operate the steering mechanism.

BRACE AND BIT

The handle of the brace moves a greater distance than the drill bit at the centre, so the bit turns with a stronger force than the handle.

SPANNER

Pulling one end of the spanner exerts a powerful force on the bolt at the other end, screwing it tight.

TAP

The handle of a tap magnifies the force of the hand to screw down the washer inside firmly and prevent the tap dripping.

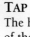

WATERWHEEL

The earliest waterwheel — the Greek mill of the first century BC — had a horizontal wheel. It was superseded by vertical wheels, which could be built to a larger size and thus developed greater power. Waterwheels obey the principle of the wheel and axle, with the force of the water on the paddles at the rim producing a strong driving force at the central shaft.

OVERSHOT WATERWHEEL

GREEK MILL

AXLE

CHUTE

PADDLES

HYDROELECTRIC TURBINE

Hydroelectric power stations contain water turbines that are direct descendants of waterwheels. An efficient turbine extracts as much energy from the water as possible, reducing a powerful intake flow to a relatively weak outlet flow. Modern turbines, such as the Francis turbine shown here, are carefully designed so that the water is guided onto the blades with the minimum of energy-wasting turbulence.

WATER INLET

GATE

DAM

POWERHOUSE

ELECTRICITY GENERATOR

TURBINE

RESERVOIR

GENERATOR SHAFT

GUIDE VANES

TURBINE BLADES

FRANCIS TURBINE

In this turbine, the water spirals horizontally around the turbine and vanes direct it to strike the curved turbine blades with maximum efficiency. When the water has given up its energy, it flows away through the turbine's centre.

WATER OUTLET

THE WINDMILL

BRAKE WHEEL

WIND-SHAFT

POST MILL

GRINDSTONE

SAIL

WALLOWER

GREAT SPUR WHEEL

The power of the wind was first put to use in a windmill built in Persia in the seventh century. Windmills use sails to develop power, just as waterwheels employ paddles. The classic windmill has four big vertical sails. It works by the principle of the wheel and axle: the force of the wind along the sails produces a stronger driving force at the central shaft. A series of bevel and spur gears (see p.37) then transmit this force, usually to turn a grindstone or to drive a pump. The power of a windmill depends on the speed of the wind on the sails and on the area that the sails present to the wind.

WINDMILL SAILS

Windmill sails have to work with a source of power that changes both its direction and its speed. In most designs of windmill, the sails can be turned so that they always face into the wind. To cope with varying wind speeds, the sails' area is changed: two ways in which this is done are the jib sail and the spring sail.

JIB SAIL

Around the Mediterranean Sea from Portugal to Turkey, windmills can still be seen with jib sails — simple triangular cloth sails like the sails of boats. To deal with a change in wind speed, the miller just furls or unfurls each sail.

SPRING SAIL

Sails composed of rows of wooden shutters replaced cloth sails in the late 1700s. The shutters pivot against a spring, opening when the wind gusts and closing when it drops. In this way, a constant wind force is maintained on the sails.

WIND
SENSORS

WIND TURBINE

This modern counterpart of the windmill drives a generator rather than a grindstone. To extract as much energy from the wind as possible, the rotor blades are huge — up to 100 metres (330 feet) across. Wind sensors enable the turbine's computer to control the movement of the rotor and produce optimum power in all wind conditions.

ELECTRIC GENERATOR

ROTATING MOUNT

GEARBOX

Electricity generation is most efficient at high speeds, so gears are used to increase the speed of the generator drive shaft.

ROTOR BLADES

These have surfaces like aircraft wings (see p.107). They are operated by the control system to work at high efficiency.

ROTATING MOUNT

The turbine assembly is rotated on its mounting under the control of a computer, which ensures that the blades always face into the wind.

TURBINE BLADES

AIR OUTLET

AIR INLET

RILL SHAFT
RILL BIT

AAAARGH!

DENTIST'S DRILL

The high-speed drill that a dentist uses to cut into your teeth is a miniature descendant of the first windmill, which turned horizontally rather than vertically. Inside is a tiny air turbine driven by compressed air which revolves at several thousand revolutions per second. In some designs, the rotor turns on two sets of ball bearings (see p.88), while in others the drill turbine floats in a cushion of high-pressure air.

GEARS AND BELTS

ON EARLY MAMMOTH POWER

As far as I can ascertain, the first use of mammoths in industry was to provide power for the famous merry-go-round experiment. The equipment consisted of two wheels, one large and one small, placed edge to edge so that when the mammoths turned one wheel, the other would turn automatically. At first seats were hung from the small wheel which was driven by the large wheel. The result was a hair-raising ride. When the wheels were reversed, the ride was far too sedate. Eventually belts connected to drive wheels of different sizes operated two rides simultaneously, one fast and one gentle. Carrot consumption during the experiment was astronomical.

TYPES OF GEARS

Gears come in a variety of sizes with their teeth straight or curved and inclined at a variety of angles. They are connected together in various ways to transmit motion and force in machines. However, there are only four basic types of gears. They all act so that one gear wheel turns faster or slower than the other, or moves in a different direction. A difference in speed between two gears produces a change in the force transmitted.

SPUR GEARS

Two gear wheels intermesh in the same plane, regulating the speed or force of motion and reversing its direction.

RACK AND PINION GEARS

One wheel, the pinion, meshes with a sliding toothed rack, converting rotary motion to reciprocating (to-and-fro) motion and vice versa.

BEVEL GEARS

Two wheels intermesh at an angle to change the direction of rotation, also altering speed and force if necessary. These are sometimes known as a pinion and crown wheel, or pinion and ring gear.

WORM GEARS

A shaft with a screw thread meshes with a toothed wheel to alter the direction of motion, and change the speed and force.

GEARS

The big wheel has twice the number of teeth, and twice the circumference, of the small wheel. It rotates with twice the force and half the speed in the opposite direction.

FORCE

SPEED

HOW GEARS AND BELTS WORK

The way gears and belts control movement depends entirely on the sizes of the two connecting wheels. In any pair of wheels, the larger wheel will rotate more slowly than the smaller wheel, but it will rotate with greater force. The bigger the difference in size between the two wheels, the bigger will be the difference in speed and force.

Wheels connected by belts or chains work in just the same way as gears, the only difference being in the direction that the wheels rotate.

SPEED   FORCE

BELTS

The big wheel has twice the circumference of the small wheel. It also rotates with twice the force and half the speed, but in the same direction.

SPUR GEARS

DERAILLEUR GEARS

The chain connecting the pedals of a bicycle to the rear wheel acts as a belt to make the wheel turn faster than the feet. To ride on the level or downhill, the rear-wheel sprocket needs to be small for high speed. But to climb hills, it needs to be large so that the rear wheel turns with less speed but more force.

Derailleur gears solve the problem by having rear-wheel sprockets of different sizes. A gear-changing mechanism transfers the chain from one sprocket to the next.

BOTTOM GEAR

REAR-WHEEL SPROCKETS

DRIVE SPROCKETS

TOP GEAR

SPRUNG ROLLERS

DRIVING GEAR

The driving gear is turned by one tooth every time the wheel rotates. The counter records how many revolutions take place, converting this figure into the distance travelled.

DRUMS

The drums bear twenty teeth — two for each numeral — on their right sides. On the left side of each drum is a gap by the numeral 2 and two projections on either side of the gap.

BICYCLE DISTANCE COUNTER

The counter is mounted on the front axle, and driven by a small peg fixed to a front wheel spoke. A reduction gear makes the right-hand numbered drum revolve once every kilometre or mile. As it makes a complete revolution, it makes the next drum to the left move by one-tenth of a revolution, and so on. The movement of the drums is produced by the row of small gear wheels beneath the drums. The wheels have teeth that are alternately wide and narrow, a feature which enables them to lock adjoining drums together when one drum completes a revolution.

GEAR WHEELS

The wheels intermesh with each drum except the one at the right-hand end.

REDUCTION GEAR

PROJECTION

DRUM TOOTH

WIDE TOOTH

NARROW TOOTH

HOW ADJOINING DRUMS LOCK

Normally, a narrow wheel tooth fits between two drum teeth and the drums do not move. When a 9 moves up into the viewing window at the top of the drums, the projection on that drum catches the narrow tooth on the gear wheel, making it rotate. The next wide tooth fits into the gap by the 2 and locks the drum and the next left drum together. As the 9 changes to 0, the gear wheel rotates and the next drum also moves up one numeral.

CAR WINDOW WINDER

The handle in a car door turns a small cog that moves a toothed quadrant (a section of a large spur gear), which in turn raises or lowers levers supporting the car window. Electrically operated windows work on the same principle, but more gears are required because the speed of the motor has to be stepped down to provide a small but powerful movement.

SALAD SPINNER

A salad spinner rotates at high speed, throwing off water by centrifugal force (see p.71). The drive mechanism consists of an epicyclic or planetary gear — a system of spur gears in which an outer gear ring turns an inner planet gear that drives a small central sun gear. Epicyclic gears can achieve a high speed magnification yet are simple and compact.

SUN GEAR

PLANET GEAR

GEAR RING

LAWN MOWER

A push-mower contains an internal pinion turned by a gear ring inside the wheel. The pinion turns the cylinder of cutting blades as the wheels move, and the grass is trapped between the spinning blades and a fixed cutting blade. The blades spin much faster than the wheels so that each blade slices only a small amount of grass, mowing the lawn neatly at a single pass.

FIXED CUTTING BLADE

CYLINDER OF CUTTING BLADES

WHEEL

PINION

THE GEARBOX

All petrol engines work best if they run at a high but limited rate of revolutions. The job of the gearbox is to keep the engine running at its most efficient rate while allowing the car to travel at a large range of speed.

The crankshaft always turns faster than the wheels — from about twelve times as fast in first gear to about four times as fast in top gear. The differential (see p.45) reduces engine speed by four times. The rest of the reduction takes place in the gearbox.

The gearbox lies between the clutch (see p.84) and the differential. The gears can only be changed when the clutch has disengaged the engine. Operating the gear lever of a manual gearbox brings a different train of spur gears into play for each gear, except fourth gear. In fourth gear, no gear wheels are engaged and transmission goes directly through the gearbox from the clutch to the differential.

The different ratios of teeth on the gears involved produce different speeds. Selecting reverse gear simply introduces an extra gear wheel which reverses the rotation of the transmission shaft.

ENGINE — CLUTCH

GEARBOX — DIFFERENTIAL

THIRD AND FOURTH GEAR SELECTOR FORK

UPPER WHEELS
In neutral (shown here), the upper gear wheels freewheel on the transmission shaft. Selecting first, second or third gear locks an upper wheel to the shaft.

DIRECT TRANSMISSION
Selecting fourth gear locks the transmission shaft directly to the clutch shaft.

CLUTCH SHAFT

CONSTANT-MESH WHEELS
This pair of wheels makes the clutch shaft drive the layshaft.

LAYSHAFT

THIRD GEAR WHEELS

SECOND GEAR WHEELS

SELECTING A GEAR

Moving the gear lever tilts it so that it pushes or pulls one of the three selector rods. Except in reverse gear, the selector fork then shifts a collar that makes the dog teeth lock the required gear wheel to the transmission shaft. The speeds of the rotating parts are matched by the synchromesh (see p.85). In reverse gear, the fork engages the idler wheel.

This illustration (right) shows first gear being selected, in which the transmission goes from the clutch shaft via the layshaft and first gear wheels to the transmission shaft.

CLUTCH SHAFT

GEAR LEVER

SELECTOR ROD

SELECTOR FORK

COLLAR

GEAR LEVER

R

3

4

1

2

LEVER PIVOT

UPPER WHEELS

LOWER WHEELS

IDLER WHEEL

LAYSHAFT

TRANSMISSION SHAFT

FIRST AND SECOND GEAR SELECTOR FORK

SELECTOR RODS

The gear lever shifts the selector rods, which move the selector forks that engage the gear wheels.

COLLAR

DOG TEETH

TRANSMISSION SHAFT TO DIFFERENTIAL

REVERSE GEAR SELECTOR FORK

IDLER WHEEL

LOWER WHEELS

The lower gear wheels are turned by the layshaft and drive the upper wheels.

FIRST GEAR WHEELS

REVERSE GEAR WHEELS

REVERSE GEAR

The idler wheel engages the reverse gear wheels, making the transmission shaft turn in the opposite direction.

MECHANICAL CLOCKS AND WATCHES

MINUTE HAND

HOUR HAND

HOUR WHEEL
(24 teeth)

PINION
(6 teeth)

MINUTE WHEEL
(10 teeth)

GEAR WHEEL
(30 teeth)

PINION

DRIVING
WHEEL

MAINSPRING

BALANCE

HAIRSPRING

ESCAPE WHEEL

PALLET

PIVOT

PALLET
LEVER

Spur gears lie at the heart of mechanical timepieces. Powered by a falling weight or an unwinding spring, they turn the two hands, ensuring that the minute hand moves exactly twelve times around the dial for every revolution of the hour hand.

The hands are turned by the driving wheel through a pinion that is geared to rotate once an hour. The pinion drives the minute hand directly. The hour hand is driven through two sets of spur gears which together reduce its speed to one-twelfth that of the hour hand.

A further train of gears controls the speed at which the driving wheel rotates by connecting it to the escapement, which is the heart of the time-keeping mechanism.

PALLET   ANCHOR

PALLET

PENDULUM

ESCAPE WHEEL

WEIGHT

ANCHOR ESCAPEMENT

Many pendulum clocks are powered by a weight that turns the escape wheel, which is itself connected through gear trains to the hands. The escape wheel moves in precise steps. The swinging pendulum rocks the anchor so that the pallets alternately engage the teeth on the escape wheel. Each swing releases the escape wheel for a short interval to allow it to move on by one tooth. As the teeth of the escape wheel move, they push the anchor to keep the pendulum swinging.

LEVER ESCAPEMENT

A mechanical watch is powered by its mainspring, which turns the driving wheel and escape wheel. The hairspring oscillates in the balance, making the lever rock to and fro so that the pallets release the escape wheel in the same way as an anchor escapement. The hairspring is kept moving by the pressure of the escape wheel teeth on the lever.

THE RACK AND PINION

CAR STEERING

In rack and pinion steering, the steering column turns a pinion that shifts a rack to the right or left. Each end of the rack moves a track rod linked to a steering arm that turns the axle of each front wheel. Overall, a wheel and axle (in the steering wheel), a rack and pinion and a lever combine to multiply the force of the hands and turn the wheels. For power steering, see p.129.

STEERING ARM

TRACK ROD

STEERING COLUMN

RACK AND PINION

STEERING WHEEL

CORKSCREW

One good design of corkscrew makes use of the screw (see p.62-3) and the rack and pinion to pull a cork from a bottle. The long handles ending in pinions produce considerable leverage on the rack, enabling the cork to be extracted without having to pull it out.

REMOVING A CORK

The corkscrew is first placed in position (1), and as it is screwed in, the handles rise (2). When the screw is fully inserted, the handles are pushed down (3), so that the pinions force up the rack, and with it, the cork.

1

2

3

BEVEL GEARS

EGG WHISK

In bevel gears, the gear wheels are often of very different sizes. This difference serves to change either the force that is applied to one of the gears, or to increase or decrease the speed of motion. An egg whisk converts a slow rotation into two much faster rotations that work in opposite directions. Its handle turns a large double-sided crown wheel, which in turn drives two bevel pinions to spin the beaters. The great increase in speed is produced by the much larger diameter of the crown wheel compared to the bevel pinions.

CROWN WHEEL
The double-sided crown wheel transmits the motion of the handle to the two bevel pinions.

BEVEL PINIONS
Because they engage opposite faces of the crown wheel, the pinions rotate in opposite directions.

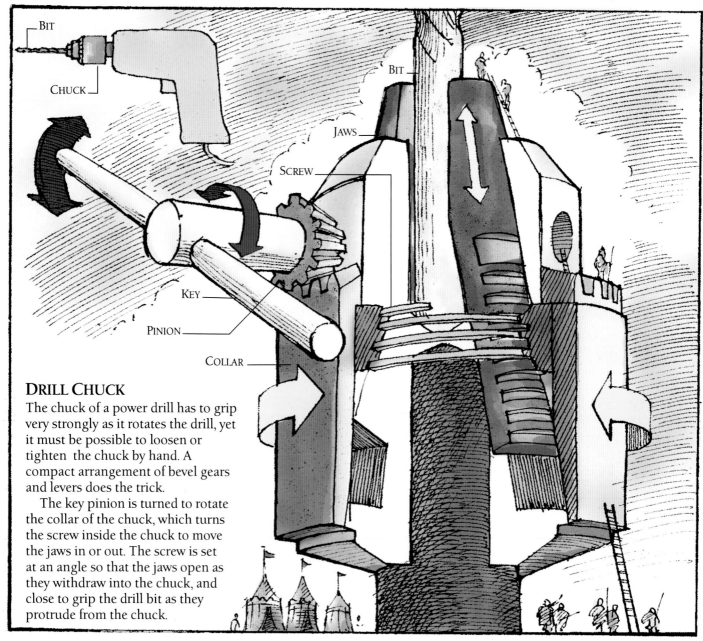

BIT

CHUCK

BIT

JAWS

SCREW

KEY

PINION

COLLAR

DRILL CHUCK

The chuck of a power drill has to grip very strongly as it rotates the drill, yet it must be possible to loosen or tighten the chuck by hand. A compact arrangement of bevel gears and levers does the trick.

The key pinion is turned to rotate the collar of the chuck, which turns the screw inside the chuck to move the jaws in or out. The screw is set at an angle so that the jaws open as they withdraw into the chuck, and close to grip the drill bit as they protrude from the chuck.

THE DIFFERENTIAL

When a car goes round a corner, the outer driving wheel must be turned at a greater speed than the inner one. This is achieved through the differential. It lies midway between the two driving wheels, linked to each wheel by a half-shaft turned through a bevel gear.

The half-shafts have sun gears connected by free-wheeling planet pinions. On the straight, the planet pinions do not spin and drive both half-shafts at the same speed. As the car corners, the planet pinions do spin, driving the sun gears and half-shafts at different speeds.

DRIVING THE DIFFERENTIAL

In a rear-wheel drive car, the transmission shaft from the gearbox (see p.40-1) turns the differential through a crown wheel and pinion.

In a front-wheel drive car, the gearbox may drive the differential directly through a pair of spur gears. Four-wheel drive cars have two differentials, one for each pair of wheels.

CROWN WHEEL

DRIVE PINION

TRANSMISSION SHAFT

SUN GEAR

HALF-SHAFT

PLANET PINION

CROWN WHEEL

The teeth on the crown wheel and the drive pinion are helical, or curved. This allows the transmission shaft to rise up and down slightly if the road surface is uneven.

ON THE STRAIGHT

The planet pinions circle around within the differential without spinning. They drive both the half-shafts at the same speed.

TURNING A CORNER

The planet pinions both circle around within the differential and spin. The half-shafts now rotate at different speeds.

WORM GEARS

ELECTRIC MIXER

An electric mixer has a pair of contra-rotating beaters, just like an egg whisk. However, electric motors rotate at very high speeds and develop heat. The speed therefore has to be reduced when the motor is put to work, rather than increased as in the hand-powered egg whisk. A worm gear is used to drive the beater shafts, and a fan attached to the motor shaft blows air over the motor to cool it.

SPEED SWITCH

WORM GEAR

ELECTRIC MOTOR

BEATER SHAFT

BEATERS

COOLING FAN

SPEEDOMETER

A car's speedometer uses worm gears to produce an enormous reduction in speed. The final drum of numbers in the distance counter turns just once every hundred thousand kilometres or miles, while the transmission shaft that drives it turns several hundred million times.

The speedometer is driven by a flexible cable. This contains a rotating wire connected to a small drive wheel which is rotated by a large worm on a shaft that drives the wheels. Inside the speedometer, the wire drives the speed indicator through magnetic induction (see pp.284-5). Its speed is further reduced by another worm gear to turn the distance counter, which itself contains reducing gears so that each numeral drum rotates at a tenth the speed of its neighbour.

CABLE CONNECTION

The speedometer cable is attached to the gearbox output shaft, transmission shaft or differential, all of which rotate at a speed that depends on the road speed.

SPEED INDICATOR

The shaft rotates a magnet inside a drag cup.

DIAL

POINTER

HAIRSPRING

NUMERAL DRUMS

DRAG CUP

MAGNET

WORM GEAR

RATCHET

DRIVE ARM

WORM

DRIVE WHEEL

ROTATING WIRE

SHAFT DRIVING WHEELS

GEARBOX

ENGINE

SPEEDOMETER

ECCENTRIC PIN

DISTANCE COUNTER

An eccentric pin, driven by a worm gear, pushes the drive arm backwards and forwards to operate the counter.

LAWN SPRINKLER

A good sprinkler not only produces a fine spray of water but also swings the spray to and fro to water a wide area of grass. No extra source of power is needed, because the mechanism is driven by the movement of the water through the sprinkler, using a system of worm gears.

As the water enters the sprinkler, it drives a turbine at high speed and then rushes to the spray tube. The turbine drives two worm gears that reduce the speed of the turbine to turn a crank at low speed. The crank moves the spray tube slowly to and fro.

SPRAY TUBE

TURBINE

CRANK

WATER HOSE

CAMS AND CRANKS

ON AN ANCIENT MACHINE

I have recently come across the remains of an extraordinary machine, the operation of which is here depicted. I believe that the machine was designed to crack the eggs of some huge and now extinct beast. Each egg was shattered by a mammoth-powered hammer, and the broken shell pushed out of the way by a shovel. My discovery prompts two observations: (a) the mammoth merry-go-round may not have been the first industrial use of mammoths after all, and (b) there must have been considerable demand for omelettes of prodigious proportions.

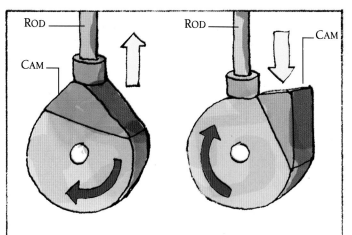

THE CAM

The egg-cracker uses a cam, a device which in its most basic form is simply a fixed wheel with one or more projections. A rod is pressed against the wheel, and as the wheel rotates, the rod moves out and in as the projection passes.

THE CRANK

The shovel is moved by a crank. This is a wheel with a pivot to which a rod is attached. The other end of the rod is hinged so that the rod moves backwards and forwards as the wheel rotates. Unlike cams, cranks may work in reverse, with the rod making the wheel rotate.

CAMSHAFT

CAM

SPRING

VALVE CLOSED

VALVE

VALVE OPEN

CYLINDER

PISTON

CONNECTING ROD

CRANK

CRANKSHAFT

CAR ENGINE CAMSHAFT

Each cylinder of a car engine contains valves that admit the fuel or expel the exhaust gases. Each valve is operated by a cam attached to a rotating camshaft. The cam opens the valve by forcing it down against a spring. The spring then closes the valve until the cam comes round again. The cam may operate the valve directly, as here, or through levers, as shown on the next page.

CAR ENGINE CRANKSHAFT

Powered by the explosion of the fuel, a piston moves down inside each cylinder of a car engine. A connecting rod links the piston to a crank on the crankshaft. The rod turns the crank, which then continues to rotate and drives the piston back up the cylinder. In this way, the crankshaft converts the movement of the pistons into rotary power.

MOTOR SHAFT

WORM GEAR

CRANK

CONNECTING ROD

WIPER BLADE

RACK

WINDSCREEN WIPERS

The windscreen wipers of a car are powered by an electric motor, and depend on a crank to move them to and fro. A worm gear reduces the motor speed, and the crank moves a rack or linking rod that drives the wiper blades.

PINION

CAMS AND CRANKS IN THE CAR

Split-second timing is essential for smooth and powerful running in a car engine. It is achieved by the engine's camshaft and crankshaft working in concert.

As the pistons move up and down in the cylinders, they drive the crankshaft which turns the flywheel and, ultimately, the wheels. But, through a chain linkage, the crankshaft also turns the camshaft. As the camshaft rotates, the cams operate the cylinder valves. In an overhead camshaft engine, the cams lie over the valves and move the valves directly. Here, the camshaft is to one side, and it operates the valves through push-rods and rockers. The cams and cranks involved open and close the valves in step with the movements of the pistons to follow the four-stroke cycle (see pp.156-7).

The camshaft and crankshaft may also drive other parts of the engine. A gear wheel on the camshaft, for example, drives the oil pump (see p.124) and the distributor.

THE SEWING MACHINE

The sewing machine is a marvel of mechanical ingenuity. Its source of power is the simple rotary movement of an electric motor. The machine converts this into a complex sequence of movements that makes each stitch and shifts the fabric between stitches. Cams and cranks play an important part in the mechanism. A crank drives the needle up and down, while two trains of cams and cranks move the serrated feed-dog that shifts the fabric.

In order to make a stitch, the sewing machine has to loop one thread around another. The first thread passes through the eye of the needle and the second thread is beneath the fabric. As the needle moves up and down, a curved hook rotates to loop the thread and form a stitch. When a stitch has been completed, the feed-dog repositions the fabric so that the next can be made. The amount of fabric moved by the feed-dog can be altered to produce long or short stitches.

DRIVE WHEEL

NEEDLE THREAD

FEED-DOG

NEEDLE

NEEDLE — 1   2   3   4   5   6

HOOK

BOBBIN

FORMING THE LOOP

The needle, carrying one thread, moves down (1). The other thread is wound on the bobbin in the rotary shuttle below the fabric. The needle pierces the fabric and then moves up, leaving a loop of thread beneath the fabric (2).

HOOKING THE LOOP

The hook on the shuttle catches the loop of needle thread (3). It then pulls the loop around the bobbin and around the bobbin thread (4). The bobbin thread is effectively put through the loop of needle thread.

COMPLETING THE STITCH

The hook continues to turn (5). The loop then slips off the hook as the needle rises above the fabric (6). The needle thread is then pulled tight by a lever on the sewing machine to form the stitch.

CAM

DRIVE WHEEL

CRANK

NEEDLE
THREAD

BELT

MOTOR

CRANK

FABRIC

NEEDLE

CAM

CRANK

HOOK

THE FEED-DOG

This moves the fabric forwards. One train of cams and cranks moves the feed-dog forwards and backwards, while the other makes it rise and fall. Both are powered by a wheel driven by the electric motor, synchronizing their movements. The feed-dog rises and moves forwards between stitches to shift the fabric and then dips and moves back.

BOBBIN THREAD

ROTARY SHUTTLE

BOBBIN

[53]

PULLEYS

ON MILKING A MAMMOTH

Although it has a rather strong flavour, mammoth milk is rich in minerals and vitamins. I have passed through countless villages of white-toothed, strong-boned folk all of whom attribute their remarkable health to a life of drinking this exceptionally nutritious fluid. The only problem in milking these creatures, besides obtaining enough buckets (they produce an unbelievable amount of milk), is the animals' great reluctance to be touched. It is necessary therefore to raise the mammoth far enough above the ground to deny it any traction. The milker is only safe when the milkee is dangling helplessly.

In many villages, I observed mammoths being lifted in a harness using a number of wheels. These wheels, around which a strong rope travelled, were hung in a given order from a very stout framework. Although the weight to be lifted was often tremendous, a system of wheels greatly reduced the effort required. I noticed that the more wheels the villagers used, the easier it was to lift the weight, but by the same token, it was also necessary to pull in much more rope to get the mammoth up to a sufficient height.

PULLEY POWER

For some, lifting a heavy weight while climbing a ladder poses no problems. For most of us, however, pulling something down is a lot easier than lifting it up.

This change of direction can be arranged with no more than a wheel and a rope. The wheel is fixed to a support and the rope is run over the wheel to the load. A pull downwards on the rope can lift the load as high as the support. And because the puller's body weight works downwards, it now becomes a help rather than a hindrance. A wheel used in this way is a pulley and the lifting system it makes up is a simple crane.

Single pulleys are used in machines where the direction of a movement must be changed, as for example in a lift (see p.61) where the upward movement of the lift car must be linked to the downward movement of a counterweight.

In an ideal pulley, the effort with which the rope is pulled is equal to the weight of the load. In practice, the effort is always slightly more than the load because it has to overcome the force of friction (see pp.82-3) in the pulley wheel as well as raise the load. Friction reduces the efficiency of all machines in this way.

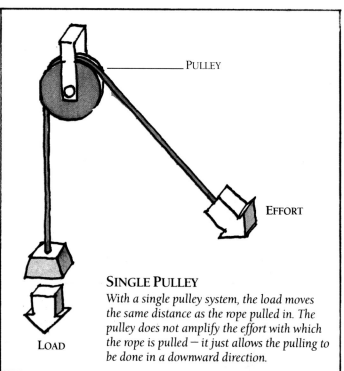

PULLEY

EFFORT

SINGLE PULLEY

With a single pulley system, the load moves the same distance as the rope pulled in. The pulley does not amplify the effort with which the rope is pulled — it just allows the pulling to be done in a downward direction.

LOAD

O ne wise old milker informed me that to avoid unnecessary delay and expenditure of energy, the gender of the mammoth should be checked before attaching the harness.

CONNECTED PULLEYS

As well as changing a pulling force's direction, pulleys can also be used to amplify it, just like levers. Connecting pulley wheels together to make a compound pulley enables one person to raise loads many times their own weight.

In a system with two pulleys, one pulley is attached to the load and the other to the support. The rope runs over the upper pulley, down and around the lower pulley and back up to the upper pulley, where it is fixed. The lower pulley is free to move and as the rope is pulled, it raises the load. This arrangement of pulleys causes the load to move only half as far as the free end of the rope. But in return, the force raising the load is doubled. As with levers, the distance moved is traded off against force — much to the puller's advantage.

The amount by which a compound pulley amplifies the pull or effort to raise a load depends on how many wheels it has. Ideally, the amplification is equal to the number of sections of rope that raise the lower set of pulleys attached to the load. In practice, the effort has to overcome friction in all the pulleys and raise the weight of the lower set of pulleys as well as the load. This reduces the amplification of the effort.

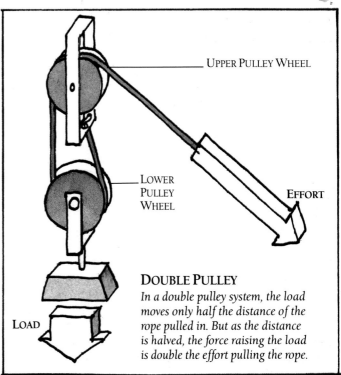

UPPER PULLEY WHEEL

LOWER PULLEY WHEEL

EFFORT

LOAD

DOUBLE PULLEY

In a double pulley system, the load moves only half the distance of the rope pulled in. But as the distance is halved, the force raising the load is double the effort pulling the rope.

CHAIN HOIST

The chain hoist consists of an endless chain looped around three pulleys. The upper two pulleys are fixed together, while the load hangs from a lower pulley, which is supported by a loop of chain. The load remains still unless the chain is moved. Just how much effort is needed to move the load depends on the difference in diameter between the two upper pulleys.

RAISING AND LOWERING THE HOIST

When the chain is pulled so that the paired pulleys rotate anticlockwise (left), the larger wheel pulls in more chain than the smaller wheel lets out, magnifying the pull exerted and raising the load a shorter distance. When the chain moves in the reverse direction (below), the load is lowered.

EFFORT

LOAD

LOAD

LOAD

TOWER CRANE

The tower crane is a modern equivalent of the shadoof, using a counterweight to balance its load in the same way.

COUNTERWEIGHT

FULCRUM

LOAD

SHADOOF

This water-raising machine, invented in antiquity, has a counterweight at one end of a pivoted beam which balances a container of water at the other end. When full, the container can be raised with little more than a light touch.

COUNTER-WEIGHT

LOAD

FORK-LIFT TRUCK

The heavy counterweight at the rear of a fork-lift truck helps raise a load high into the air by preventing the truck from toppling forward.

BLOCK AND TACKLE

COUNTERWEIGHT

COUNTERWEIGHTS

Cranes and other lifting machines often make use of counterweights in raising loads. The counterweight balances the weight of the load so that the machine's motor has only to move the load and not to support it. The counterweight may also stop the machine tipping over as the load leaves the ground. In accordance with the principle of levers (see p.18) a heavy counterweight placed near the fulcrum of a machine such as a crane has the same effect as a lighter counterweight positioned further away.

MOBILE CRANE
Once on site, a mobile crane uses outrigger beams and hydraulic jacks to relieve the suspension of the strain during lifting. The telescopic boom with its block and tackle can swivel around and extend far outwards, secured by the counterweight at the base of the boom.

COUNTERWEIGHT

HYDRAULIC
RAM

BLOCK
AND TACKLE

LOAD

BOOM

OUTRIGGER

CAB

The block and tackle is a system of pulleys that is compact yet able to raise substantial loads. It is commonly used at the end of the boom of a crane to increase the force of the crane's motor in lifting a load.

The system contains one rope wound around two separate sets of pulleys. The pulleys in each set are free to rotate independently on the same axle. The upper set is fixed to a support such as a boom, while the lower set is attached to the load. Pulling the rope raises the lower set of pulleys. The magnification of the force that the block and tackle produces is equal to the number of pulley wheels it contains.

This block and tackle contains five pulleys in each set plus a guide wheel above. The load is raised by ten pulleys, so the block and tackle increases the force applied to it by ten times.

TOWER CRANE

The aptly-named tower crane uses several sets of pulleys for precise lifting work over a wide area.

TROLLEY

TROLLEY CABLE

TROLLEY WINCH

It consists of a long, slender main jib supported by cantilever cables and balanced by a counter-weight on an opposing counter jib. The main jib carries a trolley from which a hook descends to pick up the load. The whole lifting structure is supported by a tall lattice-work tower on which the jib rotates.

LIFTING CABLE

TROLLEY PULLEYS

TROLLEY

The trolley rolls on wheels along the main jib, pulled to and fro by the trolley cable, which is driven by the trolley winch. The lifting cable extends from the end of the jib, around the trolley pulleys and hook pulley, and then over lifting pulleys to the hoist, which is powered by an electric motor.

HOOK PULLEY

THE SELF-RAISING TOWER

As a building rises, so does the crane that helps in its construction. Tower cranes do not expand telescopically like mobile cranes; instead, they extend themselves section by section. They do this by using a hydraulically operated climbing frame which raises the cab to make room for additional sections.

CAB

CLIMBING FRAME

FIRST SECTION

1 THE FIRST SECTION
The first section of the crane is a low structure erected at

2 THE CLIMBING FRAME
The frame beneath the cab uses a hydraulic ram (see pp.128-9) to extend itself, lifting the top part of the crane.

the site by a mobile crane. It is fastened to strong foundations which will hold the completed crane in position. The climbing frame is then lowered onto the top of the first section. The cab and jibs are then positioned on the frame.

MAIN JIB   LIFTING PULLEYS   HOIST

THE HOIST
The hoist winds the lifting cable in and out, raising and lowering the hook. The trolley pulleys and hook pulley together double the force exerted by the hoist by doubling the length of cable used. Extra pulleys may be incorporated to increase the force still further by quadrupling the length of cable.

CANTILEVER CABLES

COUNTERWEIGHT

MAIN JIB

3 ADDING A SECTION
The hook then lifts the next tower section, and this is bolted into position within the climbing frame.

CAB

SLEWING GEAR

CLIMBING FRAME

4 THE COMPLETE CRANE
When the tower has grown to its full height, the climbing frame can be removed.

ESCALATOR AND LIFT

Escalators and lifts are both lifting machines that make use of pulleys and counterweights. This is obvious in the lift, where the cable supporting the lift car runs over a pulley to a counterweight. The pulley also drives the cable. Although it is not so immediately apparent, the escalator works in a similar way. A drive wheel moves a chain attached to the stairs, while the returning stairs act as a counterweight.

ESCALATOR

Escalator stairs are connected to an endless chain that runs around a drive wheel. The wheel is powered by an electric motor at the top of the escalator. The descending half of the stairs acts as a counterweight to the ascending half, so that the motor moves only the weight of the people riding. Every stair has a pair of wheels on each side and each pair runs on two rails beneath the stair. The rails are in line except at the top and the bottom of the escalator. Here, the inner rail goes beneath the outer rail so that each stair moves to the level of the next stair. In this way, the stairs fold flat for people to get on and off.

ASCENDING STAIRS

HANDRAIL

OUTER RAIL

INNER RAIL

CHAIN

RETURN WHEEL

RETURNING STAIRS

ELECTRIC MOTOR

CABLE

PULLEY

CHAIN DRIVING HANDRAIL

RETURNING HANDRAIL

COUNTERWEIGHT

DRIVE WHEEL

GUIDE RAILS

LIFT CAR

CHAIN

LIFT

A lift is a single pulley lifting machine. The car is raised or lowered by a cable running over a pulley at the top of the lift shaft. At the other end of the cable is a counterweight that balances the weight of the lift car plus an average number of passengers. Both car and counterweight run up and down the shaft on guide rails. An electric motor drives the pulley to move the car, needing only enough power to raise the difference in weight between car and its passengers and the counterweight.

BELOW THE ESCALATOR

The weight of the stairs returning to the foot of the escalator offsets the weight of the stairs travelling back up to the top. All the motor has to lift is the weight of the passengers.

SHOCK ABSORBER

SCREWS

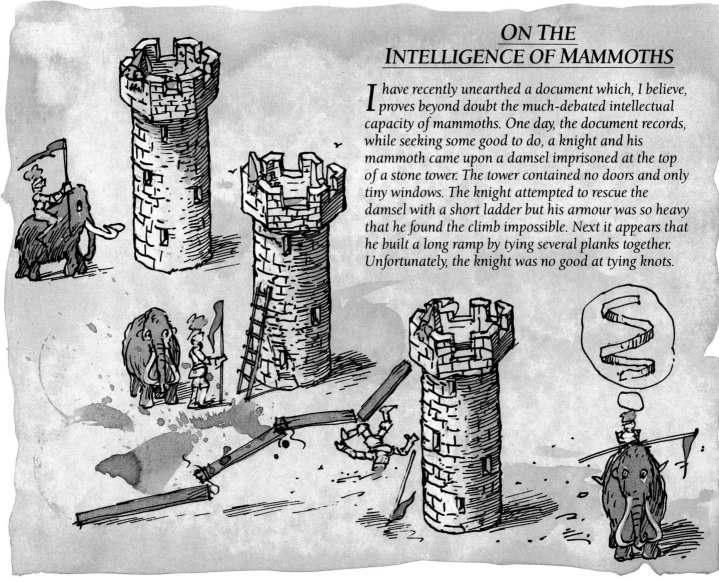

ON THE INTELLIGENCE OF MAMMOTHS

I have recently unearthed a document which, I believe, proves beyond doubt the much-debated intellectual capacity of mammoths. One day, the document records, while seeking some good to do, a knight and his mammoth came upon a damsel imprisoned at the top of a stone tower. The tower contained no doors and only tiny windows. The knight attempted to rescue the damsel with a short ladder but his armour was so heavy that he found the climb impossible. Next it appears that he built a long ramp by tying several planks together. Unfortunately, the knight was no good at tying knots.

NUTS AND BOLTS

The screw is a heavily disguised form of inclined plane, one which is wrapped around a cylinder – just as the knight's ramp encircles the tower. As we have already seen on (p.10) inclined planes alter force and distance. When something moves along a screw thread, like a nut on a bolt, it has to turn several times to move forwards a short distance. As in a linear inclined plane, when distance decreases, force increases. A nut therefore moves along the bolt with a much greater force than the effort used to turn it.

A nut and bolt hold objects together because they grip the object with great force. Friction (see pp.82-3) stops the nut working loose.

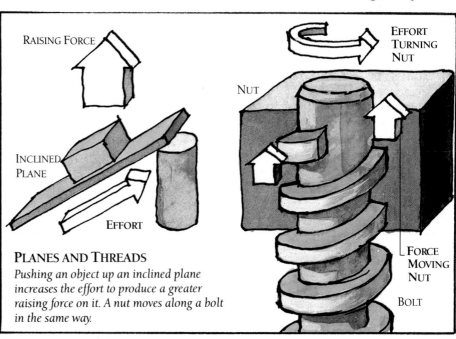

RAISING FORCE

INCLINED PLANE

EFFORT

EFFORT TURNING NUT

NUT

FORCE MOVING NUT

BOLT

PLANES AND THREADS

Pushing an object up an inclined plane increases the effort to produce a greater raising force on it. A nut moves along a bolt in the same way.

The knight's next idea was to assemble the planks into another ramp, and to fix it in a spiral around the tower. But the ramp was not long enough to reach the damsel.

At this point, the trusty mammoth acted. He picked up a nearby tree trunk, inserted it into one of the windows and turned the entire tower. Uncertain of what was going on, the knight joined in. To his amazement, the end of the ramp started to dig into the soil. By turning the tower many times they slowly screwed it into the ground. Soon the top of the tower was within easy reach of the ladder, and the dizzy damsel skipped to freedom.

SCREWS

Straight inclined planes are often used as wedges, in which the plane moves to force a load upwards. Spiral inclined planes can work like wedges too. In most kinds of screws, the screw turns and moves itself into the material – like the damsel's tower. As with the nut and bolt, the turning effort is magnified so that the screw moves forwards with an increased force. The force acts on the material to drive the screw into it.

As in the case of the nut and bolt, friction acts to hold the screw in the material. The friction occurs between the spiral thread and the material around it. It is strong because the spiral thread is long and the force between the thread and material is powerful.

WEDGES AND THREADS

A wedge produces a strong force at right angles to its movement, and a screw does the same, but at right angles to its rotation.

RAISING FORCE

WEDGE

EFFORT

FORCE ON WOOD

EFFORT TURNING SCREW

WOOD SCREW

WOOD

THE SCREW AT WORK

WOOD SCREW

The thread of a wood screw pushes strongly against the wood as it turns and drives itself into the wood. The screwdriver helps to increase the driving force even more.

NUT AND BOLT

The thread forces a nut and bolt together. The turning force is increased by the leverage of a spanner.

SCREW JACK

A screw jack uses a screw mechanism to lift a car. The handle may move fifty times further than the car, so the force on the car is fifty times greater than the effort on the handle.

MOVING PLATE

FIXED PLATE

GUIDE ROD

VICE

The vice uses a screw to grip an object tightly on a work surface.

CORKSCREW

The corkscrew works like a wood screw, but is shaped in a helix to stop the cork splitting when it is pulled from the bottle. The handle increases the turning force applied, and provides a good grip for extracting the cork.

OBJECT PLACED HERE

SPINDLE

SCALE

THIMBLE

THIMBLE

The thimble turns on a ratchet mechanism. The ratchet stops the spindle moving forward when it touches the object.

MICROMETER

This instrument measures the width of objects with great precision. The object is placed in the micrometer and the thimble turned until the spindle touches the object. The spindle and thimble gradually move along a screw thread. The movement of the spindle is read on a scale, while the graduations on the thimble itself show small fractions of a revolution. Added together, the two figures give a highly accurate measurement.

THE TAP

If you've ever tried to stop water flowing from a tap with a finger, you'll know just how much pressure the water can exert. But a tap controls the flow with little effort, using a screw (aided by the use of the wheel and axle in the handle) to drive the washer down against the water flow with great force. Once tightened, friction (see pp.82-3) acts on a screw thread to prevent the screw working loose. A steep pitch on the screw thread minimizes the turning needed to work the tap.

THE TAP CLOSED

SCREW
THREAD

WASHER

DRILLS AND AUGERS

In drills and augers, the screw is used as a means of carrying loose material. As a drill cuts forwards into a material with its sharp point, it also channels waste away backwards along its screw-shaped grooves. In large-diameter drills, the grooves that remove waste material are more pronounced and these give the drill a corkscrew shape.

BRACE AND BIT

When a lot of force is needed – for example, in drilling a wide-diameter hole – an ordinary hand drill will grind to a halt. The answer is a brace and bit. The bowed handle enables the bit to be turned with great leverage.

HAND DRILL

A hand drill uses a bevel gear (see p.37) to step up the speed at which the bit rotates. One bevel gear transmits the turning force, while the other freewheels. Hand drills are fast, but not very powerful.

POWER DRILL

An electric power drill has gears to drive the bit at high speed. It may also have an impact mechanism that hammers the drill bit through a tough material.

MOTOR

COOLING FAN

TWO-SPEED GEARING

DRILL SPINDLE

MINCER

As anyone who has trapped their finger in one will know, a kitchen mincer can reduce even the toughest chunks of meat to shreds. Turning the handle turns the cutting blades and also an auger which forces the meat into the cutters. The wheel and axle action of the handle combines with the action of the auger to magnify the turning force, moving and cutting the meat with tremendous force.

AUGER

CUTTING BLADES

CUTTER PLATE

CONSTRUCTION AUGER

Augers are used to drill holes in soft ground for the piers of large buildings. As the auger rotates, it becomes filled with soil. It is then lifted to the surface where the soil is removed, after which the auger is lowered again. In this way, an auger of limited length can excavate deep holes.

CRANE

AUGER

CUTTER HEAD

MECHANICAL MOLE

The mechanical mole is a tunnelling machine able to burrow its way through soil or soft rock. The cutting blades scour away at the workface, and as the mole advances, the tunnel behind it is lined to prevent collapsing.

The waste produced by the cutting blades is passed to one or more augers which transport it away from the workface.

TUNNEL LINING

CONVEYOR

AUGER

THE COMBINE HARVESTER

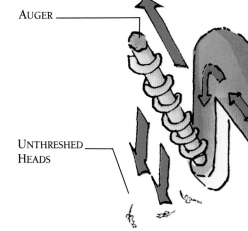

The combine harvester gets its name because it combines the two basic harvesting activities of reaping (cutting the crop) and threshing (separating out the grain). It may also bale the straw so that large fields can be harvested and cleared in one quick and tidy operation. Combine harvesters feature a number of screw mechanisms to transport the grain within the machine. Harvesters for seed crops other than grain work in similar ways.

KEY TO PARTS

1 REEL
The reel sweeps the stalks of the crop into the cutter bar.

2 CUTTER BAR
The bar contains a knife that moves to and fro between the prongs, slicing the stalks near ground level.

3 STALK AUGER
This transports the stalks to the elevator.

4 ELEVATOR
The elevator carries the stalks up to the threshing cylinder.

5 THRESHING CYLINDER
This contains a set of bars that rotates at high speed. The grain is separated from the heads and falls through the concave to the grain pan.

6 REAR BEATER
As this rotates, the straw (the threshed stalks) is moved to the straw walkers.

7 STRAW WALKERS
These carry the straw to the rear of the harvester, where it drops to the ground or is packed into bales.

8 GRAIN PAN
The vibrating surface of the pan transports the grain to the sieves.

9 SIEVES
The grain, unthreshed heads and chaff fall onto vibrating sieves. Air blows the chaff out of the rear of the harvester, while the sieves retain the unthreshed heads. The grain falls through the sieves to the base of the harvester.

10 TAILINGS ELEVATOR
This returns the unthreshed heads blown from the sieves to the threshing cylinder.

11 GRAIN AUGER AND ELEVATOR
The grain is carried by the auger and elevator to the grain tank.

12 UNLOADING AUGER
This transports the grain from the tank to a trailer or into bags.

AUGER

UNTHRESHED HEADS

5 THRESHING CYLINDER

CONCAVE

1 REEL

4 ELEVATOR

8 GRAIN PAN

3 STALK AUGER

TINES

2 CUTTER BAR

FAN

AIR BLAST

AUGER

12 UNLOADING AUGER

GRAIN TANK

6 REAR BEATER

7 STRAW WALKERS

STRAW

10 TAILINGS ELEVATOR

CHAFF

UNTHRESHED HEADS OF GRAIN

GRAIN

11 GRAIN AUGER AND ELEVATOR

9 SIEVES

AUGER

ROTATING WHEELS

ON LEARNING FROM MAMMOTH ADVERSITY

I once made the mistake of leaving my unicycle unattended in the presence of a young mammoth. Being innately curious, the mischievous creature promptly took to the road. Even as I shouted, I could not help noting the extraordinary stability of the rotating wheel which allowed the novice cyclist to make good its escape.

Although the mammoth soon lost interest in the undertaking, the wheel—now rolling along at full tilt—seemed reluctant to stop. By the time the unicycle had reached the top of a small hill, its terrified rider was being carried helplessly forward. Everything in their path was promptly and unceremoniously flattened.

PRECESSION

Precession is a strange kind of motion that occurs in wheels and other rotating objects. You can feel its effects for yourself if you hold a spinning bicycle wheel by its axle. When you try to turn it, you will find that the wheel won't turn in the way you intend it to. Instead, it will "precess", so that the axle actually turns at right angles to the direction you expect.

Precession makes a wheel rolling on its own stay upright, and it enables a cyclist (or unicyclist) to ride. We use precession instinctively by slightly swivelling the front wheel. Each swivel brings precession into play to correct tilting, helping us to keep the bicycle upright.

The force of precession increases with speed. Conversely, it decreases as a wheel slows down. This is why it is difficult to ride a bicycle that is moving slowly. Remaining upright on a stationary cycle is purely a feat of balance, and does not involve precession.

INERTIA

You'll have experienced the effects of inertia if you've ever had to push a car in order to start it. It takes a lot of effort to get a car moving, but once it is going, it will carry on for some distance without further pushing and, with luck, will start itself.

Inertia accounts for all the pushing and shoving. It is the resistance of objects to any change in their speed, even if the speed is zero. Everything has inertia, and the amount depends on mass. The greater an object's mass, the more inertia it has.

In a rotating wheel, inertia also depends on how the mass is distributed. A wheel has more inertia if its mass is concentrated near the rim than if it is concentrated around the centre. This means that two wheels of the same mass can have different inertia. Wheels designed to exploit inertia in machines often have heavy or thickened rims to provide the maximum resistance to any change in speed.

As I raced down the hill and over the wreckage, I wondered about my insurance coverage. Then I noticed the pond and its stunned occupant. The mammoth's little adventure had ended, but it was several minutes before I could approach my vehicle. Although upside down in the mud, the wheel was spinning rapidly and as it did, it flung everything attached to it a considerable distance.

CENTRIFUGAL FORCE

When an object moves in a circle, it is also always changing direction. Its inertia resists any change in direction as well as speed, and will make the object move straight on if it is free to leave the circle.

So, relative to the circle, the object is always trying to move away from the centre under an apparent outward-acting force. This is known as centrifugal force, and anything moving in a circle — like the mud on the unicycle — experiences it. The faster an object is travelling, the stronger the force is.

Centrifugal force is used in machines to throw something outwards. The simplest example is probably the spin drier, in which a spinning drum holds clothes while the water in them is forced outwards through holes in the drum. Other machines use the centrifugal force that is generated by a sudden movement to activate catches and ratchets.

INERTIA AT WORK

POTTER'S WHEEL

The potter's wheel is a heavy disc with an axle.
It is usually turned either by kicking the axle around or
by operating a treadle. The wheel has considerable inertia,
and this keeps it turning between kicks or presses of
the treadle.

Centrifugal force!

FRICTION-DRIVE TOY

Friction-drive toys store up energy in
a flywheel. When you push the toy
along the floor, the flywheel is set
spinning by the wheels. Its inertia
keeps it spinning so that
when the toy is put
down, it scoots
across the
floor.

TURNTABLE

The turntable of a record player has to rotate at a very
constant speed. To do this, it has a heavy rim so that
most of its mass is concentrated in the part that moves
fastest, thereby raising its inertia. The inertia of the
turntable cancels out any slight variation in speed that
occurs in the turntable motor.

HEAVY RIM

PLAYING ARM

SPINDLE

STARTER MOT

Inertia comes into play both in starting a car and in producing a smooth ride. A car's starter motor turns the engine by meshing with the teeth of the flywheel. An ingenious use of inertia allows the starter motor to engage and disengage the flywheel through a simple spring and screw system. Once the engine has started, the inertia of the heavy flywheel smooths out the jerky movement of the pistons.

1 STARTING UP

When the ignition key is turned, the starter motor rotates rapidly. The motor shaft turns more quickly than the pinion, which is slowed by inertia. The pinion therefore moves along the screw thread.

SPRING

SCREW THREAD

FLYWHEEL STATIONARY

PINION MOVES TOWARDS FLYWHEEL

MOTOR SHAFT

2 ENGINE RUNNING

The teeth of the pinion engage the flywheel, and through its contact with the flywheel, the starter motor turns the crankshaft.

FLYWHEEL TURNED BY PINION

PINION ENGAGES FLYWHEEL

3 STARTER DISENGAGED

When the engine starts, the pinion now begins to rotate faster than the starter motor shaft, and so it moves back along the screw thread, disengaging the flywheel.

PINION MOVES BACK

FLYWHEEL TURNED BY ENGINE

STARTER MOTOR

CRANKSHAFT

FLYWHEEL

ROLLER BLIND

A roller blind is lowered simply by pulling it down; the blind unrolls and remains in any position. To raise the blind, all that is needed is a sharp tug and the whole blind will roll up. But how can the blind tell a gentle pull from a sharp tug?

The shaft on which the blind is rolled contains a powerful spring. This winds up as the blind is lowered.

A locking mechanism — a simple ratchet — prevents the spring unwinding if it is released gently. But when the blind is pulled suddenly, the ratchet no longer holds the blind in position. The motion makes a centrifugal device in the locking mechanism release the spring: the spring unwinds, releasing the energy that it has stored, and up goes the blind.

PAWL   LOCKING DISC   SHAFT   FIXED CENTRAL ROD

PAWL

RATCHET   SPRING

LOWERING THE BLIND

As the shaft rotates, it turns the locking disc to wind up the spring. The pawls are hinged and move over the ratchet, which is fixed to the central rod and does not move.

SECURING THE BLIND

When the shaft stops, the spring pulls the locking disc back slightly. One of the pawls falls to engage the ratchet, securing the locking disc.

FREEING THE BLIND

A tug on the blind rotates the shaft sharply, making the locking pawl move back and disengage the ratchet. The locking disc is now free to move.

RAISING THE BLIND

The spring unwinds, rotating the locking disc rapidly. Centrifugal force holds the pawls away from the ratchet, and the blind rolls up.

CAR SEAT BELT

A car seat belt works in the reverse way to the roller blind. Instead of locking when the belt is pulled gently, it locks when the belt is given a sharp tug of the kind that would occur in a crash, and so secures the driver or passenger. The belt remains unlocked when pulled slowly, allowing normal movement in the seat. At the heart of the seat belt is a centrifugal clutch.

1 THE BELT MOVES FREELY
During normal use, the toothed plate is not in contact with the clutch and so the plate, and therefore the belt shaft, are free to rotate slowly.

2 THE CLUTCH ENGAGES
A sudden movement makes the toothed plate rotate quickly within the clutch. Centrifugal force makes it slide outwards to engage the inner teeth of the clutch.

3 THE BELT LOCKS
Once the clutch has engaged, it rotates to move a pawl which in turn engages the ratchet. The pawl is fixed to the car body, while the ratchet is attached to the belt shaft. The pawl prevents the ratchet turning, so locking the belt. When the belt slackens, springs return the parts to their initial positions and free the belt.

BELT

BELT SHAFT

RATCHET

PAWL
ENGAGES AND
LOCKS RATCHET

CLUTCH
MOVES PAWL

BELT SHAFT

TOOTHED PLATE

GYROSCOPE

A spinning gyroscope can balance on a pivot, defying gravity by remaining horizontal while resting just on the tip of its axle. Instead of falling off the pivot, the gyroscope circles around it. The explanation for this amazing feat lies in the effects of precession.

Like all other objects, the rotating wheel of the gyroscope is subjected to gravity. However, as long as the gyroscope spins, precession overcomes gravity by transforming it into a force that causes the gyroscope to circle instead of falling.

SPIN
SPIN AXIS

GRAVITATIONAL AXIS
FREE END
FIXED END
GRAVITATIONAL PULL

PRECESSIONAL AXIS
PRECESSIONAL MOVEMENT

1 THE GYROSCOPE STARTS SPINNING

The gyroscope is set spinning so that its axle is horizontal and the wheel is vertical. The whole gyroscope rotates around the spin axis, which runs along the axle.

2 GRAVITY BEGINS TO ACT

The gyroscope is now placed so that one end of the axle is free to move. Gravity tries to pull this end downwards, rotating the gyroscope around a second axis, the gravitational axis.

3 PRECESSION OVERCOMES GRAVITY

At this point, precession occurs. Instead of obeying the pull of gravity, precession makes the gyroscope move in a horizontal circle — in effect rotating it about a third axis, a precessional axis.

CHANGING DIRECTION

If either the wheel or the axle turns in the opposite direction, then the gyroscope precesses in the opposite direction.

ARTIFICIAL HORIZON

Gyroscopes are very important in navigation. A spinning gyroscope possesses gyroscopic inertia, which makes it resist any change in its direction. The axle of the gyroscope remains pointing in the initial direction to which it is set. In the artificial horizon – an instrument which indicates the angle at which an aircraft banks – a gyroscope controls an indicator. Gimbals allow the gyroscope axle to remain horizontal. As the aircraft banks, the indicator also remains horizontal and shows the angle of the aircraft.

ROLL AXIS

AXLE

GIMBAL MOUNTING

GYROSCOPE

OBSERVATION WINDOW

AIRCRAFT POSITION INDICATOR

GYROSCOPE CASE

PITCH AXIS

GYROCOMPASS

A gyrocompass makes use of the gyroscope to indicate direction. The axis of the gyroscope rotor is set in a north-south direction and the rotor is set spinning. The gyroscope is connected to an indicator so that as the ship or aircraft carrying the compass turns, the gyroscope keeps the indicator pointing north.

However, just as in the toy gyroscope, friction in the gyrocompass can cause it to drift out of true, and this may have to be corrected. In some gyrocompasses, this is done automatically by using the Earth's gravity. The gyroscope is connected to a weight, such as a tube of mercury, that acts as a pendulum. If the gyrocompass begins to point away from north, the pendulum tilts the axis of the rotor. Precession then occurs to bring the axis back to true north.

INDICATOR

BEARINGS

GIMBAL MOUNTING

ROTOR CASE

ROTOR

GIMBAL MOUNTING

MERCURY TUBE

THE NON-MAGNETIC COMPASS

A magnetic compass points to the north magnetic pole, which is away from true north, so correction is needed. Because gyro-compasses do not use magnetism, they always point to true north.

NORTH

SOUTH

SPRINGS

ON A MAMMOTH HARVEST

A great many mammoths, in spite of their generally placid temperament, are ill-suited to inside work. Their preference for the outdoors combined with their tremendous strength makes them marvellous helpers in the field. I well recall seeing mammoths assisting eagerly during a particularly heavy coconut harvest. Instead of climbing each tree and simply dropping the coconuts, which could damage the shells, the farmer used his mammoth to bring the coconuts within reach of a ladder for effortless picking.

SPRINGS THAT REGAIN THEIR SHAPE

Springs have two basic forms — either a coil or a bending bar — and they have three main uses in machines. The first is simply to return something to its previous position. A door return spring, for example, contracts after being stretched, while the valve springs of a car engine expand after being compressed (see p.49).

SPRINGS THAT MEASURE FORCE

The second use of springs depends on the amount by which springs change shape when they are subjected to a force. This is exactly proportional to the strength of the force exerted on the spring — the more you pull a spring, the more it stretches. Many weighing machines use springs in this way.

CONTRACTING FORCE

STRETCHING FORCE

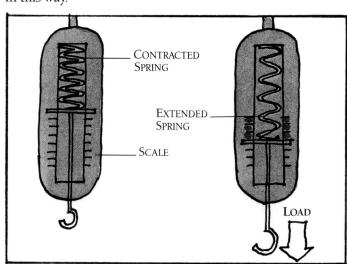

CONTRACTED SPRING

EXTENDED SPRING

SCALE

LOAD

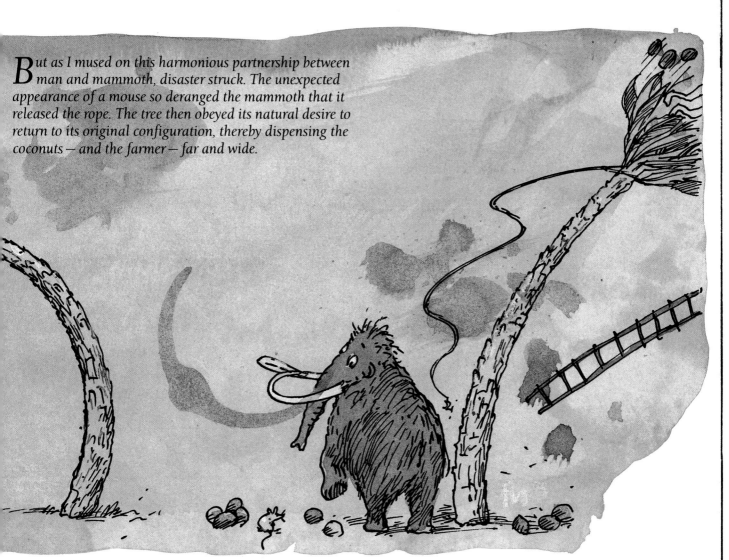

But as I mused on this harmonious partnership between man and mammoth, disaster struck. The unexpected appearance of a mouse so deranged the mammoth that it released the rope. The tree then obeyed its natural desire to return to its original configuration, thereby dispensing the coconuts — and the farmer — far and wide.

SPRINGS THAT STORE ENERGY

The third main use of springs is to store energy. When you stretch or compress a spring, you give it energy to make it move. This energy can be released immediately, as in a door spring, but if not, the energy remains stored. When the spring is released, it gives up the energy. Spring-driven clocks work by releasing the energy stored in springs.

APPLIED FORCE

SPRING CONTRACTS
TO STORE ENERGY

ELASTICITY

The special property of springs, their elasticity, is conferred on them by the way their molecules interact. Two main kinds of force operate on the molecules in a material — an attracting force that pulls molecules together, and a repelling force that pushes them apart. Normally these balance so the molecules keep a certain distance apart.

REPELLING FORCE

ATTRACTING FORCE

SPRING AT REST
The attracting and repelling forces are balanced.

SQUEEZED SPRING
Squeezing builds up the repelling force. When released, the force pushes the molecules apart again.

STRETCHED SPRING
Stretching builds up the attracting force. When released, this pulls the molecules back together.

THE STAPLER

A stapler is an everyday device that conceals an ingenious arrangement of springs. It uses both a coil spring and a leaf spring, which feed the staples along the magazine and return the stapler to its original position once it has been used. Pushing down the stapler causes the blade to descend into the magazine, forcing the front staple through the papers. The anvil bends the ends of the staple to clip the papers together. The return spring then raises the magazine and blade, allowing the magazine spring to advance the next staple into position.

BASE PLATE

A projection on the base plate flattens the return spring when the stapler is used. The spring raises the magazine away from the anvil after use.

CAR SUSPENSION

The suspension of a car allows it to drive smoothly over a bumpy road. The wheels may jolt up and down, but springs between the wheel axles and the body of the car flex and take up the force of the jolts. This ensures that the force of the bumping is not transferred to the car. Springs alone produce a bouncing motion, so the suspension also contains dampers, commonly known as shock absorbers. These slow the movement of the springs to prevent the car and its occupants bouncing up and down.

SHOCK ABSORBER

A shock absorber is fixed between the wheel axle and car body. Its piston moves up or down as the suspension spring flexes. As it does so, the oil is squeezed through channels in the piston, slowing the piston's movement.

COIL SPRING

Smaller vehicles have a coil spring and shock absorber attached to each wheel. The axle of the wheel is attached to hinged struts so that it can move up and down. The spring and shock absorber are fixed between the car body and the struts, or "wishbones".

RETURN SPRING
The return spring is a leaf spring that raises the blade from the magazine and moves the magazine and anvil apart after use.

MAGAZINE
A strip of staples is fed into the magazine of the stapler and held there by a coil spring that advances the next staple into position.

BLADE
ANVIL
STAPLE
MAGAZINE SPRING

LEAF SPRING

Larger vehicles have heavy-duty leaf springs and shock absorbers to cushion the ride. The leaf spring is a stack of steel strips; it is normally slightly curved so that the spring straightens when the vehicle is loaded. The axle is attached at or near the centre of the leaf spring, and the ends of the spring are fixed to the body. The shock absorber is fixed between the axle and body.

TORSION BAR

A torsion bar is a steel rod that acts like a spring to take up a twisting force. If the bar is forced to twist in one direction, it resists the movement and then twists back when the force is removed. Many cars contain an anti-roll bar fixed between the front axles. This rotates as the wheels go up and down. If the car begins to roll over on a tight corner, the anti-roll bar prevents the roll from increasing.

BODY MOUNTING
BODY MOUNTING
LEAF SPRING
WHEEL AXLE
BODY MOUNTING

TORSION BAR
UNTWISTING FORCE
TWISTING FORCE

ANTI-ROLL BAR
INNER WHEEL
OUTER WHEEL
ANTI-ROLL BAR
LOWER WISHBONES

FRICTION

ON MAMMOTHS AND BATHING

*L*ike children, mammoths in a domestic situation must be bathed with some regularity. Also like children, they tend to see bathing both as an annoying interruption and a needless indignity. Frequent bathing is virtually impossible, but when it must be done the most difficult part of the process is just getting the beast near the tub.

GETTING A GRIP

Friction is a force that appears whenever one surface rubs against another, or when an object moves through water, air, or any other liquid or gas. It always opposes motion. Friction happens because two surfaces in close contact grip each other. The harder they press together, the stronger the grip. The same molecular forces are at work as in springs. Forces between the molecules in the surfaces pull the surfaces together. The closer the molecules get, the stronger the force of friction.

The bathing team have to contend with the mammoth's superior weight which gives it the better grip on the ground. Only by reducing friction with the soap and marbles – a lubricant and bearings – can they move it.

You can never get the same amount of useful work from a mechanical device as you put into it: friction will always rob you of some of the energy that is transmitted through the machine. Instead of useful motion, this lost energy appears as heat and sound. Excessive heat and strange noises coming from a machine are sure signs that it is not

PULLING FORCE

FRICTION

MOLECULAR FORCES

performing well.

Designers and engineers strive to overcome friction and make machines as efficient as possible. But paradoxically, many machines depend on friction. If it were suddenly to be banished, cars would slide out of control with wheels spinning helplessly. Brakes, which depend on friction, would be of no use, and neither would the clutch. Grinding machines would not make even a scratch, while parachutes would plummet from the sky.

The bathing scene I remember most vividly was not unlike the weighing of a large mammoth in its communal atmosphere. A large sneaker-clad crowd gathered on one side of a bath filled with soap suds. A dirty mammoth sat defiantly on the other. It should be noted that a mammoth's weight is its greatest defence and that just by standing or sitting still, it is able to resist all but the most determined efforts to move it.

Once ropes had been attached to the animal, they were pulled tight. Meanwhile another team used a technique which I had not previously encountered in my researches.

First, they employed second-class levers to raise the beast slightly. Just when I had concluded that they intended to lever it all the way to the tub, some of their number poured a mixture of liquid soap and marbles between the protesting creature and the floor.

The result was astonishing: the animal's resistance was suddenly reduced, and despite its struggles it was hauled inexorably towards the water. Working simultaneously from both ends, it took little more than half an hour to get the mammoth close enough to the foam-filled tub for a good scrub behind the ears.

CAR TYRE

Car tyres use friction to provide traction and steering: they grip the road so that the force of the engine and the force you exert on the steering wheel are converted into forces that act on the tyres and propel and turn the car. Tyres must grip the road surface in all weather conditions. If a film of water becomes sandwiched between the tyre and the road, then friction – and with it traction and steering – is lost. The raised tread on the surface of a tyre is designed to maintain friction on a wet road by dispersing the water.

PARACHUTE

As a parachute opens, it develops a large force of friction with the air because it is moving rapidly. Friction is initially greater then gravity so the parachutist slows down. As the speed of the parachute lessens, friction decreases until it equals the force of gravity. At this point, there is no overall force acting on the parachutist, so he or she continues to descend without speeding up or slowing down. This constant rate of fall is slow enough for a safe landing.

FRICTION WITH AIR

GRAVITY

THE CLUTCH

In a car, the clutch makes use of friction to transmit the rotation of the engine crankshaft to the gearbox, and then to the wheels. It can take up the rotation slowly so that the car moves smoothly away.

In a car with a manual gearbox, the clutch is disengaged when the clutch pedal is pressed down. The pedal operates the thrust pad, which presses on levers at the centre of the rotating clutch cover. This raises the pressure plate away from the clutch plate, disconnecting the flywheel, which is turned by the crankshaft, from the transmission shaft. When the clutch pedal is lifted, the springs force the pressure plate and clutch plate against the flywheel. Friction linings on the clutch plate allow the plate to slide before it becomes fully engaged, which prevents jerking.

FLYWHEEL DRIVEN BY CRANKSHAFT

CLUTCH PLATE

PRESSURE PLATE

SPRING

CLUTCH COVER

CLUTCH FORK

THRUST BEARING

THRUST PAD

SYNCHROMESH

The synchromesh is a mechanism in a car's gearbox (see pp.40-1) that enables the driver to change gear easily. It prevents gear wheels inside the gearbox from engaging at different speeds and crunching together. Before any forward gear is selected, gear wheels driven by the engine freewheel on the transmission shaft. For a gear to be engaged, the wheel and shaft need to be brought to the same speed and locked together. The synchromesh uses friction to do this smoothly and quietly.

Pushed by the selector fork, the collar slides along the transmission shaft, rotating with it. The collar fits over a cone on the gear wheel, making the wheel speed up or slow down until both are moving at the same speed. The outer toothed ring on the collar then engages the dog teeth on the cone, locking the collar to the gear wheel.

ENGINE

TRANSMISSION SHAFT

GEARBOX

CLUTCH

DIFFERENTIAL

CLUTCH ENGAGED
Releasing the pedal allows the clutch springs to force the clutch plate and flywheel together, so the flywheel drives the transmission shaft.

TRANSMISSION SHAFT TO GEARBOX

CLUTCH DISENGAGED
Pressing the pedal pushes in the thrust pad, which in turn pulls back the pressure plate. The flywheel and transmission shaft are now disconnected, so the engine cannot turn the wheels.

SYNCHROMESH DISENGAGED
When the synchromesh is disengaged, the collar and gear wheel are not connected, and the gear wheel freewheels on the transmission shaft.

SELECTOR FORK

GEAR WHEEL

DOG TEETH

CONE

TOOTHED RING

COLLAR

GEAR WHEEL

TRANSMISSION SHAFT

SYNCHROMESH ENGAGED
The collar makes contact with the cone, and friction between them brings them to the same speed. The teeth mesh together. The gear wheel is now locked to the transmission shaft and so can transmit power to it from the engine, turning the wheels.

CAR BRAKES

To bring a fast-moving car and its passengers to a halt in a few seconds, car brakes must create a greater force than the engine does. Yet this force is produced by friction between surfaces with a total area only about the size of your hands.

Brakes are powerful because the brake pad or shoe and the brake disc or drum are pushed together with great force. In a car with unassisted brakes, the force of the driver's foot is amplified by the hydraulics in the braking system (see p.128). In a car with power brakes, this hydraulic system is boosted by another system that comes into operation when the brake pedal is pressed, enabling the driver to achieve quicker braking (see p.127).

BRAKE PADS
The pressure of the hydraulic fluid forces pistons in the cylinders to push the brake pads against the disc.

DISC BRAKES

In disc brakes, friction is applied to both sides of a spinning disc by the brake pads. Much heat can be generated without affecting performance, giving great braking power. This is because the heat is removed by air flowing over the disc. Disc brakes are fitted to the front wheels of a car, where more braking power is needed, or to all wheels.

CALIPER
The caliper fits around the disc and houses the brake pads and the hydraulic cylinders.

DISC
The disc plate is fixed to the wheel. It is exposed to the air so that heat generated by braking is dissipated.

DRUM BRAKES

In drum brakes, friction is applied to the inside of a spinning drum by the brake shoes. Heat build-up tends to reduce friction, causing drum brakes to "fade" and give less braking power. Drum brakes are fitted to the rear wheels of many cars. The handbrake or parking brake often operates the rear brakes via a mechanical linkage.

BRAKE LINING

HYDRAULIC CYLINDER

BRAKE SHOES
The brake shoes are either hinged at one end or moved by two hydraulic cylinders. The linings on the shoes come into contact with the brake drum.

BRAKE DRUM
The brake drum is fixed to the wheel. A return spring pulls the shoes away from the drum when the brake is released.

RETURN SPRING

OIL RIG

Drilling rigs often have to penetrate deep into hard rock. The drill bit grinds its way into the ground, breaking the rock up into small pieces. Grinding is an extreme form of friction; it develops great heat, which is removed by a cooling fluid mud that is pumped down the shaft. Oil rigs are set up above a deposit of oil or gas, which may be found under land or the seabed. Offshore rigs either stand on the seabed or on long legs, or float at the surface anchored in position.

FLOATING RIG

LAND RIG

MUD FLOW

DRILL PIPE

CONES

SEABED

SHAFT

ROCK

ROTARY BIT

The bit that drills the shaft is mounted on the end of a long drill pipe, which is rotated by an engine in the rig above. A tricone rotary bit has three cones studded with teeth that turn as the drill pipe rotates. The weight of the pipe on the bit helps it to crush and grind the rock.

MUD PUMP

MUD TANK

DRILLING MUD

The mud used on oil rigs is a special liquid developed for drilling. It is pumped into the top of the drill pipe, and from there it flows down to the drilling bit and then up the outside of the pipe back to the rig, bringing up the ground rock, before it is filtered and recycled.

SHAFT

DRILL PIPE

DRILLING BIT

FREEDOM FROM FRICTION

Machines that move themselves or that create movement are limited by friction. In the moving parts of an engine, for example, friction lowers performance and may produce overheating. Reducing friction reduces energy needs and so improves efficiency. This reduction is achieved by minimizing the frictional contact through bearings, streamlining and lubrication.

BALL BEARING

In a ball bearing, the area of contact between the balls and the moving parts is very small, and friction is therefore very low. Roller bearings contain cylindrical rollers instead of balls but work in the same way.

INNER RACE

OUTER RACE

BALLS

CAR LUBRICATION

A car has several sections with moving parts and good lubrication is essential. In the suspension, steering, gearbox and differential, filling with oil or grease is sufficient. The engine, however, needs a special lubrication system to get oil to its components as they work.

Oil is contained in the sump, which is a chamber at the base of the engine. A pump (see p.124) forces oil up from the sump through the oil filter, which removes dirt particles, and then to all the bearings and other moving parts of the engine, such as the pistons. The parts contain narrow channels that lead the oil to the moving surfaces. The oil then returns to the sump to be recirculated.

OIL PUMP

OIL FILTER

SUMP

PERPETUAL MOTION

Even with the very best bearings, lubricants and streamlining, a little friction still remains. Without a continual supply of fuel or electricity, friction gradually consumes a machine's kinetic energy (its energy of movement) and the machine slows down and stops. The mythical perpetual motion machine – one that, once started, will work forever with no energy input – must remain a myth...at least, on Earth.

In space, matters are different. No air exists to cause friction and slow a spacecraft. Once launched into space, a spacecraft is freed from friction. It can continue to move in perpetuity without ever firing its engine again. Thus, in the space probes voyaging outwards towards the stars, we have achieved perpetual motion, a pure movement governed only by the celestial mechanics of gravity.

VOLUNTEER
MOLECULES
ENTER·THE·FIRST
WHOOPEE·CUSHION

HARNESSING THE ELEMENTS

INTRODUCTION

IT WAS THE ANCIENT GREEKS who first had the idea that everything is made up of elements. They conjured up just four of them – earth, fire, air, and water. As it turned out, the idea was right but the elements wrong. Modern elements are less evocative but more numerous; they make up just over one hundred basic substances. Some are commonplace, like hydrogen, oxygen, iron, and carbon; others are rare and precious, such as mercury, uranium, and gold. Purely by the power of reason, the Ancient Greeks also made another fundamental discovery, which is that all things consist of particles called atoms. Elements are substances that contain only one kind of atom. All other substances are compounds of two or more elements in which the atoms group themselves together to form molecules. The way molecules behave governs the workings of many machines, such as ships, aeroplanes, pumps, refrigerators, and combustion engines, all of which harness the ancient elements and set molecules to work.

MORE ABOUT MOLECULES

The idea that everything is made of particles takes some imagination to understand. As you read this, molecules of oxygen and nitrogen travelling at supersonic speed are bombarding you from all directions. You are unaware of this because the molecules (which, along with those of other gases, make up the air) are on the small side. You could get about 400 million million million of them into an empty matchbox. In fact, it would be truer to say that you could get all those millions of molecules *out* of the matchbox, because the molecules of gases are so hyperactive that they will fill any space open to them. Like five-year-olds, they dash about in all directions with unflagging energy, crashing into any obstacle they meet. In liquids, the molecules are less energetic and go haphazardly about in small groups, rather like drunken dancers prone to colliding with the walls of the dance hall. The molecules in solids are the least energetic; they huddle together like a flock of sheep shuffling around in a field. However invisible molecules might be, their existence does explain the properties and behaviour of materials that are put to use in machines. In a solid, the molecular bonds are strong and hold the molecules firmly together so that the solid is hard and rigid. The weaker bonds between liquid molecules pull them together to give the liquid a set volume, but the bonds are sufficiently weak to allow the liquid to flow. The bonds between gas molecules are weaker still, and they enable the molecules to move apart so the gas expands and fills any space. In all materials, the molecules' urge to stick together or spread is very strong, and it is put to use in devices as different as the rocket, the toilet cistern, and the aqualung.

STRENGTH IN NUMBERS

Because molecules in liquids and in gases are always on the move, they have power. Each one of them may not have much, but together they become a force to be reckoned with. A liner floats because billions of moving water molecules support the hull, while a jumbo jet can fly thanks to countless air molecules clustering under its wings and holding them aloft. Molecules continually bombard any surface they encounter. Each collision produces a little force as the molecule hits the surface and bounces back. Over the whole surface, a large force builds up – this is known as the pressure of the liquid or gas. If you squeeze more molecules into the same space, you get more pressure as more molecules strike the surface. The pressure produced by this restless movement of molecules is put to work in many ways. Some machines work by producing pressure while others are powered by it.

SPEEDING THINGS UP

There is another way of strongly increasing pressure that does not involve physical effort. This is heat, which is a form of energy. We feel heat, or the lack of it, as a change of temperature. But on a molecular level, heat is just movement. If you touch something cold, the molecules in your fingers slow down as they lose heat; if you touch something hot, they gain heat and speed up. When molecules are heated, they respond by moving faster. The pressure increases unless the molecules get farther apart, in which case the material expands. If the molecules are made to move fast enough, the bonds between them start to give way: a solid melts into a liquid and a liquid forms a gas. If an object is cooled down, the speed of its molecules slows. The material loses pressure or contracts. As the bonds between molecules reassert themselves, a gas may condense to a liquid and a liquid freeze to a solid. There is a point at which all heat vanishes, although no-one can quite achieve it. If a material were cooled to -273°C (-459°F), the molecular motion would cease altogether, making this – absolute zero – the lowest temperature possible. Machines that make or use heat all get molecules on the move. The extra motion can strain relations within the families of atoms inside molecules, making them change partners and form new molecules. Fire and explosions are some of the possible results, but so too are the making of steel and toast.

BREAKING THE BONDS

The atoms of elements are made up of even smaller particles – electrons, which form the outer shells of each atom, and protons and neutrons, which make up its core, or nucleus. We tap the energy of electrons – in the form of electrical heat – in everyday devices from hairdriers to heaters. However, breaking the bonds that hold together the nucleus of an atom is a more serious business altogether. As we shall see in the last section of *Harnessing the Elements* these bonds are the strongest of all forces. Breaking them unleashes the most powerful and potentially dangerous source of energy known.

FLOATING

ON TRANSPORTING A MAMMOTH

O nce, when waiting to board a ferry, I observed further downstream a rival operator attempting to shunt a particularly large mammoth onto a sizeable raft. No sooner had the craft and its protesting cargo been launched, than both quickly sank.

Taken aback by this turn of events, I relinquished my position in the queue to enquire whether I might not be of assistance. My offer was quickly accepted by the soggy pair. After interviewing those involved and making some hasty calculations, I deduced that the spirit of the water, clearly afraid of the raft's imposing cargo, had simply moved out of the way as the raft was loaded. This left nothing below the raft and so it sank.

Clearly, a little subterfuge was necessary to keep the cargo afloat. I therefore suggested that the mammoth should be hidden from the spirit of the water by a special device of my own invention.

RAFTS AND BOATS

Although characteristically wayward, the inventor's explanation of the mammoth's adventures contains an element of truth. Water does move out of the way when anything enters it. But rather than leaving nothing below an immersed object, the water around it pushes back and tries to support the object. If the water succeeds, the object floats.

Take the case of the raft before the mammoth is on board. Its weight pulls it down into the water. But the water pushes back, supporting the raft with a force called upthrust. The amount of upthrust depends on how much water the raft displaces, or pushes aside, as it enters the water. Upthrust increases as more and more of the raft settles in the water. At some point, the upthrust becomes equal to the weight of the raft and the raft floats.

Now let's load the mammoth. The extra weight makes the raft settle deeper. Although the upthrust increases, it cannot become great enough to equal the weight of the raft and the mammoth because not enough water gets displaced. The raft and its load sink to the bottom.

The boat is a different matter. Because it is hollow, it can settle deeper in the water and displace enough water to provide the necessary upthrust to support the weight of the boat and the mammoth.

Things can also float in a gas and, like the inflated mammoth, a balloon floats in air for the same reason that a boat floats on water. In this case, the upthrust is equal to the weight of air that is displaced. If the weight of the balloon, the air that it contains and the occupants is less than the upthrust, the balloon will rise. If it is greater, the balloon will sink.

THE EFFECT OF DENSITY

Why should a heavy wooden raft float while a pin sinks? And if a steel pin sinks, why does a steel boat float? The answer is density. This factor, rather than weight, determines whether things float or sink.

The density of an object is equal to its weight divided by its volume. Every substance, including water, has its own particular density at a given temperature (density varies as a substance gets hotter or colder). Any solid less dense than water floats, while one that is more dense sinks. However, a hollow object such as a boat floats if its *overall* density — its total weight divided by its total volume — is less than the density of water.

My plans were put into effect. A wooden wall was built around the top of the raft and to everyone's amazement, except of course my own, both raft and cargo floated safely across.

In deference to the beast's obvious displeasure at even the risk of a second dunking, I had suggested that it be clothed in a rubber diving suit. I confess that I am still unable to fully explain what happened shortly after landing. The mammoth was tied up near the dock, wearing the suit and getting some sun. The suit began to expand and to my astonishment the enormous beast rose into the air. Quite why this happened is completely baffling. Perhaps it had something to do with the spirit of the air? We still have so much to learn.

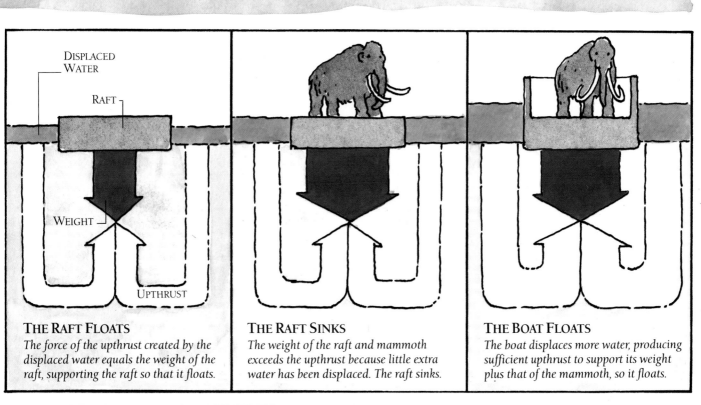

THE RAFT FLOATS

The force of the upthrust created by the displaced water equals the weight of the raft, supporting the raft so that it floats.

THE RAFT SINKS

The weight of the raft and mammoth exceeds the upthrust because little extra water has been displaced. The raft sinks.

THE BOAT FLOATS

The boat displaces more water, producing sufficient upthrust to support its weight plus that of the mammoth, so it floats.

THE SUBMERSIBLE

Submersibles are designed for use at great depths. They need to be able to sink, to rise and also to float underwater. They do this by altering their weight with a system of ballast tanks which can hold either air or water. If a craft's ballast tanks are flooded with water, the craft's weight increases. If the water is then expelled by compressed air, the weight decreases. By adjusting the amount of water in the tanks, the craft's weight and buoyancy can be precisely regulated.

Submersibles are designed to perform delicate tasks deep underwater, and are therefore designed to withstand high pressure and to be highly manoeuvrable. They do not need to move at speed and therefore, unlike submarines, they are not streamlined.

LATERAL THRUSTER
This moves the submersible from side to side.

VERTICAL THRUSTER
Small adjustments to the submersible's position above the sea floor are produced by this thruster.

CREW COMPARTMENT
The spherical pressure vessel withstands tremendous force exerted by water at great depths. The air inside is maintained at atmospheric pressure.

MAIN PROPELLER
This propeller drives the submersible forwards or backwards.

BALLAST TANK
The submersible dives or surfaces by filling the ballast tanks with water or air.

THE SUBMARINE

BALLAST TANKS

HULL

AIR EXPELLED

COMPRESSED AIR

WATER ADMITTED

UPTHRUST

HYDROPLANES

WATER FLOW

NEUTRAL BUOYANCY

WATER EXPELLED

TANKS FULL

DIVING

With its ballast tanks filled with air, the submarine has an overall density lower than seawater. As a result, it floats. To dive, the ballast tanks are flooded. This gives the submarine a density the same as seawater. The hydroplanes then steer the craft downwards as it is propelled forwards.

MANIPULATORS

The crew operate these arms, which are equipped with lights and gripping claws, from the crew compartment.

SURFACING

To reduce the submarine's density, compressed air is blown into the ballast tanks. This forces out the seawater, and the submarine begins to rise. The upward movement is increased by the action of the hydroplanes.

A submarine works in much the same way as a submersible, with the exception that it is able to use the force driving it forwards to control its depth. Fins on either side called hydroplanes swivel to deflect the flow of water around the hull. This lifts or drops the nose so that the submarine can ascend or descend under the power of its propellers. As in the submersible, buoyancy is controlled by ballast tanks. These are flooded when diving; when surfacing, the water in the tanks is expelled by compressed air.

ROBOT CAMERA

PASSENGER BOAT

All powered craft that travel in or on water move by imparting movement to the water or air around them, and they steer by altering the direction in which the water or air flows. In a large ship, power is provided by the propellers, and the direction is governed by a rudder. But large ships also need to be able to control their movement sideways when docking, and their roll during heavy seas. They do this with bow thrusters and stabilizers, two devices that act in the same way as the main propellers and the rudder.

Below the water's surface, the hull is as smooth as possible to reduce the ship's water resistance and increase efficiency. The bow thrusters are recessed, and therefore do not disturb the water flow. The stabilizers are retractable, folding away inside hatches when not in use. At the bow, the hull may project forwards beneath the water in a huge bulb. This bulb reduces the bow wave that the ship makes as it slices through the water. The water resistance of the ship is lessened, and this raises the speed or saves fuel.

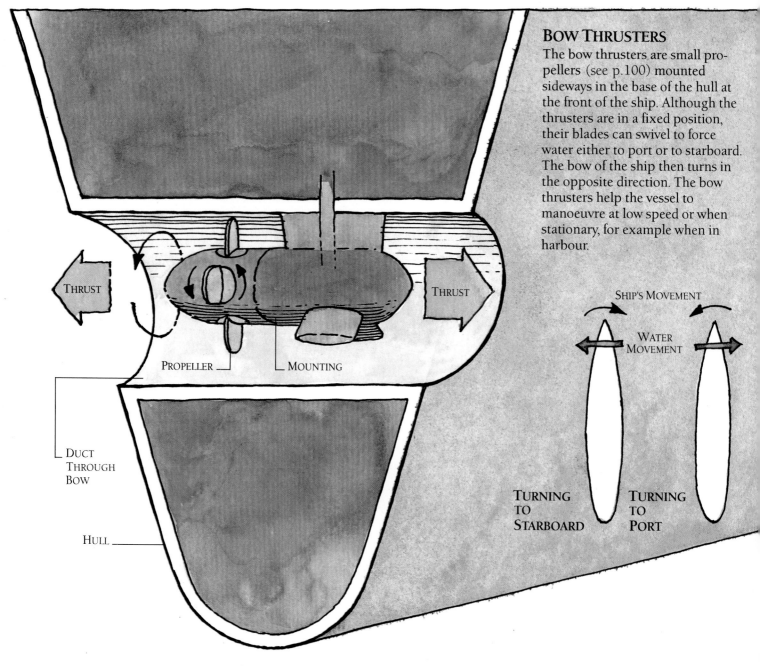

BOW THRUSTERS

The bow thrusters are small propellers (see p.100) mounted sideways in the base of the hull at the front of the ship. Although the thrusters are in a fixed position, their blades can swivel to force water either to port or to starboard. The bow of the ship then turns in the opposite direction. The bow thrusters help the vessel to manoeuvre at low speed or when stationary, for example when in harbour.

THRUST

THRUST

PROPELLER

MOUNTING

DUCT THROUGH BOW

HULL

SHIP'S MOVEMENT

WATER MOVEMENT

TURNING TO STARBOARD

TURNING TO PORT

TROPICAL FRESH WATER
NON-TROPICAL FRESH WATER

TROPICAL SEAS
SUMMER SEAS
WINTER SEAS
WINTER IN NORTH ATLANTIC

TF
F
T
S
W
WNA

PLIMSOLL LINE OR LOAD LINE

The loading of a ship is regulated by marks on the side of the hull. The lines indicate loading limits for a variety of seas and seasons. As the ship is loaded, it settles deeper in the water. For safety, it must not be loaded so that the relevant mark goes below the water.

The different levels are due to differences in the density of water, and therefore the upthrust it produces. Salt water is denser than fresh water, and cold water denser than warm water.

STABILIZERS

Ships roll from side to side as they encounter high waves. To reduce rolling, they have stabilizers. These are a pair of large fins that extend from the hull. The fins swivel as the hull begins to roll, acting like horizontal rudders (see p.101) to produce upward or downward forces that counteract the roll. The stabilizers are often controlled by a gyroscope (see p.76) that senses the ship's motion. The fins can reduce rolling movement by 90 per cent.

HULL

STABILIZER

STABILIZER

UPWARD FORCE
PRODUCED BY FIN

WATER FLOW
DEFLECTED
DOWNWARDS

PATH OF
INCOMING WATER

DIRECTION OF ROLL

EXTENDED FIN

When the hull rolls down, the front edge of the fin tilts up to deflect the water flow downwards. This produces an upward force on the fin, which stops the roll. Tilting the fin in the opposite direction stops an upward roll.

PASSENGER BOAT

Most craft that travel on water need a source of power to propel them forwards and also a means of steering. These requirements are met by propellers and rudders, two devices which work by the same pair of principles.

The first principle is action and reaction. As the blades of a propeller spin, they strike the water and make it move towards the rear of the vessel. The force with which the blades move the water is called the action. The water pushes back on the blades as it begins to move, producing an equal force called the reaction which drives the propeller forwards.

The second principle is called suction. The surface of each propeller blade is curved so that the blade has the shape of an aerofoil (see p.107). Water flows around the blade as it rotates, moving faster over the front surface. The faster motion lowers the water pressure at the front surface, and the blade is sucked forwards.

Overall, a combination of reaction and suction drives the spinning propeller through the water.

A rudder affects the water flowing around it in the same way. Reaction and suction produce a turning force that changes the boat's direction.

Propellers drive most surface vessels as well as submarines and submersibles. They also work in air, and power airships and many aircraft. Virtually all forms of water transport and most forms of air transport steer with rudders.

PROPELLER

The blades of a ship's propeller are broad and curved like scimitars to slash strongly through the water. The propeller does not turn rapidly, but, having broad blades, it moves a large amount of water to produce a powerful reaction as well as strong suction. Small high-speed vessels have fast-spinning propellers with narrow blades that move less water but which give high suction. At very high speeds the propeller may make water vaporize, causing a loss of power.

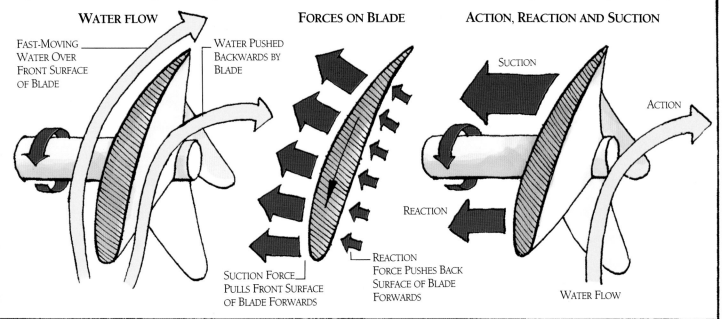

WATER FLOW

FAST-MOVING WATER OVER FRONT SURFACE OF BLADE

WATER PUSHED BACKWARDS BY BLADE

SUCTION FORCE PULLS FRONT SURFACE OF BLADE FORWARDS

FORCES ON BLADE

REACTION FORCE PUSHES BACK SURFACE OF BLADE FORWARDS

ACTION, REACTION AND SUCTION

SUCTION

ACTION

REACTION

WATER FLOW

RUDDER

The rudder acts on the water flowing past the vessel and the backward flow generated by the propeller. The rudder blade swivels to deflect this flow. As the water changes direction, it pushes back with a reaction force and the blade moves in the opposite direction. Suction produced by water flowing around the blade assists reaction. These forces move the stern of the boat and the whole vessel turns around its centre so that the bow points in a new direction.

BOAT MOVES STRAIGHT AHEAD

RUDDER

CENTRE OF BOAT

FLOW OF WATER AROUND RUDDER

RUDDER TURNED

REACTION MOVES RUDDER TO LEFT

RUDDER HANDLE MOVES TO LEFT

DEFLECTED FLOW (ACTION)

BOAT TURNS TO THE RIGHT

BOAT TURNS AROUND ITS CENTRE

BOAT ON NEW COURSE

THE WINDSURFER

Modern sailing craft from the windsurfer to the racing yacht can use the power of the wind to propel them in any direction, no matter which quarter the wind may blow from.

This versatility is achieved with a triangular sail that can be shifted around the boat's mast to engage the wind at various angles. The sail is able to propel the boat at any angle to the wind, except head-on. However, sailing boats are able to make progress into the wind, although in an indirect way. They do this by "tacking", or following a zig-zagging course which keeps the sail at an angle to the wind, and so enables it to provide power.

The windsurfer is the simplest craft with a movable sail. It is basically a raft with a sail on a tilting mast and a small keel beneath. The person aboard the windsurfer grips a curved bar to move the sail in any direction to take advantage of the wind. The sail not only drives the windsurfer forwards but also steers it.

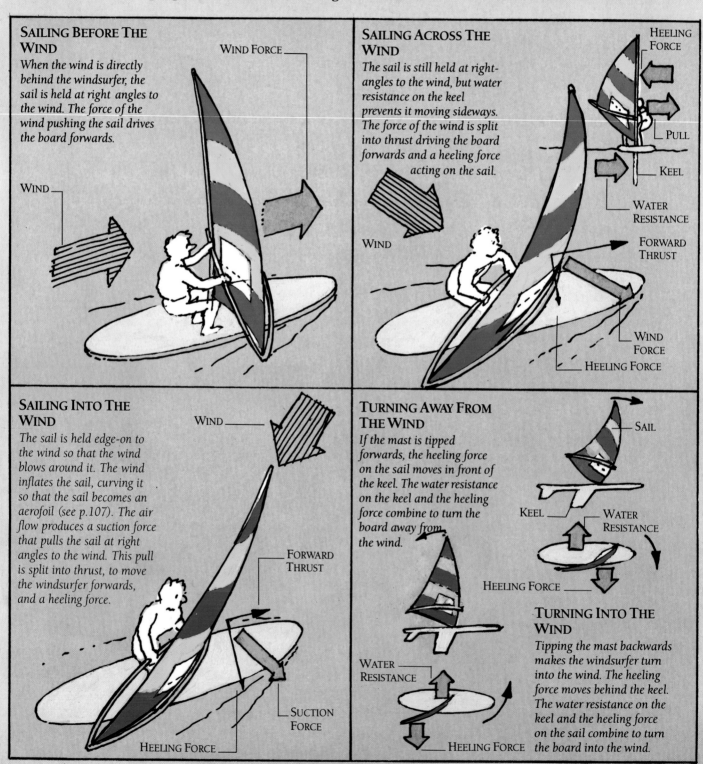

SAILING BEFORE THE WIND

When the wind is directly behind the windsurfer, the sail is held at right angles to the wind. The force of the wind pushing the sail drives the board forwards.

WIND FORCE

WIND

SAILING ACROSS THE WIND

The sail is still held at right-angles to the wind, but water resistance on the keel prevents it moving sideways. The force of the wind is split into thrust driving the board forwards and a heeling force acting on the sail.

HEELING FORCE

PULL

KEEL

WATER RESISTANCE

FORWARD THRUST

WIND FORCE

HEELING FORCE

WIND

SAILING INTO THE WIND

The sail is held edge-on to the wind so that the wind blows around it. The wind inflates the sail, curving it so that the sail becomes an aerofoil (see p.107). The air flow produces a suction force that pulls the sail at right angles to the wind. This pull is split into thrust, to move the windsurfer forwards, and a heeling force.

WIND

FORWARD THRUST

SUCTION FORCE

HEELING FORCE

TURNING AWAY FROM THE WIND

If the mast is tipped forwards, the heeling force on the sail moves in front of the keel. The water resistance on the keel and the heeling force combine to turn the board away from the wind.

SAIL

KEEL

WATER RESISTANCE

HEELING FORCE

WATER RESISTANCE

HEELING FORCE

TURNING INTO THE WIND

Tipping the mast backwards makes the windsurfer turn into the wind. The heeling force moves behind the keel. The water resistance on the keel and the heeling force on the sail combine to turn the board into the wind.

THE YACHT

A yacht usually has two triangular sails – the mainsail and the jib. The sails propel the yacht before, across or into the wind in the same way as the windsurfer. When sailing into the wind, the two sails combine to act as one large aerofoil with a slot in the centre. The slot channels air over both sails, producing a powerful suction force. This force splits into two separate forces – thrust that propels the yacht forwards and a heeling force that tilts it over. The weight of the tilting hull and keel counteracts the heeling force, while water resistance stops the yacht moving sideways.

A yacht is steered with a rudder (see p.101), which deflects the flow of water that passes the hull to turn the yacht in the required direction. As the yacht turns, the crew let out or pull in the sails so that they take up the best angle to the wind. A balloon-like spinnaker sail may be used when the yacht is sailing before the wind.

MAINSAIL

HEELING FORCE

SUCTION

THRUST

WIND

JIB

WEIGHT OF HULL AND KEEL

RUDDER

KEEL

You can't miss it. It's blue!

THE AIRSHIP

An airship has a vast envelope that creates a powerful upthrust to lift the substantial weight of the cabin, engine, fans and passengers. The bulk of the envelope contains helium, a light gas which reduces the weight of the airship so that it is equal to the upthrust, thereby producing neutral buoyancy. Inside the envelope are compartments of air called ballonets. Pumping air out of or into the ballonets decreases or increases the airship's weight and it ascends or descends. The airship also has propellers called ducted fans that drive it through the air and which swivel to manoeuvre the airship at take-off or landing. Tail fins and a rudder can tilt or turn the whole craft as it floats through the sky. In this way, the airship travels from place to place like an airborne combination of submarine and submersible.

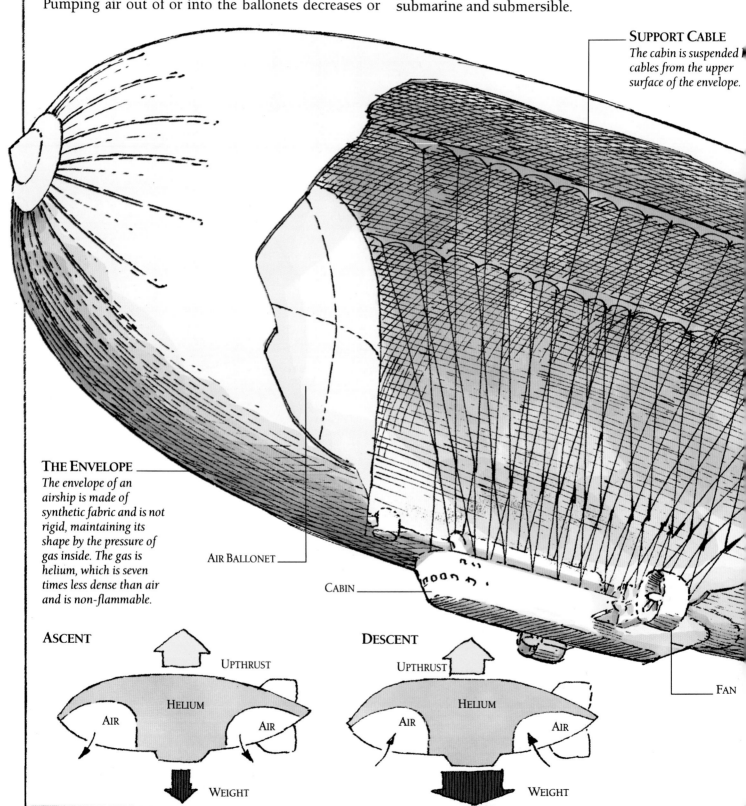

SUPPORT CABLE
The cabin is suspended cables from the upper surface of the envelope.

THE ENVELOPE
The envelope of an airship is made of synthetic fabric and is not rigid, maintaining its shape by the pressure of gas inside. The gas is helium, which is seven times less dense than air and is non-flammable.

AIR BALLONET

CABIN

FAN

ASCENT

UPTHRUST

HELIUM

AIR

AIR

WEIGHT

DESCENT

UPTHRUST

HELIUM

AIR

AIR

WEIGHT

THE HOT-AIR BALL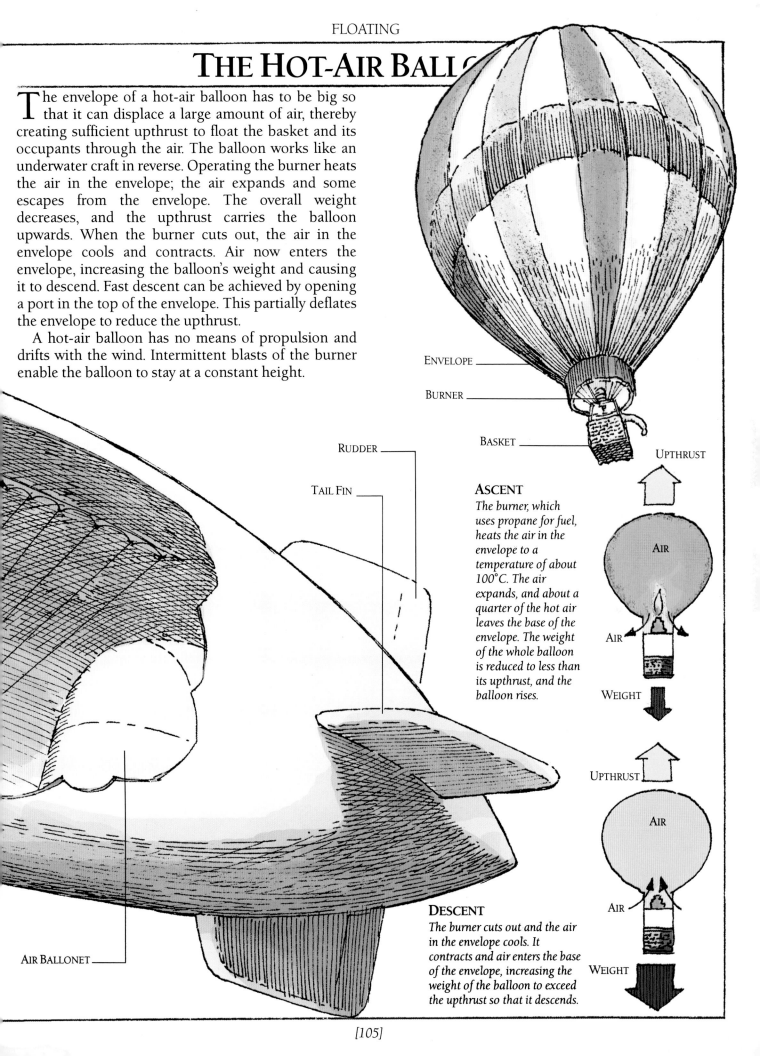

The envelope of a hot-air balloon has to be big so that it can displace a large amount of air, thereby creating sufficient upthrust to float the basket and its occupants through the air. The balloon works like an underwater craft in reverse. Operating the burner heats the air in the envelope; the air expands and some escapes from the envelope. The overall weight decreases, and the upthrust carries the balloon upwards. When the burner cuts out, the air in the envelope cools and contracts. Air now enters the envelope, increasing the balloon's weight and causing it to descend. Fast descent can be achieved by opening a port in the top of the envelope. This partially deflates the envelope to reduce the upthrust.

A hot-air balloon has no means of propulsion and drifts with the wind. Intermittent blasts of the burner enable the balloon to stay at a constant height.

ENVELOPE

BURNER

BASKET

UPTHRUST

RUDDER

TAIL FIN

ASCENT
The burner, which uses propane for fuel, heats the air in the envelope to a temperature of about 100°C. The air expands, and about a quarter of the hot air leaves the base of the envelope. The weight of the whole balloon is reduced to less than its upthrust, and the balloon rises.

AIR

AIR

WEIGHT

UPTHRUST

AIR

AIR

AIR BALLONET

DESCENT
The burner cuts out and the air in the envelope cools. It contracts and air enters the base of the envelope, increasing the weight of the balloon to exceed the upthrust so that it descends.

WEIGHT

FLYING

ON THE ADVENT OF AIRFREIGHT

*O*ne day I chanced upon a delivery mammoth from a local awning manufacturer sighing under the weight of a large wooden frame over which was stretched a piece of canvas. Apparently waiting for its driver, the mammoth was tethered to a tree with the awning firmly secured to its back. Suddenly the wind picked up, lifting the startled beast dramatically into the sky. I noticed that as long as the wind blew and the rope between tree and mammoth held, the creature remained airborne. . .

. . .but when the wind abruptly died, the mammoth returned to the ground without ceremony, destroying not only the awning but also the manufacturer's entire premises.

HEAVIER-THAN-AIR FLIGHT

In the struggle to overcome its not inconsiderable weight and launch itself into the air, the mammoth becomes in turn a kite, a glider and finally a powered aircraft. These are three quite different ways by which an object that is heavier than air can be made to fly.

Like balloons and airships, heavier-than-air machines achieve flight by generating a force that overcomes their weight and which supports them in the air. But because they cannot float in air, they work in different ways to balloons and airships.

Kites employ the power of the wind to keep them aloft, while all winged aircraft, including gliders and helicopters, make use of the aerofoil and its power of lift. Vertical take-off aircraft direct the power of their jet engines downwards and heave themselves off the ground by brute force.

The two principles that govern heavier-than-air flight are the same as those that propel powered vessels – action and reaction, and suction (see pp.100-1). When applied to flight, suction is known as lift.

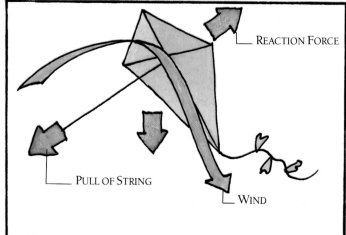

REACTION FORCE

PULL OF STRING

WIND

KITE

The kite flies only in a wind, and it is held by its string so that it deflects the wind downwards. The wind provides the force for flight. It exerts a reaction that equals the pull of the string and the weight of the kite to support the kite in the air.

*D*uring my own experiments with awning delivery, I discovered that by securing a slightly curved awning to a volunteer mammoth's back, the danger and considerable expense of crash landings could be greatly reduced. Should the wind speed drop or the rope break, the mammoth would usually glide back to Earth in a gentle spiral. I planned one further improvement in which friction-reducing foot-gear would enable the mammoth to leave the ground simply by blowing backwards with its trunk.

*H*owever, despite repeated attempts, the mammoth never got far enough off the ground to make this novel form of delivery a practical procedure. Even with the specially designed foot-gear in place, landings remained somewhat unpredictable.

I recall one most unfortunate incident in which a mammoth had to be completely bandaged after an unusually clumsy four-point landing. This resulted in the rather interesting streamlined form depicted here. It is not one that I feel could ever leave the ground.

AEROFOIL

The cross-section of a wing has a shape called an aerofoil. As the wing moves through the air, the air divides to pass around the wing. The aerofoil is curved so that air passing above the wing moves faster than air passing beneath. Fast-moving air has a lower pressure than slow-moving air. The pressure of the air is therefore greater beneath the wing than above it. This difference in air pressure forces the wing upwards. The force is called lift.

AIR FLOW

LIFT

AEROFOIL

GLIDER

A glider is the simplest kind of winged aircraft. It is first pulled along the ground until it is moving fast enough for the lift generated by the wings to exceed its weight. The glider then rises into the air and flies. After release, the glider continues to move forwards as it drops slowly, pulled by a thrust force due to gravity. Friction with the air produces a force called drag that acts to hold the glider back. These two pairs of opposing forces — lift and weight, thrust and drag — act on all aircraft.

LIFT

THRUST

LIFT

WEIGHT

DRAG

THE AEROPLANE

Adding an engine to a flying machine gives it the power to dispense with winds and air currents that govern the flight of unpowered craft such as balloons and gliders. In order to steer an aeroplane, a system of flaps is used. These act just like the rudder of a boat (see p.101). They deflect the air flow and turn or tilt the aeroplane so that it rotates around its centre of gravity, which in all aeroplanes lies between the wings.

Aeroplanes usually have one pair of wings to provide lift, and the wings and tail have flaps that turn or tilt the aircraft in flight. Power is provided by a propeller (see p.100) mounted on the nose, or by several propellers on the wings, or by jet engines (see p.160) mounted on the wings, tail, or inside the fuselage.

AILERON

PEDALS

CONTROL COLUMN

LEADING EDGE OF WING

CONTROL CABLES

The control surfaces of many aeroplanes are physically connected to the control column by cables. Hydraulic systems or electric motors operated by the cables move the surfaces. In "fly-by-wire" aircraft, the surfaces are operated by motors that respond to control signals fed along wires from a computer. The computer is connected to the control column, and it controls the surfaces to produce the required movement of the plane.

THRUST GENERATED BY REACTION OF PROPELLER

CLIMBING

To climb, the pilot pulls the control column back. This raises the elevators on the tail, which deflect the air flow so that the tail drops. The nose rises and the aircraft climbs.

DIVING

To dive, the pilot pushes the control column forwards. This lowers the elevators on the tail, which deflect the air flow so that the tail rises. The nose drops and the aircraft dives.

AIR FLOW

TURNING

To turn to the right or left, the pilot moves the control column in the required direction to raise or lower the ailerons on the wings and presses the pedals to swivel the rudder on the tail. One aileron goes up as the other goes down to bank the aircraft while the rudder turns the nose. Both movements combine to give a smooth change of direction.

AIR FLOW

RUDDER

ELEVATOR

ELEVATOR

AIR FLOW

TRAILING EDGE
OF WING

AILERON

ROLLING

Moving the control column to one side raises one aileron while lowering the other. One wing goes up, causing the plane to roll. This is necessary to turn smoothly.

FLYING MACHINES

Many different flying machines now fill our skies. They range from solo sports and aerobatic planes to wide-bodied and supersonic jet airliners which carry hundreds of passengers. Some, such as pedal-powered planes, lumber along just above the ground, while others, such as reconnaissance aircraft, streak at three times the speed of sound at a height three times that of Mount Everest.

There are also unpowered gliders, of which the returning space shuttles are the largest and hang gliders the simplest. Development in other directions has led to helicopters and vertical take-off aircraft which are capable of rising vertically and hovering in the air. There are also kites of all shapes and sizes, some large enough to carry a person.

Machines also fly through water. Hydrofoils flying through the waves employ exactly the same principles that keep winged aeroplanes aloft.

GLIDER
Being unpowered, a glider cannot travel fast and so has long straight wings that produce high lift at very low speed.

SPACE SHUTTLE
The space shuttle re-enters the atmosphere at very high speed, and so has a delta wing like a supersonic airliner. It then glides to a high-speed landing.

LIGHT AIRCRAFT
Short straight wings produce good lift and low drag at medium speed. Propellers or jet engines provide the power that produces the lift.

HANG GLIDER
The A-shaped wing inflates in flight to produce an aerofoil with low lift and drag, giving low-speed flight with a light load.

PEDAL-POWERED PLANE
Because the flying speed is very low, long and broad wings are needed to give maximum lift. Drag is at a minimum at such low speeds.

FORWARD-SWEPT WINGS
This experimental design gives high lift and low drag to produce good manoeuvrability at high speed. Two small forward wings called canards aid control.

SWING-WING AIRCRAFT
The wings are straight at take-off and landing to increase lift so that take-off and landing speeds are low. In flight, the wings swing back to reduce drag and enable high-speed flight.

SUPERSONIC AIRLINER
Aircraft that fly faster than the speed of sound often have dart-shaped delta wings. This is because a shock wave forms in the air around the aircraft, and the wings stay inside the shock wave so that control of the aircraft is retained at supersonic speed. Take-off and landing speeds are very high as lift is low.

AIRLINER
Swept-back wings are needed to minimize drag at high speed. However, lift is also reduced, requiring high take-off and landing speeds.

What's the big deal?

FLAPPING WINGS
This is a highly efficient wing design that you should look out for, particularly in places where bird feeding is encouraged.

AIRLINER WING

On a small aeroplane, the wings need little more than simple hinged ailerons to control flight. An airliner wing, however, experiences enormous and varying forces both in the air and on the ground. To cope with these, it uses an array of complex flaps that change the wing's shape.

During take-off and landing, the wing shape needs to be very different to that needed for cruising. By adjusting the area of the flaps presented to the air, and their angle to it, a pilot is able to vary the amount of lift and drag generated by the wing to suit different phases of the flight.

There are four basic kinds of flaps. Leading-edge flaps line the front edge of the wing, while trailing-edge flaps take up part of the rear edge. These flaps extend to increase the area of the wing, producing more lift and also drag. Spoilers are flaps on top of the wing that rise to reduce lift and increase drag. Ailerons are flaps at the rear edge that are raised or lowered to roll the aircraft in a turn.

GROUND SPOILERS

FLIGHT SPOILER

HIGH-SPEED AILERON

TRAILING-EDGE FLAPS

FLIGHT
SPOILERS

LOW-SPEED
AILERON

LEADING-EDGE FLAPS

ENGINE

TRAILING-EDGE FLAPS

TAKE-OFF

The leading-edge flaps extend
and the trailing-edge flaps are
raised to increase the area of the
wing. This improves lift at low
speed without incurring much
extra drag, so that take-off speed
is not high and the take-off run
not prolonged.

CRUISING

Leading-edge and trailing-edge
flaps are both retracted for
minimum drag, so the wing
presents the minimum area to
the oncoming air. The ailerons
operate to control the flight, and
may be assisted by the spoilers.

LANDING APPROACH

The leading-edge flaps extend to
increase wing area and produce
more lift at low speed. The
trailing-edge flaps extend
and droop to increase drag,
slowing the aircraft for landing.

LANDING

The ground spoilers rise
immediately on landing to reduce
lift and push the aircraft down so
that the wheels grip the runway
firmly. This enables
the brakes to work, but the
engines may reverse thrust to
assist braking.

THE HELICOPTER

ROTOR BLADES
Most helicopter rotors have from three to six blades. Each is connected to a flapping hinge and a pitch control rod.

With its whirling rotors, a helicopter looks very different to an aeroplane. Yet, like an aeroplane, it too uses aerofoils for flight (see p.107). The blades of the helicopter's main rotor have an aerofoil shape like the wings of a plane. But whereas a plane has to rush through the air for the wings to develop sufficient lift for flight, the helicopter moves only the rotor blades. As they circle, the blades produce lift to support the helicopter in the air and also to move it in the required direction. The angle at which the blades are set determines how the helicopter flies – hovering, vertical, forwards, backwards or sideways.

FLAPPING HINGES
Each rotor blade has a flapping hinge that allows it to flap up and down as it rotates. If the blades did not flap, they would develop uneven lift caused by the helicopter's motion through the air and roll the helicopter over.

ROTOR SHAFT
The rotor shaft drives the rotor blades and the upper swashplate.

PITCH CONTROL RODS
These rods are moved up or down by the upper swash-plate as it rotates. They raise or lower the front edge of the rotor blades to change the pitch of the blades.

ROTATING SCISSORS
This link turns the upper swashplate.

UPPER SWASHPLATE
The upper swashplate rotates on bearings above the lower swashplate. It is raised, lowered or tilted by the lower swashplate.

LOWER SWASHPLATE
The lower swashplate does not rotate. It is raised, lowered or tilted by links with the control columns.

HOW THE ROTOR WORKS
As the blades of the main rotor spin round, their angle or pitch can be varied to produce different amounts of lift for different modes of flight. The pitch is controlled by the swashplate, which is connected to two control columns. The swashplate moves up or down or it tilts in response to movements of the columns. It then moves control rods that alter the pitch of the blades.

MAIN ROTOR

TAIL ROTOR

VERTICAL FLIGHT

To ascend, the collective pitch control column raises the swashplate and increases the pitch of all the blades by an equal amount. The rotor lift increases to exceed the helicopter's weight so that the *helicopter rises. To descend, the swashplate is lowered. The pitch of all the blades decreases and reduces rotor lift so that the helicopter's weight now exceeds lift and causes it to descend.*

HOVERING FLIGHT

The cyclic pitch control column holds the swashplate level, so that each rotor blade has the same pitch and the helicopter does not move forwards or backwards. The collective *pitch control column raises the swashplate so that the pitch of the blades is sufficiently steep for the rotor to produce just enough lift to equal the weight of the helicopter.*

ROTOR BLADE

ROTOR BLADE

SWASHPLATE

ROTOR SHAFT

LIFT

LIFT

WEIGHT

LIFT

LIFT

WEIGHT

FORWARD FLIGHT

The cyclic pitch control column tilts the swashplate forwards. The pitch of each blade increases as it moves behind the rotor shaft then decreases as it moves in front. Lift increases over the back of the rotor, tilting the whole rotor forwards. The total rotor lift splits into a raising force that supports the helicopter's weight, and thrust that moves it forwards.

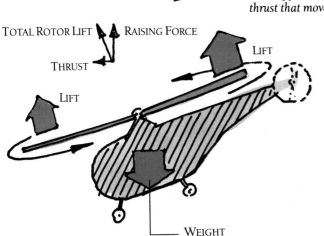

TOTAL ROTOR LIFT   RAISING FORCE

THRUST

LIFT

LIFT

WEIGHT

BACKWARD FLIGHT

The cyclic pitch control column tilts the swashplate backwards. The pitch of each blade increases as it moves in front of the rotor shaft then decreases as it moves behind. Lift increases over the front of the rotor, producing a backward thrust.

LIFT

RAISING FORCE   TOTAL ROTOR LIFT

THRUST

LIFT

WEIGHT

SINGLE-ROTOR HELICOPTER

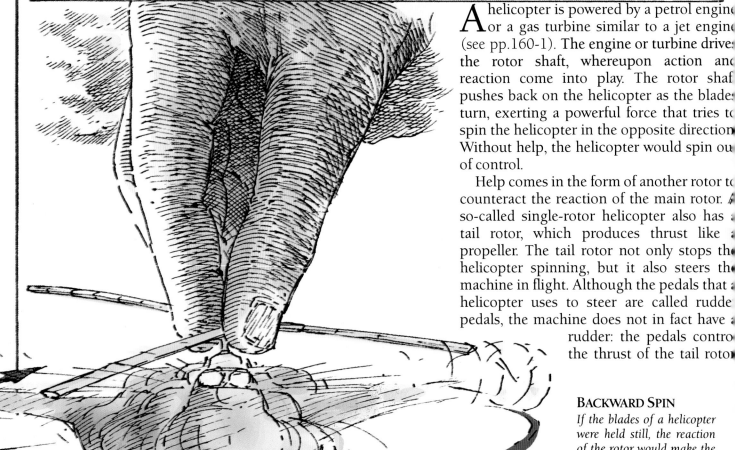

A helicopter is powered by a petrol engine or a gas turbine similar to a jet engine (see pp.160-1). The engine or turbine drives the rotor shaft, whereupon action and reaction come into play. The rotor shaft pushes back on the helicopter as the blades turn, exerting a powerful force that tries to spin the helicopter in the opposite direction. Without help, the helicopter would spin out of control.

Help comes in the form of another rotor to counteract the reaction of the main rotor. A so-called single-rotor helicopter also has a tail rotor, which produces thrust like a propeller. The tail rotor not only stops the helicopter spinning, but it also steers the machine in flight. Although the pedals that a helicopter uses to steer are called rudder pedals, the machine does not in fact have a rudder: the pedals control the thrust of the tail rotor.

BACKWARD SPIN

If the blades of a helicopter were held still, the reaction of the rotor would make the helicopter spin around in the opposite direction to the blades' normal rotation.

DIRECTION OF MAIN ROTOR

THRUST OF TAIL ROTOR

REACTION OF MAIN ROTOR

STEERING A SINGLE-ROTOR HELICOPTER

Nomally, the thrust of the tail rotor equals the reaction of the main rotor. The thrust and reaction cancel each out, and no force acts to spin the helicopter. Operating the rudder pedals to increase the thrust makes the extra thrust turn the helicopter in the same direction as the rotor blades. Decreasing the thrust of the tail rotor allows the reaction of the main rotor to turn the helicopter in the opposite direction.

TWIN-ROTOR HELICOPTER

Large helicopters often have two main rotors to give double the lift of a single main rotor and raise a heavy load or more passengers. No tail rotor is needed because the two rotors spin in opposite directions. The reaction of one rotor cancels out the reaction of the other. To turn, the rudder pedals change the speed of the rotors so that one rotor gets more power than the other. The reaction of this rotor increases, and the extra force turns the helicopter.

REAR ROTOR

REAR GEARBOX

REAR ROTOR DRIVE SHAFT

GAS TURBINE ENGINE

ENGINE DRIVE SHAFTS

MAIN TRANSMISSION SHAFT

FRONT ROTOR

FRONT GEARBOX

CABIN

OVERLAPPING ROTORS

Because the areas swept out by the front and rear rotor blades overlap, the rotors have to be designed so that their blades cannot collide. This is done by having each rotor at a different height, and by staggering their rotation, so that only one blade passes over the body of the helicopter at any one time.

FRONT ROTOR AREA

REAR ROTOR AREA

THE JUMP JET

The principle of action and reaction (see p.100) is put to use in all powered aircraft, but as a means of propulsion rather than as a direct method of producing lift. Propellers and jet engines move air backwards at high speeds, and this pushes back to force the aircraft forwards.

By using the downward thrust of its jet engine, the jump jet can dispense with the need for a runway and take off vertically from the ground. When the engine exhausts are swivelled backwards, the wings then provide lift in the normal way.

ENGINE NOZZLES

The jump jet has four engine nozzles which can be swivelled to point at any angle from vertical to horizontal. These provide the power for vertical and horizontal flight.

3 FORWARD FLIGHT

As forward speed increases to give sufficient lift for flight, the nozzles swivel to direct the air jets backwards. Reaction now only drives the jet forwards.

REACTION

COMPRESSED AIR JETS

Low-power jets at the tail, nose and wing-tips control the aircraft's angle when flying vertically or hovering – a task which is too delicate to be carried out by the main engine nozzles.

2 TRANSITION

The nozzles swivel to direct the air jets at an angle. The reaction splits into a raising force and forward thrust. As the aircraft moves forwards, the wings begin to produce lift.

AIR INTAKE

The two air intakes are connected to a single jet engine. The engine produces a stream of air at extremely high pressure which flows to the four engine nozzles.

REACTION

1 VERTICAL TAKE-OFF

The nozzles in the engine exhausts direct air jets from the engine downwards. The reaction of the moving air raises the jump jet vertically.

THRUST

Theories of Extinction: Number 37 – The Garden Hose Experiments

THE HYDROFOIL

The principles of flight do not only apply to air. An aerofoil (see p.107) in fact works better in water, which is denser than air and therefore gives more lift at lower speed. An aerofoil used in this way is called a hydrofoil, and this name is also given to a kind of boat that literally flies through the water.

A hydrofoil has a hull like a floating boat, and it does float at rest and low speed. But at high speed, wing-like foils beneath the hull rise in the water and lift the hull above the surface. Freed from friction with the water, a hydrofoil can skim over the waves at two or three times the speed of the fastest floating boats.

STRUT

WATER FLOW

FOIL

SUBMERGED FOIL

These foils remain fully submerged in the water. They are controlled by a sonar system aboard the hydrofoil that detects the height of oncoming waves. It then sends signals to the foils, which change their angle to vary the amount of lift generated. In this way, the foils adjust lift as the hydrofoil encounters waves, smoothing out the rise and fall and ensuring a steady ride.

SURFACE-PIERCING FOIL

The amount of lift generated by surface-piercing foils depends on the depth of each foil in the water. When the foil is deeper, it generates more lift. This makes the hydrofoil rise as it moves into the crest of a wave. As it enters a trough, more of the foil emerges from the water; lift decreases and the foil sinks. The hydrofoil follows the contours of the waves instead of breaking through them.

STRUT

FOIL

PRESSURE POWER
ON FIGHTING FIRES

Through careful study, I have been able to devise a way to improve both the capacity and range of mammoths in fighting fires. First the mammoth is encouraged to drink as much water as it can hold and still get to the scene of the outbreak. Meanwhile a heavy post is set into the ground a short but safe distance from the fire. The creature is then squeezed against the post in a series of rapid strokes by a large fire-fighter-operated piston.

PUMPS FOR PRESSURE

The events recorded for all time in the parchment above concern the conversion of the mammoth into a primitive but highly effective pump. Pumps are often required to raise the pressure of a fluid (a liquid or a gas), though they may alternatively reduce the pressure. The change in pressure is then put to work, usually to exert a force and make something move or to cause the fluid to flow.

A pump increases pressure by pushing the molecules in the fluid that enters the pump closer together. One way of doing this is to compress the fluid, and this is what is happening to the mammoth. The piston squeezes its stomach, so that the molecules of water inside crowd together. The pressure of the water increases as the molecules exert a greater force on the stomach walls.

If the fluid is able to move, it flows from the pump towards any region that has a lower pressure. The air around the mammoth is at a lower pressure than the water inside. The water pressure therefore forces the water along the trunk, where it emerges in a powerful jet.

SUCTION POWER

A pump may also reduce the pressure of a gas. One way is to increase the volume of the gas so that its molecules become more widely spaced. The mammoth experiences this as the piston is removed, and its empty stomach regains its normal bulk. The pressure of the air inside now becomes less than the pressure of the air outside, and air flows into the mammoth — sucking any nearby object in with it.

PRESSURE AND WEIGHT

Any liquid or gas has a certain pressure by virtue of its weight. When the weight of a liquid or gas presses against a surface within the liquid or gas or against the walls of a container, it creates a pressure on the surface or the walls. Water flows from a tap under pressure because of the weight of the water in the pipe and tank above. Air has a strong pressure because of the great weight of the air in the atmosphere. Suction makes use of this "natural" pressure of the air.

*T*ests show that my apparatus not only completely empties the mammoth, but also dramatically increases the force with which the water is discharged. The only problem with my design occurs if the piston is released too quickly when the mammoth is empty. Naturally, once the pressure is off, the mammoth expands to its original shape and size, resulting in a deep and powerful inhalation. Anyone or anything standing too close to the animal's trunk during this expansion is likely to be sucked bodily into the animal's interior.

PUMPING OUT

When the piston is pushed in a simple pump, the force creates a high pressure in the water as the water molecules crowd together. The molecules move to any point where the pressure is lower and they are less crowded. This point is the nozzle of the pump, and the water emerges from it in a jet.

SUCKING IN

As the piston is pulled back, the air pressure in the now empty pump is reduced because the air molecules move apart. The air molecules outside the pump are closer together because the air there is at higher pressure, and so they surge into the pump chamber.

RECIPROCATING PUMPS

PISTON PUMP

In the piston pump, a piston moves up and down inside a cylinder, sucking in water or air at one end and then compressing it to expel it at the other end. A hand-operated water pistol contains the mechanism shown here. A bicycle pump is another simple kind of piston pump.

Pumps increase (or decrease) the pressure of a liquid or gas in two main ways. The piston pump is a reciprocating pump, in which a part such as a piston or diaphragm moves repeatedly to and fro. Rotary pumps compress with a rotating mechanism.

PISTON IN
The piston moves in, increasing the pressure of air in the empty pump. The inlet valve closes, but the outlet valve opens as air escapes.

PISTON OUT
The piston moves back, lowering the air pressure. The outlet valve closes, while the water beneath the pump, which has a higher pressure, flows up into the pump.

PISTON IN
The piston moves in again, increasing the pressure of the water in the pump. The inlet valve closes, but the outlet valve opens to let the water out of the pump.

DIAPHRAGM PULLED DOWN
A rotating cam on the camshaft tilts a lever to pull the diaphragm down. The fuel pressure is reduced, and fuel flows through the filter and inlet valve into the pump.

DIAPHRAGM PUSHED UP
The spring moves the lever back and raises the diaphragm. The pressure of the fuel increases, opening the outlet valve to move the fuel to the engine.

DIAPHRAGM PUMP

In this pump, a flexible diaphragm replaces the reciprocating piston. The use of a diaphragm ensures that no liquid or gas leaks out of the pump, as could happen with a worn piston. The fuel pump in a car is a diaphragm pump that is driven mechanically or by an electric motor. The pump forces fuel from the tank to the carburettor or fuel injectors (see p.140).

ROTARY PUMPS

GEAR PUMP

The oil that lubricates the engine of a car must be forced at high pressure around channels in the engine (see p.88). A sturdy and durable gear pump is often used to do the job.

The rotating camshaft of the engine (see pp.50-1) normally powers the oil pump, driving a shaft that turns a pair of intermeshing gear wheels inside a close-fitting chamber. The oil enters the pump, where it is trapped in the wheels. The wheels carry the oil around to the outlet, where the teeth come together as they intermesh. This squeezes the oil and raises its pressure as it flows to the outlet. The speed of pumping is directly linked to the speed of the engine.

OIL FORCED OUT AT HIGH PRESSURE

GEAR WHEEL

OIL INLET

OUTLET

VANE

COMPARTMENT

ROTOR

INLET

ROTARY VANE PUMP

This pump contains a chamber with a rotor mounted slightly off-centre. The rotor has slots fitted with sliding vanes. As the rotor turns, the vanes are thrown outwards against the chamber wall, thereby creating compartments of changing size.

Where the liquid or gas enters the pump, the compartments expand to suck it in. As the fluid is carried around the pump, the compartments get smaller. The fluid is squeezed, and leaves the pump at high pressure. Rotary vane pumps are often used to deliver petrol at filling stations.

TO OUTLET

IMPELLER

FROM INLET

CENTRIFUGAL PUMP

The cooling system of a car engine (see p.152) requires a steady flow of cool water. The water pump raises the pressure of the water to force it through the radiator and engine. This kind of rotary pump works by centrifugal force (see p.71).

The pump contains a fan-like impeller. Liquid or gas is fed to the centre of the impeller, and flows into the rotating blades. The blades spin the liquid or gas around at high speed, flinging it outwards. As the liquid or gas strikes the wall of the chamber around the impeller, it is raised to high pressure before it leaves the outlet.

PERISTALTIC PUMP

Most pumps are likely to clog up when used with a liquid such as blood which contains particles. Furthermore, they would damage blood cells. The peristaltic pump, which is used in devices such as heart-lung machines, avoids both these problems.

The pump contains a flexible tube that is repeatedly squeezed by rotating rollers. The rollers push the blood gently along the tube. This pump has the added advantage that the blood does not come into contact with any mechanical parts and so remains clean.

FLEXIBLE TUBE

PNEUMATIC MACHINES

SUPPORTING A WEIGHT
The weight that compressed air can support depends on the pressure difference between it and the atmosphere.

DOUBLING THE AREA
The weight that can be supported also depends on the area. Doubling the area doubles the weight that the air can support.

DOUBLING THE PRESSURE
Doubling the pressure on the original area also doubles the weight that the air can support.

Air possesses considerable power when placed under pressure, and when compressed it can be used to drive machines. Pneumatic or air-driven machines all make use of the force exerted by air molecules striking a surface. The compressed air exerts a greater pressure than the air on the other side of the surface, which is at atmospheric pressure. The difference in pressure drives the machine.

RUDDER

GAS TURBINE ENGINE

HOVERCRAFT
A hovercraft exploits the power of compressed air to lift itself above the surface of the water or ground. Buoyed up by a cushion of air, it can then float and travel rapidly because there is little friction with the water or ground. The hovercraft uses propellers for horizontal movement and rudders for steering. These may operate in the air, as in an aircraft, or underwater like those in a ship. Gas turbines or piston engines drive both the lift fans that compress the air and pump it into the flexible skirt and also the propellers.

INFLATED SKIRT
Compressed air flows beneath the hovercraft. The skirt holds it in to form a high-pressure cushion.

LIFT FANS
These suck air into the hovercraft, generating enough force to lift the craft above the surface.

PROPELLER

UNINFLATED SKIRT

PNEUMATIC DRILL

The force that lifts a hovercraft above the sea is put to use on the road in the reverse direction. The ear-blasting roar which often accompanies road repairs is produced by the pneumatic drill, air hammer, or jack-hammer. This device is fed with compressed air from a pump as a source of power. The high-pressure air is used to produce a cycle of operations that delivers powerful repeated blows to the tool or blade, which hammers down into the road surface.

RAISING THE BLADE
Pressing the control lever admits air via the air duct to the base of the piston, which rises. The powerful spring raises the blade and the anvil above it.

HAMMERING THE BLADE
Air forced up above the rising piston lifts the disc valve. This diverts the incoming air to the top of the piston, pushing it down. The piston strikes the anvil, which in turn hammers the blade. The falling piston forces air back up the air duct, causing the disc valve to fall and the cycle to begin again.

POWER BRAKES

PARTIAL VACUUM
The booster unit contains air at reduced pressure (yellow) from the engine, allowing external air at atmospheric pressure to force in the main piston.

BOOSTING THE BRAKES
The brake fluid pushes up the valve piston and lifts the air control valve. Air at atmospheric pressure is admitted to the main piston, forcing it in and pushing in the slave piston to increase the pressure of the brake fluid.

Air pressure can help a driver who has to stop quickly. In a car with power brakes, the atmosphere helps to boost the brakes so that they operate with greater force. Pressing the brake pedal increases the pressure of the brake fluid in the hydraulic braking system (see p.128). The fluid first goes to the booster unit, opening a valve that admits air to the booster to increase the pressure even more. An engine-powered hydraulic system may also provide extra power to the braking system.

[127]

HYDRAULIC MACHINES

Ahydraulic machine makes use of pressure in a liquid. It does this with a set of two or more cylinders connected by pipes containing the hydraulic fluid. In each cylinder is a piston. To work the machine, force is applied to one cylinder, which is known as the "master" cylinder. This raises the pressure of the fluid throughout the whole system, and the pistons in the other cylinders – the "slave" cylinders – move out and perform a useful action. The force produced by each slave cylinder depends on its diameter.

Hydraulic machines work on the same principle as levers and gears: the wider the slave cylinder, the greater is the force that it applies, and the shorter is the distance that it moves. As with levers and gears, the converse also applies, so a narrow slave cylinder moves a large distance with reduced force.

HYDRAULIC BRAKES

Except for the hand-brake, which is operated by a cable, cars use hydraulic braking systems. The brake pedal moves the piston in the master cylinder, raising the pressure of the brake fluid evenly throughout the system. The brake fluid, its pressure boosted by the power-brakes booster unit (see p.127), then makes pistons in the wheel cylinders move out with great force. These pistons apply the brake pads or shoes to slow the car (see p.86).

BRAKE FLUID
RESERVOIR

PISTON

PIPES TO BOOSTER UNIT

MASTER
CYLINDER

HIGH-PRESSURE
BRAKE FLUID

PISTON

WHEEL
CYLINDER

BRAKE PEDAL

PISTON

WHEEL
CYLINDER

BRAKE
PAD

DISC

SPRING

BRAKE SHOE

DISC BRAKE

DRUM BRAKE

HYDRAULIC RAM

Machines such as the excavator (see p.23) and firefighter's ladder (see p.29) work with hydraulic rams. Each ram consists of a piston in a cylinder connected by pipes to a central reservoir of hydraulic fluid. The controls open valves that admit high-pressure fluid to either side of the piston, which then moves in or out with great force and precision.

HYDRAULIC LIFT

A hydraulic lift easily raises the weight of a car. It has only one piston. Air is pumped by a compressor into an oil reservoir where it increases the pressure of the oil. The oil reservoir acts as the master cylinder. The high-pressure oil then flows to the base of a cylinder, where it forces up a piston, which supports the car's weight. Closing the oil valve keeps the piston extended. To lower the car, the oil and air valves are opened. The compressed air escapes, reducing the oil pressure and allowing the piston to descend.

STABILIZER RAMS

These rams take the strain off the wheels when the machine is raising a heavy load.

SLAVE CYLINDER

The pressure of the oil in the slave cylinder increases until the pressure on the piston is greater than the weight of the load, so the piston rises. The piston moves up a greater distance than the oil in the reservoir moves down.

MASTER CYLINDER

When compressed air is pumped into the reservoir, oil is forced out of the reservoir and along the pipe to the narrower slave cylinder, which drives the piston.

LOADER BUCKET RAM

DIPPER RAM

DIGGER BUCKET RAM

LOADER LIFT RAMS

DIGGER BUCKET

BOOM LIFT RAM

AIR VALVE

COMPRESSED AIR

OIL VALVE

PISTON

HIGH-PRESSURE OIL

MASTER CYLINDER

POWER STEERING

Hydraulics can help with steering a car as well as braking. Power steering reduces the effort of turning the car by using a hydraulic system to boost the force that you apply to the steering wheel. Power-steering systems may use electric motors instead of hydraulics.

WHEEL SWIVELS TO RIGHT

RACK MOVES TO LEFT

PISTON MOVES TO LEFT

PINION

CYLINDER

TRACK ROD SWIVELS WHEEL

TRACK ROD

ROD

HIGH-PRESSURE FLUID

FLUID RESERVOIR

CONTROL VALVE

STEERING COLUMN

BELT-DRIVEN PUMP RAISES FLUID PRESSURE

STEERING WHEEL TURNS TO RIGHT

STEERING SYSTEM

A rack-and-pinion system (see p.43) transmits the rotary motion of the steering wheel to the track rods that swivel the car wheels. A control valve admits high-pressure hydraulic fluid to either side of a piston in a cylinder depending on which way the steering wheel is turned. The piston moves in or out and drives a rod fixed to the rack so that it boosts the force acting on the rack.

SUCTION MACHINES

Reducing the pressure inside a machine causes suction. The pressure of the outside air, which is created by the weight of the atmosphere, is greater than that inside the machine. This difference in pressure can then be put to work. In a vacuum cleaner, the pressure of the outside air forces material into the cleaner. Power brakes (see p.127) may use suction to boost braking.

AIR IN ATMOSPHERE

DRINKING STRAW
When you suck through a straw, the air in the atmosphere presses down on the drink and pushes it up into your mouth.

VACUUM CLEANER

Cylinder vacuum cleaners work entirely by suction. An electric motor in the cleaner drives a fan that pumps the air out of the hose. The pressure of the atmosphere pushes air into the cleaning attachment and up the hose, pulling in dust and dirt with it. The dust-laden air then passes through a dust bag, which retains the dust and dirt, before leaving the back of the cleaner. In some cleaners, the fan whirls the incoming air around at very high speed so that the dirt and dust collects on the inside walls of the cleaner. No dust bag is needed.

ELECTRIC MOTOR

FAN

DUST BAG

~MeeOW!

UPRIGHT CLEANER
Upright models have a rotating brush that beats the dust and dirt out of a carpet before it is sucked into the dust bag.

THE AQUALUNG

With the aid of an aqualung or scuba (Self-Contained Underwater Breathing Apparatus), a diver can stay underwater for long periods. This device does away with the need for a diving suit by supplying air at changing pressures during a dive.

The diver's body is under pressure from the surrounding water, which becomes greater the deeper one dives. The air inside the diver's lungs is at about the same pressure as the water. The air in the cylinder is at high pressure. The aqualung's regulator has two stages that reduce the pressure of the air coming from the cylinder to the same pressure as the water so that the diver can breathe in. The first-stage valve, worked by a spring, opens to admit air at a set pressure always greater than water pressure. The second-stage valve, worked by a lever, opens by suction to admit air at water pressure.

AIR CYLINDER

SPRING

FIRST-STAGE VALVE

SECOND-STAGE VALVE

REGULATOR

LEVER

BREATHING IN

As the diver inhales, the air pressure in the air tubes falls. The diaphragm is sucked in, pushed by the greater pressure of water on the outside of the diaphragm. The lever opens the second-stage valve, admitting more air to the diver.

DIAPHRAGM

BREATHING OUT

As the diver breathes out, the air pressure in the air tubes rises, pushing the diaphragm down to shut off the incoming air. The one-way valve opens to expel the exhaled air to the sea.

AIR TUBE

MOUTHPIECE

ONE-WAY VALVE

AIR TUBE

KEY

■	AIR FROM CYLINDER
■	AIR AT SET PRESSURE
■	AIR JUST ABOVE WATER PRESSURE
□	AIR JUST BELOW WATER PRESSURE

THE TOILET CISTERN

Many toilet cisterns work with a siphon, which accomplishes the apparently impossible feat of making water (or any other liquid) flow uphill. Provided the open end of the siphon tube is below the level of the surface, the water will flow up the tube, around the bend and then down to the open end. Operating the toilet cistern starts the siphon flowing. Once the water begins to double back down the siphon tube, air pressure makes the rest of the water follow it.

AIR PRESSURE   TUBE

WATER

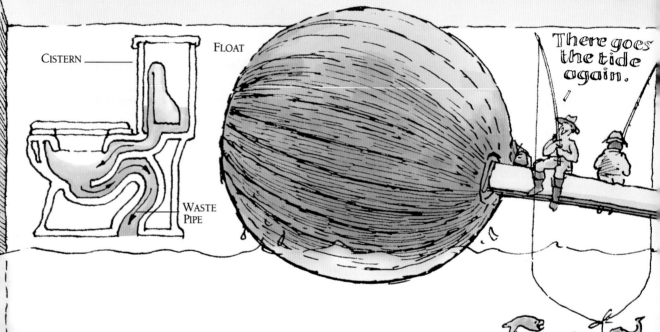

CISTERN

FLOAT

WASTE PIPE

There goes the tide again.

1 THE CISTERN FLUSHES

After the handle is pressed down, water is lifted up the siphon tube by the disc. The water reaches the bend in the siphon pipe and then travels around it. As it falls, the water in the cistern follows it.

2 THE VALVE OPENS

When the water level in the cistern falls below the bottom of the bell, air enters the bell and the siphon is broken. By this time, the float has fallen far enough to open the valve, and water under pressure enters to refill the cistern and the float begins to rise again.

3 THE VALVE CLOSES

The rising float gradually shuts the valve, cutting off the water supply. Although the cistern is full, the water cannot leave through the siphon tube until the handle is pressed down, forming the siphon once again. The float and valve work together to form a self-regulating mechanism.

CISTERN COVER

SIPHON PIPE

HANDLE

VALVE

DISC

BELL

WATER PIPE

PRESSURE GAUGES

Mechanical pressure gauges respond to the pressure of a fluid, which exerts a force to move a pointer over a dial. One of the simplest is the Bourdon gauge, which is found in the oil-pressure gauge in a car, the pressure gauge on a gas cylinder, and the depth gauge used by a diver. It works like the curled paper tubes you could find yourself blowing into at parties.

SCALE

POINTER

GEAR

LEVER

METAL TUBE

LIQUID OR GAS UNDER PRESSURE

BOURDON GAUGE

ANEROID BAROMETER

A barometer measures changes in the pressure of the air, which is an indicator of the weather ahead. The most common kind is the aneroid barometer.

At the heart of this barometer is a capsule from which air is removed. As the air pressure falls, the spring pulls the side of the capsule outwards. The arm rises, causing the rocking bar to slacken the chain. The hairspring unwinds, moving the pointer anticlockwise until the chain is pulled taut. When the air pressure rises, the capsule contracts and the pointer moves clockwise, winding up the hairspring.

POINTER

CHAIN

HAIRSPRING

SPRING

ROCKING BAR

ARM

CAPSULE

THE WATER METER

DIAL

POINTER

METER BODY

Any liquid or gas that is under pressure will flow. By detecting the rate of flow with a meter, the amount of liquid or gas that passes can be measured. A water meter often works rather like a rotary pump in reverse. As the water flows through the meter, it turns the blades of an impeller. The shaft of the impeller turns a worm gear (see p.37) that reduces the speed of the impeller. Sets of gears then turn a pointer and counters that register the total amount of water used.

COUNTERS

The counters are a series of toothed drums (see p.38). By recording the number of revolutions of the pointer, they show the total volume of water that has flowed through the meter.

GEARS

IMPELLER

Water may travel through the meter at high speed. The blades of the impeller are set at a small angle to the water flow in order to slow the rate at which the impeller spins.

IMPELLER

REDUCTION GEARS

The rate of rotation of the impeller axle is reduced by gears. A worm gear is the first in the series; the rotation rate is then further reduced by a set of spur gears.

WORM GEAR

WATER FLOW

JETS AND SPRAYS

WATER PISTOL

After being raised to a high pressure by its internal piston pump (see pp.122-3), the water is forced out of the nozzle in a powerful jet.

Forcing a liquid through a nozzle requires pressure because the narrow hole restricts the flow. The liquid emerges in a high-pressure jet which may break up into a spray of droplets as it meets the air. Jets and sprays have many uses, from delivering liquids in a useful form to providing power by action and reaction. Gases, rather than liquids, are usually employed to produce power. A pump may deliver the fluid to the nozzle, as in a dishwasher, or it may be contained under pressure, as in a spray can.

DISHWASHER

A dishwasher uses hot water under pressure both to power its spray arms, and also to do the cleaning itself. To be effective, the water has to be sprayed in powerful jets from all directions so that it reaches all the dishes and utensils. These are then rinsed by jets of clean water before drying.

THE DISHWASHER CYCLE

1 WATER TREATMENT
Cold water enters through a water softener, which treats the water so that the dishes dry without marks.

2 HEATING
The water fills the base of the dishwasher, where it is heated. Detergent is added.

3 WASHING
The hot water is pumped by the wash pump to the rotating spray arms. It sprays the dishes and returns to the base of the dishwasher, where it is recycled after being filtered.

4 RINSING AND DRYING
After washing, the dirty water is pumped out of the dishwasher and goes to the drain. The dishes are then rinsed and dried.

SPRAY ARM

COLD WATER IN

SPRAY ARM

FILTER

HEATER

WASH PUMP

PUMP

WATER SOFTENER

TO DRAIN

MANNED MANOEUVRING UNIT

W henever a jet or spray is produced, a force is generated that acts in the reverse direction to the flow of the fluid. This is an example of action and reaction (see p.100). It causes the spray arms of a dishwasher to rotate, and is also made use of in the manned manoeuvring unit (MMU). This vehicle enables astronauts to fly around in space. It is propelled by jets of nitrogen gas which spurt from small nozzles. These jets make the nozzles move backwards, thereby pushing or turning the MMU in the desired direction.

NITROGEN SUPPLY PIPE

THRUSTER SET
The MMU has eight sets of thrusters, each with three nozzles pointing at right angles to each other. The controls feed nitrogen gas to different thrusters at different pressures.

NITROGEN TANKS
The MMU has two tanks of nitrogen at high pressure that feed the thrusters. The tanks can be refuelled in space.

THRUSTER

THRUSTER

THRUSTER

THRUSTER

THRUSTER
Nitrogen gas is non-flammable. Each thruster creates movement simply by releasing the gas under pressure. A rocket engine (see p.162) has a similar effect but works by burning fuel to produce a jet of gas.

THRUSTER CONTROLS

THE NOZZLE

The nozzle is held shut by a spring. Pressing it down opens the channel inside so that the pressurized liquid escapes to form a spray. The spring reseals the can when the nozzle is released.

SPRAY

CHANNEL

GASEOUS
PROPELLANT
AT HIGH
PRESSURE

LIQUID

SPRING

TUBE

LIQUID PROPELLANT
PLUS PRODUCT

Spray cans produce an aerosol, the technical term for a very fine spray. They do this by means of a pressurized propellant, which is a liquid that boils at everyday temperatures. Inside the can, a layer of gaseous propellant forms over the liquid as it boils. The gas pressure increases, and eventually it becomes so high that boiling stops. When the nozzle is pressed, the gas pressure forces the product up the tube in the can and out of the nozzle in a spray or foam. The propellant may emerge as well but, now under less pressure, it immediately evaporates.

Theories of Extinction: Number 82 Curiosity

CURVED BASE
RESISTS PRESSURE

THE FIRE EXTINGUISHER

OPERATING LEVER

GAS CARTRIDGE
A cartridge containing carbon dioxide gas at high pressure provides the pressure needed to work the extinguisher.

1 HANDLE PRESSED

3 GAS ESCAPES
The gas then pushes down on the water, which is driven up the siphon tube to a hose connected to the nozzle.

NOZZLE

SPRING

RELEASE VALVE

2 VALVE OPENS
The release valve admits the gas to the space above the water.

An extinguisher puts out a fire by excluding oxygen so that combustion (see p.146) can no longer continue. The extinguisher must smother the whole fire as quickly as possible, and therefore produces a powerful spray of water, foam or powder. Some extinguishers produce a jet of carbon dioxide, a heavy gas that prevents burning. A fire extinguisher works in much the same way as a spray can. The extinguishing substance, such as water, is put under high pressure inside the extinguisher, and the pressure forces the substance out of the nozzle.

WATER

SIPHON TUBE

CARBURETTOR AND FUEL INJECTION

PETROL

VENTURI

FLOAT
NEEDLE

FLOAT

AIR

NOZZLE

SPRAY

THROTTLE
VALVE

FLOAT CHAMBER
*The petrol first enters
the float chamber. As
the float rises and falls,
it moves the float
needle to control the
flow of petrol to the
carburettor.*

ACCELERATOR
PEDAL

OUTLET VALVE   SPARK PLUG   INLET VALVE

INCOMING AIR

PETROL
INJECTOR

BALL OF
SPRAY

CIRCULATING
AIR

"Putting your foot down" can mean more than being firm: in a car, you speed away as you press the accelerator pedal. The car speeds up because the pedal causes more fuel to be fed to the engine (see pp.156-7). The fuel enters the engine cylinder as a spray of droplets mixed with air in just the right proportion to ignite and produce the required power. A mixture richer in fuel gives more power. However, the way in which the fuel forms a spray varies from one car to another. Older petrol-engine cars may have a carburettor, in which the spray forms before it enters the cylinder. In newer petrol-engine cars and diesel cars, the fuel is injected into the cylinder to form a spray.

PETROL DIRECT INJECTION
A fuel injector squirts petrol directly into the cylinder in a precise amount controlled electronically. The air swirls around to form a ball of spray close to the spark plug, which then fires to ignite the petrol. Direct injection can provide both fuel economy and powerful performance when required because the proportion of petrol to air can be very finely controlled.

DIESEL ENGINE
There are no spark plugs in a diesel engine. Instead, the rising piston compresses the air inside the cylinder so strongly that it becomes very hot. The diesel fuel is injected by an electronically controlled injector linked to the accelerator pedal to form a spray, often in an ignition chamber in the wall of the cylinder. There the hot air causes the fuel spray to ignite. Diesel engines use gas oil instead of petrol and are economical on fuel.

PENS

Many pens work by capillary action, which occurs in a narrow tube or channel. Liquid flows up a narrow tube because the pressure inside is lowered as the molecules at the liquid's surface are attracted to molecules in the tube. External air pressure then forces the liquid up the tube.

MENISCUS

LOW PRESSURE

GLASS TUBE

AIR PRESSURE

CAPILLARY ACTION
Molecules of water are attracted towards the glass molecules, forming a curve called a meniscus and causing the pressure to drop.

BALL-POINT PEN
At the tip of a ball-point pen is a tiny metal ball in a socket. Ink flows from the ink tube through a narrow channel to the ball, which rotates to transfer the ink to the paper. The ink dries immediately.

INK TUBE

BALL

FIBRE-TIP PEN
The tip of a fibre-tip pen contains one or more narrow channels through which ink flows by capillary action as soon as the tip touches the paper.

INK CHANNELS

INK IN GAP

DIP PEN
A dip pen's nib is split into two halves and has a gap that fills with ink as the pen is dipped in the ink. Capillary action, together with gravity, conducts ink from the gap down the narrow split in the nib to the paper.

SPLIT IN NIB

INLET VALVE

SPARK PLUG

PISTON

CYLINDER

CARBURETTOR
As the piston in the cylinder moves down, the inlet valve opens and air is sucked in through the carburettor. This contains a passage with a narrow section called a venturi. Petrol is fed from a float chamber through a nozzle to the venturi. The air speeds up as it flows through the narrow venturi, and its pressure falls. The low-pressure air sucks petrol out of the nozzle to form a spray, which goes to the cylinder. In the passage is a throttle valve linked to the accelerator pedal. The valve opens as the pedal is pressed, speeding the flow of air through the carburettor and sucking in more petrol.

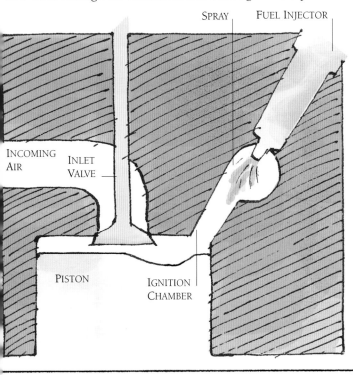

SPRAY

FUEL INJECTOR

INCOMING AIR

INLET VALVE

PISTON

IGNITION CHAMBER

EXPLOITING HEAT

fig. 1

fig. 2

ON THE USES OF MAMMOTH HEAT

*T*here are two things that mammoths enjoy above all else (with the possible exception of swamp grass). They are working at some useful task and sleeping.

During my travels, I have come across a number of situations in which the two have been successfully combined to the benefit of both man and beast.

In figure 1, heat absorbed during a long sleep in the Sun or created by chewing swamp grass is used to warm water stored in the animal's trunk. When the trunk is secured vertically, the warmest water rises to the top, making it readily available.

In figure 2, the animal is shown performing its bed-warming function. Heat absorbed or created during the day is transferred from the mammoth to the bed in anticipation of its human occupant. To rouse the beast either a mouse is slipped under the covers, or the bed's would-be occupant makes squeaking noises. In either case the terrified beast is quickly displaced.

THE NATURE OF HEAT

The mammoth receives heat from the Sun in the form of invisible heat rays and makes heat inside its vast bulk by the consumption of swamp grass and other elephantine foods. The heat travels through its body and warms its skin. In the trunk, the heated water rises of its own accord.

Heat is a form of energy that results in the motion of molecules. Molecules are constantly on the move in everything and the faster they move, the hotter is their possessor. So when anything receives heat energy, its

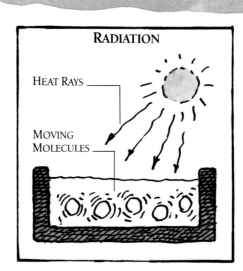

RADIATION

HEAT RAYS

MOVING MOLECULES

molecules speed up; removing heat energy slows them down. Heat travels in three ways — by radiation, conduction and convection.

RADIATION

Hot things radiate heat rays, or infra-red rays. The rays travel through air or space and strike cooler objects, which warm up. This form of heat transfer is called thermal radiation. The heat rays make the molecules in the surface of the object move about faster. Heat then spreads through the object by conduction or convection.

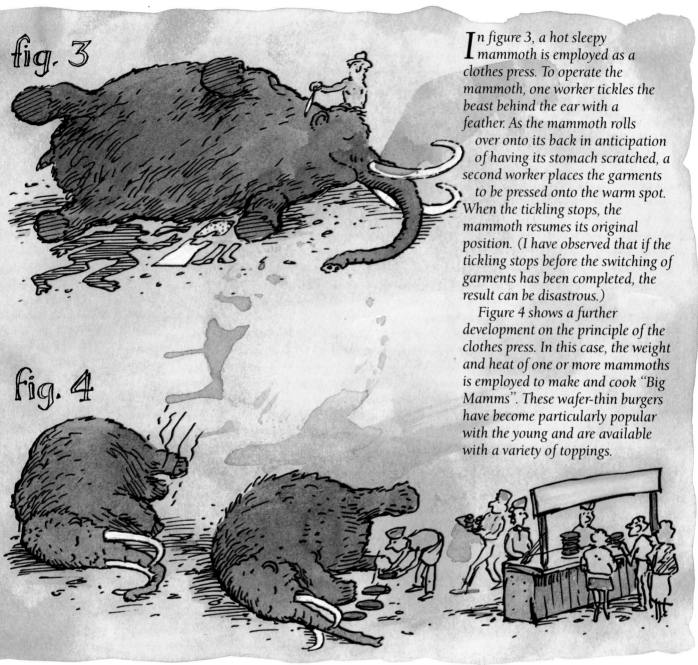

fig. 3

fig. 4

In figure 3, a hot sleepy mammoth is employed as a clothes press. To operate the mammoth, one worker tickles the beast behind the ear with a feather. As the mammoth rolls over onto its back in anticipation of having its stomach scratched, a second worker places the garments to be pressed onto the warm spot. When the tickling stops, the mammoth resumes its original position. (I have observed that if the tickling stops before the switching of garments has been completed, the result can be disastrous.)

Figure 4 shows a further development on the principle of the clothes press. In this case, the weight and heat of one or more mammoths is employed to make and cook "Big Mamms". These wafer-thin burgers have become particularly popular with the young and are available with a variety of toppings.

CONDUCTION

The molecules in solids vibrate to and fro. When part of the solid is heated, the molecules there vibrate faster. They strike other molecules and make them vibrate faster to spread the heat.

CONVECTION

In liquids and gases the molecules move about. When heated, they also move further apart. A heated liquid or gas expands and rises, while a cooled liquid or gas contracts and sinks. This movement, which is known as convection, spreads the heat.

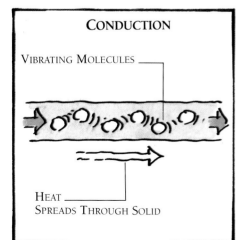

CONDUCTION

VIBRATING MOLECULES

HEAT
SPREADS THROUGH SOLID

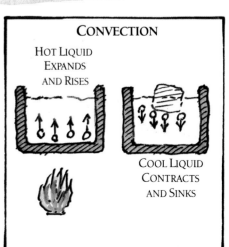

CONVECTION

HOT LIQUID
EXPANDS
AND RISES

COOL LIQUID
CONTRACTS
AND SINKS

HEAT WAVES

The Sun bombards us with a whole range of energy-carrying rays, particularly light rays and infra-red rays. These rays, and also microwaves, have similar characteristics: they pass straight through some substances, they are reflected by others and they are absorbed by the remainder. Objects that absorb rays become hot, and this is made use of in a variety of devices including the solar heater and the microwave oven.

COPPER SHEET TRANSFERS HEAT

HEAT EXCHANGER

HOT WATER

SUN'S RAYS

ALUMINIUM FOIL REFLECTS HEAT RAYS

SOLAR HEATER

A solar heater traps some of the immense heat that reaches us from the Sun. Like a closed car on a sunny day, the inside of a solar panel on a roof gets hot as infra-red rays from the Sun penetrate the glass cover. The heat passes into a copper tube through which cool water flows. The water takes up the heat and then flows directly to a hot-water tank or (as shown) to a heat exchanger.

BLACK MATERIAL ABSORBS HEAT RAYS

GLASS COVER

PUMP

COPPER TUBE

COLD WATER SUPPLY

MICROWAVE OVEN

A magnetron produces a beam of microwaves, which have high heating power. The beam strikes a spinning fan, which reflects the waves onto the food from all directions. They pass through the container and enter the food, heating it throughout and cooking the food evenly and quickly.

MICROWAVE BEAM

FAN

MAGNETRON

MICROWAVE HEATING

The microwaves strike molecules of water in the food (1). Each wave of energy causes the water molecules to align (2) and then reverse alignment (3).

1
2
3

The extremely rapid and repeated twisting produces heat.

TURNTABLE

FOOD

MICROWAVES

THE VACUUM FLASK

A vacuum flask can keep drinks piping hot – or icy cold – for hours on end. It does this by preventing as much movement of heat as possible, either out of or into the flask.

Inside the flask is a double-walled container of glass or steel. The walls are silvered on the inside to reflect heat rays (which behave like light rays) so that rays cannot leave or enter the flask. Between the container walls is a vacuum, which prevents heat conduction through the walls. The container support and stopper are made of an insulating material, such as cork, that reduces conduction.

CLOSE-FITTING STOPPER

SILVERED WALLS

VACUUM

HOT OR COLD DRINK

SUPPORT

COMBUSTION MACHINES

FIRE AND WATER

Hydrogen burns in oxygen to create great heat, producing water. Molecules of hydrogen and oxygen both contain pairs of atoms. At a sufficiently high temperature each oxygen molecule collides violently with two hydrogen molecules. The collision breaks the molecules apart, and the atoms reform as two fast-moving water molecules.

BEFORE COMBUSTION

OXYGEN MOLECULE

HYDROGEN MOLECULE

AFTER COMBUSTION

HYDROGEN ATOM

OXYGEN ATOM

WATER MOLECULE

WARM AIR

Combustion, or burning, is one common source of heat. Combustion machines allow two substances, often a fuel and oxygen in the air, to react so that the heat they produce is harnessed. The production of heat may be the sole purpose of the machine, as in a gas fire, or the heat produced may then be put to use, as in a welding torch or an engine.

GAS FIRE

The gas fire uses all three methods of heat movement — radiation, conduction and convection. Cool air enters at the base of the fire, and some of this goes to the burners. The flames heat the fireclay radiants which produce heat by radiation. The waste gases travel through the heat exchanger which warms the air behind the fire by conduction. The warmed air rises by convection and flows out into the room.

HEAT EXCHANGER

FIRECLAY RADIANTS

FLUE

HEAT RAYS

GAS BURNERS

AIR

WELDING TORCH

Metal parts can be joined with great strength by melting or welding them together. A welding torch may work by combustion. Cylinders of oxygen and hydrogen, acetylene or another gaseous fuel are connected to the torch. The oxygen and fuel burn to give a very hot flame.

In electric welding, a strong electric current or a hot electric spark heats the two parts at the join.

FILLER ROD

The welder uses a filler rod to add metal to the join.

TORCH

OXYGEN

GASEOUS FUEL

GUN CARTRIDGE

A cartridge contains two explosives to fire a bullet from the barrel of a gun at very high speed. Explosives are materials that burn very quickly; they produce lots of gas that rapidly expands with great power.

The first explosive in a cartridge (the detonator) is a sensitive explosive that is set off by the firing mechanism of the gun. It ignites the second explosive (the propellant). The resulting gas can only expand in one direction, and it drives the bullet out of the cartridge and along the barrel.

FIRING PIN

BULLET

PROPELLANT

TONATOR

FLARES

Combustion gives light as well as heat but is nowadays mostly used for emergency lighting only. Flares contain materials that burn brightly to light up the night. When used as distress signals, flares contain chemicals that produce intense colours.

BLAST FURNACE AND STEEL CONVERTER

Steel depends on combustion at several points in its manufacture. It is basically iron mixed with a precise but small quantity of carbon, and it is made from iron ore and carbon in the form of coke. Iron ore is a compound of iron and oxygen. To remove the oxygen and free the iron, the ore is heated with coke in a blast furnace. The oxygen in the iron is released and taken up by the coke during combustion.

SKIP HOIST

FURNACE GAS
The waste gases from the top of the furnace contain carbon monoxide, which burns in air. This furnace gas goes to the stove.

BLAST FURNACE
Inside the blast furnace, the carbon in the coke burns in a blast of hot air. The great heat makes more carbon combine with the oxygen in the iron ore as it slowly descends.

AIR BLAST
Hot air from the stove blasts into the base of the blast furnace.

PIG IRON
Molten pig iron, which is rich in carbon, collects at the bottom of the blast furnace. It is piped into containers and taken to the converter.

SLAG

In the blast furnace, the iron mixes with too much carbon to make good steel. A steel converter removes this extra carbon. The most common kind of converter blows oxygen gas onto the molten iron. The oxygen burns away the extra carbon to give steel. Scrap steel may be added to the converter for recycling.

Other kinds of steel converters include the open hearth furnace, in which flames of burning fuel play on a charge of iron to burn away the excess carbon, and electric furnaces powered by a strong electric current.

— STOVE
The stove heats the air that goes to the blast furnace. Furnace gas burns to heat the interior of the stove.

— STEEL CONVERTER
Molten pig iron is placed in the converter, which is tilted upright. Oxygen is then blown onto the iron through a tube. The carbon in the pig iron burns, providing heat to keep the iron molten. Waste gases from the converter are cleaned and discharged.

— OXYGEN

— MOLTEN PIG IRON

AIR IN

WASTE GASES OUT

STEEL INGOTS
When the steel-making process, which is called the basic oxygen process, is finished, the converter tilts over and discharges the steel. It is then cast into ingots ready for use.

ELECTRIC HEAT

No form of heating is as convenient as electric heating. It's available at the click of a switch and is totally clean to use, although its generation may very often produce polluting waste through combustion and nuclear fission (see p.166).

Like all other sources of heat, electricity hastens the motion of molecules, giving them extra energy that appears as heat. When an electric current flows along a wire, billions of tiny particles called electrons move among the metal atoms in the wire. The electrons are smaller than the atoms, and jostle the atoms as they pass. The vibration of the metal atoms increases, and the wire gets hotter.

Many machines contain electric heating elements that work in this way. Heat may radiate from the element, as in an electric fire, or the element may be enclosed in an electrically insulating container that heats water, for example, by conduction and convection.

ELECTRIC KETTLE

An electric kettle contains a long heating element coiled so that it fits into the base of the kettle. The element is long so that it gives plenty of heat and boils the water quickly. The kettle may also contain a thermostat (see p.154). This stops the supply of current to the element when the water boils so that the kettle will not boil dry if unattended. The thermostat may also cut off the power if the kettle is switched on without any water so that the element does not overheat.

SWITCH

HEATING ELEMENT

FAN

FAN MOTOR

HEATING ELEMENT

HAND GRIP

SWITCH

HOT AIR

HAIR DRIER

A hair drier produces an instant blast of hot air, yet is light enough to be held in one hand so the air can be directed. It contains a very long coil of thin wire that develops great heat. A jet of air blown by a fan behind the heating element carries away this heat. If the air flow is obstructed and the air becomes too hot, a thermostat cuts off the power.

SPRING

HEATING ELEMENTS

TOAST

RACK HANDLE

RACK

HEAT SENSOR

A metal strip expands and bends outwards as the temperature increases and the toast browns. When the toast is ready, the strip meets the trip plate, completing an electric circuit and activating the solenoid.

CATCH

LEVER

TRIP PLATE

TIMING MECHANISM

SOLENOID

The solenoid contains an electromagnet (see p.275) that attracts the catch. As the catch moves, it trips the lever which releases the toast rack.

THE TOASTER

An electric toaster is designed to pop up toast browned to perfection. The slices of bread descend into the toaster on a spring-loaded rack. This switches on heating elements that brown all sides. A timing mechanism then switches off the elements when the toast is ready. The rack, released by an electromagnetic catch, springs back up.

BROWNING CONTROL

Operating the control shifts the trip plate. For lighter toast, the plate moves towards the heat sensor.

REFRIGERATOR

The refrigerator is a machine that makes heat move. It takes heat out of the inside, which in losing its heat becomes cold. The refrigerator moves this heat to the outside, where the heat flows into the air and is lost. Refrigerators work by evaporation. When a liquid turns to vapour, it loses heat and gets colder. This is because the molecules of vapour need energy to move and leave the liquid. This energy comes from the liquid; the molecules left behind have less energy and so the liquid becomes colder.

COMPRESSOR
An electric refrigerator contains a compressor to move a refrigerant (a volatile liquid) around a pipe. The compressor pumps the liquid from the evaporator into the condenser. It then returns through the expansion valve.

EVAPORATOR
The refrigerant leaves the expansion valve at low pressure, causing it to evaporate inside the pipe and get cold. The evaporator is inside the refrigerator and heat flows into the evaporator, making the refrigerator cold.

EXPANSION VALVE

CAR COOLING SYSTEM

Most cars have water-cooled engines. A pump (see p.125) drives the water around channels inside the engine. The hot water then passes through the thermostat to the radiator, where it loses its heat to the air before returning to the pump. In some cars, the hot water also flows through the car's heater.

RADIATOR
Air blowing through the radiator cools the water.

THERMOSTAT
(SEE P.154)

FAN

COOLED WATER

FAN BELT

WATER PUMP

CYLINDERS

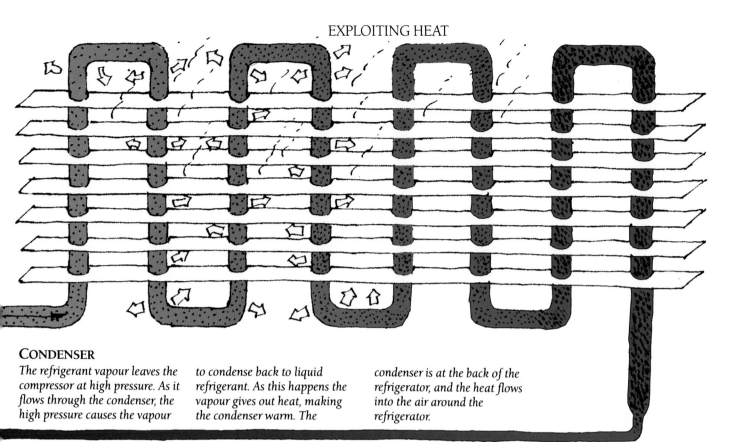

CONDENSER

The refrigerant vapour leaves the compressor at high pressure. As it flows through the condenser, the high pressure causes the vapour to condense back to liquid refrigerant. As this happens the vapour gives out heat, making the condenser warm. The condenser is at the back of the refrigerator, and the heat flows into the air around the refrigerator.

AIR CONDITIONER

This machine works in the same basic way as a refrigerator. A compressor circulates a refrigerant from an evaporator through a condenser and expansion valve and back to the evaporator. The evaporator is placed over a fan that extracts hot and humid air from the room. It takes heat from the air, making its moisture condense into water droplets. The cool dry air then returns to the room. A fan removes the heat from the condenser outside the room.

HEATER

The car heater may be part of the cooling system. It contains a heat exchanger, in which the hot water from the engine heats air driven by a fan in the passenger compartment. The warm air then returns to various parts of the passenger compartment.

HOT HUMID AIR

EXPANSION VALVE

EVAPORATOR

FAN

WATER DROPLETS

HEATED AIR

COOL DRY AIR

COMPRESSOR

CONDENSER

INSIDE

OUTSIDE

THERMOSTATS

Thermostats are devices that regulate heaters and cooling machines, repeatedly turning them on and off so that they maintain the required temperature. They work by expansion and contraction. As something heats up, its molecules move further apart. The object expands in size. When the object cools, the force pulling the molecules together reasserts itself; the molecules close ranks and the object contracts.

EXPANSION   CONTRACTION

BIMETAL THERMOSTAT

This common thermostat contains a strip of two different metals, often brass and iron. The metals expand and contract by different amounts. The bending produced by heating or cooling the thermostat can be used to activate a heater switch.

BIMETAL STRIP

CONTACT OPEN

SWITCH OPEN

The strip bends as it gets hotter, opening the contact. The current stops flowing and the heater switches itself off.

CURRENT IN

CURRENT OUT

CONTACT CLOSED

SWITCH CLOSED

The strip bends back as it cools and makes contact. The current passes and the heater switches itself back on.

ROD THERMOSTAT

Gas ovens and heaters often contain rod thermostats. The control is connected to a steel rod housed in a brass tube. The tube expands or contracts more than the rod, which closes and opens a valve in the flow of gas.

SPRING
GAS
VALVE
BRASS TUBE
STEEL ROD
BYPASS
CONTROL

TEMPERATURE INCREASES

The tube expands more than the rod, allowing the spring to close the valve at the required temperature and cut off most of the gas supply. A little gas reaches the burner through a bypass so that the burner does not go out, which would be dangerous.

TEMPERATURE DECREASES

The tube contracts, pushing back the rod so that it opens the valve. The full supply of gas begins to flow to the burner.

CAR THERMOSTAT

The thermostat in a car cooling system (see p.152) controls the flow of cooling water to the radiator. Most car thermostats contain wax, which melts when the water gets hot. The wax expands, opening a valve in the water flow. A spring closes the valve when the water cools and the wax solidifies.

ROD
WAX
CONTAINER

VALVE CLOSED

When the engine is cool, the rod is seated in the wax inside the brass container.

VALVE OPEN

The wax melts and expands, pushing against the rod and forcing the container down.

THERM

As things expand or contract, they change size by an amount that depends on the temperature. A rise of twenty degrees, for example, gives twice the expansion produced by ten degrees. Expansion and contraction can therefore be used to measure temperature.

In a common thermometer (*left*), coloured alcohol or mercury rises in a narrow tube as the liquid gets hotter and expands. The level falls as it gets colder and contracts. The maximum-minimum thermometer (*right*) makes use of both to record extremes of temperature.

MAXIMUM TEMPERATURE

The U-shaped tube contains alcohol with mercury in the centre. At high temperatures, the alcohol in the bulb above the minimum scale expands, pushing the mercury up the maximum scale. A metal marker remains at the highest point reached.

MINIMUM TEMPERATURE

The alcohol in the bulb above the minimum scale contracts. The air in the other bulb pushes the mercury up the minimum scale, moving the marker up the scale.

ALCOHOL

MARKERS

The steel markers each have a small spring that stops them falling back down the tube. A magnet is used to pull the markers back to the mercury to reset the thermometer.

ALCOHOL

MERCURY

PETROL ENGINE

1 INDUCTION STROKE
The piston moves down and the inlet valve opens. The fuel and air mixture is sucked into the cylinder.

2 COMPRESSION STROKE
The inlet valve closes and the piston moves up. The mixture is compressed.

In the petrol engine, we put heat to use by converting it into motive power. A petrol engine is often called an internal combustion engine, but this means only that the fuel burns inside the engine. The jet engine and rocket engine are also internal combustion engines.

A petrol engine works by burning a mixture of petrol and air in a cylinder containing a piston. The heat produced causes the air to expand and force down the piston, which turns a crankshaft linked to the wheels.

Most cars have a four-stroke engine. A stroke is one movement of the piston, either up or down. In a four-stroke engine, the engine repeats a cycle of actions (shown above) in which the piston moves four times.

Many light vehicles, such as motorcycles, have two-stroke engines. This kind of engine is simpler in construction than a four-stroke engine, but not as powerful. A two-stroke engine has no valves. Instead there are three ports in the side of the cylinder that the piston opens and closes as it moves up and down. A diesel engine is similar to the petrol engine, but has no spark plugs (see pp.140-1).

The exhaust gases that leave the engine contain harmful polluting gases, and may first pass through a catalytic converter. This converts the harmful substances to harmless products. The cleaned-up gases finally go to the silencer before leaving the exhaust.

3 POWER STROKE
The electric spark plug produces a spark and the fuel ignites, forcing the piston back down the cylinder.

4 EXHAUST STROKE
The outlet valve opens and the piston rises, pushing the exhaust gases out of the cylinder.

CATALYTIC CONVERTER

The harmful gases include carbon monoxide, nitrogen oxides, and hydrocarbon fuel. In the converter, surfaces coated with catalyst metals change the gases into carbon dioxide, nitrogen, and water vapour. The metals are platinum, palladium, and rhodium.

SILENCER

The exhaust gases leave the engine at high pressure, and would produce intolerable noise if allowed to escape directly. The silencer contains a series of plates with holes, which reduce the pressure of the gases so that they leave the exhaust pipe quietly.

EXHAUST PIPE

STEAM POWER

The first engine to make use of heat to drive a machine was the steam engine. It employed steam raised in a boiler to drive a piston up and down a cylinder. This engine was vital in the development of the Industrial Revolution, but is now obsolete.

However, the age of steam is by no means over because steam power provides us with the bulk of our electricity. Thermal power stations, which burn fuels such as coal (shown here) and oil, contain steam turbines to drive the electricity generators – as do nuclear power stations (see pp.170-1). All power stations are designed to pass as much energy as possible from the fuel to the turbines.

INCOMING AIR

STEAM REHEATER

CHIMNEY
The flue gases from the burning coal pass through the reheater, economizer and preheater before going to the chimney.

FLUE GASES

PREHEATER
To extract as much heat as possible from the fuel, the hot flue gases from the boiler pass through the preheater and heat the incoming air.

PRECIPITATOR
The flue gases contain dust and grit that are removed by the electrostatic precipitator before the gases are discharged to the atmosphere. Inside the precipitator are electrically charged plates that attract the dust and grit particles. (See p.262)

ECONOMIZER
The water from the condenser is first heated in the economizer before it returns to the boiler.

COAL CONVEYOR

COAL MILL
The coal is ground to a fine powder inside the coal mill. Air heated in the preheaters blows the powdered coal along pipes to the furnace.

SUPERHEATER

STEAM DRUM

OUTGOING STEAM AT LOWER PRESSURE

INCOMING STEAM

STATIONARY BLADES

ROTATING BLADES

STEAM TURBINE

A steam turbine works in the same basic way as a windmill (see p.34). The high-pressure steam strikes the blades of the turbine and makes them rotate, just as the wind blows the sails of a windmill. The turbine contains sets of stationary blades attached to the inner wall that direct the steam on to the rotating blades.

The steam expands as it drives the blades, lowering its pressure and temperature. The turbine has three stages with separate sets of blades that work at high, intermediate and low steam pressures. In this way, the maximum amount of heat energy is turned into motive power.

BOILER

Water flows through tubes inside the furnace, producing steam at high pressure in the steam drum. This steam then flows to the superheater at the top of the furnace.

HIGH-PRESSURE STAGE

INTERMEDIATE-PRESSURE STAGE

LOW-PRESSURE STAGE

HIGH-VOLTAGE GENERATOR

BURNING COAL

CONDENSER

The steam from the turbine is condensed to water in the condenser. It then returns to the boiler. In the condenser, the steam flows through pipes surrounded by cold water. This cooling water may then be piped to cooling towers.

COOLING WATER

THE JET ENGINE

Without the jet engine, many of us would have little experience of flight. Superior both in power and economy to the propeller engine, it has made mass worldwide air travel possible.

A jet engine sucks air in at the front and ejects it at high speed from the back. The principle of action and reaction (see p.100) forces the engine forwards as the air streams backwards. The engine is powered by heat produced by burning kerosene or paraffin.

THE TURBOFAN

The engine that drives big airliners is a turbofan engine. At the front of the engine, a large fan rotates to draw air in. Some of this air then enters the compressors, which contain both rotating and stationary blades. The compressors raise the pressure of the air, which then flows to the combustors or combustion chambers. There, flames of burning kerosene heat the air, which expands. The hot, high-pressure air rushes towards the exhaust, but first passes through turbines which drive the compressors and the fan.

The rest of the air sucked in by the fan passes around the compressors, combustors and turbines. It helps to cool and quieten the engine, and then joins the heated air. A large amount of air speeds from the engine, driving the aircraft forwards with tremendous force.

BYPASS AIR

FAN SHAFT

ROTATING FAN BLADES

ENGINE COWLING

STATIONARY FAN BLADES

Can I have your boots, Señor?

COMPRESSOR SHAFTS

HEATED AIR

EXHAUST

COMBUSTOR

COMPRESSOR TURBINES

COMPRESSORS

FAN TURBINE

BYPASS DUCT

OUTGOING BYPASS AIR

ROCKET ENGINES

The rocket is the simplest and most powerful kind of heat engine. It burns fuel in a combustion chamber with an open end. The hot gases produced expand greatly and rush from the open end or exhaust at high speed. The rocket moves forwards by action and reaction (see p.100) as the gases exert a powerful force on the chamber walls.

Rockets can work in space because, unlike other heat engines, they do not require air for combustion. Their fuel burns without the need for an external oxygen supply.

SOLID-FUEL ROCKET

Many spacecraft are launched by solid-fuel boosters, which are rocket engines that, like firework rockets, contain a solid propellant. A circular or star-shaped channel runs down the centre of the propellant. The propellant burns at the surface of this channel, so the channel is the combustion chamber. A solid-fuel booster develops more power if the channel is star-shaped. This is because the channel's area is larger, and a greater volume of hot gases is produced. Solid-fuel rockets can produce great power but, once ignited, they cannot be shut down; they fly until all the propellant has burned.

PAPER CONE

COLOURED STARS

EXPLOSIVE CHARGE

CLAY

ROLLED PAPER TUBE

PROPELLANT

FUSE

STICK

FIREWORK ROCKET
Firework rockets are the simplest form of heat engine. They are packed with a propellant, a powder that burns fiercely. The smoke and hot gases stream from the base and drive the rocket upwards, while the long stick keeps the rocket's flight straight. The propellant is slowly consumed by combustion, and finally the burning powder ignites an explosive charge which expels the glowing stars.

IGNITER

PROPELLANT

CHANNEL

NOZZLE
The rocket can be steered by swivelling the nozzle at the base of the rocket.

LIQUID-FUEL ROCKET

Spacecraft that require repeated firings of their engines, often for manoeuvring in space, have liquid-fuel rocket engines. Unlike solid propellants, liquid propellants are fed to the combustion chamber and are burned for as long as necessary. The propellants consist of two liquids, usually called the fuel and the oxidizer. Liquid hydrogen and liquid oxygen are often used.

FUEL TANK

OXIDIZER TANK

PUMPS

The rocket may contain pumps that feed the propellants to the combustion chamber. The pumps are driven by a turbine often powered by gas produced by the propellants. In some rockets, the propellants are delivered under gas pressure, so pumps are not needed.

VALVES

These control the flow of the propellants, enabling the engine to work at different degrees of power.

COMBUSTION CHAMBER

The propellants generally have to be ignited in the combustion chamber, but some rockets use propellants which ignite on contact.

NOZZLE

EXTERNAL TANK

SOLID-FUEL BOOSTER

ORBITER

MAIN ENGINES (LIQUID FUEL)

SPACE SHUTTLE

The space shuttle has five principal rocket engines. These are two huge solid-fuel boosters fixed alongside the orbiter, and three liquid-fuel main engines at the rear of the orbiter. The external tank contains liquid hydrogen and liquid oxygen for the main engines. These five engines only take the shuttle into space. Other smaller liquid-fuel engines are used to attain and leave orbit and to manoeuvre the shuttle in space.

NUCLEAR POWER

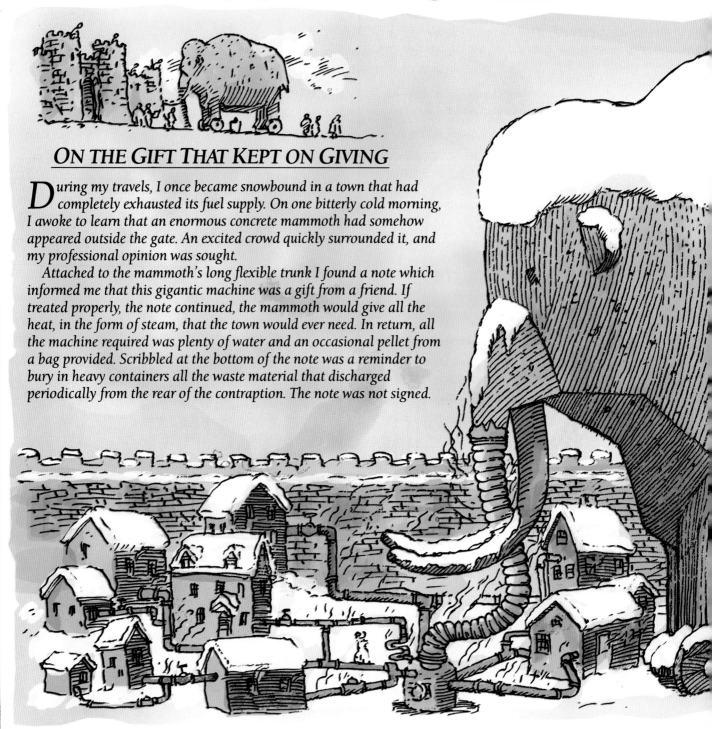

ON THE GIFT THAT KEPT ON GIVING

During my travels, I once became snowbound in a town that had completely exhausted its fuel supply. On one bitterly cold morning, I awoke to learn that an enormous concrete mammoth had somehow appeared outside the gate. An excited crowd quickly surrounded it, and my professional opinion was sought.

Attached to the mammoth's long flexible trunk I found a note which informed me that this gigantic machine was a gift from a friend. If treated properly, the note continued, the mammoth would give all the heat, in the form of steam, that the town would ever need. In return, all the machine required was plenty of water and an occasional pellet from a bag provided. Scribbled at the bottom of the note was a reminder to bury in heavy containers all the waste material that discharged periodically from the rear of the contraption. The note was not signed.

NUCLEAR REACTIONS

The mechanical mammoth is able to supply such prodigious amounts of energy from so little fuel because it is a nuclear machine. Inside is a nuclear reactor that converts the fuel into heat, but it does not burn the nuclear fuel.

Burning or combustion is a chemical reaction. The elements present in the fuel and the oxygen in the air merely rearrange themselves as burning progresses. The new arrangement of elements, which yields ash, smoke and waste gases, has less energy then the original fuel and oxygen. The leftover energy appears as heat.

A nuclear reaction exploits the elements to produce heat in a totally different manner.

When a nuclear reaction occurs, the elements in the fuel do not remain the same. Instead, the nuclear reactor changes the elements in the fuel into other elements. The waste products of the nuclear reaction have less mass than the fuel, and the lost mass turns into heat energy. A nuclear reaction in fact creates energy; it does not convert one form of energy into another. A little mass gives a lot of energy, which is why nuclear power is so abundant.

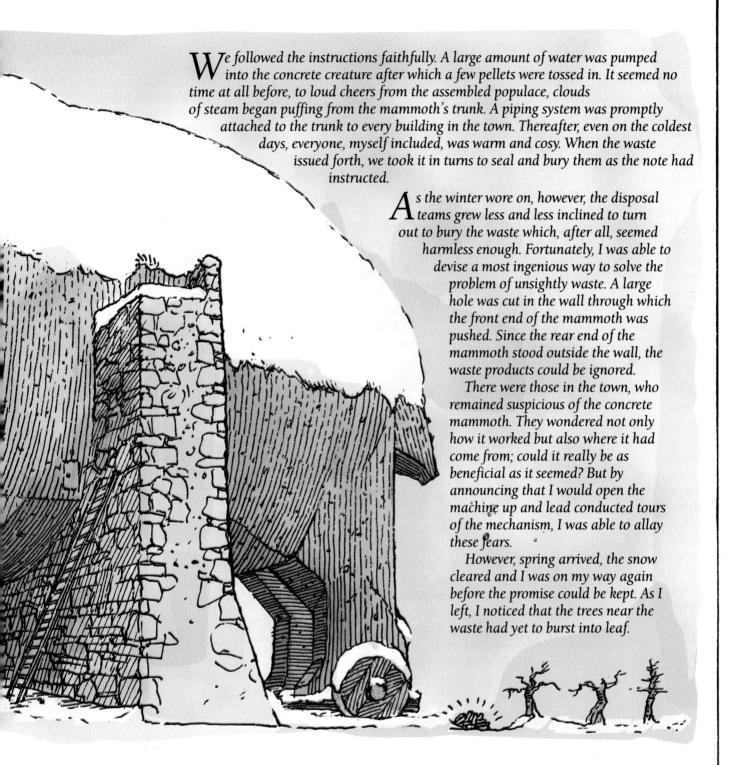

We followed the instructions faithfully. A large amount of water was pumped into the concrete creature after which a few pellets were tossed in. It seemed no time at all before, to loud cheers from the assembled populace, clouds of steam began puffing from the mammoth's trunk. A piping system was promptly attached to the trunk to every building in the town. Thereafter, even on the coldest days, everyone, myself included, was warm and cosy. When the waste issued forth, we took it in turns to seal and bury them as the note had instructed.

As the winter wore on, however, the disposal teams grew less and less inclined to turn out to bury the waste which, after all, seemed harmless enough. Fortunately, I was able to devise a most ingenious way to solve the problem of unsightly waste. A large hole was cut in the wall through which the front end of the mammoth was pushed. Since the rear end of the mammoth stood outside the wall, the waste products could be ignored.

There were those in the town, who remained suspicious of the concrete mammoth. They wondered not only how it worked but also where it had come from; could it really be as beneficial as it seemed? But by announcing that I would open the machine up and lead conducted tours of the mechanism, I was able to allay these fears.

However, spring arrived, the snow cleared and I was on my way again before the promise could be kept. As I left, I noticed that the trees near the waste had yet to burst into leaf.

CONTROLLING NUCLEAR POWER

The people are right to be wary of the nuclear mammoth. A nuclear reaction can, if uncontrolled, produce an enormous explosion as the immense release of energy takes place almost instantaneously. This occurs in nuclear weapons. Nuclear reactors achieve the controlled release of nuclear power. However, the reaction itself and also its waste products give out harmful rays known as radiation, and the reactor has to be encased in concrete and the waste stored well away from people for safety. The production of radiation is also a nuclear reaction, for it changes the elements in the waste. However, it takes place at a much slower rate than in a nuclear reactor, and the radioactive waste can continue to emit harmful radiation for many years.

It is ironic then that we all depend ultimately on nuclear power, because the heat and light that support life on Earth come from a gigantic nuclear reaction that is taking place in the Sun. Indeed, the production of energy on such a vast scale is possible only by nuclear reactions. Every second, the Sun losses four million tonnes of its mass to sustain its huge output of energy.

NUCLEAR FISSION

Nuclear power gets its name because the process of power production takes place inside the nucleus. Each atom of fuel contains a central particle called the nucleus, which is itself made up of even smaller particles called protons and neutrons.

The kind of nuclear reaction that happens inside a nuclear reactor is called nuclear fission. The fuel is uranium or plutonium, two very heavy elements which have many protons and neutrons in their nuclei. Fission starts when a fast-moving neutron strikes a nucleus. The nucleus cannot take in the extra neutron, and the whole nucleus breaks apart into two smaller nuclei. Several neutrons are also released and these go on to break more nuclei, which produce more neutrons and so on. Because the first neutron sets off a chain of fissions, the nuclear reaction is called a chain reaction. Without control, it can multiply rapidly and produce enormous heat in a fraction of a second.

FISSION FRAGMENTS
Each fission produces two smaller nuclei called fission fragments. As the chain reaction proceeds, the fragments and neutrons move at high speed, agitating the atoms of fuel and producing great heat.

FREE NEUTRON

CHAIN REACTION
Free neutrons in the fuel strike nuclei of uranium or plutonium, causing them to break apart and produce more neutrons. If there are sufficient nuclei, the neutrons produce a chain of further fissions as more and more nuclei break apart.

NUCLEUS OF URANIUM OR PLUTONIUM

RADIATION
As each fission occurs, gamma rays are released. This form of radiation is harmful and highly penetrating, requiring a concrete shield for safety.

NUCLEAR FUSION

Nuclear power can be produced by a process called fusion as well as by fission. In this kind of reaction, the nuclei of the fuel come together and do not break apart. Unlike fission, nuclear fusion occurs only with small atoms whose nuclei contain very few protons and neutrons. The gaseous fuel consists of two different forms of hydrogen, which is the lightest of the elements. To produce nuclear fusion, pairs of nuclei meet so that their protons and neutrons fuse together and become a single nucleus. A spare neutron is left over. The fused nuclei and neutrons move off at high speed, producing great heat. Radiation is not emitted, but the neutrons are harmful.

To get the nuclei to meet and fuse, the atoms must be banged together with tremendous force. This can only be done by heating the fuel to temperatures of millions of degrees. Nuclear fusion powers the Sun, and it also occurs in thermonuclear weapons.

NEUTRON

DEUTERIUM
One gas in the fuel is deuterium, which is a form of hydrogen. Its nuclei each contain one proton and one neutron. Deuterium is made from water.

TRITIUM
The other gas in the fuel is tritium, another form of hydrogen. It has one proton and two neutrons in each nucleus. Tritium is made by bombarding lithium, a common metal, with neutrons.

HELIUM
When the nuclei of deuterium and tritium fuse, they first produce a nucleus containing two protons and three neutrons. This nucleus is an unstable form of the element helium. It breaks apart to give normal helium, which has two protons and two neutrons, and the extra neutron escapes.

NUCLEAR WEAPONS

ATOM BOMB

An atom bomb is better known as a fission bomb because it works by nuclear fission. The bomb contains a hollow sphere of uranium or plutonium. The sphere is too big to initiate a chain reaction because neutrons that occur naturally escape from the surface of the sphere without causing fission.

To detonate the bomb, a source of neutrons is shot by the detonator into the centre of the sphere. Explosives then crush the sphere around the neutron source. The neutrons cannot now escape. A chain reaction occurs and fission flashes through the uranium or plutonium in a fraction of a second. The bomb explodes with a power equal to thousands of tonnes (kilotonnes) of TNT. Intense radiation is also produced.

DETONATOR

NEUTRON SOURCE

URANIUM OR
PLUTONIUM SPHERE

EXPLOSIVE

CASING

HYDROGEN BOMB

The hydrogen bomb or H-bomb is a thermonuclear weapon which works partly by nuclear fusion. Two forms of hydrogen — deuterium and tritium — are compressed at very high temperature to produce instant fusion. These conditions of ultra-high temperature and pressure can only be created by a fission bomb, which is used to trigger fusion in a thermonuclear weapon. Explosives crush all the nuclear materials around a neutron source to detonate the bomb.

Some thermonuclear weapons also contain a jacket of uranium, which produces a blast equal to millions of tonnes (megatonnes) of TNT. The neutron bomb, on the other hand, is a fusion weapon of relatively low power that produces penetrating neutrons. The neutrons released by the bomb would kill people while most buildings would survive the weak blast.

NUCLEAR TESTING

The fallout or debris produced by the explosion of a nuclear weapon is so radioactive that the weapons must be tested in chambers dug deep underground in remote areas. In this way, the atmosphere is not contaminated by the fallout.

EXPLOSIVE

CASING

NEUTRON SOURCE

FUSION FUEL

URANIUM JACKET

URANIUM OR
PLUTONIUM TRIGGER

FALLOUT

A future nuclear war would not only reduce cities and towns to ruins. Fallout from the nuclear explosions would spread through the atmosphere, bombarding the land with lethal amounts of radiation. The only means of escape would be to live in deep underground shelters away from the fallout. This imprisonment would have to last until the radiation decreased to an acceptable level, which could take many years. Even then, climatic changes, shortage of food and the threat of disease would make life above ground a grim business.

NUCLEAR REACTOR

The heart of a nuclear power station is its nuclear reactor. Here, immense heat is generated by the fission of uranium fuel. The heat is transferred from the reactor to a steam generator, where it boils water to steam. The rest of the nuclear power station works in the same way as one powered by coal (see pp.158-9).

In all nuclear reactors, a liquid or gas flows through the core of the reactor and heats up. Its purpose is to take away the heat generated by fission in the reactor core, so it is called a coolant. The main kind of nuclear reactor used in nuclear power stations, the pressurized water reactor (PWR), uses water as the coolant.

FUEL RODS

The fuel consists of pellets of uranium dioxide loaded into long metal tubes. Clusters of these fuel rods are then inserted into the reactor core.

CONTROL RODS

Among the fuel rods are control rods, which contain a substance that absorbs neutrons. Moving the rods in or out of the core controls the flow of neutrons so that fission progresses steadily and provides a constant supply of heat. The reactor is shut down by fully inserting the control rods.

REACTOR CORE

A steel pressure vessel surrounds the core of the pressurized water reactor, which contains the fuel rods and control rods. Neutrons, which occur naturally, start a chain reaction in the fuel and fast neutrons are produced by fission. The coolant (pressurized water) flowing through the core slows the neutrons down. The slow neutrons cause further fission and keep the chain reaction going. Heat produced by fission is passed to the coolant.

FUEL PELLET

FUEL ROD

FUEL PELLET

METAL TUBE

CONTROL ROD

HOT COOLANT OUT

NEUTRON SHIELD

COOLANT IN

FUEL ROD

CONTROL ROD

STEEL PRESSURE VESSEL

CIRCULATING COOLANT

REACTOR BUILDING

The reactor core and steam generators are housed in a steel containment vessel surrounded by a thick layer of concrete. The concrete absorbs radiation while the steel vessel seals off the reactor and steam generators to prevent the escape of any radioactive water or steam. The spent fuel is also highly radioactive; its radioactivity may take decades or even centuries to decline to a level where it can be considered safe. Spent fuel may be stored at the power station, or alternatively, it may be sealed and buried either underground or beneath the sea.

CONTAINMENT
VESSEL
(STEEL)

REACTOR
SHIELD
(CONCRETE)

HOT STEAM
TO TURBINES

CORE SHIELD

The core has a concrete shield which reduces the levels of radiation inside the reactor building. Within the shield, the top of the reactor core may be immersed in water to absorb radiation.

STEAM GENERATOR

The temperature of the core is far above the normal boiling point of water, and the coolant water is placed under high pressure to stop it boiling. This superhot water then goes to the steam generators, where it gives up its heat to boil unpressurized water flowing through the steam generators. This steam then travels to the turbines.

COOLANT PUMP

Powerful pumps circulate the hot coolant from the reactor core to the steam generators.

REACTOR CORE

HOT COOLANT

CONDENSED WATER FROM TURBINES

FUSION POWER

Nuclear fusion could provide us with almost unlimited power. The fuels for fusion come from materials that are common. Deuterium is made from water and tritium is produced from lithium, which is a metal that occurs widely in minerals. All that is needed is a machine to make them fuse under controlled conditions.

In practice, these conditions are extremely difficult to achieve. The two gases must be heated to a temperature of hundreds of millions of degrees, and kept together for a few seconds. No ordinary container can hold them, and several different systems based on magnetic fields or lasers are being tried.

However, progress is being made; fusion has been achieved on a limited scale but the amount of energy produced is much less than the energy fed into the fusion machine to create the conditions. Scientists hope that fusion power will advance to become reality early in the next century. If so, we shall possess a source of energy that not only has tremendous power but uses fuels that are abundant. Although a fusion reactor would not be likely to explode and release radioactivity, it would produce radioactive waste in the form of discarded reactor components.

THE TOKAMAK

Most fusion research uses a machine called a tokamak, which was originally developed in Russia. At its heart is a torus – a doughnut-shape tube that contains the gases to be fused. A huge electrical transformer and coils of wire surround the tube. The transformer produces an electric current in the gases, which heats them up to produce an electrically charged mixture, or plasma. At the same time, strong magnetic fields produced by the current and the coils act on the hot gases.

The magnetic fields confine the gases to the centre of the torus so that they do not touch the walls. They can then become very hot indeed and begin to fuse. Extra heating can be achieved by bombarding the gases with powerful radio waves, and by injecting beams of particles into the torus.

TORUS
The torus contains a vacuum into which the fuel gases are injected.

MAGNETIC FIELD COILS
These coils are wound around the torus and are supplied with a powerful electric current. A magnetic field is created in the torus.

TRANSFORMER
Electric current supplied to the transformer coils at the centre of the machine is stepped up by the transformer coils to create a powerful current in the plasma. This current heats the plasma and produces a second magnetic field around the plasma. The two magnetic fields combine to give a field that confines the plasma to the centre of the torus.

PLASMA
The gases fed into the torus are heated to such high temperatures that they become a plasma, a form of superhot gas that is affected by magnetism. The magnetic field squeezes the plasma into a narrow ring at the centre of the torus. The high temperature and pressure cause fusion to occur.

FUSION REACTOR

This is how a fusion reactor of the future could work. Deuterium and tritium are fed into the torus, where they fuse together. Fusion produces non-radioactive helium, which leaves the torus, and high-energy neutrons. Around the torus is a blanket of lithium metal. The neutrons enter the blanket and convert some of the lithium into tritium, which is extracted and goes to the torus. The neutrons also heat up the blanket. This heat is removed by a heat exchanger and goes to a boiler to raise steam for electricity generation. The reactor shield absorbs the low-energy neutrons leaving the blanket.

DEUTERIUM

TRITIUM

TRITIUM EXTRACTION

HELIUM EXHAUST

MAGNETIC FIELD COILS

SHIELD

LITHIUM BLANKET

TORUS

HOT GASES

HEAT EXCHANGER

STEAM TO TURBINE

WATER FROM TURBINE

STEAM BOILER

SOLAR FUSION

Several forms of power make use of the heat and light that come from the Sun. None are yet the principal providers of our energy, but they may become important in the future. Solar power makes use of nuclear fusion, which produces the Sun's heat and light.

THE·FIRST
SON·ET·LUMIÈRE
ATLANTIS

WORKING WITH WAVES

INTRODUCTION

A T EVERY MOMENT OF OUR LIVES, we are bombarded with waves of energy. Painful though this may sound, it is actually nothing to get alarmed about, because most of this energy passes by us, or in some cases, right through us, without having any harmful effect. However, not all of these waves escape our notice. Through our senses, we can detect a small but important part of this ceaseless barrage. We can feel heat energy through our skin, we can see light energy with our eyes, and we can detect sound energy with our ears. But with the help of the machines described in this part of *The New Way Things Work* we can do far more than this: we can communicate over unimaginable distances, bring hidden worlds – both microscopic and astronomic – into view, and reconstruct sights and sounds that would otherwise be locked away in the past.

STRETCHING OUR SENSES

Machines that work with waves use wave energy to amplify and extend our eyes and ears. Telescopes and microscopes upgrade the lenses in our eyes to reveal the extraordinary amount of fine detail that is actually present in light rays, but which unaided our eyes cannot see. Printing and photography put words and pictures on paper in full colour, while in holograms, lasers exploit the clash of light waves to produce astonishing images that are so real you think you can put your hands around them. Methods of recording sound and moving images recreate waves of sound and light to produce a potent means of illusion.

What most of these machines do is quite easy to describe, because many of them, for example the camera, tape recorder, video recorder, and telephone, are familiar objects found in almost every home. More difficult is understanding how wave energy allows them to do it.

ENERGY ON THE MOVE

When a sewing machine or a petrol engine is used, it is easy to see where the energy comes from and where it goes to. Machines that work with waves are different. You cannot hold waves of energy in order to examine them, and to make things trickier, energy waves behave according to a separate set of principles from those that govern physical matter.

The important feature of energy waves is that when they are conducted through matter, it is only the energy itself that moves. When a stone is dropped into a pond, for example, the ripples spread out from the point where the stone hits the water. But these miniature waves are not made up of water travelling outwards. Instead, the water at the surface of the pond just rises and falls, and only the energy moves outwards. The waves used by machines work in just the same way. Every passing wave consists of a regular rise and fall of energy. The distance between successive energy rises is the wavelength, and the rate at which they pass is the wave's frequency. Both are very important in our perception of waves.

WAVES THROUGH MATTER

The machines in the following pages use two different types of waves. Of the two, sound waves are easier to understand because they consist of vibrations in matter. They can only travel through matter – air, water, glass, steel, bricks and mortar; if it can be made to vibrate, sound will travel through it. An individual sound wave is a chain of vibrating molecules – the tiny particles in the air, water, or solid materials. When a loudspeaker vibrates, the molecules in the air around it also vibrate. But like the water in the pond, the molecules do not themselves move with the sound. Instead, they just pass on the vibration. Regions of high and low pressure move through the air and spread out from the source. Sound is simply our perception of this vibration. If something vibrates faster than about 20 times a second, we can hear it – this is the deepest note that human ears can detect. As the vibration speeds up, the pitch gets higher. At 20,000 vibrations a second, the pitch becomes too high for us to hear, but not too high for machines such as the ultrasound scanner, which uses high-pitched sound in the same way as a flying bat to create an image built up of echoes.

WAVES THROUGH SPACE

The second category of waves includes light and radio waves – members of a family known as electromagnetic waves. These mobile forms of energy are often called rays instead of waves – heat rays are also family members. The only way these waves differ is in their frequency. Rather than vibrating molecules, electromagnetic waves – light, heat rays, and radio waves – consist of vibrating electric and magnetic fields. Because these fields can exist in empty space, electromagnetic waves can travel through nothingness itself. Like sound waves, each wave has a particular frequency. In light, we see different frequencies as different colours just as higher and lower sound frequencies give treble and bass notes. All electromagnetic waves travel at the speed of light, while sound waves crawl along at a millionth of that speed.

COMMUNICATING WITH WAVES

In travelling to us and through us, waves and rays may not just bring energy but may also communicate meaning. Waves that are constant, as in the beam of a torch, cannot convey any information. But if that beam is interrupted, or if its brightness can be made to change, then it can carry a message. This is how all wave-borne communications work. Patterns of energy arrive from energy sources that are high or low, loud or soft, light or dark, different colours. In this way, sound waves and light rays bring us music, voices, words on a page and expressions on faces. By converting these waves to radio waves and electrical waves that can travel great distances, sounds and images can flash around the world. The machines on the following pages show something of the vast range of wave communications – from a telephone conversation with a next-door neighbour to the feeble signals from a space probe hurtling towards the Solar System's distant edge.

LIGHT AND IMAGES

ON SEEING THINGS

My life as an inventor has not been without its setbacks. Perhaps the most distressing was the failure of my athletic trophy business. Having perfected the folding rubber javelin and the stunning crystal discus, I entrusted their production to an apprentice. His initial enthusiasm however soon gave way to strange delusions of giant mammoths.

LIGHT RAYS

All sources of light produce rays that stream out in all directions. When these rays strike objects, they usually bounce off them. If light rays enter our eyes, we either see the source of the light or the object that reflected the rays towards us. The angle of the rays gives the object its apparent size.

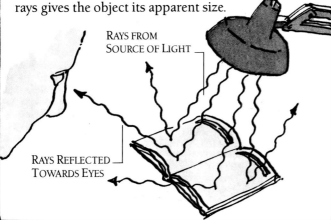

RAYS FROM
SOURCE OF LIGHT

RAYS REFLECTED
TOWARDS EYES

EYESIGHT

The lens of the eye bends the light rays that come from an object. It forms an image of the object on the light-sensitive retina of the eye, and this image is then changed to nerve impulses which travel to the brain. The image is in fact upside down on the retina, but the brain interprets it as upright.

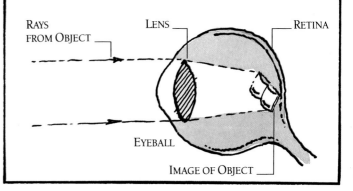

RAYS
FROM OBJECT

LENS

RETINA

EYEBALL

IMAGE OF OBJECT

Assuming that he was simply overworked, I reduced his hours and improved ventilation in the workshop. But his condition deteriorated and one day he confronted me in my laboratory, claiming that miniature mammoths had invaded the premises. He insisted that a procession of these creatures was making its way across the wall,

accompanied by a trail of smoke. Within the hour, word reached us that the workshop and all its contents had mysteriously burned to the ground. I realized that the frightened youth must have knocked over a candle as he fled, and although very disappointed at the loss, I decided to humour him and attribute the disaster to the spirits.

FORMING IMAGES

As light rays enter and leave transparent materials such as glass, they bend or refract. Seen through a lens, a nearby object appears to be much bigger because the rays enter the eye in a wider angle than they would without it. This is why the mammoth's eye is magnified by the discus.

Lenses can also throw images onto a surface. Cones of rays from every point on the object are bent by the lens to meet at the surface. The cones cross, inverting the mammoths, while the sun's rays meet to form a hot spot on the wall.

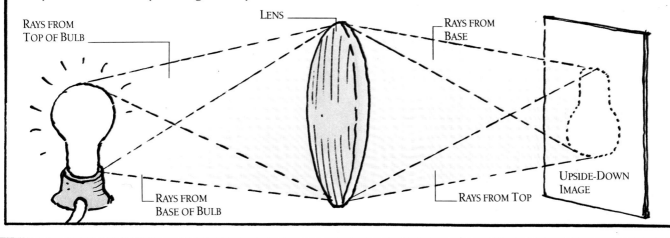

RAYS FROM TOP OF BULB

LENS

RAYS FROM BASE

RAYS FROM BASE OF BULB

RAYS FROM TOP

UPSIDE-DOWN IMAGE

LIGHTING

There are two basic methods of producing artificial light. The first is to heat something so hot that it glows. The flame of a candle or oil lamp contains particles of carbon that have been made white-hot by the combustion of the wax or oil. In a light bulb, the filament is heated so much that it glows. The second method is to pass an electric current through a gas or vapour so that the gas or vapour lights up. Both methods cause electrons, the tiny charged particles inside atoms, to emit energy in the form of light rays.

STABLE ATOM
Inside an atom, electrons move in a number of concentric orbits around the nucleus.

ELECTRONS MOVE OUT
Heat or electricity provides enough energy to make the electrons "jump" to higher orbits.

ELECTRONS FALL BACK
When the electrons fall back, their extra energy is emitted as a ray of light.

ELECTRODE — PHOSPHOR COATING — GLASS TUBE — ELECTRODE

FREE ELECTRONS

MERCURY VAPOUR

FLUORESCENT LAMP

A fluorescent lamp contains a glass tube that glows with white light when an electric current is passed through it. At each end of the tube are electrodes that are heated by the current and emit free electrons. The electrons strike atoms of mercury vapour in the tube, and cause the atoms to emit rays of ultraviolet light. The ultraviolet rays, which are invisible, strike a phosphor coating on the inside of the tube. The rays energize the electrons in the phosphor atoms, and the atoms emit white light. The conversion of one kind of light into another is known as fluorescence.

STREET LAMP
The colour of fluorescent street lamps depends on the substance inside the tube. Sodium lights contain sodium vapour which glows a bright yellow-orange when electricity is passed through it. Neon signs work with a number of gases: neon itself glows red.

ELECTRONIC FLASH
The electronic flash on a camera is similar to a fluorescent lamp. A capacitor inside the camera builds up a strong electric charge and then discharges it as the shutter is pressed. The charge produces a bright but very brief spark of light inside the flash tube.

LIGHT BULB

An electric light bulb consists of a filament of tungsten wire wound in a tight coil. The passage of electricity through the filament heats the coil so that it becomes white hot. The filament reaches a temperature of about 2,500°C (4,500°F). Tungsten is chosen because it has a very high melting point and will not melt as it heats up. The bulb contains an inert gas such as argon to prevent the metal combining with oxygen in the air, which would cause the filament to burn out. The gas is usually under reduced pressure.

In modern light bulbs each coil of the filament is often made up of even tinier coils. The filament is therefore very long but very thin. This arrangement increases its light output.

GLASS BULB

INERT GAS AT LOW PRESSURE

TUNGSTEN FILAMENT

ELECTRICAL CONTACTS

ADDING COLOURS

Many of the colour images we see are not quite what they seem. Instead of being composed of all the colours that we perceive, they are actually made of three primary colours mixed together. Images that are sources of light, such as colour television pictures (see p.246), combine colours by "additive" mixing. Stage lights produce a range of colours by additive mixing of three primary colours at various brightnesses.

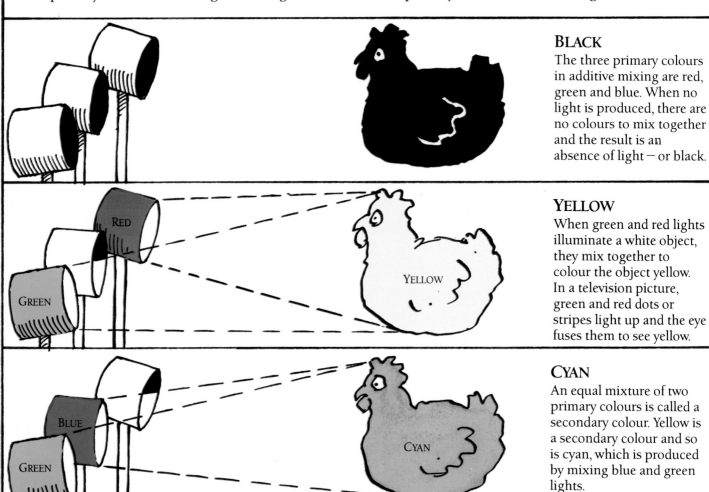

BLACK
The three primary colours in additive mixing are red, green and blue. When no light is produced, there are no colours to mix together and the result is an absence of light – or black.

YELLOW
When green and red lights illuminate a white object, they mix together to colour the object yellow. In a television picture, green and red dots or stripes light up and the eye fuses them to see yellow.

CYAN
An equal mixture of two primary colours is called a secondary colour. Yellow is a secondary colour and so is cyan, which is produced by mixing blue and green lights.

MAGENTA
Magenta is a third secondary colour, produced by mixing red and blue. Other colours are formed by mixing the primary colours in different proportions.

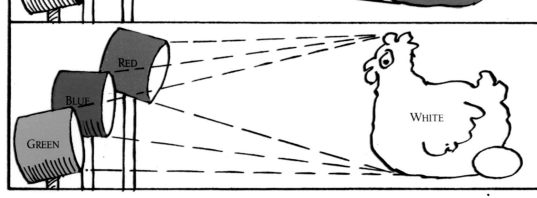

WHITE
White is produced by mixing all three primary colours together. White light is given by an equal mixture of red, green and blue lights.

SUBTRACTING COLOURS

Images produced by mixing printing inks (see pp.214-5) and paints form colours by "subtractive" mixing. This gives different colours to additive mixing because the pictures themselves are not sources of light. The pictures reflect some of the primary colours in the white light that illuminates them, and absorb or subtract the other primary colours. We see the reflected primary colours added together.

WHITE
A white surface reflects all the light falling on it and absorbs none. No subtraction takes place and all three colours are reflected, mixing together to give white.

YELLOW
A yellow surface absorbs the blue light in the white light striking it. Blue is subtracted and red and green are reflected, which combine to give yellow.

CYAN
A cyan surface subtracts red from the light that illuminates it. Blue and green are reflected and combine together to give cyan. Mixing yellow and cyan subtracts blue and red respectively, leaving green.

MAGENTA
A magenta surface absorbs green from the white light that strikes it. Red and blue are reflected and mix together to give magenta. Mixing magenta with yellow subtracts green and blue, leaving red.

BLACK
A black "colour" is given by a pigment that absorbs all the colours falling on it. All three primary colours are subtracted and none reflected, causing the surface to appear black.

MIRRORS

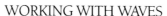

A flat mirror reflects the light rays which strike it so that the rays leave the surface of the mirror at exactly the same angle that they meet it. The light rays enter the eye as if they had come directly from an object behind the mirror, and we therefore see an image of the object in the mirror. This image is a "virtual" image: it cannot be projected on a screen. It is also reversed. Images formed by two mirrors, as in the periscope, are not reversed because the second mirror corrects the image.

PERISCOPE

The periscope makes it possible to see around corners. It has one mirror to capture light rays from an object and sends them to another mirror which directs the rays into the eye.

IMAGE

CONVEX MIRROR

OBJECT

DRIVING MIRROR

A driving mirror is a convex mirror, which curves towards the viewer. It reflects light rays from an image so that they diverge. The eye sees an image which is reduced in size, giving the mirror a wide field of view.

CONCAVE MIRROR

BULB

PARALLEL RAYS IN LIGHT BEAM

HEADLAMP MIRROR

In headlights and torches, a concave mirror is placed behind the bulb. The light rays are reflected by the curved surface so that they are parallel and form a narrow and bright beam of light.

ENDOSCOPE

FIBRE OPTICS

Fibre optic devices depend on internal reflection, which allows light to pass along a narrow filament of very pure glass. The light-conducting fibres used by instruments such as the endoscope have a glass coating that reflects light rays along the fibre core. An image formed by a lens on one end of a cable of fibres appears at the other end, no matter how much the cable twists. Each fibre carries part of the image. Optical fibres also carry light signals over long distances in telecommunications (see pp.234-5).

LIGHT PATH

IMAGE LENS

LIGHT

By using an endoscope, a doctor can easily see what is going on inside a body without cutting it open. A narrow tube containing fibre optic cables or guides is inserted into a channel in the body, such as the throat. Light guides transmit light along the fibres to light up the interior. The image guide sends a picture of the interior back along the tube, where it is viewed in an eyepiece. The tube also contains air and water pipes as well as a channel for small surgical instruments. Wires control the bending of the tube.

EYEPIECE

CONTROLS

CONNECTOR
Light sources and air, water and suction pipes are attached to the connector, which links them to the endoscope tube.

INSTRUMENT CHANNEL

CONTROL WIRE

WATER PIPE

AIR PIPE

LIGHT GUIDE

IMAGE GUIDE

ANGLE KNOB
Operating the angle knob moves the control wires to bend the tube.

TUBE

LENSES

Lenses are of great importance in devices that use light. Optical instruments such as cameras, projectors, microscopes and telescopes all produce images with lenses, while many of us see the world through lenses that correct poor sight. Lenses work by refraction, which is the bending of light rays that occurs as rays leave one transparent material and enter another. In the case of lenses, the two materials involved are glass and air. Lenses in glasses and contact lenses are used to supplement the lens in the eye (see p.178) when it cannot otherwise bend the rays by the angle required to form a sharp image.

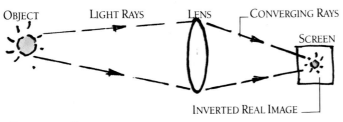

CONVEX LENS

A convex lens is thicker at the centre than the edges. Light rays from an object pass through it and converge to form a "real" image – one that can be seen on a screen.

CONCAVE LENS

A concave lens is thicker at the edges than the centre. It makes light rays diverge. The eye receives these rays and sees a smaller "virtual" image (see p.184) of the object.

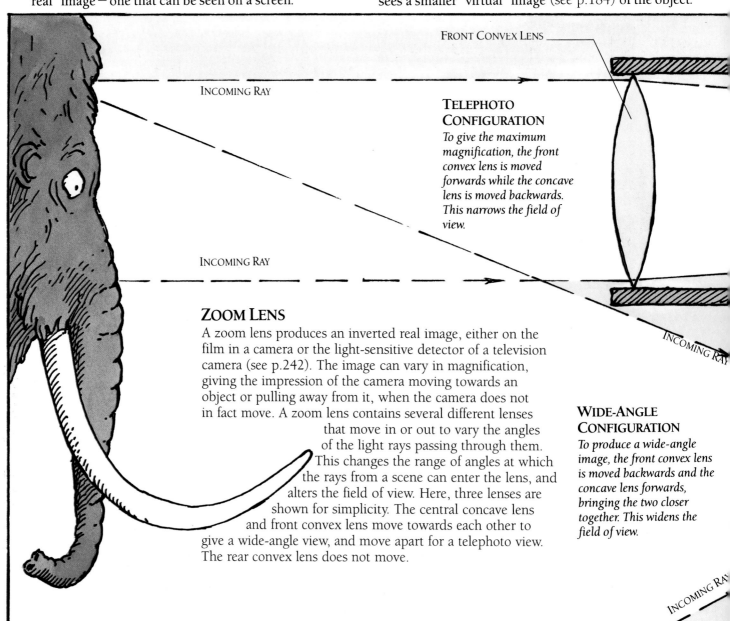

TELEPHOTO CONFIGURATION

To give the maximum magnification, the front convex lens is moved forwards while the concave lens is moved backwards. This narrows the field of view.

ZOOM LENS

A zoom lens produces an inverted real image, either on the film in a camera or the light-sensitive detector of a television camera (see p.242). The image can vary in magnification, giving the impression of the camera moving towards an object or pulling away from it, when the camera does not in fact move. A zoom lens contains several different lenses that move in or out to vary the angles of the light rays passing through them. This changes the range of angles at which the rays from a scene can enter the lens, and alters the field of view. Here, three lenses are shown for simplicity. The central concave lens and front convex lens move towards each other to give a wide-angle view, and move apart for a telephoto view. The rear convex lens does not move.

WIDE-ANGLE CONFIGURATION

To produce a wide-angle image, the front convex lens is moved backwards and the concave lens forwards, bringing the two closer together. This widens the field of view.

MAGNIFYING GLASS

A magnifying glass is a large convex lens. When held near a small object, a magnified virtual image can be seen in the lens. The lens makes the rays from the object converge as they enter the eye. The part of the brain that deals with vision always assumes that light rays arrive at the eye in straight lines. For this reason, it perceives the object as being larger than it really is.

VIRTUAL IMAGE

ASSUMED PATH OF LIGHT RAYS

LIGHT RAYS

LENS

EYE

OBJECT

CONCAVE LENS

REAR CONVEX LENS

TELEPHOTO IMAGE

In the telephoto configuration, the magnification is increased, giving a close-up view of the object. However, because the field of view is decreased, only a small part of it can be seen.

WIDE-ANGLE IMAGE

In the wide-angle image, the field of view is big enough to take in large objects. To balance this, the magnification is much reduced.

TELESCOPES

A telescope gives a close-up view of a distant object, which, in the case of an astronomical telescope viewing a far-off planet or galaxy, is very distant indeed. Most telescopes work in the same basic way, which is to produce a real image of the object inside the telescope tube. The eyepiece lens then views this image in the same way as a magnifying glass (see p.187). The viewer looks at a very close real image, which therefore appears large. The degree of magnification depends mainly on the power of the eyepiece lens.

REFRACTING TELESCOPE

In a refracting telescope, an objective lens forms the real image that is viewed by the eyepiece lens. The image is upside down but this is not important in astronomy. A terrestrial telescope gives an upright view. It contains an extra convex lens that forms an upright real image and the eyepiece lens views this image.

REFLECTING TELESCOPE

In a reflecting telescope, a large concave primary mirror forms the real image that is then viewed by an eyepiece lens. Usually, a secondary mirror reflects the rays from the primary mirror so that the real image forms beneath the mirror or to the side. This is more convenient for viewing.

Reflecting telescopes are important in astronomy because the primary mirror can be very wide. This enables it to collect a lot of light, making faint objects visible. Collecting light from an object is often more important than magnifying it because distant stars do not appear bigger even when magnified.

LIGHT RAYS FROM OBJECT

OBJECTIVE LENS

REAL IMAGE

EYEPIECE LENS

PRIMARY MIRROR

SECONDARY MIRROR

LIGHT RAYS FROM OBJECT

CASSEGRAIN FOCUS

The light rays pass through a hole in the primary mirror and meet behind it to form the real image. This is then viewed with an eyepiece lens or photographed with a camera.

COUDÉ FOCUS

Two extra mirrors are inserted to form the real image at the side of the telescope, where it can be easily viewed or photographed.

SECONDARY
MIRROR

MOTION ABOUT
HORIZONTAL AXIS

CASSEGRAIN
FOCUS

PRIMARY
MIRROR

TELESCOPE MOUNTING

*In astronomy, a telescope
must move to counteract the
motion caused by the
rotation of the Earth if it is
to keep a distant object
continuously in view. Most
modern telescopes have an
altazimuth mounting, in
which the telescope tube
pivots on a vertical axis and
horizontal axis. Motors
controlled by a computer
move the telescope about
both axes at the same time.*

MOTION ABOUT
VERTICAL AXIS

BINOCULARS

A pair of binoculars is basically two small refracting telescopes that together produce a stereoscopic or three-dimensional view. Each eye sees a separate close-up view, but the brain combines them to perceive an image that has depth.

Binoculars are different from telescopes in one respect. They contain a pair of prisms between the objective and eyepiece lenses. The faces of the prisms reflect the light rays internally so that an upright non-reversed image is seen. The prisms also lengthen the light path between the lenses, which narrows the field of view and increases magnification in a short tube. In addition, the two objective lenses may be farther apart than the eyes, which enhances stereoscopic vision.

EYEPIECE LENSES

PRISMS

The objective lens gives an upside down reversed image. The first prism reverses this image again so that it appears the right way around, and the second prism inverts it so that the image is upright.

OBJECTIVE LENS

MICROSCOPES

An optical microscope (*left*) gives a highly enlarged view of an object that is invisible to the unaided eye. The microscope works in the same way as a refracting telescope, but the object or specimen is very close to the objective lenses instead of being distant. The objective lenses form an enlarged real image of the specimen near the eyepiece lenses, and this image is viewed through the eyepiece lenses which further enlarge it. The specimen is illuminated by a beam of light reflected from a mirror and concentrated by condenser lenses.

EYEPIECE

REAL IMAGE OF SPECIMEN

OBJECTIVE LENSES

SPECIMEN

CONDENSER

MIRROR

MAGNETIC CONDENSER
The condenser concentrates the electrons into a beam that strikes the specimen.

MAGNETIC OBJECTIVE
The objective deflects the electrons that pass through the specimen. Denser or thicker parts of the specimen allow fewer electrons through.

MAGNETIC PROJECTOR
The projector further deflects the electrons to form an electron image on the fluorescent screen.

ELECTRON SOURCE

SPECIMEN

FLUORESCENT SCREEN

ELECTRON MICROSCOPE

An optical microscope magnifies as much as 2,000 times, but an electron microscope (*above*) can make things look a million times bigger. Instead of using light, it uses a beam of moving electrons (see p.180). It has magnetic lenses, which are electric coils that produce magnetic fields to deflect the electrons in the same way that glass lenses bend light rays. In the transmission electron microscope (shown here), the beam passes through the specimen. In the scanning electron microscope, the beam is reflected from the specimen.

POLARIZED LIGHT

Light rays are electromagnetic waves: their energy consists of vibrating electric and magnetic fields (see p.239). In normal light rays, these fields vibrate in planes at random angles. In polarized light, all the rays vibrate in the same plane. The direction of this plane is the plane in which the electric field vibrates. Polarizing filters are found in, among other things, anti-glare sunglasses and liquid crystal displays.

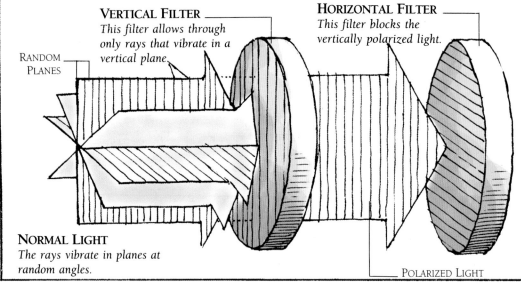

VERTICAL FILTER
This filter allows through only rays that vibrate in a vertical plane.

HORIZONTAL FILTER
This filter blocks the vertically polarized light.

RANDOM PLANES

NORMAL LIGHT
The rays vibrate in planes at random angles.

POLARIZED LIGHT

POLARIZING FILTERS

A polarizing filter blocks all rays except those vibrating in a certain plane. If polarized light strikes a filter whose plane is at right angles to the plane of the rays, then no light passes.

Polarizing sunglasses work in this way. Light reflected from shiny surfaces is partly polarized, and the sunglasses are polarizing filters. They block the polarized light and reduce glare.

MIRROR

REAR (VERTICAL) POLARIZER

LIQUID CRYSTALS

FRONT (HORIZONTAL) POLARIZER

POLARIZED LIGHT

REAR ELECTRODE

FRONT ELECTRODE

NORMAL LIGHT (RANDOM POLARIZATION)

LIQUID CRYSTAL DISPLAY

A sandwich of liquid crystals lies at the heart of the liquid crystal display (LCD) in, for example, a calculator or watch. Light striking the display is first polarized, and then passes through the transparent electrodes and liquid crystals to a second polarizer at right angles to the first. At the rear of the display is a mirror.

The liquid crystals affect the polarized light so that it is either blocked or reflected by the segments of the display, which go dark or light.

LIQUID CRYSTALS

Liquid crystals are liquid materials with molecules arranged in patterns similar to those of crystals. The molecules are normally twisted and when polarized light passes through liquid crystals, its plane of vibration twists through a right angle.

A weak electric current changes the pattern of molecules in liquid crystals. It causes the molecules to line up so that polarized light is no longer affected. The liquid crystals are sandwiched between two transparent electrodes, which pass light rays and deliver the electric current.

By arranging liquid crystals in separate segments, numbers and letters can be produced in a liquid crystal display. The display is controlled by microchips (see pp.359).

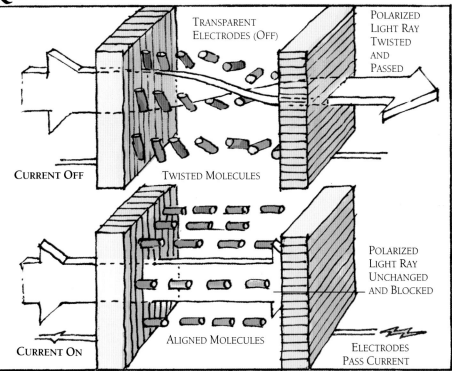

TRANSPARENT ELECTRODES (OFF)

POLARIZED LIGHT RAY TWISTED AND PASSED

CURRENT OFF

TWISTED MOLECULES

POLARIZED LIGHT RAY UNCHANGED AND BLOCKED

ALIGNED MOLECULES

CURRENT ON

ELECTRODES PASS CURRENT

CURRENT OFF
The liquid crystals twist the polarized light so that it passes through the rear polarizer to the mirror. The reflected light is twisted back to emerge from the front polarizer. The segment remains light.

LIGHT REFLECTED   LIGHT BLOCKED

CURRENT ON
A current passes through the portion of liquid crystals in the segment. The liquid crystals do not affect the polarized light, which is blocked by the rear polarizer. The segment goes dark.

SEGMENTS
A number or letter is produced by a group of segments linked to a battery or solar cell. Each segment is normally light and cannot be seen. When an electric signal passes to it, the segments darken in patterns that form numbers or letters.

FIGURE "3"
Seven segments can produce the numbers from 0 to 9. Here, five darken to give a 3.

LASER

A laser produces a narrow beam of very bright light, either firing brief pulses of light or forming a continuous beam. Laser stands for Light Amplification by Stimulated Emission of Radiation. Unlike ordinary light, laser light is "coherent", meaning that all the rays have exactly the same wavelength and are all in phase, vibrating together to produce a beam of great intensity.

A laser beam may either be of visible light, or of invisible infra-red rays. Visible light lasers are used in digital recording and fibre-optic communications as well as in surveying and distance measurement, and give results of very high quality and accuracy. The intense heat of a powerful infra-red laser beam is sufficient to cut metal.

1 EXCITING THE ATOMS

In a laser, energy is first stored in a lasing medium, which may be a solid, liquid or gas. The energy excites atoms in the medium, raising them to a high-energy state. One excited atom then spontaneously releases a light ray. In a gas laser, shown here, electrons in an electric current excite the gas atoms.

MIRROR · ELECTRODE · POWER SOURCE · SEMI-SILVERED MIRROR

EXCITED ATOM · ELECTRON

2 LIGHT BUILDS UP

The ray of light from the excited atom strikes another excited atom, causing it also to emit a light ray. These rays then strike more excited atoms, and the process of light production grows. The mirrors at the ends of the tube reflect the light rays so that more and more excited atoms release light.

3 THE LASER FIRES

As each excited atom emits a light ray, the new ray vibrates in step with the ray that strikes the atom. All the rays are in step, and the beam becomes bright enough to pass through the semi-silvered mirror and leave the laser. The energy is released as laser light.

LASER BEAM

GAS LASER

A gas laser produces a continuous beam of laser light as the gas atoms absorb energy from the electrons moving through the gas and then release this energy as light.

ELECTRODE

GAS

MIRROR · ELECTRODE · GLASS TUBE · SEMI-SILVERED MIRROR

HOLOGRAPHY

One very important application of lasers is holography, the production of images that are three-dimensional and that appear to have depth just like a real object. Holography requires light of a single exact wavelength, which can only be produced by a laser.

In holography, the light beam from a laser is split into two beams. One beam, the object beam, lights up the object. The second beam, the reference beam, goes to a photographic plate or film placed near the object. When developed, the plate or film becomes a hologram, in which a three-dimensional image of the object can be seen (see pp.196-7).

MAKING A HOLOGRAM

The photographic plate or film receives laser light from the object and from the reference beam. The arrangement here produces a reflection hologram, which gives an image in ordinary light. For a transmission hologram, which is viewed with a laser, the two beams strike the same side of the plate or film.

OBJECT

BEAM SPREADER
The laser beam is spread so that it can illuminate the object.

MIRROR

OBJECT BEAM

PHOTOGRAPHIC FILM

REFERENCE BEAM

BEAM SPREADER
A diverging lens widens the laser beam so that it can illuminate the hologram.

BEAM SPLITTER
A semi-silvered mirror passes part of the laser beam and reflects the other part to split the laser beam into two beams.

MIRROR

MIRROR

SHUTTER

LASER BEAM

HOLOGRAM

A reflection hologram is made with a photographic plate or film and laser light (see p.195). In the plate or film, light first reflected by the object meets light coming directly from the laser. Each pair of rays – one from every point on the surface of the object and one in the reference beam – interferes. The two rays give light if the interference is "constructive" or they cancel each other out to give dark if the interference is "destructive". Over the whole hologram, an interference pattern forms as all the pairs of rays meet. This pattern depends on the energy levels of the rays coming from the object, which vary with the brightness of its surface.

RAYS REFLECTED BY POINT ON OBJECT

PLATE OR FILM

RAYS IN REFERENCE BEAM

INTERFERENCE PATTERNS PRODUCED WHERE PAIRS OF RAYS MEET

DESTRUCTIVE INTERFERENCE

In destructive interference, th two rays meet so that the energy crests of one ray alwa coincide with the energy troughs of the other ray. Eacl crest cancels out a trough, an there is no light at the interference point.

CONSTRUCTIVE INTERFERENCE

When two light rays meet, they interfere. The energy level of each ray rises and falls like a wave. In constructive interference, the energy crests or energy troughs always coincide, producing bright light at the interference point.

LIGHT RAY

INTERFERENCE POINT

LIGHT RA

LIGHT RA

ENERGY CREST (POSITIVE MAXIMUM)

LIGHT RAY

ENERGY TROUGH (NEGATIVE MAXIMUM)

INTERFERENCE POINT

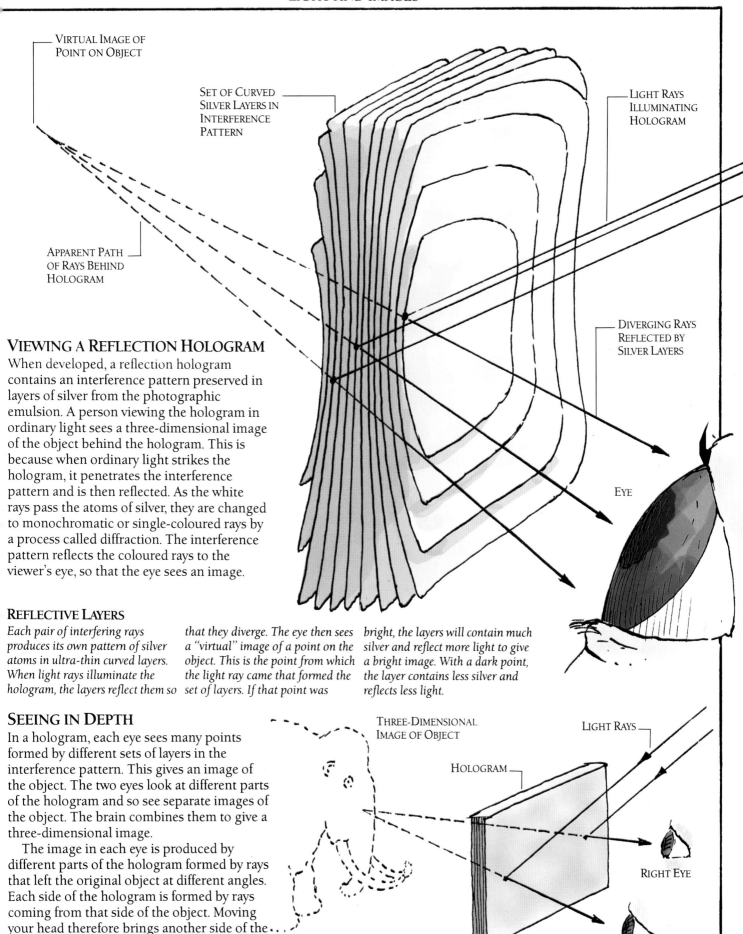

VIRTUAL IMAGE OF
POINT ON OBJECT

SET OF CURVED
SILVER LAYERS IN
INTERFERENCE
PATTERN

LIGHT RAYS
ILLUMINATING
HOLOGRAM

APPARENT PATH
OF RAYS BEHIND
HOLOGRAM

DIVERGING RAYS
REFLECTED BY
SILVER LAYERS

EYE

VIEWING A REFLECTION HOLOGRAM

When developed, a reflection hologram
contains an interference pattern preserved in
layers of silver from the photographic
emulsion. A person viewing the hologram in
ordinary light sees a three-dimensional image
of the object behind the hologram. This is
because when ordinary light strikes the
hologram, it penetrates the interference
pattern and is then reflected. As the white
rays pass the atoms of silver, they are changed
to monochromatic or single-coloured rays by
a process called diffraction. The interference
pattern reflects the coloured rays to the
viewer's eye, so that the eye sees an image.

REFLECTIVE LAYERS

*Each pair of interfering rays
produces its own pattern of silver
atoms in ultra-thin curved layers.
When light rays illuminate the
hologram, the layers reflect them so*
*that they diverge. The eye then sees
a "virtual" image of a point on the
object. This is the point from which
the light ray came that formed the
set of layers. If that point was*
*bright, the layers will contain much
silver and reflect more light to give
a bright image. With a dark point,
the layer contains less silver and
reflects less light.*

SEEING IN DEPTH

In a hologram, each eye sees many points
formed by different sets of layers in the
interference pattern. This gives an image of
the object. The two eyes look at different parts
of the hologram and so see separate images of
the object. The brain combines them to give a
three-dimensional image.

   The image in each eye is produced by
different parts of the hologram formed by rays
that left the original object at different angles.
Each side of the hologram is formed by rays
coming from that side of the object. Moving
your head therefore brings another side of the
object into view and your view of the image
changes.

THREE-DIMENSIONAL
IMAGE OF OBJECT

LIGHT RAYS

HOLOGRAM

RIGHT EYE

LEFT EYE

PHOTOGRAPHY

ON MAMMOTH PICTURES

While playing golf one day, I noticed that the grass in the specified caddy waiting areas was considerably lower and less green than the grass in the sunlight. I played on, but my mind was no longer on the game. If the image of a mammoth could be made on the grass accidentally, I reasoned, then perhaps images of other things could be made intentionally?

Returning to my workshop, I begged the assistance of the family next door for my first experiment. I asked them to sleep in a line on the grass outside. They were reluctant. I offered to pay them and they were soon snoring away.

PRESERVED IN SILVER

Rather than grass, black-and-white photography uses silver to preserve images permanently. Tiny crystals of light-sensitive silver compounds are suspended in an emulsion of gelatin, which coats a transparent plastic film. In a camera, the lens forms an image of a scene on the film. This exposure to light, even for a fraction of a second, is enough to start a chemical change in the crystals, and they begin to break down into black specks of metallic silver. Developing the film then completes the formation of silver to produce a negative of the scene.

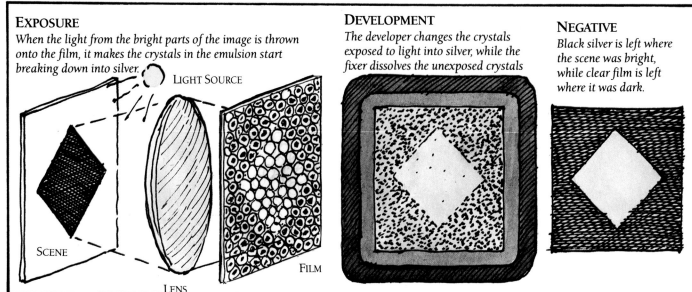

EXPOSURE
When the light from the bright parts of the image is thrown onto the film, it makes the crystals in the emulsion start breaking down into silver.

LIGHT SOURCE

SCENE

LENS

FILM

DEVELOPMENT
The developer changes the crystals exposed to light into silver, while the fixer dissolves the unexposed crystals

NEGATIVE
Black silver is left where the scene was bright, while clear film is left where it was dark.

fig 1

fig 2

fig 3

I had them return for the next five days and lie in exactly the same spot. By the end of the week I had a perfect image of my neighbours. The procedure soon caught on, and eventually even school groups could be seen lying motionless on the workshop's lawns.

However, several drawbacks arose which I had not forseen. The images required continuous trimming once the subjects left the picture. They were also difficult to display as well as being astronomically expensive to frame. Had I been able to shrink people before they were recorded, I am convinced that my discovery would have had a bright future.

PRINTING THE PICTURE

A print is made on photographic printing paper, which bears a light-sensitive emulsion like that on a film. The negative is used to expose the paper, often with an enlarger that projects a magnified image of the negative. The paper is then developed to create a picture made up of black silver. Light areas in the negative now appear dark in the print and vice-versa — the same as in the original scene. Using a different process, a positive picture can be made directly on photographic film or paper without producing a negative.

EXPOSURE
An image of the negative is formed on printing paper by placing the negative in an enlarger. Moving the lens enables the image size to be enlarged.

LENS

LAMP

NEGATIVE

PRINTING PAPER

DEVELOPMENT
The paper is developed and fixed in red light, to which the emulsion is not sensitive.

POSITIVE
Light areas on the negative create black silver on the print, while dark areas create white paper.

THE SINGLE-LENS REFLEX CAMERA

PENTAPRISM

VIEWFINDER EYEPIECE

SMILE.

RELEASE
BUTTON

TAKE-UP SPOOL

FOCAL PLANE SHUTTER

*The shutter consists of two spring-loaded
blinds in front of the film. The first blind
normally covers the film. As the shutter
release is pressed, the first blind moves
across to expose the film to the light beam
from the lens. The second blind then follows to
cover the film again.*

FILM

GAP BETWEEN
BLINDS

FIRST BLIND

FILM
CASSETTE

FOCUSING
SCREEN

*The focusing screen is
made of ground glass.
The lens and mirror
form an image on the
screen, which is seen
in the eyepiece. The
screen and film are
both the same
distance away from
the mirror. Focusing
the image on the
screen therefore also
focuses it on the film.*

HINGED
MIRROR

SECOND BLIND

Some cameras have two different sets of lenses: one to view the image and one to throw it onto the film. Many photographers prefer to view the actual image that will fall on the film before taking a picture. The single-lens reflex (SLR) camera is so named because it uses a single collection of lenses both for viewing and for taking the picture. The SLR camera has a hinged mirror that rests at an angle of 45 degrees in front of the film, and reflects the light beam from the lens onto a focusing screen above the mirror. The image forms on this screen, and light from it is reflected by the faces of the pentaprism into the viewfinder eyepiece. The various reflections turn the viewfinder image upright and the right way round. When the shutter release is pressed, the mirror rises and the light beam strikes the film.

VIEWFINDER EYEPIECE

FOCUSING SCREEN

LENS

PENTAPRISM

MIRROR

FILM

IRIS DIAPHRAGM

This controls the aperture of the lens, regulating the amount of light that enters the camera. The diaphragm is at the centre of the lens, and contains a set of hinged blades that move to open or close the central hole. Opening the diaphragm, which gives a lower f number, lets more light in.

LENS

A high-quality lens is made up of several lens elements that work together to form a sharp image on the film. The field of view depends on the focal length of the lens, which is the distance from the lens to the film when an object at infinity is in focus. The lens surfaces are often coated to reduce reflections.

LIGHT BEAM

COLOUR PHOTOGRAPH

No matter how multicoloured prints or slides may appear, they are made of only the three secondary colours (see p.183) arranged in layers. When you look at a photograph light passes through the layers and combines to give full colour. Developing a print film produces a colour negative, while in a slide, a process called colour reversal (*below*) forms positive colour image on the film.

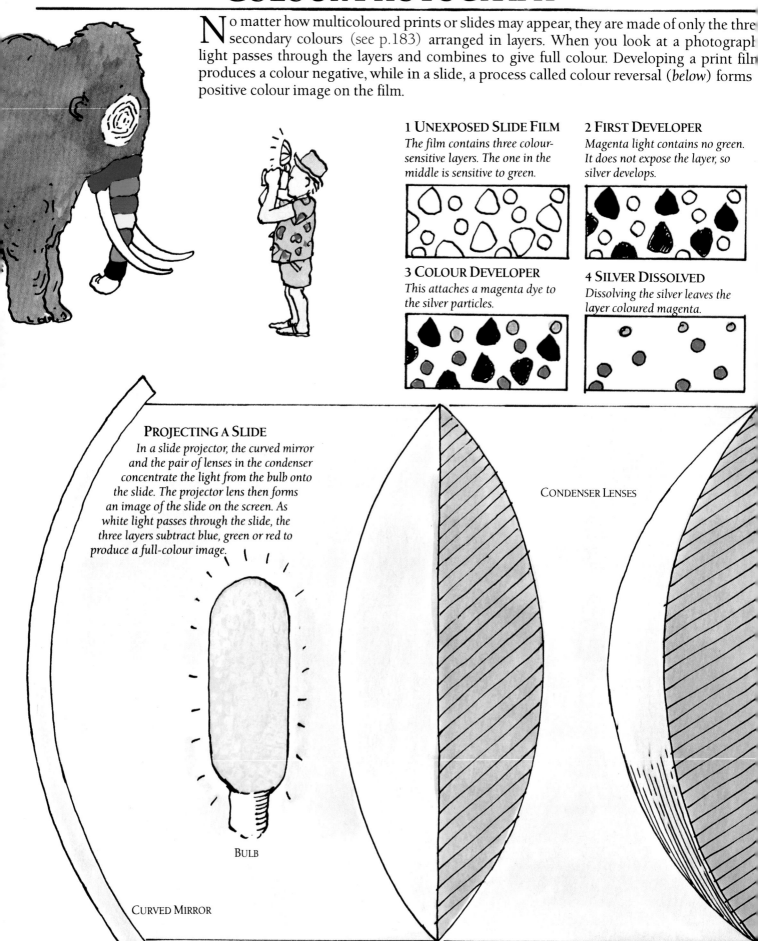

1 UNEXPOSED SLIDE FILM
The film contains three colour-sensitive layers. The one in the middle is sensitive to green.

2 FIRST DEVELOPER
Magenta light contains no green. It does not expose the layer, so silver develops.

3 COLOUR DEVELOPER
This attaches a magenta dye to the silver particles.

4 SILVER DISSOLVED
Dissolving the silver leaves the layer coloured magenta.

PROJECTING A SLIDE
In a slide projector, the curved mirror and the pair of lenses in the condenser concentrate the light from the bulb onto the slide. The projector lens then forms an image of the slide on the screen. As white light passes through the slide, the three layers subtract blue, green or red to produce a full-colour image.

CONDENSER LENSES

BULB

CURVED MIRROR

COLOUR SLIDE
BEFORE COLOUR
DEVELOPMENT

THE THREE-LAYER SYSTEM

Each of the colour-sensitive layers in a colour film is similar to a black-and-white film, except that the top layer is sensitive only to blue light, the middle layer to green and the bottom layer to red. The three layers detect the amounts of these colours in the image formed on the colour film by the camera lens.

Developers for colour films contain dye couplers, which attach dyes to the silver that forms in the emulsion during development. The silver is then dissolved, leaving a layer of dye. The top layer becomes yellow, the middle layer magenta and the bottom layer cyan.

In colour slide film, colour reversal, shown on the opposite page, changes the *unexposed* layers into layers of dye. Green, for example, exposes only the middle layer, so the first and third layers become yellow and cyan. These two layers mix to give green. Each piece of film becomes a colour slide.

In colour print film, the *exposed* layers are changed into layers of dye. Yellow, for example, appears as a mixture of magenta and cyan which gives blue. The negative is then printed on colour paper, which contains the same three layers as a film, and which is developed in the same way.

BLUE-
SENSITIVE
LAYER

GREEN-
SENSITIVE
LAYER

RED-
SENSITIVE
LAYER

PROJECTOR LENS

COLOUR SLIDE
AFTER
DEVELOPMENT

IMAGE ON SCREEN

ALMOST INSTANT PICTURES

Immediately on taking a photograph with an instant camera, a plastic sheet emerges. After a minute, the picture begins to appear and a little later a full-colour photograph is in your hand. Instant photography uses basically the same process as a colour slide (see p.202). The film contains layers of silver compounds sensitive to blue, green and red light that develop to give layers of yellow, magenta and cyan dyes. It also contains the developing chemicals. As an instant photograph develops, the three dyes leave their layers and move up through the film. They collect in a layer beneath the surface, where the dyes mix to form the picture.

ROLLERS

RED LIGHT STRIKING FILM

REAGENT POD

1 FILM EXPOSED

The film contains nine separate chemical layers. When it is exposed, light penetrates to the layers of silver compounds sensitive to blue, green and red light. Here, red light is shown exposing the red layer.

CLEAR PLASTIC SURFACE

ACID LAYER

TIMING LAYER

IMAGE LAYER

BLUE-SENSITIVE LAYER (UNEXPOSED)
YELLOW DYE DEVELOPER
SPACER
GREEN-SENSITIVE LAYER (UNEXPOSED)
MAGENTA DYE DEVELOPER
SPACER
RED-SENSITIVE LAYER (EXPOSED)
CYAN DYE DEVELOPER
BLACK BASE

2 FILM LEAVES CAMERA

The sheet of film passes through the rollers, which squeeze a thin pod of reagent in the borders around the picture area. The reagent contains white pigment, opacifiers that prevent light passing, water and alkali. It enters the film just above the light-sensitive layers, and the opacifiers

REAGENT LAYER ENTERS FILM

stop light getting to these layers as the film emerges. The reagent spreads down through the light-sensitive layers, but its progress upwards is slowed by the timing layer.

3 IMAGE BEGINS TO FORM

The reagent activates the dye developers in the light-sensitive layers. Where the silver compounds were not exposed, the dyes dissolve and begin to diffuse through the other layers to the image layer. But in the exposed layers, the developer produces silver, which prevents the dye moving. Here, the cyan dye in the exposed red-sensitive layer cannot move. Yellow and magenta dyes formed in the other two unexposed layers diffuse upwards.

YELLOW AND MAGENTA DYES DIFFUSE
SILVER IMMOBILIZES CYAN DYE

4 IMAGE CLEARS

The reagent reaches the acid layer, which neutralizes the alkali and makes the opacifiers clear. The dyes in the image layer are seen against the white pigment, giving a clear picture.

YELLOW AND MAGENTA MIX IN IMAGE LAYER TO FORM RED

REAGENT ENTERS ACID LAYER

WHITE LAYER

PHOTO BOOTH

PAPER SPOOL

1 SUBJECT LIT
Electronic flashes (see p.180) light up the sitter as the shutter opens.

2 LIGHT REFLECTED
The prism reverses the image formed by the lens on the paper, so the picture is the right way around.

PAPER STRIP

LENS

3 PAPER CUT
The paper strip moves down after each exposure, and the cutter slices the strip after four exposures.

LIGHT FROM SITTER

A photo booth produces a strip of pictures soon after the flashes fire. It uses photographic printing paper, which the machine dips into several tanks of chemicals that form a positive image directly on the paper. The booth can develop several strips separately, so that more customers can use the booth while others are waiting for their pictures.

4 PAPER DEVELOPED
The exposed paper travels through nine or more tanks. It is first developed to form a negative and then the dark silver in this image is dissolved. The unexposed emulsion that remains is then treated and developed to form silver, giving a positive image on the paper. The strip is then washed.

5 DELIVERY
After washing, the developed photographs are dried by a fan. When this process is almost complete, they emerge through the slot in the side of the booth.

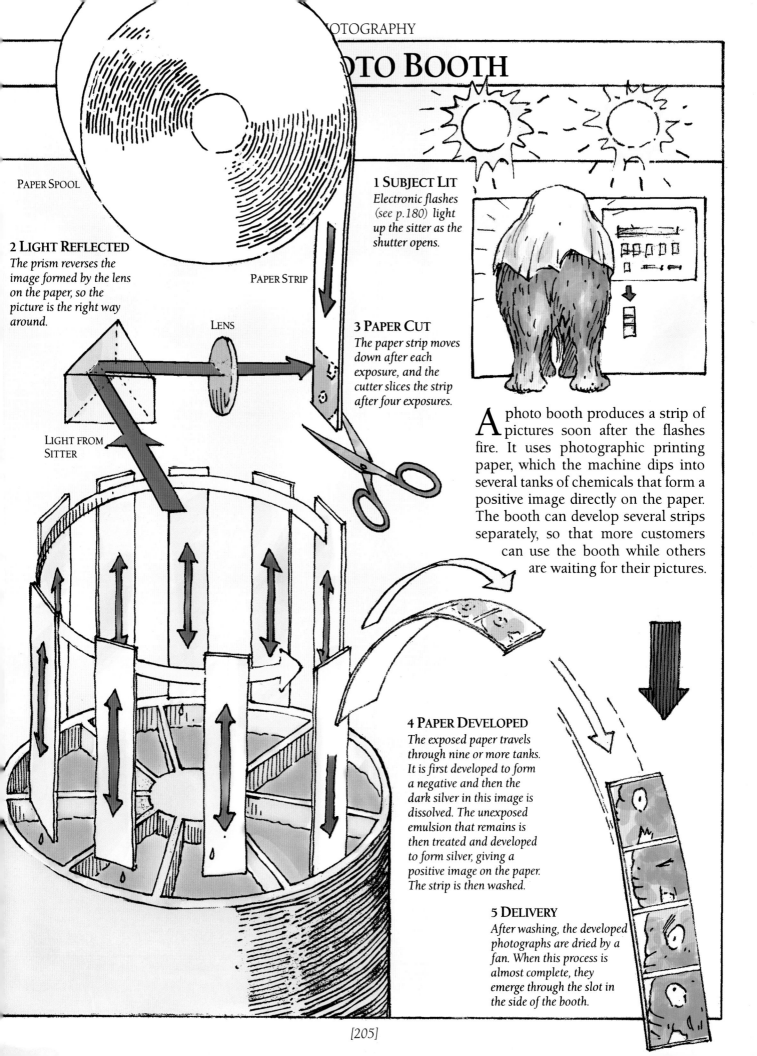

MOVIE CAMERA

Moving pictures depend on illusion, not only in the acting but in our eyes. A movie film consists of a series of still pictures seen in rapid succession. After it leaves the screen, each image persists in the eye until the next image arrives. Our eyes merge the separate images together to give an illusion of motion.

A movie camera photographs a sequence of still images on a strip of film. It normally takes 24 pictures or frames every second. The film is still when each picture is taken, and moves on between exposures.

FEED SPOOL

TAKE-UP SPOOL

SHUTTER

LIGHT PATH

LENS

MOVIE FILM
Movie film comes in four standard widths: 35mm (cinema), 16mm (television) and 8mm and Super-8 (home movies). 70mm film is used for wide-screen cinema films.

GATE

CLAW

FILM LOOP
The film makes a loop before and after the gate. The loops enable the film to be moved intermittently through the gate by the claw.

SPROCKET WHEEL
Teeth on the sprocket wheel engage the sprocket holes in the film and move the film from one spool to the other.

SHUTTER

LIGHT PATH

GATE

PRISM

VIEWFINDER

REFLEX VIEWFINDER
The shutter's surface reflects the light beam from the lens as it covers the film, sending the light into the viewfinder. The camera operator sees the moving scene that is being photographed by the lens.

MAKING MOVIES

GATE

SPROCKET HOLE

FILM

IMAGE

CRANK

CLAW

SHUTTER

1 EXPOSURE BEGINS
The claw is disengaged from the sprocket holes in the film. The gap in the rotating shutter moves in front of the still film, allowing the lens to form an image on the film.

SHUTTER MOVES INTO LIGHT PATH

2 EXPOSURE ENDS
The shutter begins to cut off the light reaching the film. Meanwhile the crank has turned to raise the claw.

MOVIE PROJECTOR

A movie projector works like a movie camera in reverse. A claw moves the film intermittently through the projector gate, allowing the lens to project a still image on the screen for a fraction of a second. A rotating shutter allows light to reach the film, and then cuts off the light source so that the image disappears as the film moves. As in the movie camera, the projector shows 24 frames in every second. But it projects each frame twice so that the eye sees 48 separate pictures, which reduces flicker.

FEED SPOOL

LAMP

CONDENSER

MIRROR

FAN

ROTATING SHUTTER

GATE

CLAW

CRANK

FILM LOOP

LENS

TAKE-UP SPOOL

LIGHT SOURCE

The light from a bright lamp is reflected by a curved mirror and concentrated by a condenser to illuminate the film. A fan cools the lamp.

SHUTTER BLOCKS LIGHT PATH

3 CLAW ENGAGES

The claw engages the sprocket holes in the film. The shutter prevents light reaching the film as it begins to move.

SHUTTER BLOCKS LIGHT PATH

FILM PULLED DOWN

4 FILM MOVES

As the crank turns, the claw pulls the film down by one frame. The light path is still blocked by the shutter.

PRINTING

MODERN METHODS OF PRINTING

The mammoth mint works by a printing process known as letterpress, the oldest of the three main methods now in use. The other two are gravure and lithography. Here we show flat printing plates for simplicity. Printing presses often have curved plates that rotate to print multiple copies on sheets or strips of paper, but the principles involved are the same.

LETTERPRESS

1 *The plate has raised letters.*

2 *Ink sticks to the letters.*

3 *Paper is pressed against the plate.*

4 *The ink transfers to the paper.*

GRAVURE

1 *The plate has recessed letters.*

2 *Ink fills the letter recesses.*

3 *Paper is pressed against the plate.*

4 *The ink transfers to the paper.*

ON A MAMMOTH MINT

*F*ollowing a rash of particularly skilful boulder forging, I was asked to suggest a more secure and if possible more portable medium of exchange. The result was my mammoth mint.

High quality leaves of predetermined size were carefully centred on a mat, one at a time, by trunk suction. A large pad containing a herbal dye of my own concoction was kept at the required level of moisture by the chief squirter. After pressing a patterned stamp down on the pad, the master minter then brought the same stamp down onto the pre-centred leaf transferring the impression. Each leaf was then thoroughly dried, checked and counted before shipment to one of several mammoth banks.

Although technically flawless, the mint suffered insurmountable staffing difficulties. Losses which I had initially attributed to pilfering were later explained by the toothsome character of the new currency to mammoths.

The processes here show printing in a single colour. In full-colour printing, a number of inks are applied one after the other by different rollers. Three coloured inks, together with black, can produce a complete range of hues by the process of colour subtraction.

LITHOGRAPHY

1 An image of the letter is projected onto the plate.

2 The plate is treated to deposit lacquer on the letter.

3 The plate is wetted and the lacquer rejects water.

4 The plate is inked. The lacquer accepts ink, but the wet surface rejects ink.

5 Paper is pressed against the printing plate.

6 The ink transfers from the lacquer to the paper.

PRINTING ON STONE

Lithography first used stone printing plates, hence its name which means "writing on stone". An artist can draw on the stone with a greasy substance that attracts ink, and the ink is transferred to paper in a press. Modern litho printing uses light-sensitive plates on which text and images can be deposited by photography. In offset litho printing, the ink is first transferred to a cylinder that then prints the paper.

PAPERMAKING

Printing is of little use without paper. A sheet of paper is a flattened mesh of interlocking plant fibres, mainly of wood and cotton. Making paper involves reducing a plant to its fibres, and then aligning them and coating the fibres with materials such as glues, pigments and mineral fillers.

1 FELLING
Trees are felled and then transported to paper mills as logs.

2 DEBARKING
The bark has first to be stripped off the logs without damaging the wood.

BELT

6 PRESSING
Belts move the web between the press rolls, which remove more water and compress the paper.

DANDY ROLL

DECKLE STRAPS
These hold the layer o[f] pulp down on the mesh belt.

PRESS ROLLS

WET WEB

Where's Fred?

MESH BELT

DAMP PAPER

7 DRYING
The damp web moves through the drier, where it passes between hot cylinders and felt-covered belts that absorb water. It then passes through the calender stacks before being wound on reels or cut into sheets.

LOWER FELT-COVERED BELT

HOT CYLINDERS

DIGESTER
Materials other than wood, such as cotton rags, may be pulped in the digester.

3 PULPING
Pulping reduces the wood to a slurry of loose fibres in water. The logs are first sliced into chips and then treated with chemicals in a digester. These dissolve the lignin binding the wood fibres together. Alternatively, machines may grind the logs in water to produce pulp. The pulp is then bleached.

5 FORMING THE WEB
Liquid pulp is fed from the flowbox onto the mesh belt. Water drains through the holes in the mesh; the drainage is accelerated by suction. The dandy roll presses the fibres together into a wet ribbon known as a web.

MIXER

FLOWBOX

LIQUID PULP

SUCTION BOX

UPPER FELT-COVERED BELT

4 MIXING
The pulp goes to the mixer, where materials are added to improve the quality of the paper. The additives include white fillers such as china clay, size for water-proofing, and coloured pigments. The mixer beats the fibres into a smooth pulp.

DRIED PAPER

Where's the switch?

CALENDER STACKS
These stacks of rollers smooth the surface of the paper.

PRINTING PLATE

When a book like *The New Way Things Work* is printed, all the colour pictures in it are produced by just four inks. These are the three secondary colours – yellow, magenta and cyan (see p.183) – and black. Each ink is printed by a separate printing plate. Producing these plates involves two processes, colour scanning and typesetting. Colour scanning breaks the illustrations down into the three secondary colours and black, while typesetting converts the text into print.

OPTICAL SYSTEM —   — LIGHT SOURCE

COLOUR SCANNING

A colour scanner breaks down each illustration into the four separate images or separations which together will re-create the full-colour picture. In each separation, the picture is broken up into many separate dots. The computer in the scanner controls the size of the dots, producing large dots where the ink must be dense and small dots in other parts of the separation. Breaking the picture up into dots enables the printing plate to print any colour at any intensity.

COLOUR SEPARATIONS

FILM

LASER BEAM

TYPESETTING

The text of this book has been set into print using a laser typesetter. The operator keys in the text, together with codes that specify the typeface and type size. The operator's keyboard is linked to a computer whose memory contains all the type characters in a variety of different typefaces and sizes. The computer then sends signals to the typesetter, in which a laser beam forms lines of text on film or paper.

DRUM

LASER BEAM

FILM OR PAPER

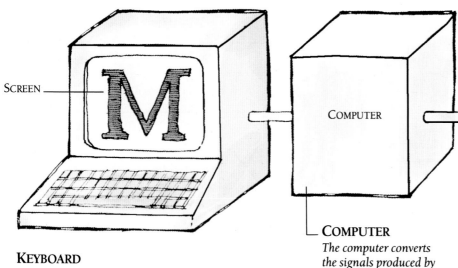

SCREEN

COMPUTER

KEYBOARD

The text appears on a screen as the operator keys it into the typesetter. Alternatively, a disc from the author's word processor may by inserted directly into the typesetter.

COMPUTER

The computer converts the signals produced by the keyboard into signals that operate the laser.

LASER TYPESETTER

Photographic film or paper rotates on a drum as a laser beam moves across the film or paper. The computer switches the beam on and off so that each character is formed by a set of close-spaced vertical lines. The film or paper is then developed.

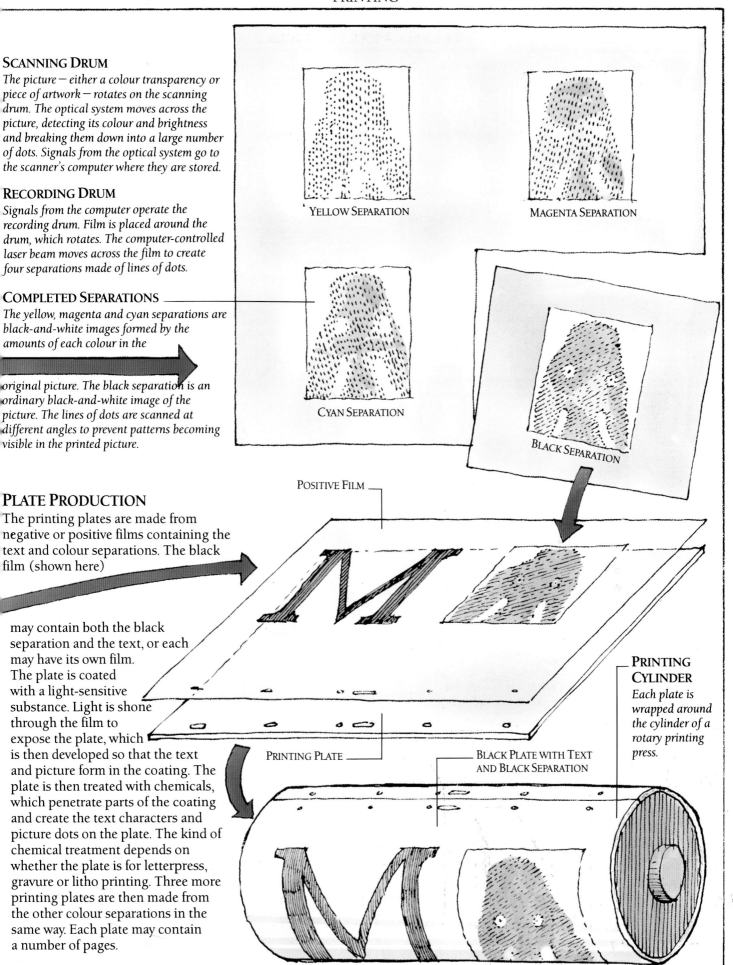

SCANNING DRUM

The picture – either a colour transparency or piece of artwork – rotates on the scanning drum. The optical system moves across the picture, detecting its colour and brightness and breaking them down into a large number of dots. Signals from the optical system go to the scanner's computer where they are stored.

RECORDING DRUM

Signals from the computer operate the recording drum. Film is placed around the drum, which rotates. The computer-controlled laser beam moves across the film to create four separations made of lines of dots.

COMPLETED SEPARATIONS

The yellow, magenta and cyan separations are black-and-white images formed by the amounts of each colour in the

original picture. The black separation is an ordinary black-and-white image of the picture. The lines of dots are scanned at different angles to prevent patterns becoming visible in the printed picture.

YELLOW SEPARATION

MAGENTA SEPARATION

CYAN SEPARATION

BLACK SEPARATION

PLATE PRODUCTION

The printing plates are made from negative or positive films containing the text and colour separations. The black film (shown here)

may contain both the black separation and the text, or each may have its own film. The plate is coated with a light-sensitive substance. Light is shone through the film to expose the plate, which is then developed so that the text and picture form in the coating. The plate is then treated with chemicals, which penetrate parts of the coating and create the text characters and picture dots on the plate. The kind of chemical treatment depends on whether the plate is for letterpress, gravure or litho printing. Three more printing plates are then made from the other colour separations in the same way. Each plate may contain a number of pages.

POSITIVE FILM

PRINTING CYLINDER

Each plate is wrapped around the cylinder of a rotary printing press.

PRINTING PLATE

BLACK PLATE WITH TEXT AND BLACK SEPARATION

PRINTING PRESS

The printing press, as its name implies, prints by pressing paper against an inked plate. Large printing presses are rotary machines in which the printing plate is fitted around a cylinder. As the cylinder rotates, cut sheets or a web (continuous strip) of paper pass rapidly through the press and are printed while on the move. Presses which print in colour have four or more printing cylinders so that the colour separations are printed immediately one after the other. Quick-drying inks prevent smudging.

SHEET-FED OFFSET PRESS

This book, like many books and magazines, has been printed by offset lithography, a process which combines speed with quality printing. Sheet-fed presses are mainly used for printing books because print quality is very high. Sheets of paper are fed into the press and pass through four printing units that print in yellow, magenta, cyan and black. The three colours form colour pictures, while the black plate adds contrast to the pictures and prints black text. The sheets are printed first on one side, and are then fed back into the machine for printing on the reverse side.

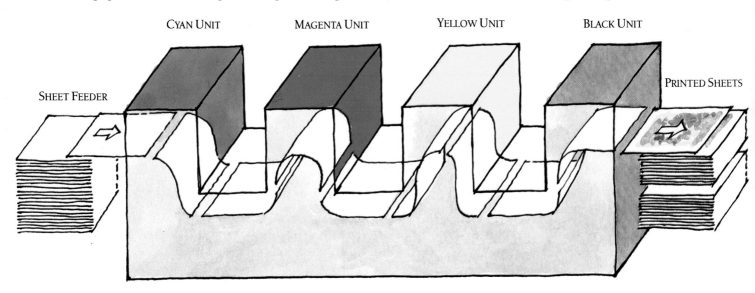

CYAN UNIT   MAGENTA UNIT   YELLOW UNIT   BLACK UNIT

SHEET FEEDER   PRINTED SHEETS

WEB OFFSET PRESS

Web offset presses achieve very high speed as well as good quality, and are often used to print magazines and newspapers. Large reels feed the web into the press, which is then printed with four or more colours. Each printing unit usually contains two sets of printing cylinders so that both sides of the paper are printed at the same time. After leaving the press, the web continues on to folding and cutting machines (see p.216).

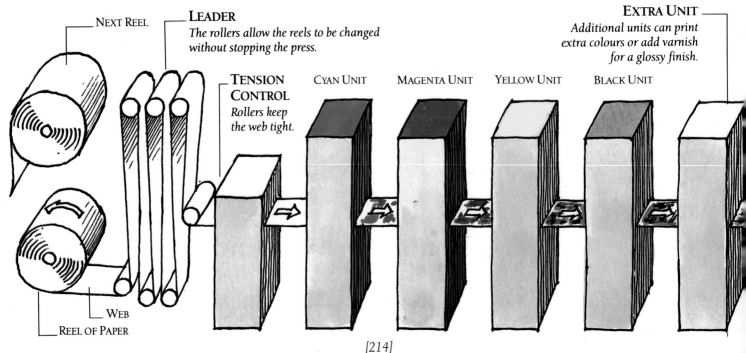

NEXT REEL

LEADER
The rollers allow the reels to be changed without stopping the press.

EXTRA UNIT
Additional units can print extra colours or add varnish for a glossy finish.

TENSION CONTROL
Rollers keep the web tight.

CYAN UNIT   MAGENTA UNIT   YELLOW UNIT   BLACK UNIT

WEB

REEL OF PAPER

COOLING WATER

INK FEED

INKING ROLLERS

OFFSET LITHO PRINTING

The dampening roller first wets the printing plate on the plate cylinder, which is then inked by the inking rollers. The ink then transfers to the rubber blanket cylinder, and the impression cylinder presses the paper against the blanket cylinder. The blanket cylinder prints the paper, its flexible rubber surface overcoming any irregularities in the paper.

PRINTED WEB MOVES TO FOLDER AND CUTTER

OSCILLATING ROLLERS

These rollers are cooled to chill the ink and prevent moisture loss. They oscillate back and forth to pass the ink evenly to the inking rollers.

DAMPENING ROLLERS

BLANKET CYLINDER

PAPER

WATER

PLATE CYLINDER

IMPRESSION CYLINDER

DRIER

The printed web passes through a heated tunnel in which the ink is dried.

CHILLING UNIT

Chilled rollers cool the paper, which gets very hot in the drier.

MOISTURE UNIT

Water is applied to the paper to replace moisture lost in the drier.

BOOKBINDING

The printed sheets or webs that roll off the press have to be folded and, if necessary, cut to produce sections of the book called signatures. Then all the signatures in the book must be collated, or assembled in the correct order. Next, the signatures are bound together and their edges trimmed. Finally, the cover – which is printed separately – is attached and the book is ready to use.

SHEET FOLDER

A sheet from a sheet-fed press usually contains one signature and is folded several times.

SHEET

SLOT

1 ENTERING THE FOLDER
Rollers feed the sheet into the slot of the folder, which stops it moving.

2 BUCKLING THE SHEET
The rollers force the sheet forwards so that it begins to buckle in the centre.

3 FOLDING THE SHEET
The lower rollers grip the buckle and pull the sheet through to fold it in two.

WEB FOLDER

Web signatures are printed one after another, and the folder separates each signature as well as folding it.

1 FIRST FOLD
The web passes over a pointed metal "nose" and then between rollers that fold the web along the centre.

2 SEPARATION
A serrated blade pierces the folded web so that the signature is torn loose.

3 SECOND FOLD
A folder blade pushes the centre of the signature between a pair of folding rollers.

FOLDING ROLLERS

SIGNATURE

FOLDER BLADE

4 THIRD FOLD
The signature is folded again and the pages are now in the correct order.

FAN WHEEL

Signatures are fed into the fan wheel, and the wheel delivers them to a conveyor belt which takes them to be bound into books.

FAN WHEEL

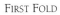

FRONT   BACK

SIGNATURES

The pages in the signature are printed on the sheet or web in a particular order. When folded the right way the pages in each signature will be in the correct sequence. Signatures may contain various numbers of pages: most books have signatures of 16, 24 or 32 pages.

FIRST FOLD   SECOND FOLD

THIRD FOLD

16-PAGE SIGNATURE
The sheet or web is four pages wide and the signature two pages deep. It is folded in the centre three times.

HAND BINDING

1 *The set of signatures is aligned in the correct order.*

2 *The backs of the signatures are sewn together.*

3 *Glue is applied to hold the signatures together. The pages are then trimmed.*

4 *A lining is glued to the spine (back) of the book.*

SIGNATURES

CASE

LINING

5 *The case (cover) is glued to the lining.*

THE FINISHED BOOK
Machine binding follows much the same sequence of operations as hand binding, although sometimes glueing is used without sewing.

SOUND AND MUSIC

ON PLAYING THE MAMMOTH

While I do not profess to understand the "modern" music, I have long been involved in the development of the mammoth as an instrument. In my earliest experiments, a trio of courageous musicians produced the most remarkable assortment of sounds from a single properly tuned and securely tethered beast. The tusks, when struck by wooden mallets, gave a rich melodic chime. The great belly, played with leather-covered mallets, offered a sonorous thud. The tail, secured by a flexible tree trunk, produced a soothing twang when plucked. By moving the tree trunk to either stretch or relax the tail, the plucker could achieve many different notes. But perhaps the most extraordinary sound was that produced voluntarily by the animal itself. As the mammoth slipped into the spirit of the music, it issued periodic trumpet blasts from its great trunk. The trio became a quartet in which man and nature achieved an unforgettable harmony.

MAKING SOUND

All sound producers emit sound by making something vibrate. As a vibrating object moves to and fro, it sets up sound waves in the air. The waves consist of alternate regions of high and low pressure, which are known as compressions and rarefactions. As the object's surface moves forwards into the air, it produces a compression. The surface then moves back, producing a rarefaction. Together each compression and rarefaction makes up a sound wave, and the waves move out in all directions at high speed. The stronger the vibrations, the greater the pressure difference between each compression and rarefaction and the louder the sound.

The vibrations that set up sounds can be produced in a number of different ways. The simplest is hitting an object: the energy from the blow vibrates the object and these vibrations are transmitted to the air. Plucking a taut string (or tail) makes it vibrate, while releasing air under pressure into a hollow tube (such as a trunk) can also set up vibrations in the air.

SETTING UP SOUND WAVES

Hitting an object like a tusk makes it vibrate, and this vibration is then transmitted to the air around the object. The vibration needed to create an audible sound wave has to have a rate of more than 20 compressions and 20 rarefactions per second.

*M*ore recent experiments have focused on the mammoth as an ensemble instrument. Perhaps the best known of these undertakings was my arrangement for four mammoths, tethered in order of size. Although the instruments often grew restless during rehearsals, the twelve musicians, comprising four tusk-tappers, four stomach-thumpers and four tail-twangers, became highly proficient at playing them. The performance was a feast not only for the ears but also for the eyes.

*T*he popularity of massed mammoth music reached its peak with the creation of the Mammoth Tabernacle Choir. While I personally never saw or heard it, I am assured that the effect, especially at close range, was nothing short of stunning.

SOUND REFLECTIONS

As well as travelling directly to listeners, sound waves may also bounce off nearby surfaces. The ear receives a mixture of the direct sound and echoes. If the reflecting surfaces are fairly distant, the reflected sound will take much longer to reach the ear and separate echoes will be heard.

REFLECTED SOUND WAVES

HEARING

EAR DRUM COCHLEA

AUDITORY NERVE TO BRAIN

SOUND WAVES

INNER EAR

As sound waves enter the ear, the pressure differences between successive compressions and rarefactions set the ear drum vibrating. These vibrations pass to the cochlea in the inner ear, where they are converted into electric signals. The signals travel along the auditory nerve to the brain, and the sound is heard.

WOODWIND INSTRUMENTS

Woodwind instruments are not necessarily made of wood, many of them, like the saxophone, being metal, but they do require wind to make a sound. They consist basically of a tube, usually with a series of holes. Air is blown into the top of the tube, either across a hole or past a flexible reed. This makes the air inside the tube vibrate and give out a note. The pitch of the note depends on the length of the tube, a shorter tube giving a higher note, and also on which holes are covered. Blowing harder makes the sound louder.

AIR IN — VIBRATING AIR — HOLES

ALL HOLES COVERED

Covering all seven holes in a simple pipe makes the air in the whole tube vibrate, giving the note middle C.

FIRST THREE HOLES COVERED

This shortens the vibrating air column to two-thirds of the tube, giving the higher note G.

FIRST FIVE HOLES COVERED

This extends the vibrating air column to four-fifths of the total length of the tube, giving an E.

KEYS AND CURVES

To produce deep notes, woodwind instruments have to be quite long. The tube is therefore curved so that the player can hold the instrument, as in this alto saxophone. Keys allow the fingers to open and close holes all along the instrument.

EDGE-BLOWN WOODWINDS

In the flute and recorder, the player blows air over an edge in the mouthpiece. This sets the air column inside the instrument vibrating.

SINGLE-REED WOODWINDS

In the clarinet and saxophone, the mouthpiece contains a single reed that vibrates to set the air column inside the instrument vibrating.

DOUBLE-REED WOODWINDS

The oboe, cor anglais and bassoon have a mouthpiece made of a double reed that vibrates to set the air column inside the instrument vibrating.

FINGERHOLES

In a short and simple woodwind instrument, such as the recorder, the fingers can cover all the holes directly.

PADS

Several woodwinds have holes that are larger than the fingers, requiring the fingers to press pads to cover the holes.

KEYS

Holes that are out of reach of the fingers are covered by pressing sprung keys attached to pads.

BRASS INSTRUMENTS

Brass instruments are in fact mostly made of brass, and consist of a long pipe that is usually coiled and has no holes. The player blows into a mouthpiece at one end of the pipe, the vibration of the lips setting the air column vibrating throughout the tube. The force of the lips varies to make the vibrating column divide into two halves, three thirds, and so on. This gives an ascending series of notes called harmonics. Opening extra lengths of tubing then gives other notes that are not in this harmonic series.

LOW PRESSURE
With low lip pressure, the air column vibrates in two halves and each half gives the note middle C. The length of the tube is therefore twice as long as a woodwind instrument sounding the same note.

INCREASED PRESSURE
Raising the lip pressure makes the air column vibrate in three thirds. Each vibrating section is two-thirds the length of the previous section, raising the pitch of the note to G.

INCREASED LENGTH
To play an E, which is not in the harmonic series, the player keeps the air vibrating in three thirds and increases the total length of the tube. Each vibrating section becomes four-fifths the length for middle C.

THE TROMBONE
The trombone has a section of tubing called a slide that can be moved in and out. The player pushes out the slide to lengthen the vibrating air column and produce notes that are not in the harmonic series.

MOUTHPIECE

SLIDE

THE TRUMPET
The trumpet has three pistons that are pushed down to open extra sections of tubing and play notes that are not in the harmonic series. Up to six different notes are obtained by using different combinations of the three pistons.

PISTON

VALVE CLOSED

AIR COLUMN

HOW VALVES WORK
On instruments such as the trumpet and tuba, each valve has a loop of tubing attached to it. Normally, the spring pushes against the piston, keeping the valve closed and shutting off the loop. But when the piston is depressed, the air column is diverted through the loop.

MOUTHPIECE   PISTONS

EXTRA SECTIONS
OF TUBING

LOOP
SPRING

LOOP

VALVE OPEN

STRING AND PERCUSSION INSTRUMENTS

String instruments form a large group of musical instruments which includes the violin family and guitar, and also harps, zithers and the piano. All these instruments make a sound by causing a taut string to vibrate. The string may be bowed, as with the violin family, plucked as in guitars, harps and zithers, or struck by a hammer as in the piano (see pp.26-7). The pitch of the note produced depends on three factors – the length, weight and tension of the string. A shorter, lighter or tighter string gives a higher note.

In many string instruments, the strings themselves do not make much sound. Their vibration is passed to the body of the instrument, which resonates to increase the level of sound that is heard.

STRING   FINGERBOARD

TUNING PEG

Percussion instruments are struck, usually with sticks or mallets, to make a sound. Often the whole instrument vibrates and makes a crack or crash, as in castanets and cymbals. Their sound does not vary in pitch and can only be made louder or softer. Drums contain stretched skins, which may vibrate to give a pitched note. As with strings, tightening the skin makes the note higher in pitch and smaller drums give higher notes.

Tuned percussion instruments, such as the xylophone, have sets of bars that each give a definite note. The pitch of the note depends on the size of the bar, a smaller bar giving a higher pitch.

THE KETTLE-DRUM

Kettledrums or timpani make sounds with a definite pitch, which can be varied. Pressing a pedal or turning screws pulls the hoop down to tighten the skin and raise the pitch, or releases the hoop to slacken the skin and lower the pitch.

SKIN

SC

THE VIOLIN

The violin and its relatives are the most expressive of string instruments. The violin has four strings of different weights. These are wound around tuning pegs to produce the correct amount of tension, and they sound four "open" notes when they are plucked or bowed. The performer stops the strings to obtain other notes, pressing one or more strings against the fingerboard to shorten the section that vibrates, thus raising the pitch of the string.

The front and back of the violin are connected by a short sound post, which transmits vibrations to the back. The whole body vibrates and the sound emerges through the f-shaped sound holes on the front of the instrument.

SKIN

HOOP

TENSIONING SCREW

SHELL

RESONATORS
Air inside tubes called resonators under the bars vibrates to make the notes louder.

BAR

RESONATOR

THE XYLOPHONE

The xylophone and similar instruments such as the vibraphone and marimba have sets of bars arranged like a piano keyboard. Each bar gives out a particular note when struck with a mallet, the longer bars sounding deeper notes.

A microphone is a kind of electric ear in that it too converts sound waves into an electric signal. The voltage of the microphone signal depends on the pressure of the sound wave – or in other words, on the volume of sound. The frequency at which its voltage varies depends on the other important characteristic of the sound wave, the frequency or pitch.

MICROPHONE SIGNAL

The weak signal produced by the microphone travels to a mixer, then to an amplifier (see pp.226-7) and finally to a loudspeaker (see pp.228-9).

CONDENSER MICROPHONE

All microphones have a diaphragm that vibrates as sound waves strike it. The vibration then causes electrical components to create an output signal. The condenser microphone (shown here) uses a capacitor for high-quality sound.

METAL DIAPHRAGM
(NEGATIVE CHARGE)

FIXED PLATE
(POSITIVE CHARGE)

OUTPUT SIGNAL
ZERO

ELECTRON FLOW

OUTPUT SIGNAL
POSITIVE

OUTPUT SIGNAL
NEGATIVE

BATTERY

NO SOUND
The battery produces equal charges on the diaphragm and fixed plate. Together, they form a capacitor. No further current flows.

COMPRESSION
As the diaphragm moves in, the plate attracts electrons from the diaphragm. Electrons in the output signal flow to the diaphragm.

RAREFACTION
As the diaphragm moves out, electrons in the diaphragm repel each other and flow away from it. The output signal reverses.

SYNTHESIZER

Electronic music makes great use of the synthesizer, which is an instrument that produces an electric sound signal similar to that of a microphone. Inside the synthesizer are electronic components that create the signal. The keyboard controls the voltage rate or frequency of the signal to determine the pitch of the sound, which emerges from a loudspeaker connected to the synthesizer. (See also p.316 and p.360.)

ECTRIC GUITAR

STRINGS

PICK-UPS

VOLUME AND
TONE CONTROLS

An electric guitar makes little sound of its own.
Playing the metal strings makes pick-ups beneath
the strings generate electric sound signals. The signals
go to volume and tone controls, which determine the
loudness and the kind of sound, and then to an
amplifier and loudspeaker.

PICK-UP

STRING AT REST
The pick-up produces no signal.

MOVING STRING
*When the string moves out
(above) or in (below) it produces
a signal in the pick-up.*

METAL STRINGS

MAGNET

COIL

BASE PLATE

CONNECTIONS TO
VOLUME AND TONE
CONTROLS

PICK-UPS
*Magnets in the pick-up produce
magnetic fields around the metal
strings and the coil of wire. As the
metal strings vibrate, they cause
the fields to vary in strength. The*
*changing field in turn creates a
varying electric current in the coil
(see pp.284-5), and this is the
sound signal that goes to the
guitar controls.*

MIXER

A mixer takes sound signals from several different
sources and mixes them together. The tone and
volume of each signal is controlled so that a good

sound balance results. One combined signal
(or two for stereo sound) then goes to the
amplifier and loudspeakers.

VOLUME METERS

GUITAR SIGNAL

MICROPHONE SIGNAL

TONE CONTROLS

VOLUME CONTROLS

STEREO SIGNAL

AMPLIFIER

An amplifier increases the voltage of a weak signal from a microphone, mixer, electric instrument, radio tuner, tape or CD player, giving it enough power to drive a loudspeaker or earphone. It works by using the weak signal to regulate the flow of a much stronger current, which normally comes from a battery or the mains supply. The key components that regulate the flow of the strong current are usually transistors. These two pages show the principles of amplification with a basic single-transistor amplifier.

RAREFACTION IN SOUND WAVE

A transistor is a small sandwich of two types of semiconductor, so-called because their conductivity changes as the transistor works. The two n-type (negative) pieces have some free electrons, while the p-type (positive) piece has "holes" into which the electrons can fit. The three pieces are known as the emitter, base and collector. When the microphone diaphragm moves out, electrons from the weak sound signal fill holes in the p-type semiconductor. This blocks the electrons from the power supply.

BLOCKED ELECTRONS

LOUDSPEAKER RECEIVES NO SIGNAL

POWER SUPPLY

NO CURRENT FLOWS

EMITTER (N-TYPE)

BASE (P-TYPE)

COLLECTOR (N-TYPE)

ELECTRONS FILL HOLES

FREE ELECTRONS

HOLES

FREE ELECTRONS

ELECTRONS ENTER BASE

DIAPHRAGM MOVES OUT

NEGATIVE OUTPUT SIGNAL

AMPLIFIED STEREO SIGNAL

INCOMING WEAK SIGNAL
In stereo sound, four wires conduct the weak incoming signal to the amplifier – a pair of wires for each channel.

AMPLIFIER
An amplifier usually contains many transistors and other components that enable the amount of amplification and also the tone of the sound to be varied.

POWER SUPPLY
This provides the energy that is needed to amplify the signal.

COMPRESSION IN SOUND WAVE

When the microphone diaphragm is pushed in by a compression in the sound wave, it reverses the flow of electrons in the weak signal. Electrons leave the base semiconductor in the centre of the "sandwich" and create holes. Forced by the power supply, many electrons enter these holes from the emitter and then move on into the collector. The result is a flow of electrons much larger than that in the weak signal, but exactly in step with it: the weak signal has been amplified.

LOUDSPEAKER RECEIVES STRONG SIGNAL

MOVING ELECTRONS

STRONG CURRENT FLOWS

ELECTRONS MOVE FROM EMITTER ACROSS BASE

ELECTRONS LEAVE BASE

DIAPHRAGM MOVES IN

POSITIVE OUTPUT SIGNAL

LOUDSPEAKER

SIGNAL FROM AMPLIFIER

MAGNETIC FIELD
BETWEEN COIL
AND MAGNET

CONE

MAGNET

MOVING COIL

A loudspeaker reproduces sound by responding to the electrical signal produced by an amplifier (see pp.226-7). It contains a thin but rigid cone fixed to a coil. The electric signal goes to the coil, which sits inside a magnetic field created by a circular permanent magnet around the coil. The coil also produces its own magnetic field, which varies in strength as the varying signal passes through it. The two magnetic fields push and pull on each other, causing the coil to vibrate in step with the variations of the signal. The cone vibrates at the same frequencies as the original sound waves that struck the microphone (see p.224), causing the surrounding air to vibrate and reproduce the original sound waves.

EARPHONE

An earphone is basically a miniature loudspeaker, and works in the same way. Just as two loudspeakers are normally used, a pair of earphones are usually worn, and these can reproduce stereophonic sound. Two pairs of wires carry a pair of sound signals originating from two or more microphones or other sound sources (see pp.224-7). Although the sounds go directly to each ear, the stereophonic effect causes the voices or instruments to spread out and have locations in space between the two earphones or loudspeakers.

INSIDE AN EARPHONE

The signal goes to a coil fixed to a diaphragm and suspended around a magnet. The coil and diaphragm vibrate to reproduce the sound.

GRILL

SOFT COVER

MAGNET

COIL

DIAPHRAGM

PLUG

The wires from the amplifier end in a socket. The earphone plug fits in the socket and contacts in the plug transfer the electric signal to the wires leading to each earphone.

THE RECORD PLAYER

A record player takes discs that revolve at 33 or 45 revolutions per minute, each side containing one spiral groove. The recording system, now obsolescent, is analog. The number and depth of the contours in the groove wall correspond to the varying frequency and loudness of the sound waves being recorded.

The record rests on a rotating turntable, and the pick-up arm in the player has a cartridge with a stylus that rests in the groove and vibrates as the record revolves. The vibrations of the stylus make the cartridge produce a stereo electric signal. This signal then goes to an amplifier and pair of loudspeakers to reproduce the recorded sound.

SPINDLE

TURNTABLE

BELT DRIVE
Many turntables are driven by a belt that runs around a drive spindle turned by the motor. This system prevents motor vibration reaching the record.

MAKING A RECORD

A metal stereo master disc is made from a stereo master tape. The master disc is made by a cutter that produces a spiral groove on its surface. Plastic copies of the master disc are then pressed.

CUTTING HEAD

The cutting head has two blades that vibrate at right angles in response to the stereo signals on the master tape. The blank disk moves past the head, and the blades cut a V-shaped groove in the surface so that the right-hand signal is recorded in one wall and the left-hand signal in the other

PICK-UP ARM

AMPLIFIER

LOUDSPEAKERS

RIGHT-HAND SIGNAL

LEFT-HAND SIGNAL

FIXED COILS

MOVING MAGNET

CARTRIDGE

The moving-magnet cartridge contains a magnet attached to the stylus. The magnet is surrounded by a pair of coils fixed at right angles. As the groove walls vibrate the stylus, the magnet also vibrates and generates electric signals in the coils. In moving-coil cartridges, the magnet is fixed and the coils vibrate.

GROOVE

DIAMOND OR SAPPHIRE STYLUS

Theories of Extinction: No. 6 The Fox-Trot.

PRESSURE PAD
The pressure pad is mounted in the cassette, and presses the tape against the record/replay head when the cassette is inserted into the player.

ERASE HEAD
A high-frequency electric signal is fed to the erase head when recording. It produces a magnetic field (*see p.275*) that alternates rapidly, disorientating the magnetic particles on the tape and erasing any previous recording.

TAPE SPOOL

UNMAGNETIZED TAPE

MAGNETIZED TAPE

GUIDE PILLAR

TAPE SPOOL

DRIVE MECHANISM
A capstan driven by the motor in the player and a pinch wheel move the tape past the heads from one spool to the other.

CAPSTAN

GUIDE PILLAR

PINCH WHEEL

CORES

STEREO TRACKS
A pair of stereo tracks is recorded on each side of an analog tape so that the tape cassette can be turned over and used.

COILS

STEREO SIGNALS

THE TAPE RECORDER

A tape recorder can record and replay voices and music on tape cassettes, which contain set lengths of magnetic tape. Analog tape players (shown above) record an incoming sound signal, such as that from a microphone, directly on the tape. Digital tape players first convert the sound signal to digital form before recording it (see p.322 and p.334)

On inserting the cassette into the machine, the centres of the tape spools fit over the spindles in the tape recorder. Pressing the PLAY button brings the record/replay head and drive mechanism into contact with the tape. The tape moves and the head records or replays the sounds. When recording, the erase head wipes off any previous recording on the tape.

RECORD/REPLAY HEAD
A coil of wire is wound around each core, causing it to act as an electromagnet. When recording, two stereo electric signals are amplified and go to the pair of coils in the head. They produce magnetic fields that *magnetize the particles in the tape. On replay, the magnetic particles in each track produce a pair of stereo electric signals in the coils, and these go to an amplifier and pair of loudspeakers or earphones to reproduce the sound.*

TELECOMMUNICATIONS

ON THE CONVEYING OF MESSAGES

While on a mammoth watch in the mountainous southern area, I was asked for some advice in the matter of communication between remote villages. It appeared that the age-old system of conveying messages — which relied on catapulting couriers from one place to another — was critically threatened by a shortage of both volunteers and also paper. After inspecting the catapults and calculating certain distances and elevations, I devised a completely new system. Instead of relying on dwindling manpower, I suggested that the messages could be carried through the air in the form of stones.

INSTANT SOUNDS AND IMAGES

Telecommunications are communications at a distance beyond the range of unaided hearing or eyesight. In order to send messages without delay over long distances, a fast-moving signal carrier is required. The method of telecommunication recorded above uses catapulted rocks as the signal carriers. The rocks are hurled aloft in a sequence that encodes a message, and when they land, the sequence is decoded and the message read.

Modern telecommunications use electricity, light and radio as very swift signal carriers. They carry signals representing sounds, images and computer data, which may be either analog signals that vary continuously in level, or digital signals made up of on-off pulses. The carrier – an electric current, light beam or radio wave – is often "modulated" by combining it with the analog or digital signal so that the carrier is made to vary in the same way as the signal. The modulated current, beam or wave is then sent to a receiver. A detector in the receiver extracts the signal from the carrier and reproduces the sound, image or data. For digital communications, see pages 349-351.

POWER SOURCE

AMPLIFIER

SOUND SIGNAL

OSCILLATOR

TRANSMITTER

MICROPHONE

LASER

MODULATOR

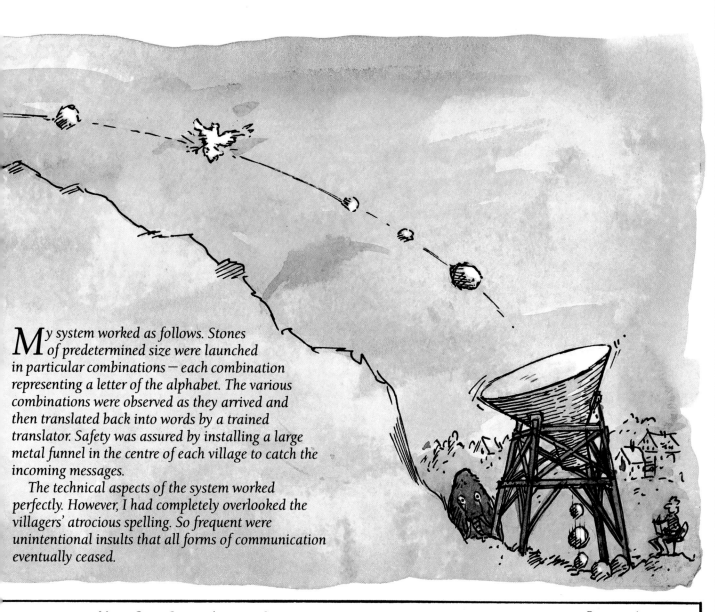

*M*y system worked as follows. Stones of predetermined size were launched in particular combinations — each combination representing a letter of the alphabet. The various combinations were observed as they arrived and then translated back into words by a trained translator. Safety was assured by installing a large metal funnel in the centre of each village to catch the incoming messages.

The technical aspects of the system worked perfectly. However, I had completely overlooked the villagers' atrocious spelling. So frequent were unintentional insults that all forms of communication eventually ceased.

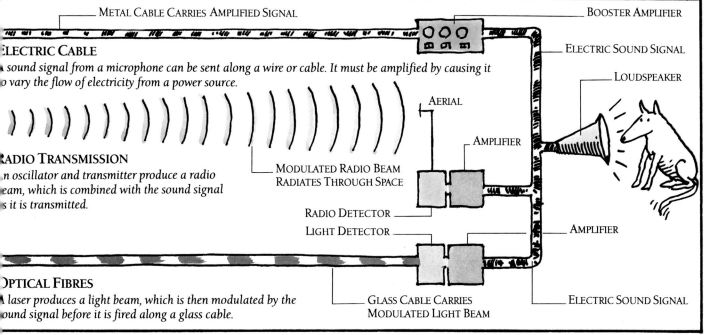

METAL CABLE CARRIES AMPLIFIED SIGNAL

BOOSTER AMPLIFIER

ELECTRIC SOUND SIGNAL

ELECTRIC CABLE

A sound signal from a microphone can be sent along a wire or cable. It must be amplified by causing it to vary the flow of electricity from a power source.

AERIAL

AMPLIFIER

LOUDSPEAKER

RADIO TRANSMISSION

An oscillator and transmitter produce a radio beam, which is combined with the sound signal as it is transmitted.

MODULATED RADIO BEAM
RADIATES THROUGH SPACE

RADIO DETECTOR

LIGHT DETECTOR

AMPLIFIER

OPTICAL FIBRES

A laser produces a light beam, which is then modulated by the sound signal before it is fired along a glass cable.

GLASS CABLE CARRIES
MODULATED LIGHT BEAM

ELECTRIC SOUND SIGNAL

TELEPHONE

The global telephone network enables us to speak to anyone in the world. Using metal cables, radio links, or fibre-optic cables, a call from a fixed telephone goes through a series of local and main exchanges that route it to another telephone. A mobile phone connects by radio to a nearby base station, which is at the centre of a hexagonal cell. Each cell has a base station and varies in size depending on the number of callers in the cell. As a mobile phone moves from one cell to another, it automatically connects to the base station in the next cell. Each base station then sends the call to a mobile exchange, which connects to a main exchange in the network. The mouthpiece and earpiece in a telephone handset work in the same way as a microphone (see p.224) and earphone (see p.229). The telephone network also supports fax machines (see p.326), computer communications (see pp.349-351), and text and picture messaging for mobile phones.

LOCAL EXCHANGE
All the telephones in a small area are connected to a local exchange.

TELEPHONE HANDSET

FAX MACHINE

PHONE SOCKET

CALL BOX

CELL

BASE STATION

MAIN EXCHANGE

BASE STATION

RADIO LINK

MOBILE PHONE

RADIO LINK

CELL

BASE STATION

BASE STATION

BASE STATION

BASE STATION

BASE STATION

CELL

MOBILE EXCHANGE

CELL

RADIO LINK

BASE STATION

MOBILE PHONE

RADIO
LINK

COMMUNICATIONS
SATELLITE

INTERNATIONAL
EXCHANGE

INTERNATIONAL EXCHANGE
A call to another country goes through an international exchange connected to the main exchanges in the caller's country. This sends the call to the international exchange in the other country.

UNDERSEA CABLE

RADIO
LINKS

MAIN EXCHANGE
All the local exchanges in a wide area are connected to a main exchange.

RELAY TOWER
Radio links at microwave frequencies connect distant exchanges via a high relay tower.

BASE
STATION

LOCAL EXCHANGE

CELL

TELEPHONE
HANDSET

SOCKET

FAX MACHINE

SOCKET

RADIO TRANSMITTER

Sunny and mild..

Radio waves are produced by feeding an electric signal to the mast or antenna of a transmitter. The signal makes the electrons in the metal atoms of the mast or antenna change energy levels and emit radio waves. They do this in the same way that electrons in atoms emit light rays (see p.180). Radio transmitters broadcast radio waves that are modulated. This means that the original sound signal is superimposed on the radio wave so that the radio wave "carries" the sound.

Like all waves, radio waves have a particular frequency or wavelength. Frequency is a measure of the number of waves that are transmitted per second, and it is measured in hertz. Wavelength is a measure of the length of each complete wave, and is expressed in metres. Frequency and wavelength are directly linked: a radio wave with a high frequency has a short wavelength, and one with a low frequency has a long wavelength.

MICROPHONE

ELECTRIC SOUND SIGNAL

SOUND SIGNAL

A microphone responds to sound waves by producing an electric sound signal that changes in voltage at the same rate or frequency. The curved line represents the variation of voltage in the signal.

CARRIER SIGNAL

The radio wave that carries the sound signal is called the carrier wave. It is produced by a radio-frequency (rf) carrier signal, which is an electric signal generated by a component called an oscillator. The frequency of the rf signal is constant and very much greater than the frequency range of the sounds being carried.

MODULATED SIGNAL

The sound signal from the microphone and the rf carrier signal from the oscillator are amplified and then combined in the modulator of the transmitter. This is done by amplitude modulation (AM) or by frequency modulation (FM). In AM radio, the waves are modulated so that the amplitude (energy level) of the carrier wave varies at the same frequency as the changing voltage in the sound signal. In FM radio, the waves are modulated so that that frequency of the carrier wave varies with the voltage level of the sound signal.

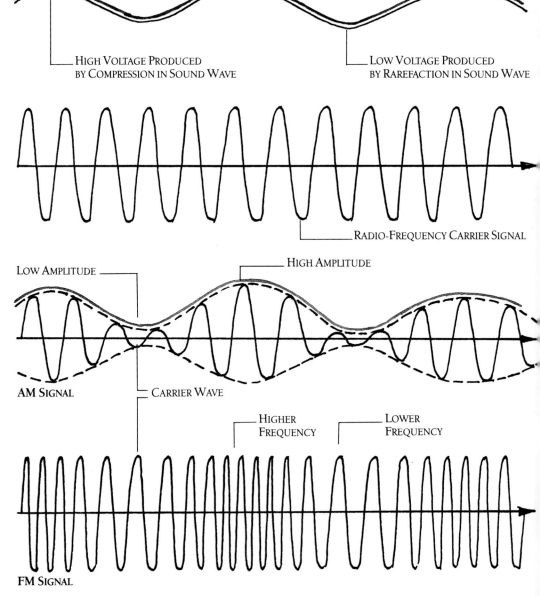

HIGH VOLTAGE PRODUCED BY COMPRESSION IN SOUND WAVE

LOW VOLTAGE PRODUCED BY RAREFACTION IN SOUND WAVE

RADIO-FREQUENCY CARRIER SIGNAL

LOW AMPLITUDE

HIGH AMPLITUDE

AM SIGNAL

CARRIER WAVE

HIGHER FREQUENCY

LOWER FREQUENCY

FM SIGNAL

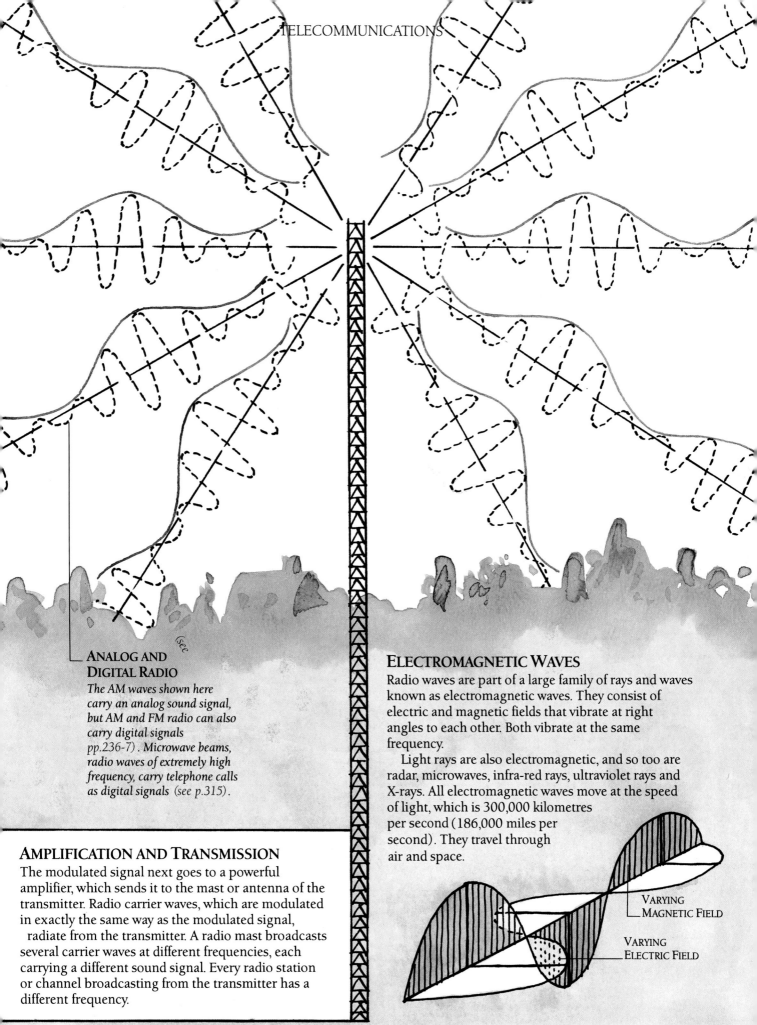

ANALOG AND DIGITAL RADIO

The AM waves shown here carry an analog sound signal, but AM and FM radio can also carry digital signals pp.236-7). Microwave beams, radio waves of extremely high frequency, carry telephone calls as digital signals (see p.315).

AMPLIFICATION AND TRANSMISSION

The modulated signal next goes to a powerful amplifier, which sends it to the mast or antenna of the transmitter. Radio carrier waves, which are modulated in exactly the same way as the modulated signal, radiate from the transmitter. A radio mast broadcasts several carrier waves at different frequencies, each carrying a different sound signal. Every radio station or channel broadcasting from the transmitter has a different frequency.

ELECTROMAGNETIC WAVES

Radio waves are part of a large family of rays and waves known as electromagnetic waves. They consist of electric and magnetic fields that vibrate at right angles to each other. Both vibrate at the same frequency.

Light rays are also electromagnetic, and so too are radar, microwaves, infra-red rays, ultraviolet rays and X-rays. All electromagnetic waves move at the speed of light, which is 300,000 kilometres per second (186,000 miles per second). They travel through air and space.

VARYING
MAGNETIC FIELD

VARYING
ELECTRIC FIELD

RADIO RECEIVER

A radio receiver is essentially a transmitter in reverse. Radio waves strike the aerial connected to the receiver. They affect the metal atoms, producing weak electric carrier signals in the aerial.

The receiver then selects the carrier signal of the required station or channel. It extracts the sound signal from the carrier signal, and this signal goes to an amplifier and loudspeaker to reproduce the sound.

VHF (FM)
87-108mHz

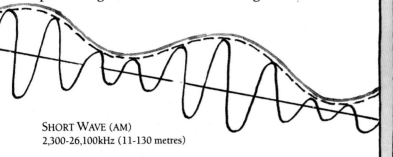

SHORT WAVE (AM)
2,300-26,100kHz (11-130 metres)

MEDIUM WAVE (AM)
525-1,700kHz (180-570 metres)

LONG WAVE (AM)
150-300kHz (1,000-2,000 metres)

WAVE BANDS

Radio waves are broadcast in several wave bands, often called long wave, medium wave, short wave and VHF (Very High Frequency) bands. Each band contains a range of radio frequencies or wavelengths, and each station or channel has its own particular frequency or wavelength within a band.

Stations are shown on a radio dial either in metres, which indicates the wavelength of the carrier wave, or in hertz, which gives its frequency. Radio frequencies are so high that they are shown in kilohertz (kHz) or megahertz (mHz), which are thousands and millions of hertz. The long, medium and short wave bands broadcast in AM; VHF radio is FM.

REPRODUCING THE SOUND

The carrier signal selected by the tune is modulated with the original sound signal. The detector in the receiver removes the carrier frequency to produce the sound signal. This signal then amplified and goes to the loudspeaker in the receiver. In stereo radio, left and right signals are combined and broadcast on one carri A stereo receiver has a decoder that separates them into two sound signal while an ordinary receiver reproduces the combined signal.

TUNER

The tuner selects a particular station or channel by removing all other frequencies. The required carrier signal passes through the tuner and then goes to the detector.

RADIO SIGNALS

VHF AND MEDIUM WAVES

VHF waves (*below*) travel a short distance, bouncing off the ground or large objects.

DIRECT WAVE

REFLECTED WAVE

SKY WAVE

Medium waves are reflected by the ionosphere.

SURFACE WAVE

REFLECTED SKY WAVE

IONOSPHERE

LONG WAVES

A surface wave curves around the Earth's surface, giving a range of thousands of kilometres or miles.

SURFACE WAVE

SHORT WAVES

Multiple reflections of a sky wave between the ionosphere and the Earth's surface give worldwide communications by short waves.

REFLECTED SKY WAVE

IONOSPHERE

MODULATED CARRIER SIGNAL

SOUND SIGNAL

AMPLIFIER

Sunny and mild..

LOUDSPEAKER REPRODUCES SOUND

[241]

TELEVISION CAMERA

Television transmits a sequence of 25 still images per second, and the eyes merge these into a moving picture as with a movie (see p.206). A colour television camera produces three images of each still picture in the three primary colours – red, green, and blue. Each image forms on a detector that converts it into an electric signal. The detector scans the image, splitting it into 625 horizontal lines. It puts out an electric image signal whose voltage varies with the brightness of the image along each line The signals from the three detectors are then combined into one signal that is transmitted to the home by radio or cable. For digital television, see pages 326 and 352.

STUDIO CAMERA

Mirrors separate the image formed by the lens into three images in red, green, and blue. Each detector is a CCD (see opposite) or, in older cameras, a light-sensitive tube.

REVERSING MIRROR

RED DETECTOR

SEMI-TRANSPARENT BLUE MIRROR

GREEN DETECTOR

SEMI-TRANSPARENT RED MIRROR

BLUE DETECTOR

LENS

LIGHT FROM SCENE

REVERSING MIRROR

GREEN SIGNAL

RED SIGNAL

BLUE SIGNAL

LUMINANCE SIGNAL
The image signals from the three detectors go to a colour mixer, which mixes them to produce a luminance signal. This gives the overall brightness of each part of the picture scanned by the three detectors.

CHROMINANCE SIGNAL
The three colour signals are combined together in a colour encoder to give a chrominance signal. This contains the amounts of the three colours in each part of the picture.

SYNCHRONIZATION SIGNAL
A pulse unit produces a signal which synchronizes the three detectors so that they scan exactly together. The three signals are then combined into one video signal.

MICROPHONE

SOUND SIGNAL
The sound signal is added to the video signal before transmission.

SOUND FROM SCENE

SOUND SIGNAL

VIDEO AND SOUND SIGNALS

CAMCORDER

You can make your own movies with portable camcorders. The camera has a lens and special CCD that separates the picture into three colour images. This CCD has red, green, and blue colour filters over adjacent light-sensitive elements. The video signal from the CCD and sound signal from the camcorder's microphone are then recorded. These are either recorded in analogue on to a tape in the same way as a video recorder (see pp.244-5) or, in digital camcorders, are converted into digital bits and stored on a memory card (see p.326), hard disk, or tape.

VIDEO HEAD DRUM

VIDEO TAPE

MICROPHONE

LENS

CCD

VIEWFINDER
In the viewfinder is a tiny television screen, which shows the picture being taken by the camcorder.

CCD (CHARGE-COUPLED DEVICE)

The image to be scanned falls on a CCD, which is a microchip with an array of thousands of tiny light-sensitive elements containing photodiodes (see p.272). In each one, the light striking the element frees electrons to produce a certain level of negative electric charge that varies according to the light intensity. Each row of elements gives one line of the picture. Electrodes behind the photodiodes move the charges from the rows to the CCD's output to form the image signal.

MASKING STRIP

DARK

IMAGE OF LINE 1

BRIGHT

FREED ELECTRONS

CHARGES IN LINE 1

CHARGES IN LINE 2

POSITIVE CHARGE MOVES ALONG ELECTRODES

ELECTRODES

POSITIVE CHARGE MOVES UP

MAST

1 CHARGES FORM
Red light making up lines 1 and 2 of the picture falls on two rows of elements in the red CCD of a camera. Electrons are freed to give levels of electric charge that depend on the intensity of the light.

CHARGES IN LINE 2

2 CHARGES MOVE UP
A positive charge moves up the electrodes behind the rows. It pulls the electrons to the next higher row of elements, so that the sequence of negative charges in line 1 enters the top masked row of elements.

CHARGES IN LINE 1

DISH

3 CHARGES MOVE OUT
A positive charge now moves along the electrodes behind the top row. It pulls the charges into the output path. The charges from each subsequent row move up and out in turn to produce the image signal.

CABLE

OUTPUT PATH

VIDEO RECORDER

GUIDE ROLLER

LOADING POLES

VIDEO HEAD DRUM

ERASE HEAD
Any previous recording on the tape is wiped off by the erase head.

Like a television receiver (see pp.246-7), a video recorder first extracts the video (picture) signal from the television carrier signal that is either broadcast or cabled to the home. But instead of sending the video signal to the television tube to be seen, the video recorder preserves the signal on tape. It does this with a tape cassette in much the same way that a tape recorder records a sound signal (see pp.232-3).

The video signal goes to a record-replay head that records it on the magnetic tape, and the video recorder replays the tape to send the recorded signal to the television set. However, the tape must pass the head at a very high speed to record a video signal, because so much information has to be stored. The head therefore rotates rapidly as the tape passes, recording video signals in diagonal tracks across the tape.

The VHS (Video Home System) arrangement shown here has become the main system used in home video cassette recorders. Other video systems use the same basic method of a rotating head to record the signals on tape.

DIAGONAL VIDEO TRACKS

VIDEO HEAD DRUM

HEAD

TAPE

HEAD

ROTATING VIDEO HEADS
The drum contains two video record/replay heads on opposite sides of the drum, and it is tilted relative to the tape. The pair of heads records one complete picture in each revolution in the form of a pair of diagonal tracks across the tape.

SUPPLY REEL

VIDEO TAPE

LOADING POLES

GUIDE ROLLER

PINCH ROLLER

VIDEO CASSETTE

VIDEO (PICTURE) TRACKS

AUDIO (SOUND) TRACK

PINCH ROLLER

LOADING THE TAPE

When the cassette is inserted into the recorder, the loading poles take the tape out of the cassette and move it into contact with the heads and rollers in the recorder.

CAPSTAN

The pinch roller brings the tape into contact with the rotating capstan to transport the tape from the supply reel to the take-up reel.

UDIO AND
ONTROL HEAD
*he head records and replays
e sound signal and
e synchronization
gnal that controls
e picture. The
acks are recorded
ong the top and
ottom of the tape.
some video recorders,
gh quality stereo sound
recorded on diagonal
udio tracks.*

CAPSTAN

CONTROL SIGNAL

AKE-UP REEL

TELEVISION SET

A television set receives a video signal from a television station or video recorder. It works like a television camera in reverse to form a succession of still pictures on the screen. It does this by scanning in the same way as a camera tube to build up the picture in horizontal lines on the screen. In a colour picture, each line contains a series of red, green and blue stripes. At viewing distance, the lines and stripes cannot be made out. The eye merges them together, and we see a sharp picture in full colour (see p.182).

AERIAL
Radio waves modulated with video signals strike the aerial or dish, producing electric video signals that go to the set. Alternatively, the electric signals may arrive through a cable.

TUNER
The tuner selects a tv channel by selecting a video signal at a particular carrier frequency in the same way as a radio tuner.

LUMINANCE DETECTOR

LUMINANCE SIGNAL

PRODUCING THE PICTURE
The detectors separate the luminance, chrominance and synchronization signals from the video signal. The chrominance decoder produces the three colour signals. All these signals go to the picture tube and control three electron beams, which scan the inner surface of the screen to form a picture.

RED SIGNAL

GREEN SIGNAL

BLUE SIGNAL

CHROMINANCE DETECTOR AND DECODER

ELECTRON GUNS

SYNCHRONIZATION SIGNAL

SYNCHRONIZATION DETECTOR

LOUDSPEAKER

SOUND SIGNAL

SOUND DETECTOR

PHOSPHOR COATING

SCANNING ELECTRON BEAMS

DEFLECTION COILS MOVE BEAMS

SHADOW MASK

SCREEN

PICTURE TUBE

INTERLACING
Each still picture is made up of two scans consisting of alternate lines. The camera and picture tubes first scan the odd-numbered lines and then scan the picture again to form the even-numbered lines. We see 50 scans a second, which reduces flicker in the moving picture.

FIRST SCAN

SECOND SCAN

BLUE BEAM

OVEMENT OF
LECTRON BEAMS

GREEN BEAM

SHADOW MASK

RED BEAM

COLOUR SCREEN

The screen contains tiny stripes of phosphors that light up in red, green or blue. The three electron beams, one for each colour, scan across the shadow mask behind the screen. The mask contains holes that allow each beam to strike only stripes of the correct colour. These light up as each beam passes, and vary in brightness with the strength of the beam. A black-and-white set contains only one electron beam, which is controlled by the luminance and synchro-nization signals, and no shadow mask.

PHOSPHOR
STRIPE

SATELLITE

Artificial satellites orbit the Earth, communicating with us from a unique vantage point high above the atmosphere. Weather and Earth observation satellites look down and astronomy satellites peer outwards, while communications satellites link distant parts of our planet and beam television channels to our homes. Some satellites have orbits that take them over different parts of the Earth, while others are "parked" in geostationary orbits above a particular point on the equator.

GROUND STATION

SATELLITE PHONE

GROUND STATION

PASSENGER PHONE ON AIRCRAFT

SOLAR CELLS

IMAGING SYSTEM

COMMUNICATIONS EQUIPMENT

HORN   HORN

DISH   RADIO BEAM   DISH

RADIO LINKS

All satellites communicate with ground stations by radio, sending back images and measurements and receiving instructions and information. Many satellites and ground stations have a curved dish that reflects outgoing signals from a central horn to form a narrow beam, and reflects signals in an incoming beam to meet at the central horn.

WEATHER SATELLITE

The Meteosat family of satellites sends back images of the Earth that reveal cloud formations together with measurements of weather conditions such as winds and surface temperatures. Images and information from weather satellites enable forecasters to make accurate predictions of the weather.

COMMUNICATIONS SATELLITE

The Inmarsat-3 series of communications satellites in geostationary orbit provides worldwide coverage of telephone, fax, and data communications. They link not only large ground stations but portable terminals known as satellite phones, and terminals on aircraft, ships, and vehicles. Inmarsat is used for disaster and emergency communications and news reporting from remote areas.

GEOSTATIONARY ORBIT

At a height of 35,880 kilometres (22,295 miles), a satellite takes exactly 24 hours to orbit the Earth.

RADIO DISH

SOLAR PANEL

WIND
DETECTOR

WAVE HEIGHT
DETECTOR

**SYNTHETIC
APERTURE RADAR**
*High-resolution radar
images of the Earth reveal
different kinds of features
on the surface.*

EARTH OBSERVATION SATELLITE

The ERS (European Remote Sensing) satellites look
down to record and measure many aspects of the
Earth's surface and climate. As well as producing
detailed pictures of the Earth's surface for mapping,
an observation satellite can locate mineral deposits;
monitor crops and forests; study the ozone layer; detect
surface movements, such as those involved in
earthquakes and volcanic eruptions; and measure ocean
movements to learn more about ocean winds and waves.

SHIELD AND SENSORS
The heat sensors on COBE had to
be kept extremely cold in order to
measure the very weak background
radiation in space. Liquid helium
maintained the instruments close
to absolute zero. The sensors were
surrounded by a conical shield that
protected them from the heat and
light of the Sun and the Earth.

RADIO
COMMUNICATIONS
ANTENNA

HEAT SENSORS

SHIELD

SOLAR PANELS

SOLAR PANEL
*Solar cells (see p.271)
in panels or on the side
of a satellite convert
sunlight into electricity
to power the equipment
in the satellite.*

ASTRONOMY SATELLITE

COBE (Cosmic Background Explorer), an American
satellite, was launched in 1989 and over several years
measured the background radiation in the Universe.
This radiation consists of the heat rays produced by
the Big Bang that formed the Universe about 15 billion
years ago. COBE found regions that are slightly cooler
than others, indicating places where galaxies began
to form. COBE provided the first evidence of the
evolution of the Universe from the Big Bang towards
the form we observe today.

RADIO TELESCOPE

Many objects in the universe send out radio waves, and a radio telescope can be used to detect them. A large curved metal dish collects the radio waves and reflects them to a focus point above the centre of the dish, rather as the curved mirror of a reflecting telescope gathers light waves from space (see p.188). At this point, an aerial intercepts the radio waves and turns them into a weak electric signal. The signal then goes to a computer. Radio telescopes detect very weak waves, and can also communicate with spacecraft.

By detecting radio waves coming from galaxies and other objects in space, radio telescopes have discovered the existence of many previously unknown bodies. It is possible to make visible images of radio sources by scanning the telescope or a group of telescopes across the source. This yields a sequence of signals from different parts of the source, which the computer can process to form an image. Differences in frequency of the signals give information about the composition and motion of the radio source.

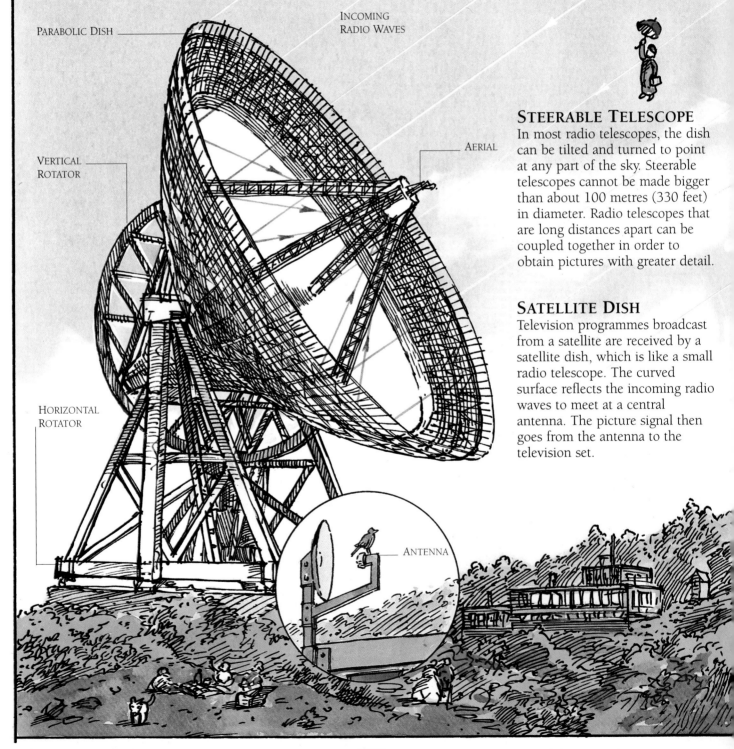

PARABOLIC DISH

INCOMING RADIO WAVES

AERIAL

VERTICAL ROTATOR

HORIZONTAL ROTATOR

ANTENNA

STEERABLE TELESCOPE

In most radio telescopes, the dish can be tilted and turned to point at any part of the sky. Steerable telescopes cannot be made bigger than about 100 metres (330 feet) in diameter. Radio telescopes that are long distances apart can be coupled together in order to obtain pictures with greater detail.

SATELLITE DISH

Television programmes broadcast from a satellite are received by a satellite dish, which is like a small radio telescope. The curved surface reflects the incoming radio waves to meet at a central antenna. The picture signal then goes from the antenna to the television set.

SPACE TELESCOPE

The Hubble space telescope is part optical telescope and part satellite. It orbits the Earth and, under radio control from the ground, takes pictures and measurements of planets, stars, galaxies and other bodies in space. Operating in the total clarity of space, above the obscuring effects of the atmosphere, the space telescope produces sharper pictures then those of Earth-bound telescopes. It has detected faint and distant objects and produced more detailed pictures of known objects, greatly expanding our knowledge of the Universe. The space telescope was launched by the space shuttle in 1990 and improved in 1993 and 1997. It should operate until at least 2005.

RADIO DISH
The dish sends telescope images and measurements from instruments back by radio to ground stations below.

EQUIPMENT SECTION
Light detectors change the visual images produced by the mirrors into television signals. The space telescope also contains scientific instruments.

APERTURE DOOR

SECONDARY MIRROR

LIGHT RAYS FROM STAR OR GALAXY

PRIMARY MIRROR
The space telescope is a Cassegrain reflecting telescope (see p.188) with a main mirror 2.4 metres (8 feet) in diameter.

BAFFLES
These ridges reduce the reflection of stray light from surfaces in the tube.

TELESCOPE TUBE
The main body of the telescope is 13 metres (43 feet) long and 4.3 metres (14 feet) across.

SPACE SHUTTLE

SOLAR PANELS
The pair of panels provides electricity (see p.271) to work the instruments aboard the space telescope.

SPACE PROBE

The ultimate limits of communication are reached with space probes, which have sent us detailed pictures and information from every planet in the Solar System except Pluto, the most distant. Probes have also surveyed our Moon and many of the moons that orbit distant worlds, and one has flown to the heart of Halley's comet.

Radio waves, travelling at the velocity of light, have brought their discoveries to Earth. Such is their speed that signals reach us from the farthest worlds in just a few hours. These signals include geological and atmospheric data, and video signals that give close-up pictures of distant worlds and details of their surfaces. The signals are extremely weak, and ground stations train large dishes on a probe to pick them up. The stations can also beam powerful command signals back to the space probe. Space probes may either fly past a world, or enter an orbit around it and survey it over a long period. Some probes may land on the surface or send down separate landers.

MARS PATHFINDER

Launched from Earth in December 1996, the Mars Pathfinder space probe arrived at Mars in July 1997. The probe did not orbit Mars but landed directly on the surface. It cushioned the landing with air bags, and then opened to deploy a small six-wheeled robot explorer called Sojourner. As the main Pathfinder lander surveyed a rusty-red desert plain littered with rocks, Sojourner set out to examine the terrain. The controllers on Earth could tell Sojourner to proceed to rocks seen in Pathfinder's pictures. But the robot used its on-board computer, camera, and laser scanner to find its way to each rock. There, Sojourner put a probe against the rock to analyze it.

The results radioed back to Earth by Pathfinder show that the rocks on Mars are like those on Earth and probably formed in a similar way. Sojourner found rocks that appear to have formed in water, suggesting that this part of Mars was covered in an ocean. Although Mars is now dry and very cold, it may once have been wet and warm and living organisms like bacteria may have evolved there long ago. These may possibly still survive.

SOJOURNER   SOLAR PANEL   CAMERA   MAIN PATHFINDER LANDER

RADAR
IMAGER

CAMERAS AND SENSORS

HUYGENS LANDER

NUCLEAR-POWERED
ELECTRICITY GENERATOR

RADIO
DISH

ROCKET ENGINES

ELECTRIC FIELD
AND MAGNETIC
FIELD DETECTOR

MAGNETOMETER
BOOM

LANDING ON TITAN
In November 2004, the Huygens lander is due to parachute down to the surface of Titan, one of Saturn's moons.

CASSINI

With its breathtaking system of rings, Saturn is the most beautiful planet in the Solar System. Little is known of Saturn and its many moons and it has been visited only by two passing Voyager space probes. But in 2004, after a seven-year journey from Earth, the space probe Cassini will arrive and go into orbit around Saturn. It will move in close to the planet to observe its clouds, and then soar out to look down on the planet's poles and the famous rings. Cassini will also make more distant orbits out among Saturn's moons, and will skim over the surface of some of them. Over a four-year period of observations, Cassini will answer many tantalizing questions about how Saturn and its rings and moons formed and evolved. The information could hold vital clues about the origin of the Solar System.

The highlight of the mission will come with Cassini's visit to Titan, Saturn's biggest moon. Titan is a large moon and has a hazy orange atmosphere that obscures the surface. Cassini will release a lander called Huygens, which will parachute down through the atmosphere to the surface. It will detect the different gases, take images, and measure the conditions. The results will go by radio back to Cassini, which will send them on to Earth. The atmosphere of Titan is thought to be like that of Earth long ago, and Huygens' observations could throw light on how life began on Earth.

THE
DISCOVERY
OF·MAGNETIC
NORTH

ELECTRICITY & AUTOMATION

INTRODUCTION

THE POWER BEHIND ELECTRICITY comes from the smallest things known to science. These are electrons, tiny particles within atoms, that each bear a minute electric charge If a million million of them were lined up, they would scarcely reach across the head of a pin. When an electric current flows through a wire, these tiny particles surge through the metal in unimaginable numbers. In a current of 1 ampere, sufficient to light a torch bulb, for example, 6 million million million electrons pass any point in just one second. Each electron moves relatively slowly, but the charge transfers from electron to electron at the speed of light. If the nineteenth century was the heyday of mechanical machines, then the twentieth century has belonged to machines powered by electricity. This does not mean that the age of mechanical machines is behind us. Machines that move will always be needed for doing work, but they have come increasingly to be driven by electric motors and governed by electrical control devices. And the twentieth century has also seen the rise of machines that use electricity to carry information and which may contain few moving parts. These include the various communications devices that store or carry sounds and images and which occupy the later pages of Part 3 of this book. This branch of technology assumes greater and greater importance as machines go digital, a subject that is explored in depth in Part 5.

EXPLOITING ELECTRONS

The machines in this part of *The New Way Things Work* either produce electricity or use it in various ways. Many use the ability of moving electrons to create a magnetic field around them. Magnetic fields attract and repel each other with great force. Machines that use electric motors move by harnessing the push and pull of magnetic fields created around wires that carry electricity. Electric generators, which produce our main supply of electricity, also make use of magnetic fields. And magnets themselves are magnetic and possess a magnetic field because of the motion of the electrons within their atoms. So all machines that exploit magnetism in one way or another are ultimately using electrons. Electrons also produce electric fields, which have the same ability to attract and repel as magnetic fields do. Some machines, such as the photocopier and ionizer, work by shifting electrons about so that electrical attraction and repulsion come into play. Yet more machines use electrons as a means to carry information. But despite these differences, the principles that govern the flow of electricity are exactly the same in all electrical machines. The electrons always need energy to make them move. They always travel in a set direction (from negative to positive) at a set speed. Furthermore, they will always produce particular effects while they are on the move. Magnetism is one. So too are heat and light, as we have already seen in Part 2. Electrons have other ways of producing light as well as rays that are invisible and even sounds that cannot be heard, but all are highly useful.

ELECTRICITY AND MOVEMENT

As a source of power, electricity has no rival. It is clean, silent, can be turned on and off instantly, and can be fed easily to where it is needed. Electric machines that produce movement are extraordinarily diverse. At first sight, there is little similarity between, for example, a quartz wristwatch and an electric locomotive. However, both use the motive force produced by the magnetic effects of an electric current – although the current used by a train is hundreds of thousands of times greater than that which flows in a watch. Like all electrical machines, those that use electricity to produce movement take only as much power as they need. An electric motor will only take a set amount of current. This means that one source can power many machines with each one taking only the current it needs and no more.

MACHINES THAT CONTROL THEMSELVES

Electrons can be forced into a wire in varying quantities, and they give rise to varying levels of electric charge that travel almost instantly along the wire to a machine. This varying charge constitutes an electric signal, and it can govern the way in which a machine works. The signal may simply switch the machine on or off, or it may control the performance of the machine. Many machines contain devices that produce control signals that enable the machines to control themselves so effectively that they can work totally unaided. Everyday examples are automatic doors and traffic lights. Sensors and detectors are often the source of these control signals. They can detect the presence of physical objects, like a piece of metal or a whiff of smoke, and they can also measure quantities, such as speed. The signal goes from the detector to the machine, which reacts accordingly. Automatic machines respond in two main ways. In the simpler ones, the control signal triggers a set operation: automatic doors, for example, open the moment one approaches and an air bag inflates instantly in a car crash. These machines do nothing more – they don't need to. But some automatic machines are much more sophisticated and have sensors or detectors that measure the machine's own performance. Their signals keep the machine working properly, correcting its performance if necessary. An aircraft is such a machine: the autopilot senses any deviation in flight and operates the aircraft controls to correct it, while the guidance system continually checks the aircraft's position and ensures that it follows the correct route.

More and more aspects of our everyday lives now depend on the flow of billions of controlling electrons along wires or through circuits inside machines. Automatic machines take tasks out of our hands, make life more convenient and often much safer. Some give us abilities that we would otherwise not possess or find hard to learn; an automatic camera, for example, makes photography much easier. Many such machines are controlled by digital devices because these can produce highly complex sequences of control operations, as the next part of *The New Way Things Work* will make clear.

ELECTRICITY

ON MAMMOTH ATTRACTION

*O*ne day, I happened upon a mammoth whose hair had been lovingly combed. The hairdresser, in fact, was just about to return her creation to its owner. No sooner had the perfectly coiffed animal stepped into the street, however, than a combination of litter, loose laundry and stray cats flew into the air and secured themselves to the startled beast's freshly combed coat. It is common knowledge that a well groomed individual is more attractive, but never before had I seen this so forcefully illustrated.

STATIC ELECTRICITY

All things are made up of atoms, and within atoms are even smaller particles called electrons. Electrons each have an electric charge, and this charge, which is considered to be negative, is the fundamental cause of electricity.

Static electricity is so-called because it involves electrons that are moved from one place to another rather than ones that flow in a current. In an object with no static electric charge, all the atoms have their normal number of electrons. If some of the electrons are then transferred to another object by, for example, vigorous rubbing or brushing, the other object becomes negatively charged while the object that loses electrons becomes positively charged. An electric field is set up around each object.

Unlike charges always attract each other and like charges always repel each other. This is the reason why the mammoth finds itself festooned with rubbish after its brushing, and why a comb rubbed with a cloth will attract pieces of paper. Rubbing or brushing creates a charge and therefore an electric field. The field affects objects nearby, producing an unlike charge in them, and the unlike charges are drawn together.

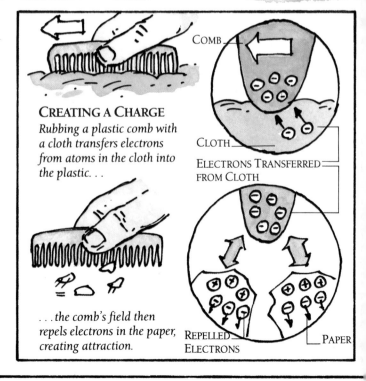

CREATING A CHARGE

Rubbing a plastic comb with a cloth transfers electrons from atoms in the cloth into the plastic. . .

. . .the comb's field then repels electrons in the paper, creating attraction.

COMB

CLOTH

ELECTRONS TRANSFERRED FROM CLOTH

REPELLED ELECTRONS

PAPER

ON MAMMOTH LEMONS

*A*t harvest time, I once watched with great admiration as lemons were gathered with mammoth assistance. Large specimens were harpooned, the mammoths being equipped with copper lances, and their riders with zinc ones — a lightweight improvement of my own devising. During my visit, the riders did complain of suffering powerful shudderings which they somehow attributed to their new equipment, but I was able to assure them that of course there could be no connection.

As each team boldly rode into action, the air was almost electric.

CURRENT ELECTRICITY

Current electricity is produced by electrons on the move. Unlike static electricity, current electricity can only exist in a conductor — that is, a material such as a metal that allows electrons to pass freely through it.

In order to make electrons move, a source of energy is needed. This energy can be in the form of light, heat, or pressure, or it can be the energy produced by a chemical reaction. Chemical energy is the source of power in a battery-powered circuit. The mammoth and its rider suffer a surge of electric current because they inadvertently form this type of circuit. Lemons contain acid, which reacts with the zinc and copper in the lances. Atoms in the acid take electrons from the copper atoms and transfer them to the zinc atoms. The electrons then flow through the materials connected to the two metal lances. The zinc lance, which releases the negatively charged electrons, is the negative terminal of the lemon battery. The copper lance, which receives the electrons, is the positive terminal. Whereas an ordinary lemon would not produce sufficient electrons to give a big current, the giant lemon yields enough to produce a violent shock.

ZINC

ACID

COPPER

FLOW OF ELECTRONS (CURRENT)

BATTERY CIRCUIT

Electrons travel from the negative terminal through the wire to the positive terminal.

ACID TAKES POSITIVE CHARGES FROM ZINC

ACID TAKES ELECTRONS FROM COPPER

DOCUMENT

TONER BRUSHES APPLY
TONER TO DRUM

MIRRORS

LENS

IMAGE OF
STRIP OF DOCUMENT

DRUM

DRUM CHARGER

CLEANER

FIRST ERASE LAMP
*This lamp removes the
charge on the drum.*

TRANSFER CHARGER
*The transfer charger applies negative
charge to the piece of paper so that
it attracts the toner particles.*

SECOND ERASE LAMP
*This removes the charge on
the drum after the toner
has been deposited
on the paper.*

THE PHOTOCOPIER

Static electricity enables a photocopier to produce almost instant copies of documents. At the heart of the machine is a metal drum which is given a negative charge at the beginning of the copying cycle. The optical system then projects an image of the document on the drum. The electric charge disappears where light strikes the metal surface, so only dark parts of the image remain charged. Positively charged particles of toner powder are then applied to the drum. The charged parts of the drum attract the dark powder, which is then transferred to a piece of paper. A heater seals the powder to the paper, and a warm copy of the document emerges from the photocopier. A colour copier works in the same basic way, but scans the document with blue, green, and red filters and no filter. Using coloured toner, the drum forms four images in yellow, magenta, cyan, and black that overlap to give a full colour copy (see p.214)

GLASS WINDOW

LAMP

MIRRORS

CARRIER BELT

HEATER
The heater warms the paper so that the toner particles soften and are pressed into the surface of the paper.

OPTICAL SYSTEM
Beneath the glass window, a lamp, set of mirrors and a lens scan the document, moving across it to project a strip onto the rotating drum. The optical system may enlarge or reduce the size of the image on the drum.

AIR CLEANER

The most effective kind of air cleaner uses an electrostatic precipitator to remove very fine particles, such as cigarette smoke and pollen, from the air in a room. The precipitator works by giving a positive charge to particles in the air and then trapping them with a negatively charged grid. The cleaner may also contain filters to remove dust and odours, and finally an ionizer to add negative ions to the clean air.

PRE-FILTER
A mesh in the pre-filter first removes large dust and dirt particles from the air.

DIRTY AIR

ELECTROSTATIC PRECIPITATOR
Opposite high-voltage charges are placed on the two grids. The first grid gives the remaining fine particles a positive charge, and the negative grid attracts the particles.

CLEAN AIR

FAN

CARBON FILTER
A filter containing activated carbon absorbs odours from the air, which is pulled through the cleaner by a fan.

LIGHTNING CONDUCTOR

CHARGE BUILD-UP
A thunderstorm creates regions of strong negative electric charge at the base of clouds. These charges cause strong positive charges to form in the ground.

NEGATIVE CHARGE IN CLOUD BASE

POSITIVE CHARGE IN GROUND

LIGHTNING DISCHARGE
The very strong electric fields produce ions and free electrons in the air. The air can then conduct electricity and a flash of lightning surges through it.

IONIZER

CHARGED NEEDLE

Atoms that have an electrical charge are called ions. Ions occur naturally; they make up many solid substances and they are also found in the atmosphere. Air that contains a high concentration of negative ions is reputed to be beneficial; ionizers are designed to produce them. An ionizer supplies a strong negative charge to one or more needles. An intense electric field is developed at the point of a needle, and it creates ions in the atoms in the air. Positive ions are attracted to the needle, while negative ions flow outwards.

POSITIVE IONS

NEGATIVE IONS

CAPACITORS

DIODE

CHARGED NEEDLE

VOLTAGE MULTIPLIER

This converts the alternating current of the mains supply to a high-voltage direct current that charges the ionizer needles. The diodes change the alternating current to direct current (see p.267) which charges the capacitors. The capacitors store increasing amounts of charge to raise the voltage.

REDUCING THE CHARGE

A lightning conductor helps to prevent lightning. Intense positive charges at the pointed tips of the conductor create positive ions that flow upwards to reduce the negative charge in the thundercloud while negative charges are attracted downwards.

LIGHTNING CONDUCTOR

ELECTRONS ENTER GROUND

CONDUCTING THE CHARGE TO EARTH

If lightning does strike, it tends to follow the ion path and hits the lightning conductor. The powerful current flows down the cable and enters the ground without causing any damage.

SELF-WINDING WATCH

PIEZOELECTRICITY

Exerting pressure on certain crystals and ceramics can cause them to produce an electric charge. This effect is called piezoelectricity, from the Greek word *piezein* meaning to press, and it is put to use in several electrical devices. In many substances, the atoms are in the form of ions (see p.263) which are held together very tightly by their electric charges. Quartz, for example, has positive silicon ions and negative oxygen ions. Pressing the quartz displaces the ions so that negative ions move towards one side of the crystal and positive ions towards the other. The opposite faces develop negative and positive charges, which can be very powerful. The reverse happens too: applying an electric signal to a crystal makes it vibrate at a precise natural frequency, as in a quartz oscillator.

NORMAL QUARTZ CRYSTAL CRYSTAL UNDER PRESSURE

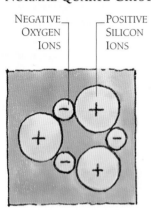

NEGATIVE OXYGEN IONS

POSITIVE SILICON IONS

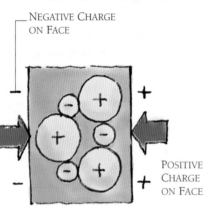

NEGATIVE CHARGE ON FACE

POSITIVE CHARGE ON FACE

QUARTZ OSCILLATOR

INCOMING SIGNAL

REGULAR SIGNAL

VIBRATING CRYSTAL

A quartz watch (see opposite page) consumes very little power, but its battery will eventually run out and have to be replaced. The self-winding, or kinetic watch, is a quartz watch that uses the principles of piezoelectricity to keep good time, but does not require a battery. It generates its own electricity simply by using the movement of the wearer's wrist. Inside the watch is an oscillating weight that swings to and fro as the watch moves. The oscillating motion is transferred through a set of gears to a tiny magnetic rotor that rotates at speeds of up to 100,000 revolutions per minute and induces bursts of electric current in a generating coil. The current then goes to the capacitor of the watch to be stored for use by the watch's quartz oscillator and motor.

WIRES TO CAPACITOR IN WATCH

GENERATING COIL

MAGNETIC ROTOR

GEARS

OSCILLATING WEIGHT

QUARTZ CLOCK

Piezoelectricity provides a simple method of accurate time-keeping. Many clocks and watches contain a quartz crystal oscillator which controls the hands or display. Power from a small battery makes the crystal vibrate and it gives out pulses of current at a very precise rate or frequency. A microchip reduces this rate to one pulse per second, and this signal controls the motor that turns the hands or activates the display.

CAPACITOR

QUARTZ OSCILLATOR

MICROCHIP
The microchip divides the oscillator's very high vibration frequency to produce a control signal exactly once a second.

MOTOR
The motor rotates 180° every second, and drives the train of gears that turns the hands.

ELECTROMAGNET

BATTERY

TRAIN OF GEARS TURNING HANDS

COIL
The coil receives control signals and powers the electromagnet that drives the motor.

THE CURRENT CART

Because electricity cannot be seen as it flows around a circuit, it is easier to understand by comparing it with something else. The machine on this page is a fictional, water-powered equivalent of an electric circuit. Water, rather than electrons, circulates and provides power. Each part of the cart has a counterpart in the simple circuit on the opposite page.

SLUICE GATE

Opening the sluice gate increases the flow of water so that more water strikes the paddle wheel and speeds up the machine. This is the counterpart of the resistance of the light bulb in the circuit. Fitting a brighter bulb gives less resistance and more current flows through it.

WATER CHANNEL

The amount of water passing through the channel is the equivalent of the current. This varies depending on the height of the water-raiser (the voltage) and the position of the sluice gate (the resistance).

WATER-RAISER

The water-raiser, which gives the water the force to flow back to the trough at the bottom of the machine, is the equivalent of the battery. The top of the screw is equivalent to the negative terminal, which sends out electrons with sufficient force to flow around the circuit and light the bulb. The height of the water-raiser is equivalent to the voltage.

TROUGH

The water flows into the trough, at which point it has lost all its energy. This is equivalent to the positive terminal of the battery, where electrons return to their source after completing the electric circuit.

ELECTRIC CIRCUIT

All devices and machines powered by current electricity contain an electric circuit. A source of electricity, usually a battery or generator, drives electrons through a wire to the part of the machine that provides power or releases energy. The electrons then return along a wire to the source and complete the circuit. The source produces a certain number of volts, which is a measure of the electrical force that sends the electrons around the circuit. The current, which is the amount of electricity that flows, is measured in amps or amperes. The working part of the circuit has a resistance measured in ohms.

BATTERY

BULB

ELECTRON FLOW

ONE-WAY FLOW

LOOSE ELECTRONS MOVE FROM ONE ATOM TO NEXT

METAL ATOM

ELECTRON FROM SOURCE

ELECTRIC CHARGE

ELECTRIC CHARGE

DIRECT CURRENT (DC)

The electric current produced by a battery and solar cell is direct current. The electrons flow in one direction from the negative terminal of the source to the positive terminal. Although individual electrons move very slowly, the electric charge travels very much faster. This is because the arriving electrons collide with loose electrons in the metal atoms, making them leave one atom and collide with the next. Like shunting railway trucks, the shift in electrons progresses very rapidly along the wire, making the electric charge move very quickly.

TWO-WAY FLOW

ELECTRIC CHARGE

ELECTRIC CHARGE

ALTERNATING CURRENT (AC)

The mains supply is usually not direct current but alternating current. Here, the electrons move to and fro 50 times a second, because the terminals of the supply repeatedly change from positive to negative and vice-versa. This makes no difference to a light bulb, which lights up when the current flows in either direction.

BATTERIES

A battery produces an electric current when its terminals are connected to each other to form a circuit. All batteries contain two electrodes and an electrolyte, which produces the chemical reaction with the electrodes resulting in a current. In "dry" batteries, the electrolyte is a paste of powdered chemicals. "Wet" batteries, like those in cars, contain a liquid electrolyte.

A battery's voltage depends on the metals that are used in its electrodes.

LONG-LIFE BATTERY

Within the strong steel case is powdered zinc and a form of manganese oxide, both mixed with an alkaline electrolyte. The electrolyte causes a chemical reaction in which zinc changes to zinc oxide, causing zinc atoms to lose electrons and become positive zinc ions, and the manganese ions in the manganese oxide gain electrons. The battery produces 1.5 volts.

POSITIVE TERMINAL

POWDERED ZINC

MANGANESE OXIDE PLUS CARBON TO CONDUCT CURRENT

ELECTROLYTE

ABSORBENT SEPARATOR

STEEL CASE PASSES ELECTRONS TO MANGANESE

STEEL "NAIL" COLLECTS ELECTRONS FROM ZINC

NEGATIVE TERMINAL

NEGATIVE TERMINAL

POWDERED ZINC

MERCURY OXIDE

POSITIVE TERMINAL

ABSORBENT PAD CONTAINING ELECTROLYTE

BUTTON BATTERY

The battery contains powdered zinc and mercury oxide with an alkaline electrolyte. The zinc loses electrons as it becomes zinc oxide, while the mercury atoms gain electrons as the mercury oxide changes to mercury. The battery produces 1.35 volts.

CAR BATTERY

The battery in a car is designed to produce the strong current needed to turn the starter motor (see p.73). It does this by using a number of cells linked together. When running, the engine turns a generator which feeds current back into the battery to recharge it.

A car battery contains plates of lead oxide and lead metal, immersed in a sulphuric acid electrolyte. As the battery produces current, both kinds of plate change to lead sulphate. Feeding a current into the battery reverses the chemical reaction.

ELECTRON FLOW DURING DISCHARGE

ELECTRON FLOW DURING RECHARGE

SULPHURIC ACID

LEAD OXIDE

LEAD METAL

LEAD SULPHATE

LEAD SULPHATE

SULPHURIC ACID

CELL DIVIDER

NEGATIVE TERMINAL

CELL 1

CELL 2

CELL 3

CELL 4

CELL 5

CELL 6

CAR TEMPERATURE GAUGE

Electrical temperature gauges and thermometers depend on the changing resistance of a heat-sensitive element. The resistance varies with temperature, so that the amount of current flowing depends on how hot the element gets.

DIAL

NEEDLE

STABILIZER

LOW CURRENT

COIL

BIMETALLIC STRIP

BATTERY

COOL WATER

THERMISTOR

A thermistor is made of a semiconductor (see opposite page). Heat makes its atoms vibrate more, freeing electrons that carry current and thereby lowering its resistance. The stabilizer ensures that a constant voltage is fed to the thermistor.

ENGINE COOL

Before the engine has warmed up (*above*), only a small current flows through the gauge. From the battery, it passes through the stabilizer, coil and the thermistor in the water jacket of the car's engine. The thermistor's high resistance restricts the current and the needle indicates that the engine is cool.

ENGINE HOT

As the water in the engine heats up (*below*), the resistance of the thermistor decreases. This enables a larger current to flow through it, and the current heats the coil in the gauge. The heat bends the bimetallic strip (see p.154) which is linked to the needle.

HIGH CURRENT

STRIP BENDS AS TEMPERATURE INCREASES

HOT WATER

SOLAR CELL

A solar cell turns light into electricity. Large panels of cells power satellites while strips of a few cells provide the much smaller current needed to power calculators. Like many electronic devices, solar cells depend on semiconductors. These are materials in which the flow of electrons can be controlled – in this case, to generate a low current. Each cell contains two layers of different types of silicon. The silicon atoms are arranged in a lattice in which other atoms containing extra or fewer atoms are inserted.

ARRAY OF CELLS

SINGLE CELLS

CONTACT

N-TYPE LAYER

LIGHT RAYS

NEGATIVE TERMINAL

POSITIVE TERMINAL

P-TYPE LAYER

ATOMIC LATTICE

In n-type silicon some atoms have an extra or free electron, while in p-type silicon some have one less electron or a "hole". At the junction between the two, the extra electrons move from the n-type to the p-type silicon to fill the holes. This gives the p-type silicon a negative charge and the n-type a positive charge.

N-TYPE SILICON

ATOM WITH FREE ELECTRON

OUTER ELECTRONS

SILICON ATOMS

ATOM WITH HOLE

P-TYPE SILICON

INSIDE A CELL

An individual solar cell (above) is made of two kinds of silicon – an upper n-type layer and a lower p-type layer. When light strikes the cell (below), the rays penetrate the silicon and free electrons from the atoms. The charges on the two layers make the electrons move. The electrons are collected by the contact and the cell generates a current as the electrons flow.

N-TYPE

P-TYPE

HOLES

ELECTRON FLOW (CURRENT)

LIGHT STRIKES THE CELL

The light ray frees an electron which is pulled into the n-type layer by the positive charge there.

FILLING THE HOLE

An electron from an adjoining atom moves upwards to fill the hole left by the freed electron.

CURRENT FLOWS

Electrons produce a current as light frees them. Returning electrons fill the holes that they have left.

REMOTE CONTROL UNIT

DIODE

A diode allows current to flow in one direction but not in the other. It consists of a *p-n* semiconductor junction (see p.271). When a positive terminal is connected to the *p*-type layer (*far right*), the positive charge of the terminal attracts electrons and a full current flows. On reversing the connections (*right*), the negative charge of the *p*-type layer opposes electron flow. A low current flows as a few electrons freed by atomic vibrations cross the juction.

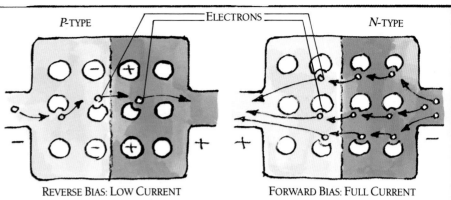

P-TYPE — ELECTRONS — N-TYPE

REVERSE BIAS: LOW CURRENT   FORWARD BIAS: FULL CURRENT

PHOTODIODE

P-TYPE   N-TYPE

RAY

ELECTRON FLOW INCREASES

POWER SOURCE

DECODER

A microchip connected to the photodiode receives a series of electrical pulses in binary code as the beam flashes on and off. A bar-code reader, digital film sound, and compact disc player work in a similar way (see pp.334-7).

POWER LEADS

Pressing a button on the remote control unit for a television or video recorder transmits a beam of invisible infra-red rays to the set. The beam contains a digital code signal similar to that given when a key on a computer keyboard is pressed (see p.317). The receiver unit in the set detects the signal and decodes it, for example to change channel or volume. Both the transmitter and receiver work with diodes, but in each case the diodes function in opposite ways.

RECEIVER UNIT

The receiver unit contains a photodiode, which is a diode sensitive to light or infra-red rays. It is connected in reverse bias so that normally only a low current flows through it. When rays strike the diode, they free some electrons, increasing the current to produce a signal which goes to the decoder.

INFRA-RED BEAM

PHOTODIODE

CIRCUIT BOARD

RESISTORS

INDICATOR LED

CAPACITOR

KEY

MICROCHIP

CONNECTOR

TRANSISTOR

TRANSMITTER LED

LIGHT-EMITTING
DIODE (LED)

ELECTRONS AND
HOLES COMBINE

N-TYPE

LIGHT OR
INFRA-RED
RAYS

ELECTRONS
ENTER DIODE

P-TYPE

ELECTRONS
LEAVE DIODE

ENCODER CHIP

POWER SOURCE

RANSMITTER UNIT

his hand-held transmitter unit contains keys
nd electronic components similar to those in
computer keyboard (see p.317). Pressing
key routes a signal to the encoder chip, which
ends a series of electrical pulses to the LED (light-
mitting diode). The pulses form a signal in binary
de, and the LED flashes on and off to send the
gnal to the receiver. An indicator LED lights up
the key is pressed.
A light-emitting diode is connected to a
ower source in forward bias. Electrons leaving
e semiconductor atoms create holes that are
en filled by arriving electrons. As the electrons
d atoms combine, they produce light or
fra-red rays.

MAGNETISM

ON SHOEING A MAMMOTH

Working mammoths wear out their shoes with great rapidity, so it was with extreme interest that I watched a blacksmith fitting new improved shoes to a volunteer beast. The test had mixed results. Shoe wear was reduced to zero, but only because a strange and powerful attraction between opposite shoes prevented all movement on the part of the wearer.

WHERE NORTH MEETS SOUTH

A magnet is a seemingly ordinary piece of metal or ceramic that is surrounded by an invisible field of force which affects any magnetic material within it. All magnets have two poles. When magnets are brought together, a north pole always attracts a south pole, while pairs of like poles repel each other. Bar magnets are the simplest permanent magnets. Horseshoe magnets, which have such an unfortunate effect when used as mammoth footwear, are bar magnets bent so that their poles are brought close together.

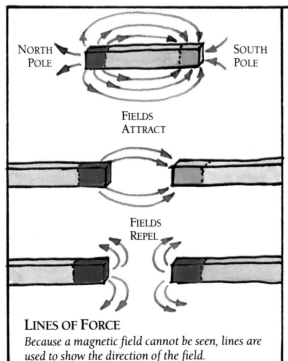

NORTH POLE

SOUTH POLE

FIELDS ATTRACT

FIELDS REPEL

LINES OF FORCE

Because a magnetic field cannot be seen, lines are used to show the direction of the field.

MAGNETIC ATTRACTION

The lines of force extend from the north pole of one magnet to the south pole of the other, pulling the magnets together.

ON A MAMMOTH CLOTHES-DRIER

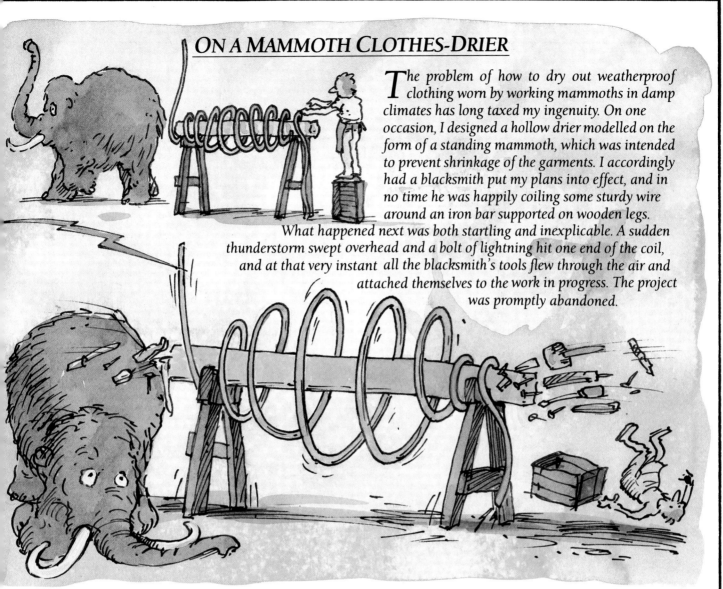

*T*he problem of how to dry out weatherproof clothing worn by working mammoths in damp climates has long taxed my ingenuity. On one occasion, I designed a hollow drier modelled on the form of a standing mammoth, which was intended to prevent shrinkage of the garments. I accordingly had a blacksmith put my plans into effect, and in no time he was happily coiling some sturdy wire around an iron bar supported on wooden legs.

What happened next was both startling and inexplicable. A sudden thunderstorm swept overhead and a bolt of lightning hit one end of the coil, and at that very instant all the blacksmith's tools flew through the air and attached themselves to the work in progress. The project was promptly abandoned.

ELECTRICAL MAGNETS

When an electric current flows through a wire, a magnetic field is produced around it. The field produced by a single wire is not very strong, so to increase it, the wire is wound into a coil. This concentrates the magnetic field, especially if an iron bar is placed in the centre of the field. Electromagnets can be very powerful — as the blacksmith finds out. A sudden burst of current momentarily transforms his clothes-drier into a powerful electromagnet which attracts all nearby iron objects to its poles.

MAGNETIC FIELD — WIRE

FLOW OF ELECTRONS

MAGNETIC FIELD — FLOW OF ELECTRONS

WIRE

SINGLE WIRE
The lines of force form circles around the wire.

COIL OF WIRE

The lines of force of all the loops in a coil combine to produce a field that is similar to the field around a bar magnet. The poles of the electromagnet are at either end of the coil.

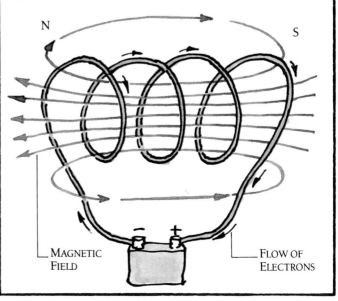

N   S

MAGNETIC FIELD   FLOW OF ELECTRONS

MAGNETS AT WORK

MAGNETIC COMPASS

The Earth has its own magnetic field. A compass needle will align itself so that it points towards the north and south magnetic poles, along lines of force which run in the direction of the field. The magnetic poles are situated away from the geographical poles.

MAGNETIC INDUCTION

A magnet is able to pick up a piece of steel or iron because its magnetic field flows into the metal. This turns the metal into a temporary magnet, and the two magnets then attract each other.

NORTH MAGNETIC POLE

NORTH POLE

LINES OF FORCE

COMPASS

SOUTH POLE

SOUTH MAGNETIC POLE

POLE OF PERMANENT MAGNET OR ELECTROMAGNET

LINES OF FORCE

DOMAINS

Inside the metal are small magnetic regions called domains. The magnetic field lines up their poles, which otherwise cancel each other out, so that the metal becomes a magnet.

UNMAGNETIZED IRON

MAGNETIZED IRON

SUSPENSION CABLE

STEEL CASING

POWER LINE

COIL

NON-MAGNETIC COIL PLATE

ELECTROMAGNET

An electromagnet is a coil of wire wound around an iron core. When current flows through the coil, it creates a magnetic field. The strength of the field depends on the current. Large electromagnets are strong enough to lift scrapped cars; much smaller electromagnets are used medically for tasks such as extracting metal splinters.

METAL BAR   MAGNET

SPRING

ELECTRICAL CONTACTS

BURGLAR ALARM

A magnetic sensor can detect the opening of a door or window. A permanent magnet is mounted on the window or door and a special switch on the frame. When the window or door is closed, the magnetic field attracts a metal bar, keeping the switch on.

ALARM SOUNDS

If the window or door is opened, the magnet moves and no longer attracts the metal bar. The spring pulls the bar back, opening the contacts. This cuts the circuit, which activates a mechanism that rings the alarm.

MAGNETIC MACHINES

A great number of machines contain electromagnets. Many use them in their electric motors (see pp.300–1) to provide power. Electromagnets are also used to store signals in tape recorders, video recorders and computer disc drives, to produce sound in bells, buzzers, loudspeakers and telephones, and to deflect electron beams in television cameras and receivers.

THE ELECTRIC BELL

BELL

HAMMER

ARMATURE

CONTACTS

SPRING

ELECTRO-MAGNET

CURRENT FLOWS

BATTERY

BUTTON

O ne of the many everyday uses of electromagnetism is the electric bell. The button at the door is an electric switch that sends current from a power source such as a battery to the striking mechanism. This makes a hammer move to and fro several times a second, sounding a metal bell. An electromagnet and a spring alternately pull the hammer.

PRESSING THE BUTTON

When the button is pressed, the contacts are first closed. Current flows through the contacts and the spring to the electromagnet, which produces a magnetic field. This field attracts the iron armature, which moves towards the electromagnet against the spring and makes the hammer strike the bell.

THE BELL SOUNDS

As the hammer strikes the bell, the movement of the armature opens the contacts. The current stops flowing to the electromagnet, which loses its magnetism. The spring pulls the armature back, and the hammer moves away from the bell. The contacts then close again, and the cycle repeats itself for as long as the button is pressed.

HORN

THE ELECTRIC HORN

COIL OF
ELECTROMAGNET

MOVING BAR

CONTACTS

WIRES FROM
BATTERY

DIAPHRAGM

The horn of a motor vehicle is another example of the use of magnetism to produce sound by a simple vibration. The mechanism of a horn is rather similar to that of an electric bell, with a set of contacts repeatedly closing and opening to interrupt the flow of current to an electromagnet. Here, an iron bar moves up and down inside the coil of the electromagnet as the magnetic field switches on and off. The bar is attached to a diaphragm, which vibrates rapidly and gives out a loud sound.

The horn, as here, may have an actual bell-shaped horn attached to the diaphragm. This resonates to give a penetrating note and projects the sound forwards.

TO POWER SUPPLY

STATOR COIL

COMMUTATOR

BRUSH

ELECTRIC MOTOR

ROTOR
The central rotor contains several coils. As it rotates, each coil is in turn supplied with current by the brushes on the commutator.

STATOR
The stator contains coils that are fed with the electric current supplied to the rotor. This produces the magnetic field that interacts with the field of the electrified rotor coil.

The electric motor is the most convenient of all sources of motive power. It is clean and silent, starts instantly, and can be built large enough to drive the world's fastest trains or small enough to work a wristwatch. Its source of energy can be delivered along wires from an external power source or contained in small batteries.

There are several different kinds of electric motors. Many household machines contain the universal motor shown here. This motor gets its name because it can run on both the direct current provided by a battery and the alternating current supplied by the mains. It is like a direct current motor but has an electromagnet called a stator instead of a permanent magnet, and a rotating set of coils called a rotor. When direct current is used, the rotor field reverses every half turn and the stator field does not. With alternating current, the opposite happens. Either way, the rotor keeps on turning.

LINES OF FORCE
At these points, all the lines of magnetic force are close together and have the same direction. This produces a strong repulsion between the magnet and the coil.

DIRECT CURRENT MOTOR
In a simple electric motor, direct current is fed to a coil that can rotate between the poles of a magnet. The magnetic field of the coil and that of the magnet interact and force the coil to turn. The coil drives the shaft of the motor.

NORTH POLE OF MAGNET

COIL

ELECTRON FLOW

SOUTH POLE OF MAGNET

POWER SUPPLY

BATTERY

COMMUTATOR
The commutator reverses the flow of current every half turn of the coil. This is necessary to reverse the magnetic field of the coil and keep the coil moving.

MAGLEV TRAIN

A maglev has no wheels, instead using magnetic fields to levitate itself above a track. Thus freed from friction with the rails, the train can float along the track. The train shown here uses the attractive system of levitation, in which electromagnets attached to the train run below the suspension rail and rise towards it to lift the train.

SUSPENSION RAIL

ELECTROMAGNET

LINEAR MOTOR

REACTION RAIL

MOTOR COILS

REACTION RAIL

S N S N

N S N S N

LINEAR INDUCTION MOTOR

A form of electric motor called an induction motor drives the maglev train. Coils on the train generate a magnetic field in which the poles shift along the train. The field induces electric currents in the reaction rail, which in turn generates its own magnetic field. The two fields interact so that the shifting field pulls the floating train along the track.

The disk drive of a computer uses electromagnetis to "write" or store programs and data. The rea write head converts electric code signals from t computer into magnetic codes recorded on the surfa of the disk; the drive then reverses this process to "rea the disk (see p.333).

A disk drive contains two electric motors – a di motor to rotate the disk at high speed and a head mot to move the head across the disk. The drive

SECTORS OF MAGNETIC CODE SIGNALS

FLOPPY DISK
A floppy disk is inserted into the drive by hand. The disk is protected by a sleeve in which a window is cut to expose the surface of the disk. Inside the drive, the head travels along the window as the disk rotates inside the sleeve.

TIMING HOLE
Some disks contain a hole through which a light shines onto a detector so that the drive can find the required sectors.

SLEEVE

WINDOW

DRIVE

STEPPER MOTOR

The stepper motor in a disk drive contains a rotor that is permanent cylindrical magnet with many poles around it circumference. It rotates inside two sets of stator coils, each of which has a row of metal teeth. Sending an electr current to a coil (*right*) magnetizes its teeth with alternate north and south poles. Reversing the current (*far right*) reverses the sequence of the poles. The two rows of teeth on the upper and lower stators are placed out of alignme and the rotor moves to position each pole with a pair of overlapping teeth having the opposite pole. Signals from the drive controller to the stator coils change the teeth poles so that the rotor turns to follow them.

DISK DRIVE

must work with very great precision, because a tiny error in the position of the head could corrupt the program or data and stop the computer. The head is therefore moved by a stepper motor which, instead of turning constantly, obeys a control signal to rotate by an exact amount.

DISK MOTOR

PRESSURE PAD

BELT

GUIDE RAILS

RINGS GRIP DISK

BELT

READ-WRITE HEAD
The head contains a small electromagnet to produce magnetic signals.

STATOR COILS

ROTOR

HEAD MOTOR (STEPPER MOTOR)

UPPER TEETH

LOWER TEETH

UPPER STATOR

LOWER STATOR

CURRENT

COIL

REVERSED POLES

FIRST SIGNAL
Each north pole on the rotor lines up with an overlapping pair of south poles on the stator teeth, while each south pole on the rotor lines up with a pair of north poles on the teeth.

COIL

ROTOR POLES

ROTOR

ROTOR TURNS

SECOND SIGNAL
The current to the upper stator reverses so that the sequence of poles on the upper teeth reverses. Each pole shifts by one tooth clockwise, relative to the lower teeth. The rotor turns by one tooth as its poles line up with the new pairs.

CURRENT REVERSES

ELECTRIC GENERATOR

MAGNET

COIL

NORTH POLE

SOUTH POLE

NORTH POLE

SOUTH POLE

LINES OF FORCE

ELECTRON FLOW

CARBON BRUSHES

DRIVE

COMMUTATOR

SLIP RINGS

ELECTRON FLOW

BRUSHES

DC GENERATOR

In the coil of a generator, the flow of electrons in the wire reverses every half turn. The split ring of the commutator also rotates, contacting each half with alternate brushes. In this way, one brush is always negative and the other positive so that direct current is produced.

A n electric generator works by electromagnetic induction – it uses magnetism to make electricity. The power source spins a coil between the poles of a magnet or electromagnet. As it cuts through the lines of force, an electric current flows through the coil.

AC GENERATOR – FIRST HALF TURN

An alternating current (AC) generator contains two slip rings connected to the end of the coil. As the current reverses in the coil, an alternating current emerges from the brushes. When part of the coil cuts the lines of force near the magnet's north pole, the electrons move up the wire, producing a positive charge at the lower slip ring.

POWER SUPPLY

T he large generators in power stations are powered by steam turbines, water turbines or gas turbines, which work like the turbines in jet engines (see p.160). The electricity reaches our homes through a network of power lines carrying current at a very high voltage, which reduces energy losses in transmission. Transformers then step down the voltage to different levels for use in industry and in the home.

POWER LINE

At high voltage, the current is capable of sparking considerable distances through air. For safety, the lines are suspended from high pylons by long insulators.

GENERATOR

The generator produces a powerful current at several thousand volts.

TRANSMISSION TRANSFORMER

This steps up the voltage to several hundred thousand volts to reduce energy losses.

TRANSFORMER

LOW VOLTAGE

HIGH VOLTAGE

IRON CORE

NORTH POLE

SOUTH POLE

SLIP RINGS

ELECTRON FLOW

BRUSHES

AC GENERATOR – SECOND HALF TURN

The same part of the coil has now turned to cut the lines of force near the magnet's south pole. Electrons now flow down the wire to produce a negative charge at the lower slip ring, reversing the current flow. The frequency of the current reversal produced by an AC generator depends on the speed at which the coil rotates.

A transformer changes the voltage of an alternating current. The input current goes to a primary coil wound around an iron core. The output current emerges from a secondary coil also wound around the core. The alternating input current produces a magnetic field that continually switches on and off. The core transfers this field to the secondary coil, where it induces an output current. The degree of change in voltage depends on the ratio of turns in the coils; the tranformer shown here steps up or steps down the voltage three times.

DISTRIBUTION TRANSFORMER

This transformer steps the voltage down to several thousand volts for distribution. The current may go directly to factories with high-voltage machines and to high-speed electric trains.

HOME SUPPLY TRANSFORMER

Before the current reaches the home, a further transformer steps the distribution voltage down to 240 volts.

THE TWO-WAY SWITCH

Once a supply of electricity has entered the nome, it is metered and then distributed to power points and light switches. The two-way switch is a common part of a domestic electric circuit. In it, a pair of switches is connected so that pressing either turns a light on or off. Each switch has two sets of contacts linked by a pair of wires. Moving the switch up or down closes one set of contacts and opens the other set. To turn the light on, the sets of contacts at the ends of either of the two wires must close.

Many appliances have a third wire connected to their metal casing which links through the wiring circuit to the ground. If the appliance is faulty and a live wire touches the case, the strong current is immediately conducted to the ground.

OPEN CONTACTS

CLOSED CONTACTS

METER AND SAFETY SYSTEM

The current flows through a meter, which works like an electric motor to turn an indicator. It then enters a box of fuses or circuit breakers. If the current in any part of the circuit surges to a dangerously high level, a fuse will melt and break the circuit. A circuit breaker cuts off the supply by using an electromagnetic switch activated by the high current.

OPEN CONTACTS

CLOSED CONTACTS

POWER SOCKETS

EARTH SOCKET

EARTH WIRE

CAR IGNITION SYSTEM

Electromagnetism enables a car to start and also keeps it running by producing the sparks that ignite the fuel. At a twist of the ignition key, the starter motor draws direct current from the battery to start the engine. Producing the powerful magnetic field needed in the starter motor requires a hefty current, one which is too strong to pass through the ignition switch. So a solenoid, activated by a low current passing through the ignition switch, passes a high current to the starter motor.

In electromechanical ignition systems, like the one shown here, the contact breaker in the distributor opens and interrupts the supply of low-voltage current to the induction coil. The magnetic field around the primary winding collapses, inducing a high voltage in the secondary winding. The distributor then passes the current to the spark plugs. In electronic ignition, the contact breaker is replaced by an electronic switch.

CURRENT TO INDUCTION COIL

LOW CURRENT TO SOLENOID

IGNITION SWITCH
The key has two positions. It first activates the solenoid, and then passes current to the induction coil.

SOLENOID
In the solenoid, the low current from the ignition switch flows through a coil, producing a magnetic field. This moves the iron plunger to close the contacts and pass a high current to the starter motor. A spring returns the plunger as soon as the ignition key is released, breaking the circuit.

CONTACTS

COIL

PLUNGER

FLYWHEEL

HIGH CURRENT TO STARTER MOTOR

STARTER MOTOR
A very large current flows through the motor to produce the powerful force needed to start the flywheel turning (see p.73).

BATTERY
One terminal of the battery is connected to the car body, which serves as a return path for the circuits in the car's electrical systems.

TERMINAL CONNECTED TO CAR BODY

CURRENT

ROTATING ARM

SPARK PLUG TERMINALS

SPRING

CAPACITOR

CONTACT BREAKER POINTS

DISTRIBUTOR

DISTRIBUTOR SHAFT

INDUCTION COIL

PRIMARY WINDING (FEW TURNS)

SECONDARY WINDING (MANY TURNS)

CAMSHAFT TURNED BY ENGINE

HIGH-VOLTAGE CURRENT TO SPARK PLUG

CERAMIC INSULATOR

SPARK PLUG

ELECTRODE

CYLINDER HEAD

CYLINDER

SPARK GAP

ELECTRODE

SPARK

SENSORS AND DETECTORS

ON MAMMOTH SENSITIVITY

*E*motionally and physically, mammoths are highly sensitive creatures. Their physical sensitivity can be exploited in numerous ways, assuming always that their emotional sensitivity can be controlled. A selection of such applications is here depicted. In figure 1, the trunk of a sleeping mammoth is used as a pressure-operated alarm to frighten away burglars.

*I*n figure 2, the trunk of a sleeping mammoth is secured to the ceiling to act as a smoke detector. Plants obscure the creature's bulk and also provide it with occasional snacks.

fig 1

fig 2

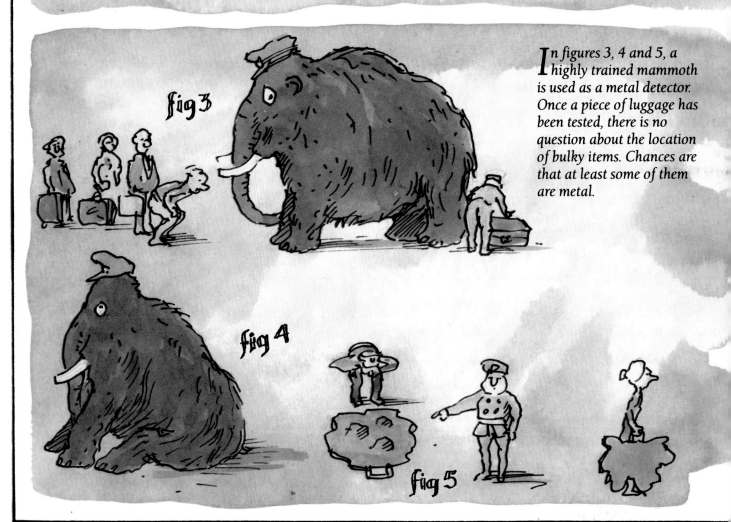

fig 3

fig 4

fig 5

*I*n figures 3, 4 and 5, a highly trained mammoth is used as a metal detector. Once a piece of luggage has been tested, there is no question about the location of bulky items. Chances are that at least some of them are metal.

*I*n figures 6 and 7, the mammoth's trunk is employed as a highly sensitive mobile breath analyser.

fig 6

fig 7

*F*igure 8 illustrates my automated ski lift. By continually consuming water, the mammoth's weight increases until it exceeds that of the loaded car, which automatically ascends.

fig 8

*F*igure 9 shows the specially designed squeezer. This forces the water out of the mammoth so the car automatically descends.

fig 9

DISCOVERY AND MEASUREMENT

Sensors and detectors are devices that are used to detect the presence of something and often to measure it. Alarm systems sense the direct evidence of unwanted visitations, such as the tell-tale tread of a burglar or the airborne particles of smoke from a fire. Other sensors and detectors employ penetrating rays or magnetic fields to locate and reveal objects that cannot be seen. Measuring instruments, from seismographs to radar speed traps, are sensors and detectors that react to something specific and then register its quantity.

Sensors and detectors are also very important as essential components of automatic machines. Many machines, for example the autopilot in an aircraft, use feedback. This means that their sensors measure the machine's performance and then feed the results back to control the power output. This in turn affects the performance, which is measured by the sensors... and so on in an endless loop. By sensing their own performance, automatic machines keep within set limits. The mammoth-powered weight-sensing ski lift is a simple automatic machine.

SEISMOGRAPH

Seismographs can locate the origin of an earthquake and measure its force. The sudden movement of underground rock in an earthquake generates seismic waves that travel through the Earth and shake the ground. A seismograph is very sensitive to vibrations, even those far from the earthquake where the vibrations are extremely weak and records them as zigzag lines on paper.

VERTICAL VIBRATIONS

VERTICAL PENDULUM

PEN

SPRING

MOVEMENTS OF PAPER

GROUND VIBRATIONS

THREE AT ONCE
Two of the pendulums record horizontal vibrations in two directions at right angles, and the third records vertical vibrations.

HORIZONTAL PENDULUM

HORIZONTAL PENDULUM

HORIZONTAL VIBRATIONS

HORIZONTAL VIBRATIONS

AIR BAG

In front of and possibly to each side of the occupants of a car is a concealed bag and gas generator containing an igniter and solid propellant. If the car crashes, a crash sensor triggers the igniter, which fires the propellant. A large volume of nitrogen gas (not air) is generated and inflates the bag in about 30 milliseconds. The bag emerges, and then deflates gently as the head of the occupant sinks into it.

AIR BAG WARNING LIGHT

CRASH SENSOR

AIR BAG INFLATES

SEAT BELT HOLDS BODY

By comparing the arrival times of the seismic waves at several seismographs in different places, the location of the earthquake can be pinpointed. The strength of the vibrations enables the intensity of the earthquake to be estimated. Seismographs can also detect vibrations from underground nuclear tests. The simple seismograph shown here operates mechanically; more advanced seismographs have vibration detectors that work electromagnetically.

BASIC SEISMOGRAPH

The seismograph is basically a pendulum mounted horizontally or vertically. It has a heavy mass with a high inertia (see p.70). As the ground shakes, the rest of the detector vibrates around the mass and a pen fixed to the pendulum marks the vibrations on a moving roll of paper.

CRASH SENSOR

The sensor that detects the sudden deceleration of the car in a crash is a microchip containing a tiny square linked by thin strips to a frame.

STRIPS

SQUARE

Because of the square's inertia, the movements of the car stretch or compress the strips, changing their electrical resistance in the same way as a strain gauge (see p.321). In a crash, the sensor puts out a strong signal and this triggers the air bag.

AUTOPILOT

The guidance system of an aircraft operates the controls to correct drifting and keep it on course. It has two main parts. The autopilot keeps the aircraft flying at a set height and direction, using gyroscopes (see p.76) to detect changes in height or direction. The other part of the guidance system continually checks the position to keep the aircraft to its route, altering height and direction when required. In it, accelerometers mounted on a level platform stabilized by gyroscopes measure the forces acting on the plane. Inertia causes a spring-mounted armature to remain still as coils beneath it move, inducing an electric signal in the coils that measures the force.

ARMATURE

SPRING

COILS

ALTERNATING CURRENT

OUTPUT SIGNAL

MOTION SIGNAL
The alternating current produces a magnetic field that is disturbed when the coils move relative to the armature. The changing field produces a signal in the outer coils.

STEADY FLIGHT

DECELERATION

ACCELERATION

NORTH-SOUTH ACCELEROMETER

EAST-WEST ACCELEROMETER

VERTICAL ACCELEROMETER

INERTIAL GUIDANCE
Inertial guidance systems contain three accelerometers mounted on a stable platform. They sense vertical forces and north-south and east-west horizontal forces. In this way, the accelerometers can detect all the movements of the aircraft. Their signals go to a computer that calculates the aircraft's current altitude and latitude and longitude to keep it on course.

BREATH TESTER

Several sensors are designed to detect the presence of specific substances. A breath tester detects and measures the concentration of alcohol in the breath, which is an accurate indication of the amount of alcohol in the blood. Breath testers use either a fuel cell (shown here) or infra-red rays, which are absorbed by alcohol vapour. Testing drivers with a breath tester enables police to check alcohol levels in a matter of seconds.

DIAPHRAGM   SET BUTTON

READ BUTTON

AIR

ELECTRODES

MICROCHIP

1 PREPARING THE TESTER
The SET button is pressed first to lower the diaphragm and empty the fuel cell of air. The fuel cell contains two platinum electrodes connected to a microchip.

DISPLAY READS ZERO

BATTERY

LIGHT A   LIGHT B

TIMER

PRESSURE SENSOR

2 TAKING A READING
The driver blows into a tube until first light A and then light B come on. The lights are linked to a pressure sensor and timer to provide the correct breath sample. The READ button is then pressed, which raises the diaphragm to admit the sample to the fuel cell. Alcohol in the air causes the fuel cell to produce a current.

BREATH SAMPLE

3 ALCOHOL LEVEL
The microchip measures the voltage of the cell and converts it into a signal that goes to the display. This shows the alcohol level.

265

SMOKE DETECTOR

MICROCHIP

BATTERY

ELECTRODES

DETECTION CHAMBER

RADIOACTIVE SOURCE

ALARM

ELECTRODE

IONS

ELECTRODE

Smoke detectors can sense the small particles of smoke that rise from a smouldering object, and raise the alarm before fire breaks out. They work in two ways. Optical detectors use a light beam and light sensor that react to anything obscuring the beam. Ionizing detectors of the kind shown here are electrical sensors that can detect smaller particles than their optical equivalents.

The ionizing smoke detector contains a chamber in which a low electric current flows through the air. Smoke particles entering the chamber increase its electrical resistance so that less current flows. A microchip responds to the drop in current (and a failing battery) by switching on an alarm.

IONIZING RAYS

Rays from the radioactive source ionize the atoms in the air of the detection chamber, giving them positive and negative electric charges. The charged atoms or ions carry an electric current between the charged electrodes. Smoke particles entering the chamber attract the ions and reduce the current.

SMOKE
ATTRACTS IONS

HIGH-VOLTAGE SUPPLY

OIL

COPPER ANODE

X-RAY BEAM

TUNGSTEN TARGET

ELECTRON BEAM

FILAMENT

CATHODE
A heated filament produces the beam of electrons. The X-ray tube works at a very high voltage produced by a transformer.

OIL

DENTAL X-RAY TUBE

Inside the X-ray tube, a negatively charged electrode, or cathode, produces a beam of electrons that strikes a tungsten target in a positively charged copper anode. The electrons make the tungsten atoms emit X-rays, and the surface is angled so that an X-ray beam emerges from a window in the machine. The window is transparent to X-rays but the rest of the tube is encased in lead, which absorbs the other rays produced. The copper anode conducts the considerable heat created in the target to the oil bath that surrounds the glass envelope.

WINDOW

FILM HOLDER

VACUUM INSIDE GLASS ENVELOPE

LEAD CASING

FILLING

X-RAY IMAGE OF TEETH

X-RAY PRODUCTION

Millions of high-speed electrons bombard the tungsten target to create a powerful X-ray beam. As the electrons meet the atoms of tungsten in the target, they interact with the electrons and nucleus in each atom. An incoming electron may be slowed and deflected by the nucleus, giving off X-rays as it loses energy. It may also knock an inner electron out of a tungsten atom; an outer electron then moves in and takes its place, emitting X-rays as it does so.

X-RAYS

Most of us are familiar with X-rays from pictures that the dentist takes to examine our teeth. The X-ray machine produces a beam of invisible rays. These penetrate the teeth and strike a piece of photographic film mounted in a holder clenched between the teeth. The dentist develops the film and sees a picture that shows the interior of the teeth and also any defects that need attention.

X-rays are used to look inside many things in the same kind of way. They are electromagnetic rays similar to light rays (see p.178) but with greater energy. They easily penetrate materials made of light atoms, which include the atoms in flesh. Heavier atoms, such as those of most metals, absorb them. Teeth and bones contain some calcium, which is a metal, and so the teeth and metal fillings inside them show up.

HIGH-VOLTAGE SUPPLY

FILM HOLDER

The plastic holder contains a piece of film that is exposed by X-rays, which pass straight through the outer covering. The parts of the teeth that absorb the rays show up in white on the X-ray picture.

FILM

X-RAY TUBE

SCREEN

BAGGAGE SCANNER

Airport security requires both rapid and effective searching of passenger's baggage by a scanner. This uses X-rays to penetrate the baggage and show up metal objects inside. A very sensitive detector is used so that a low dose of X-rays is given, thereby avoiding exposure of films in the baggage.

THIN X-RAY BEAM

LOW-DOSE SCREENING

The baggage moves along a conveyor belt beneath an X-ray tube that generates a pencil-thin beam of X-rays. The beam scans the baggage and strikes a row of photodiode sensors (see p.272) under the belt. Signals from the photodiodes go to a computer, which builds up an image of the interior of the baggage on the inspection screen.

PHOTODIODES

CONVEYOR BELT

SONAR

Sonar, which stands for SOund Navigation And Ranging, is a sensing system that detects objects with sound waves. It is mainly used underwater, where other kinds of waves and rays do not travel so well. Ships employ sonar to measure the depth of water, to find shoals of fish and to detect wrecks. A transducer emits a pulse of sound, which travels down through the water and is reflected back. The transducer picks up this echo, and the sonar converts the time it takes the sound to return into a value for the object's distance.

ECHO SOUNDING

It takes 1 second for an echo to return from an object 750 metres (2,500 feet) deep. The returning echoes of sound produce an electric signal that goes to a screen display. The time differences of the echoes show on the display as points of light in different positions. In this way, a profile of the water beneath the ship is seen complete with depth scale, giving the location of the bottom and shoals of fish.

HULL OF SHIP

SWIVEL MOUNTING

TRANSDUCER

A transducer is a device that converts one kind of signal into another. In sonar, a transducer on the hull of a ship converts an electric pulse into a pulse of sound; it then converts the returning sound waves back into an electric signal. It is similar to a combined loudspeaker and microphone.

TRANSDUCERS

OUTGOING SOUND PULSES

RETURNING ECHOES

HORIZONTAL SWEEP OF SCANNING BEAM

FORWARD MOVEMENT OF BEAM

SCANNING SONAR

It is possible to obtain images of the ocean floor by scanning a sonar beam at an angle across the floor. A computer can build a hazy image from the intensity of the echoes. The beam may scan forwards and to the side.

ULTRASOUND SCANNER

The principles of sonar are put to important use in the ultrasound scanner. This machine can produce an image of an unborn child inside its mother. Pulses of sound from a probe scan across the interior of the body. A computer uses the returning echoes to build up a cross-section image of the mother and baby.

The scanner produces pulses of ultrasound, which is sound with a frequency range that lies above the limit of human hearing. Ultrasound is used, not to spare the ears of doctor, mother and baby, but because it has a shorter wavelength and so enables the computer to produce more detail in the image.

1 PROBE *emits ultrasound pulse.*

WOMB
PULSE
ABDOMEN
BODY OF BABY
PROBE

2 ECHO *returns from womb.*

PULSE
CONTINUES
ECHO FROM WOMB

3 ECHO *returns from baby.*

ECHO FROM BABY

VERTICAL SWEEP OF SCANNING BEAM

COMPUTER

A computer receives electrical signals from the probe as the echoes return. The computer plots points of light on the screen that show echoes from various depths. As the ultrasound beam scans across, the points build into lines that form an image.

WHALE'S BACKBONE
BABY WHALE

SCREEN DISPLAY

FORWARD MOVEMENT OF BEAM

RADAR

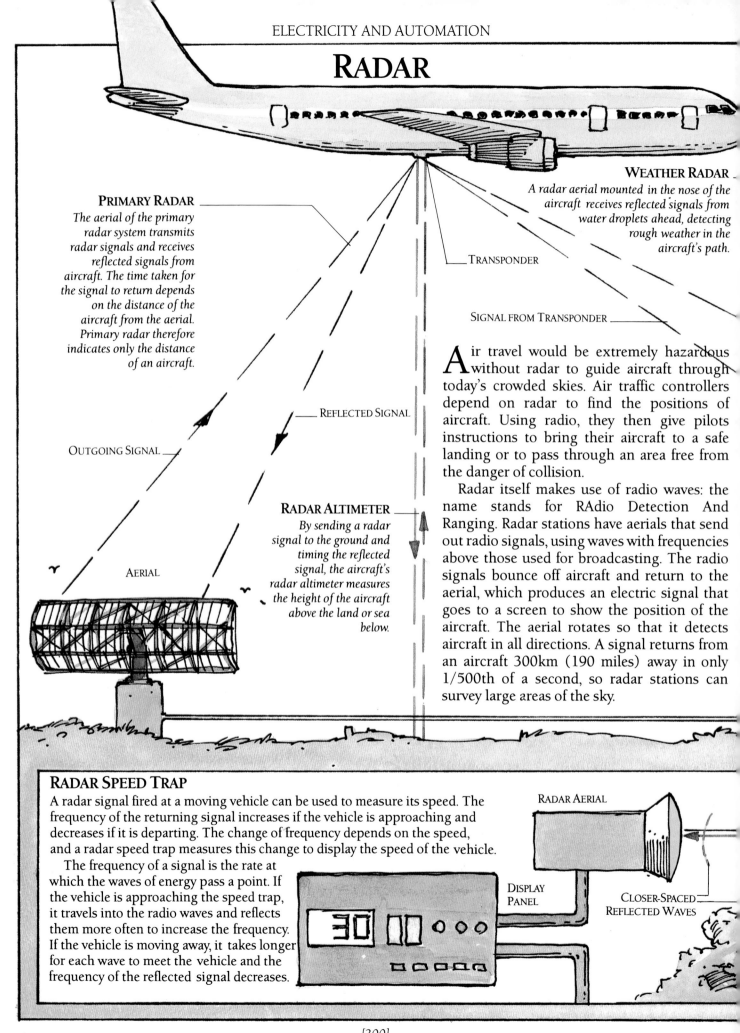

WEATHER RADAR
A radar aerial mounted in the nose of the aircraft receives reflected signals from water droplets ahead, detecting rough weather in the aircraft's path.

PRIMARY RADAR
The aerial of the primary radar system transmits radar signals and receives reflected signals from aircraft. The time taken for the signal to return depends on the distance of the aircraft from the aerial. Primary radar therefore indicates only the distance of an aircraft.

TRANSPONDER

SIGNAL FROM TRANSPONDER

REFLECTED SIGNAL

OUTGOING SIGNAL

RADAR ALTIMETER
By sending a radar signal to the ground and timing the reflected signal, the aircraft's radar altimeter measures the height of the aircraft above the land or sea below.

AERIAL

Air travel would be extremely hazardous without radar to guide aircraft through today's crowded skies. Air traffic controllers depend on radar to find the positions of aircraft. Using radio, they then give pilots instructions to bring their aircraft to a safe landing or to pass through an area free from the danger of collision.

Radar itself makes use of radio waves: the name stands for RAdio Detection And Ranging. Radar stations have aerials that send out radio signals, using waves with frequencies above those used for broadcasting. The radio signals bounce off aircraft and return to the aerial, which produces an electric signal that goes to a screen to show the position of the aircraft. The aerial rotates so that it detects aircraft in all directions. A signal returns from an aircraft 300km (190 miles) away in only 1/500th of a second, so radar stations can survey large areas of the sky.

RADAR SPEED TRAP

A radar signal fired at a moving vehicle can be used to measure its speed. The frequency of the returning signal increases if the vehicle is approaching and decreases if it is departing. The change of frequency depends on the speed, and a radar speed trap measures this change to display the speed of the vehicle.

The frequency of a signal is the rate at which the waves of energy pass a point. If the vehicle is approaching the speed trap, it travels into the radio waves and reflects them more often to increase the frequency. If the vehicle is moving away, it takes longer for each wave to meet the vehicle and the frequency of the reflected signal decreases.

RADAR AERIAL

DISPLAY PANEL

CLOSER-SPACED REFLECTED WAVES

OUTGOING SIGNAL

SECONDARY RADAR

The aerial of the secondary radar system sends signals to transponders on aircraft. In reply, each transponder sends back a signal giving the aircraft's height and identity.

AERIAL

RADAR DISPLAY

In a radar display (*below*), the positions of aircraft within range of the radar station appear on a screen marked with a map of the area. As the primary aerial rotates, the positions of aircraft returning radar signals light up. The computer displays the information from secondary radar beside the position of the aircraft. This information gives the aircraft's flight number (in this case TW754), its destination (LL or London) and its current height (300 or 30,000 feet). In this way, the screen displays the information that the air traffic controller requires.

TW 754
300 LL

OUTGOING
RADIO WAVES

METAL DETECTOR

The technology that enables us to discover buried treasure also tests coins in ticket machines or vending machines, invisibly frisks people at airports and controls traffic lights. All these machines are basically metal detectors, and they work by electromagnetic induction (see pp.284-5).

When a piece of metal passes through a magnetic field or the field passes through the metal, the field produces electric eddy currents that circulate in the metal. The eddy currents in turn produce their own magnetic field, and metal detectors work by detecting this field.

DETECTOR COILS
The transmit and receive coils overlap so that each induces a current in the other. Normally the two currents cancel out, but the magnetic field of a metal object distorts this balance and a low current appears in the receive coil.

TRANSMIT COIL

RECEIVE COIL

DETECTOR HEAD
In the metal detector head, one coil usually transmits a magnetic field and another coil picks up the magnetic field produced by a metal object below. The receive coil produces an electric signal that goes to a light, earphones or a meter to indicate a find.

PULSE OF CURRENT

MAGNETIC FIELD OF COIL

COIL

CAN LID

SINGLE-COIL DETECTOR
A brief pulse of current fed to the coil produces a magnetic field around the coil (above). The field enters the buried can lid. Eddy currents induced in the metal generate a magnetic field that in turn induces an opposite current in the now inactive coil (below). Sensitive electronic components detect this current.

MAGNETIC FIELD OF LID

OPPOSITE CURRENT

EDDY CURRENTS

COIN TESTER

ELECTRICAL TEST
An electric current passes through the coin to measure its metal content and size. Only proper coins conduct the right amount of electricity.

MAGNET

LEDs

LIGHT SENSORS

ELECTRIC CURRENT

REJECT MECHANISM

E lectronic coin testers in ticket machines and vending machines can instantly identify coins and reject fakes. As the coin enters the slot, it is first tested for metal content and size. Fake coins fail this test and are rejected. The second test uses a magnet and light sensors to detect the coin's value. Invalid coins are rejected.

MAGNETIC TEST
The coin passes between the poles of a magnet. Eddy currents induced in the coin produce an opposing magnetic field, slowing the coin. The change of speed depends on its size.

LIGHT TEST
The coin passes an array of light-emitting diodes or LEDs (see p.272) and light sensors that measure its speed and diameter. Each value has its own particular speed and diameter, which identify the coin.

REJECT MECHANISM

AIRPORT DETECTOR
The gateways of metal detectors in airports contain coils similar in principle to the coils in a treasure finder. A receiver detects distortions of the transmitted field caused by metal possessions on the person passing through the gateway. The coils are shielded on the outside so that people passing nearby do not trigger the detector.

LOOP IN ROAD

MAGNETIC FIELD INDUCED IN CAR BUMPER

TRAFFIC LIGHTS
Traffic lights may sense the arrival of vehicles. Some work like upside-down treasure finders. A loop of wire in the road surface is connected to the box that controls the lights. A current passes through the loop. As a vehicle moves overhead, it produces a signal in the loop. The signal goes to the control box to register the vehicle's arrival. Other lights use radar detectors to sense a vehicle.

CURRENT

LOOP IN ROAD

MAGNETIC FIELD OF LOOP

BODY SCANNER

Doctors can see into any part of the body with the aid of body scanners. These can produce images of any internal organ, locating defects and diseases. Some scanners work by passing X-rays or gamma rays through the body. The most useful scanner works by nuclear magnetic resonance (NMR). When a patient lies inside an NMR scanner, the body is bombarded first by a strong magnetic field and then by pulses of radio waves. Unlike X-rays and gamma rays, these are harmless. The nuclei in the atoms of the body produce magnetic signals that are picked up by detectors, and a computer forms an image from the signals.

POLE OF ELECTROMAGNET

NUCLEAR MAGNETIC FIELD

NUCLEUS OF ATOM IN BODY

STRONG MAGNETIC FIELD

POLE OF ELECTROMAGNET

1 MAGNETIC FIELD APPLIED

FIELD BEGINS TO ROTATE

COIL

RADIO PULSE

2 RADIO PULSE FIRED

ROTATING FIELD CUTS THROUGH COIL

COIL

3 NMR SIGNALS PRODUCED

INSIDE A BODY SCANNER
The patient enters the scanner on a sliding couch. Inside, he or she is surrounded by curved panels that contain the coils that produce the radio pulses and NMR signals. Around the panels are ring-shaped electromagnets, which may be made superconducting by cooling them with liquid helium. Scanning gives no sensation, not even a tingle.

HOW THE SCANNER WORKS
Atomic nuclei each have their own tiny magnetic field. The scanner applies a strong magnetic field (1) to line up the nuclear fields of the body's atoms. Coils then send out a pulse of radio waves (2) which make the nuclear fields rotate. The rotating fields induce electric signals in the scanner coils (3), which are built up by a computer into an image showing the distribution of the atoms of certain elements. As the amounts of these elements vary from one part of the body to another, an image of the internal organs is produced.

ELECTROMAGNETS

CURVED PANEL

SLIDING COUCH

ADVANCED BURGLAR ALARMS

PHOTODIODES

LENSES

Burglar alarms can detect even the slightest movement made by an intruder. There are two kinds of alarms – active detectors and passive detectors. They usually sit high in the corner of a room, silently checking that all is well.

An active detector sends invisible beams of microwaves or ultrasonic waves throughout the room. Every object in the room reflects the beams back to the detector. A beam reflected from a stationary object, such as furniture, is unchanged in frequency. But a moving object causes a change in frequency. This is the same effect as that used by a radar speed trap (see p.300). The detector registers the change in frequency and sounds the alarm.

A passive detector works with infra-red rays. All objects give off invisible infra-red rays (or heat rays) depending on their temperature. Warmer objects give off stronger rays than cold objects. The detector senses any change in the level of infra-red rays received from the room. The body heat of an intruder increases the level and activates the alarm.

PASSIVE INFRA-RED MOVEMENT DETECTOR

The detector contains a line of lenses that focus infra-red rays on a set of photodiodes (see p.272). Each one collects infra-red rays from a different part of the room. The alarm is triggered only when the level of infra-red rays received by any photodiode changes over a period of time. The body heat of an intruder moving across the room causes the level on some photodiodes to increase and then decrease.

INFRA-RED RAYS
FROM WARM
MOVING TAIL

RAYS FROM COOL
STATIONARY OBJECTS

MICROWAVE
DETECTOR

MICROWAVE
BEAM

SAFETY BEAM

AUTOMATIC DOOR

When you approach an automatic door, an invisible and harmless beam of microwaves from a detector above the door strikes you. Because you are moving towards the door, the frequency of the beam increases as it returns to the detector – like the active burglar alarm above. The detector registers the increase and triggers a mechanism to open the door. An invisible safety beam and detector in the door detect your presence in the doorway and prevent the door closing until you have passed through.

LINE TO OIL PUMP

VALVE MOVES OUTWARD
Oil passes to the shift valve at ᵃ
pressure that depends on the sp︎
of the car.

GOVERNOR
The drive shaft that turns the wheels also turns the governor. As the car accelerates, the governor rotates faster. Centrifugal force moves the valves outwards, sending oil from the pump to the shift valve. Reducing speed makes the valves move inwards, sending oil in the opposite direction.

OIL FROM
OIL PUMP

LINE TO
OIL PUMP

ACCELERATOR
PEDAL

OIL FROM THROTTLE VALVE

CHANGING DOWN
As the governor rotates more slowly or the accelerator pedal is pressed, the throttle valve pressure exceeds the governor pressure. The shift valve moves back, and the low-gear piston engages low gear while the high-gear piston disengages high gear.

GOVERNOR

LOW-GEAR PISTON   HIGH-GEAR PISTON

THROTTLE VALVE

SHIFT VALVE

OIL PUMP

THROTTLE VALVE
The accelerator pedal moves the piston, increasing oil pressure in the valve. A spring returns the pedal, decreasing the oil pressure.

AUTOMATIC TRANSMISSION

Automatic transmission makes driving easy because there is no gear lever and clutch pedal to operate. The mechanism responds to the speed of the car, and automatically changes to a higher or lower gear as the car's speed rises and falls. It can also sense the position of the accelerator pedal.

The control system works by oil pressure. Each gear change is controlled by a shift valve. A governor linked to the wheels and a throttle valve operated by the pedal supply oil at different pressures to the shift valve. The valve moves accordingly and routes oil to the gear change mechanisms in the transmission.

LOW-GEAR PISTON
The piston moves in to disengage low gear.

PISTONS
The two pistons operate the clutches or brake bands that change gear (see next page). Oil at pump pressure from the shift valve moves one of the pistons out to engage a new gear. A spring (not shown) returns the other piston, sending oil back to the pump at low pressure and disengaging its gear.

HIGH-GEAR PISTON
The piston moves out to engage high gear.

OIL RETURNING TO OIL PUMP

OIL FROM OIL PUMP

OIL FROM GOVERNOR

SPRING

SHIFT VALVE
One end of each shift valve receives oil from the governor and

the other end from the throttle valve. When governor pressure is greater (as here), the shift valve moves to send oil from the oil pump to the high-gear piston. Oil flows away from the low-gear piston to return to the pump.

OIL PUMP
The pump (see p.124) circulates oil throughout the transmission and also the engine.

OIL FROM OIL PUMP
(MAXIMUM PRESSURE)

HIGH-PRESSURE OIL

LOW-PRESSURE OIL

OIL RETURNING TO OIL PUMP
(MINIMUM PRESSURE)

AUTOMATIC TRANSMISSION

An automatic transmission contains two main parts, the torque converter and automatic gearbox. The torque converter passes power from the engine flywheel to the gearbox. It does this progressively and smoothly so that starting and changing gear are not jerky, acting rather like the clutch in a manual gearbox (see p.84).

The automatic gearbox contains two sets of epicyclic gears (see p.39) in which gear wheels rotate at different speeds. Overall, except in top gear, the speed of the flywheel is reduced so that the car wheels turn more slowly but with more force. Reverse gear reverses the direction of the wheels.

SECOND ANNULUS

COMMON SUN WHEEL

GOVERNOR

DRIVE SHAFT TO WHEELS

SECOND PLANET WHEEL

PLANET WHEEL

SECOND PLANET CARRIER

FIRST ANNULUS

FIRST PLANET WHEEL

FIRST PLANET CARRIER

INPUT SHAFT

CLUTCH 2
The plates lock to connect the input shaft to the first annulus.

BRAKE BAND 1
The band engages to stop the common sun wheel.

CLUTCH 1
The plates lock to connect the input shaft to the common sun wheel

BRAKE BAND 2
The band engages to stop the second planet carrier.

PLANET CARRIER

SUN WHEEL

ANNULUS

PLANET WHEEL

EPICYCLIC GEAR
Each part either rotates or is locked so that other parts rotate around it.

AUTOMATIC GEARBOX

This gearbox has three forward gears and one reverse gear. The various parts are controlled by multiplate clutches, which lock to transmit power, and brake bands that engage to stop a part rotating.

	Clutch 1	Clutch 2	Band 1	Band 2
First gear	Unlocked	Locked	Off	On
Second gear	Unlocked	Locked	On	Off
Third gear	Locked	Locked	Off	Off
Reverse gear	Locked	Unlocked	Off	On

CASING OIL FLYWHEEL

IMPELLER

REACTOR

OIL FLOW

TURBINE

CRUISE CONTROL

Many cars are fitted with cruise control, which at the press of a button automatically maintains a set speed. In this way, the driver can cruise at a speed limit or economic speed without continually checking the speedometer. The automatic system required is an example of a feedback mechanism. A sensor measures the car's speed and controls the carburettor or fuel injectors (see p.140) that admit fuel to the engine cylinders and govern the speed. It boosts fuel flow if speed begins to drop on climbing a slope, or feeds less fuel into the engine if the car begins to speed up. The sensor may be an electromagnet on the drive shaft, which produces an electric signal related to the speed. A microprocessor continually checks the speed signal and sends a fuel signal to the carburettor or fuel injectors. The advantage of a microprocessor is that it can do more than simply control speed. It is given the car's speed and can therefore calculate the distance travelled. From this and the amount of fuel consumed, the microprocessor can calculate and display the rate of fuel consumption, and can control the engine in order to improve consumption.

SPEED SIGNAL

SPEED SENSOR

CRUISE CONTROL BUTTON

MICRO-PROCESSOR

FUEL SIGNAL

ENGINE CARBURETTOR

TORQUE CONVERTER

The torque converter contains three parts – an impeller turned by the engine flywheel, a turbine that turns the input shaft of the automatic gearbox, and a reactor between. The converter is filled with oil, which is moved by the impeller blades. The vanes of the reactor deflect this oil to move the turbine blades. As the impeller rotates, the speed of the turbine increases to match the impeller speed. This provides a fluid coupling between the engine and gearbox that smooths out speed changes. It also increases torque (turning force).

PART 5

THE DIGITAL DOMAIN

& *THE LAST MAMMOTH*

THE LAST MAMMOTH

CHAPTER ONE

Mammoth stood in the stream stuffing clumps of swamp grass into his mouth. As the tender juices trickled down his throat, he contemplated the pros and cons of the solitary life. On the one hand, he didn't have to share the dwindling harvest with any other mammoths — because there were no other mammoths. But, on the other hand, he was terribly lonely. He wondered how he had come to be the last mammoth and where the rest of his proud species had gone. A large oil slick floated by. He marvelled at its iridescence before ambling off in search of more food.

The trail of dwindling swamp grass led to an imposing wall and an entrance presided over by a character who introduced himself as Bill. Bill announced that this was his "digital domain" and that it was full of wonderful and amazing things all of which were intended to improve the quality of life but none of which had been fully tested. While Bill spoke with enthusiasm about the future, Mammoth could only dwell on the past. Lonely thoughts filled his tiny brain, releasing a single tear which inadvertently saturated Bill's tennis shoes. Recognizing the mammoth's distress, Bill suggested they work together. He and his digital staff needed someone (or some thing) to process. And the mammoth was obviously desperate for companionship. So it came to pass that Mammoth, who generally distrusted high walls, warily entered Bill's gates.

He was immediately surrounded by enthusiastic white-coated workers who began recording every aspect of his considerable being. This was not exactly the kind of companionship he'd been hoping for. One group measured him from top to bottom while another tackled him head to tail. A third group was assigned to gauge his considerable weight. Even those things that could not be so easily measured, such as voice and smell, were meticulously noted.

Within hours, everything about the last mammoth had been reduced to numbers, which Bill copied on to large white cards. He informed Mammoth that although they were very good numbers indeed, they weren't actually the right kind of numbers for the digital domain. If they were going to be useful in helping find true companionship, these numbers would first have to be changed.

Along one side of an enormous pumpkin patch, eight rows of crates had been laid out. Each row was half as long as the one that preceded it. The first and longest row contained one hundred and twenty eight crates, the second contained sixty-four and so on. When Bill held up the card inscribed with the number 237 (the mammoth's height in centimetres), a team of farm hands quickly harvested exactly 237 pumpkins.

Then, moving row by row from longest to shortest, they placed one of these pumpkins into each crate. If they couldn't fill an entire row completely, they simply skipped it. As soon as all the pumpkins had been appropriately crated, Bill drew Mammoth's attention to the pattern of pumpkins along the bottom of all eight rows.

He explained that in the language of the digital domain, the relatively simple number 237 was now "pumpkin, pumpkin, pumpkin, no-pumpkin, pumpkin, pumpkin, no-pumpkin, pumpkin." "That's progress," he added proudly. Mammoth was having a little trouble with this concept, but really shook his head when Bill suggested that "pumpkin" and "no-pumpkin" were equally important. To Mammoth this was like saying swamp grass and no swamp grass were equally filling.

Bill supervised as the pumpkins from the first crate of each row were hung on a long clothes-line. Special care was taken to keep them in exactly the same order. For each "no-pumpkin", a space was left. However, since this happened to be a Tuesday, these spaces were filled with single pieces of wet laundry. When pumpkin, pumpkin, pumpkin, sock, pumpkin, pumpkin, pants, pumpkin had been secured to the line, the whole thing began to move slowly out of view. "Come on, Mammoth," shouted Bill. "We've got work to do."

MAKING BITS

Like the mammoth, we too are entering the digital domain as a new millennium dawns. Digital machines and systems serve us with abilities hitherto only dreamt of. They are able to outstrip previous machines because digital machines work in a completely new way – by numbers. The mammoth finds its dimensions, image, and sound changed into numbers as it goes digital. Similarly, all digital machines begin a task by converting things like these into numbers. Instead of the decimal form that uses ten digits, numbers in the digital domain are binary numbers, which use only two digits and which are much more convenient for machines. These digits are called bits – short for "binary digits" – and a digital machine starts work by making bits.

The mammoth observes that its height, measured in decimal centimetres as 237 becomes, in the digital domain, a set of eight crates, some containing a pumpkin and others empty. The sequence of full and empty crates is a binary number containing eight digits or bits: 237 is full-full-full-empty-full-full-empty-full. When writing binary numbers, we use the two numerals 1 and 0 to represent bits, 1 meaning full or yes and 0 empty or no, so that the decimal number 237 becomes 11101101. But in a digital machine, bits take a form just as physical as pumpkins. They manifest themselves primarily as electric charges in which the electricity is switched either on or off. Here, 237 becomes on-on-on-off-on-on-off-on. So when a machine or system makes bits, it produces on-off sequences of electric charge that are the bits in binary numbers. The bits then progress through the digital domain inside a machine or system, being stored, processed, possibly sent elsewhere, and finally converted back into a form that we can use or understand, such as writing, sounds, even bank notes.

Numbers represented by on-off electrical signals and on-off light signals flash to and fro along the pathways of digital machines in huge quantities at great speed. Because the vast amounts of numbers can be arranged in countless ways, digital machines can carry out a huge variety of complex tasks very quickly. Furthermore, bits are rugged: they do not easily degrade as they rush about the digital domain. Being born survivors, bits enable digital machines to work at superior levels of quality and reliability.

FINGERTIP INPUT

The part of a digital machine or system that makes bits is called the input unit. It is often this unit that gives you entry to the digital domain and gets a digital machine or system working for you. You need to use your fingers to operate some input units, pressing keys or buttons to feed data into the machine. This data can be a code number, such as a key number to open an electronic lock or a PIN number (see p.330) to use a cash machine. You may also tap in an amount of money, letters forming words, or even the notes in a piece of music. A lock or cash machine compares the code number tapped in with the correct key number or PIN number to check if they are the same. Find out how it does this on page 341.

CASH MACHINE AND ELECTRONIC LOCK

Getting cash out of a machine is simply a matter of tapping your PIN number and the amount required on the keypad. You also tap a code number in on a similar keyboard to open an electronic lock. Like the number keys on the computer keyboard opposite, the keys act as switches to generate a sequence of on-off electric pulses forming the bits in the numbers. From a cash machine, these bits go to the bank's central computer, which checks the PIN number and debits your account before instructing the machine to pay out (see p.365). In the lock, the bits go to a chip that checks the number. If it is correct, the chip produces an electric signal which frees the bolt so that the door can be opened.

KEYPAD
The CANCEL button enables you to delete any wrong key presses and start again.

ELECTRIC KEYBOARD

Electronic music equipment, such as keyboards and synthesizers, conforms to a standard called MIDI (Musical Instrument Digital Interface). When you play a MIDI keyboard, it works in the same way as a computer keyboard and sends out a digital code number that identifies each key. Each number has seven bits, and middle C is 0111100 (decimal 60), C# is 0111101 (61), and so on. Another seven-bit digital code number gives the force with which the key is pressed. The bits go to a synthesizer in the keyboard or a separate synthesizer (see p.360), and you hear the note played loudly or softly.

INSTANT MUSICAL SCRIBE
The MIDI bits can go to a computer, which displays the music in written form on the screen as you play.

CONTROLS
You can operate the sound controls with one hand as you play with the other.

COMPUTER KEYBOARD

Only about half of the hundred or so keys on a computer keyboard produce characters – letters, numbers, and signs. Pressing the other keys makes the computer take action, and more options become available by pressing two or even three keys at once. This versatility is possible because pressing a key causes the keyboard to generate an electric signal forming a code number that identifies the key. The code number is in the form of bits made up of on-off electric pulses. This digital signal goes along the cable connecting the keyboard to the computer's main box. The computer interprets the code number or combination of numbers either to display a character or take action.

3 KEYBOARD CHIP
The chip (see p.343) sends out a scanning signal along the pairs of lines to all the key contacts. When the signal in one pair changes, the chip generates a code for the key connected to that pair of lines. Key B produces the bits 00110000 (decimal 48).

4 LETTER b APPEARS
Bits for key number 48 go along the wire to the computer box. There a chip converts the bits to 01100010 (98), the code number for the lower-case letter b.

RUBBER DOME
RETURNS KEY TO
ORIGINAL POSITION

RUBBER SHEET UNDER
THE KEYS PROTECTS
INTERNAL WORKINGS

1 PRESSING KEY B
A metal contact in a rubber dome under key B touches two contacts at the ends of a pair of lines from the keyboard chip.

DOME AND
METAL CONTACT

2 SCANNING SIGNAL
As the contacts meet, a scanning signal sent along the lines from the keyboard chip changes strength.

CONTACTS AT ENDS OF PAIR
OF LINES FROM KEYBOARD CHIP

PHOTODIODE

HORIZONTAL WHEEL

SLOTS

LIGHT-EMITTING
DIODE (LED)

BUTTON

ROLLER BALL

LIGHT-EMITTING
DIODE (LED)

PHOTODIODE

VERTICAL WHEEL

CONNECTING
CABLE

INSIDE THE MOUSE

The mouse rolls on a ball that turns two slotted wheels
mounted at right angles. Each wheel has one or two pairs of
light-emitting diodes (see p.273) and photodiodes (see p.272).
As the wheel turns, light shines through the slots and produces
an electric signal in the photodiodes. The signals from the
wheels give the changes in the mouse's position.

MOUSE

Operating a computer is simplified by using a "mouse", which controls the position on the screen of the cursor, often a sloping arrow. You move the mouse over a mat or the desk top, and the cursor on the screen mirrors its motion. Shift the cursor to an icon or other image representing an action, and click the mouse button. Immediately, the computer carries out the required command.

ICONS AND HOT SPOTS

On the screen there may be a display of icons, which are small images representing programs or operations of some kind. Other parts of the screen may also be "hot", which means they respond to mouse clicks. Every part of the screen has two position numbers that give its horizontal position (from left to right) and vertical position (from top to bottom).
The computer initially gives the cursor two position numbers, and it appears at that position. Moving the mouse sends signals to the computer that change the position numbers, and the cursor shifts accordingly.

CLICKING THE MOUSE

When the cursor reaches a particular icon, its position numbers are the same as that icon. Clicking the mouse button makes the computer compare the position numbers of the cursor with those of all the icons. (Find out on page 341 how the computer does this.) It performs the action of the icon that has the same position numbers as the cursor.

BUTTONS

The mouse may have two buttons, which can produce different actions.

FINAL POSITION OF CURSOR

GROUPS OF ICONS

FIRST POSITION OF CURSOR

VERTICAL MOVEMENT

ACTUAL MOVEMENT OF MOUSE

HORIZONTAL MOVEMENT

MOUSE

MOUSE MAT

TIME APPEARS ON LIQUID CRYSTAL DISPLAY (SEE P.359)

Timer keeps time using a quartz crystal oscillator (see p.265).

HOUR BUTTON   MINUTE BUTTON   START BUTTON

DIGITAL TIMER

Pressing the buttons of a digital timer feeds in bits giving the desired time. A chip then counts down the time, and sets off the alarm when it reaches zero. An electronic parking meter works in the same way; inserting coins triggers an input unit that feeds in the required time bits.

SIGNAL INPUT

There are many digital machines and systems that do not need fingertip input of information. They set about making bits unaided, needing little or no control. Digital thermometers and electronic scales constantly measure temperature and weight. Many digital machines respond to incoming sound waves or light rays, changing them into sequences of binary numbers so that you can capture speech or music digitally or take digital pictures. Once sound and light are in digital form, machines can process the numbers and do amazing things.

One very special device makes this possible: the analog-digital converter. It is the main gateway from our environment – the analog world – to the digital domain. Ours is a world of movement and forces, of heat, light, and sound. All these are analog quantities, meaning that they vary continuously, rising and falling in level or intensity.

These variations are turned into sequences of numbers, or sets of bits, in a digital machine or system. First, a detector or sensor converts the varying levels of heat, weight, sound, or light into an analog or varying electric signal. Then an analog-digital converter chip measures the voltage of this signal at frequent intervals, and changes each number of volts into a binary number made up of bits in the form of on-off electric pulses. These bits then progress through the digital domain.

ANALOG-DIGITAL CONVERTER (ADC)

This converter produces three bits for simplicity. In practice, ADCs produce binary numbers with 8, 16, or more bits.

1 ANALOG INPUT

An analog signal of five volts is fed to the ADC, which will convert it to the three-bit number 101 (decimal five). The ADC contains two parts. The signal goes to the comparator-register, which is linked by three lines to a digital-analog converter (DAC).

2 FIRST BIT

The comparator-register sends an electric signal along line one to the DAC, which receives the binary number 100 (decimal four) and generates a four-volt signal. This returns to the comparator-register, which compares the DAC signal with the input signal.

3 SECOND BIT

The comparator-register now opens line two to the DAC. The DAC receives the binary number 110 (decimal six) and converts it to six volts, which returns to the comparator-register.

4 THIRD BIT

As the second bit was an off-bit (0), the comparator-register closes line two and opens line three. The DAC receives the binary number 101 (decimal five) and converts it to five volts.

DIGITAL THERMOMETER

The heat-sensing probe of a digital thermometer contains a thermistor (see p.270), which produces an electric signal that increases or decreases in voltage as the temperature changes. The signal goes to an analog-digital converter, which changes each measurement into bits. Using chips like those in the electronic scales, the thermometer displays the temperature as a number.

C/F button gives temperature in degrees Celsius or degrees Fahrenheit.

HI and LO buttons give highest and lowest temperatures previously measured. These are stored as bits in the thermometer's memory.

PROBE

VOLTAGE

DISPLAY (SEE P.359)

Analog electric signal from thermistor varies in voltage as temperature rises, steadies, then falls.

MEASUREMENTS OF VOLTAGE

TIME

ELECTRONIC SCALES

DETECTING WEIGHT
The weight of the purchase very slightly bends the beam, which stretches or compresses the thin wire in the strain gauge. This changes the electric resistance of the wire so that the voltage of the current flowing through the gauge also changes.

STRAIN GAUGE CONTAINS TWO WIRE LOOPS

SECOND STRAIN GAUGE UNDER BEAM

ANALOG-DIGITAL CONVERTER

PROCESSOR CHIP

DISPLAY CHIP

MEMORY CHIP

BUTTON CONTROLLER CHIP

OFF BUTTON

DISPLAY (SEE P.359)

OUNCES/GRAMS BUTTON

RESET BUTTON

ON BUTTON

VOLTAGE

MEASUREMENTS OF VOLTAGE

WEIGHT OF PAN PLUS PURCHASE

STRAIN GAUGE SIGNAL

WEIGHT OF PAN

TIME

Like this postal scale, electronic weighing machines used in shops contain a strain gauge that detects the weight of a purchase. The gauge sends out an analog electric signal that varies in voltage with the weight, and an analog-digital converter changes the voltage into a binary number consisting of on-off electric pulses. These bits go to the scale's processor, which calculates the weight, subtracts the weight of the pan (stored in the memory), and may also calculate the price. The result goes to the display.

SOUND TO BITS

A microphone begins the process by which the sounds of voices or music are turned into bits. As it passes through the air to the microphone, a sound wave causes the pressure of the air to rise and fall – rather as a water wave ripples, but far more quickly. The variations in air pressure cause the microphone (see p.224) to produce an electrical sound signal in which the voltage varies at the same rate. The sound signal then goes to an analog-digital converter (see p.320). This measures the voltage of the sound signal, and converts each number of volts into a binary number in the form of on-off electric pulses. For CD quality sound, the converter makes 44,000 measurements each second. Each one is changed to a 16-bit number, which gives 65,536 levels of voltage. The resulting digital signal is a very accurate representation of the sound wave, which is why digital sound reproduction is of very high quality.

VOLTAGE

MEASUREMENTS OF VOLTAGE

SOUND SIGNAL
The sound signal from a microphone varies rapidly in voltage. This sound lasts about 1/2000 of a second.

TIME

SOUND CARD

Computers and digital machines that use sound contain a sound card. A microphone or other sound equipment that produces a sound signal, such as a CD player, tape player or radio, is plugged into the card's input socket. One of the chips on the sound card is an analog-digital converter. It turns the incoming sound signal into bits, which may then be stored, processed, or sent elsewhere.

INPUT SOCKET

THE SOUND CARD IS INSIDE THE COMPUTER'S MAIN BOX

MICROPHONE

ANALOG-DIGITAL CONVERTER

VOICE RECOGNITION
Talk to your computer. You can feed in words by speaking, and the computer can obey spoken commands. The memory contains a dictionary of words as sets of bits, and the computer recognizes a spoken word by matching the bits to an identical or similar set in the memory. It can also translate spoken words and test your accent in speaking other languages.

DIGITAL SOUND RECORDING
The sound bits can be stored to record voices or music. They may go to the computer's hard disk (see p.333), or to a digital tape, digital film, or compact disc (see pp.334-7). NICAM video recorders can record digital sound on a videotape.

DIGITAL RADIO
The sound bits are converted to radio waves and broadcast from the radio station's transmitter to digital radio receivers in cars and homes (see p.352).

MOBILE PHONE
Many mobile phones are digital, and contain sound circuitry that converts the sound signal produced by the microphone in the mouthpiece to bits. These bits are then transmitted by radio to a base station (see pp.236 and 352).

BITS IN DIGITAL SOUND SIGNAL

!***!!!"?

THE VOICE RECOGNITION SOFTWARE IN THIS COMPUTER CANNOT SPELL THE WORD SPOKEN.

PLEASE TRY AGAIN.

LIGHT TO BITS

Computers and other digital machines are able to capture the light in images and turn it into bits. The machine must first scan the original. It may project the image on a CCD (charge-coupled device) containing an array of tiny light-sensitive detectors (see p.243). Each detector deals with a tiny part of the image and produces a voltage proportional to the brightness of that part. The rows of detectors then read out their sequences of voltage one after the other. Alternatively, the image may pass over a CCD containing a single row of detectors. Successive strips of the image fall on the detectors, and the voltages flow out from the row in sequence. Overall, the image is converted into an electric signal of which the varying voltage represents the varying brightness along strip after strip of the whole image. These voltages are then measured and converted into bits by an analog-digital converter (see p.320).

Measurements of voltage along strip of image falling on central row of CCD. Brighter parts give higher voltage.

CCD CONTAINING ARRAY OF LIGHT DETECTORS

IMAGE OF EYE FALLING ON CCD

OPTICAL CHARACTER RECOGNITION (OCR)

You can make your computer read with OCR software. Using a scanner (see pp.324-5), it first scans a document containing written words and turns the image of the lines of words into bits. The software then enables the computer to recognize the shapes of individual letters in each word and other characters, such as numerals and punctuation marks, just as if you had keyed them in with the keyboard. In this way, you can feed a document directly into the computer instead of having to key in the words, and then send it by e-mail, for example (see pp.350-1). Even better, the computer can read books aloud to blind people. It scans the words on each page and converts the bit sequences of the written words into the bits of spoken words, and sends these bits to a digital-analog converter and loudspeaker to speak the words (see p.360).

1 SCANNING D
The written letter D is turned into a sequence of bits.

2 COMPARING D
The computer compares the bits with the bit sequences of all possible characters.

3 MATCHING D
The bits of the D character sequence are most similar to the bits of the written letter.

4 DISPLAYING D
The D character bits go to the screen and the computer displays a D.

RECOGNIZING CHARACTERS

The computer scans each written character, turning its shape into a sequence of on-bits and off-bits. The computer's memory contains the bit sequences of all characters, and matches the scanned bit sequence to an identical or similar character sequence in its memory.

HAND-HELD TRANSLATOR

Roll the translator along a line of foreign words, like a dish on a menu. Each foreign word and its English translation appear on the display. The translator scans the words and uses OCR to recognize each foreign word. Its memory contains all the words of both languages in bit form, so it can swiftly change the foreign bits to English bits.

3 FIRST MIRROR
A mirror moves with the light source, reflecting each strip of the picture as it passes to a second mirror.

2 LIGHT SOURCE
As the picture is scanned, a source of bright light beneath the window moves along the picture and lights up successive narrow strips of the picture.

SCANNER

You use a scanner to feed photographs, drawings, paintings, and documents into a computer. Once it is in digital form, an image can be altered and used in many ways. It may be stored for future viewing, included in a document and printed out, sent in digital form to another computer, or incorporated in a web site. A scanner may be a separate machine connected to a computer, like the flatbed scanner shown here, or it may be part of an all-purpose machine that also contains a fax, printer, and photocopier. The scanner breaks up the image into many rows of tiny pixels (picture elements), each one having a certain colour. It then converts each pixel into bits which form a binary number representing that particular colour, so that the image becomes a long sequence of colour numbers in binary form.

CABLE CONNECTS SCANNER TO COMPUTER

1 USING THE SCANNER
A picture of the sun and sky is placed face down on the window of the scanner.

MAKING BITS

PICTURE FACE DOWN

WINDOW

24-BIT NUMBER FOR
YELLOW PIXEL IN SUN

8-BIT
BLUE NUMBER

8-BIT
GREEN NUMBER

8-BIT
RED NUMBER

ANALOG-DIGITAL CONVERTER

4 SECOND MIRROR
*The second mirror
is fixed and reflects
each passing strip
of the picture to a lens.*

8 DIGITAL COLOUR OUTPUT
*The analog-digital converter changes
the three voltage levels
for each pixel into three
eight-bit numbers. The
resulting sequence of 24-
bit numbers goes to the
computer for storage or
processing, and will go to a
computer screen to display the
image (see p.361).*

7 ANALOG COLOUR SIGNAL
*Three lines carry the varying
voltage from the red, green,
and blue rows of the CCD to the
scanner's analog-digital converter
(see p.320).*

YELLOW PIXEL IN SUN

YELLOW PIXEL IN SUN

*Part of the picture
showing the edge of the
yellow sun and blue sky
passes the CCD and is
broken up into an array
of 11 rows each of
11 pixels.*

RED ARRAY

GREEN ARRAY

YELLOW PIXEL IN SUN

BLUE ARRAY

BLUE ANALOG SIGNAL

5 LENS
*The lens projects
an image of each
passing strip
on a CCD.*

RED ANALOG SIGNAL

GREEN ANALOG SIGNAL

6 CCD
*The CCD (see p.243) contains three rows of
hundreds of tiny light detectors with red, green, and
blue filters. As the image passes, each detector produces
an analog electric signal of varying voltage, depending on
the brightness of the light falling on it. Each group of three
red, green, and blue detectors gives one pixel.*

DIGITAL COLOUR
*Colours are reproduced by mixing
red, green, and blue light in different
levels of brightness. Red and green
mix to form yellow, as here. Many
scanners use eight-bit numbers to
measure each of the three levels of
brightness. This gives 256 shades
each of red, green, and blue, which
combine to produce over 16 million
different shades of colour.*

FAX MACHINE

A document passes through a fax machine as it is sent. The page passes over a CCD containing a single row of light detectors (see p.243). The CCD scans the page, producing an electrical signal of varying voltage representing the dark and light parts of the page. This analog signal is then changed to bits by an analog-digital converter (see p.320). The bits are sent along a telephone line to the receiving fax machine (see p.352).

DOCUMENT PASSES OVER CCD

CCD

ANALOG-DIGITAL CONVERTER

ANALOG SIGNAL

DIGITAL SIGNAL GOES TO TELEPHONE LINE

DIGITAL STILL CAMERA

Photography enters the digital domain with the digital still camera, which uses no film and takes pictures in digital form. These can be viewed on the camera's display, a television set, or computer screen, or printed out on a computer printer. The camera has the usual lens, flash, and viewfinder. The image formed by the lens falls on a CCD containing an array of a million or so light detectors. The CCD produces an analog colour signal that is converted to a 24-bit digital colour signal (see p.325). When you press the button, the picture bits are stored in the camera's memory.

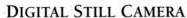

PROCESSOR

ANALOG-DIGITAL CONVERTER

MEMORY CHIP
The flash memory chip (see p.332) stores a set number of pictures. Any picture can be erased and replaced, so you can keep on taking a picture until you are satisfied with it.

CCD

LENS

MEMORY CARD SOCKET

MEMORY CARD
A flash chip in each memory card stores an extra set of pictures for as long as required.

COMPUTER CABLE

DIGITAL-ANALOG CONVERTER (SEE P.360)

ANALOG PICTURE SIGNAL

TELEVISION SOCKET

DIGITAL PICTURE SIGNAL

COMPUTER SOCKET
The picture bits can go from the camera processor to a computer. This can store the pictures on its hard disk, alter the pictures with graphics software, send the pictures to others via e-mail or post them on a web site, and print out the pictures.

COLOUR SCREEN
At the back of the camera is a liquid-crystal screen (see p.361) that displays the picture being taken, and any picture in the camera's memory. It receives an analog picture signal direct from the CCD, or from the digital-analog converter.

DIGITAL TELEVISION

A television camera contains CCDs similar to that in a digital still camera. These produce an analog picture signal that is transmitted to TV sets (see p.242-3). In digital television, the signal is converted to bits by an analog-digital converter and the bits are transmitted (see p.352). This digital system gives high-quality reception and many more channels.

CHAPTER TWO

The other end of the rope was attached to a rolling stepladder behind which stood a tall set of shelves. Every shelf was individually numbered and divided into eight compartments. A worker placed each arriving pumpkin into its own compartment once again, taking special care to maintain their order. Where there was a no-pumpkin or piece of laundry, that compartment was left empty. Even to the mammoth this seemed a somewhat overly complicated way of drying clothes, but this too he assumed must be "progress".

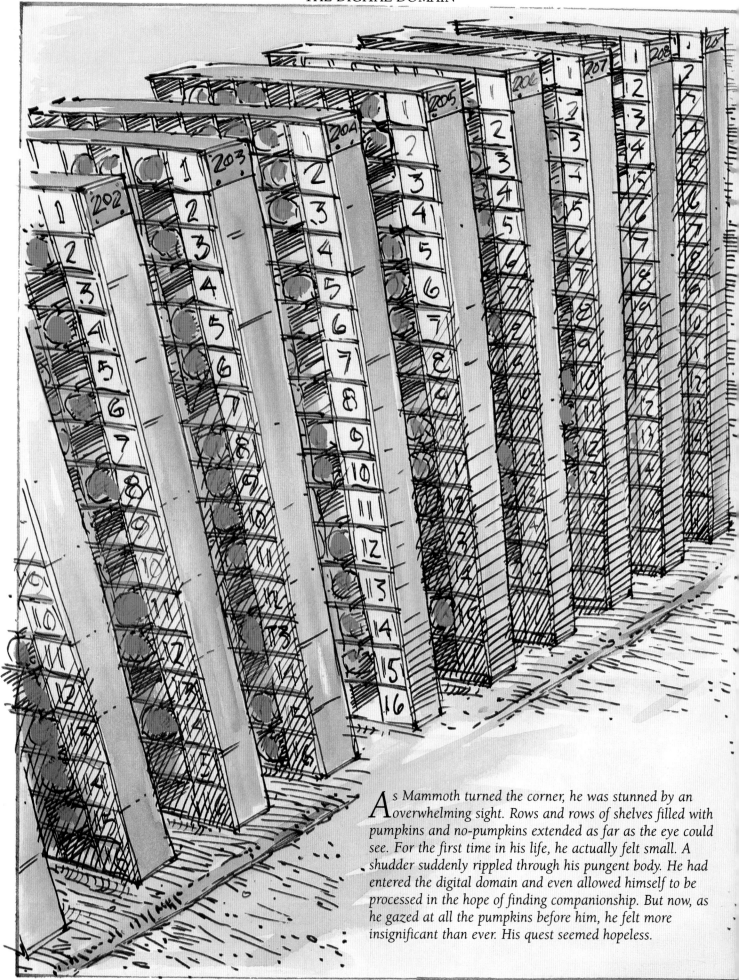

As Mammoth turned the corner, he was stunned by an overwhelming sight. Rows and rows of shelves filled with pumpkins and no-pumpkins extended as far as the eye could see. For the first time in his life, he actually felt small. A shudder suddenly rippled through his pungent body. He had entered the digital domain and even allowed himself to be processed in the hope of finding companionship. But now, as he gazed at all the pumpkins before him, he felt more insignificant than ever. His quest seemed hopeless.

Even though every shelf had its own number, he wondered how anyone, including Bill, could possibly keep track of all these pumpkins – never mind the no-pumpkins. As Mammoth looked around for reassurance, he noticed that all the shelves were served by another even larger ladder. When Bill called out a particular shelf number, the ladder was rolled against that bank of shelves and then the entire eight compartment pattern was removed. It was then attached to one of two moving ropes and carried off.

STORING BITS

The mammoth watches as its personal details are stored for future use. The eight-bit sequences of pumpkins are placed in numbered racks so that any sequence can be found and sent elsewhere.

Bits enter and leave storage as on-off electric pulses. But in its memory units, a digital machine or system stores the bits in other forms. The bits may be parked in the memory just for a short time, or the memory may hold the bits for a long time or even permanently.

Digital machines store two classes of bits: programs and data. A program is a set of instructions that direct the machine to carry out a particular task, such as word processing, taking pictures, or playing a game. The instructions consist of bits that form code numbers for actions to be taken. Data consists of bits that make up information required by the program or produced as the program runs, such as words, images, or points scored.

KINDS OF STORAGE

MEMORY CHIPS
Bits are stored as off-on sequences of electric charge.

DISKS AND TAPES
Magnetic fields pointing forwards or back store bits.

BAR CODES
White spaces and black bars represent off-bits and on-bits.

DIGITAL FILM SOUND
Bits are stored in the form of tiny transparent dots on the film.

COMPACT DISCS
Bits are stored as tiny pits and non-pits in the disc surface.

RECORDABLE CDS
Bits are stored as dark marks and non-marks in the surface.

BITS AND BYTES

Every memory device has a certain storage capacity that is measured in bytes. A byte is a tiny amount – just eight bits – that stores in binary form any decimal number from 0 to 255; larger numbers require two or more bytes. Memory capacity is measured in units bigger than single bytes. One kilobyte (1 Kb) is 1,024 bytes; one megabyte (1 Mb) is 1,048,576 bytes; and one gigabyte (1 Gb) is 1,073,741,824 bytes. Each byte has its own location in the memory, and this is identified by an address number. A digital machine keeps a record of which byte is stored where, and works through a list of address numbers to retrieve the bits in a set of bytes.

ONE BYTE
Eight bits make up one byte. Letters, numerals, and signs are represented by eight-bit code numbers: the letter "a" is 01100001 (decimal 97). So one byte stores one letter.

ONE KILOBYTE
One kilobyte is just over a thousand bytes. This amount of memory can store the letters in about 150 words, or half a page of a novel.

CD-ROM
A CD-ROM has a memory capacity of 650 megabytes, which is equivalent to several hundred novels. However, CD-ROMs contain images, which take up more memory than words do. One CD-ROM can store the contents of an encyclopedia including several thousand pictures.

FLOPPY DISK
A floppy disk has a storage capacity of approximately one megabyte or a million or so bytes. This is enough to store some 150,000 words – the average length of a novel.

HARD DISK
The memory capacity of the hard disk in a home computer is usually several gigabytes. A hard disk can contain thousands of novels – enough to fill a small bookshop!

Do you have a copy of 'The Typewriter's Revenge'?

Shhhhhhh . . . . .

SQUEEZING BITS
The amount of data that can be stored in a memory device can be greatly increased by data compression. This system uses a mathematical process. For example, rather than store all the original numbers produced by the input unit, the machine may store the first number and then calculate and store only the differences between each successive number. This difference can be very small, or even zero (as in adjacent parts of a picture of the same colour). This compression process greatly reduces the number of bits to be stored – by a factor of 200 to 1 in video images. When the compressed bits are retrieved from the memory, the digital machine decompresses them. It reconstitutes the original sets of bits by reversing the mathematical process.

PINS AND PASSWORDS
Secure digital machines and systems, such as cash machines and e-mail, ask you to key in a PIN (personal identification number) or a password. The machine or system contains the PIN or password stored in its memory as a set of bits. It compares the bits that you key in with the set in its memory. Only if they match does the machine allow you to proceed.

ELECTRICAL STORAGE

Microchips store bits in electrical form. A memory chip consists of a grid of tiny electronic memory cells that each store one bit. The cells are arranged in groups of eight, each holding one byte (eight bits). Each group has an address number, and an address decoder opens lines to groups of cells in order to store or retrieve bits. The grid of cells is like a vast city of long roads containing numbered houses. Sets of eight bits flash along the roads to occupy the eight rooms in each house.

MEMORY CHIP

RANDOM-ACCESS MEMORY (RAM)

The main working memory of a digital machine consists of RAM chips. These hold data and programs, but only for as long as these bits are required; they are constantly replaced by new sets of bits as the machine is used. The bits can be stored at any available groups of memory cells, hence the name "random-access". More RAM may make the machine work faster.

ADDRESS LINE 0 CLOSED

DATA LINE ON

TRANSISTOR OFF

TRANSISTOR OFF

ADDRESS LINE 1 OPEN

TRANSISTOR ON

CAPACITOR STORES PULSE (1)

DATA LINE OFF

TRANSISTOR ON

NO PULSE STORED (0)

ADDRESS DECODER

BITS STORED AT ADDRESS 1

FOUR MEMORY CELLS ENLARGED RIGHT

ADDRESS NUMBER

INSIDE A RAM CHIP

Each memory cell contains a transistor (see p.341) and a capacitor, and is connected to an address line and a data line. To store bits, the address decoder opens an address line, switching on all the transistors at that address. On-off electric pulses forming the bits then go along the data lines. Each on-bit (1) passes through the cell's transistor to charge its capacitor. To retrieve the bits, the cells discharge and send on-off electric pulses back along the data lines.

READ-ONLY MEMORY (ROM)

The bits held in a ROM chip are permanent and cannot be changed. A computer's BIOS (basic input-output system) is a ROM containing start-up routines that spring into action when the computer is switched on. A ROM chip contains a grid of memory cells consisting of transistors that are linked to address lines and data lines as in a RAM chip. Some of the address line links are cut when the chip is made. To retrieve bits, power goes to all the cells. It passes only through the linked transistors at an address, which are switched on to give the on-pulses in the bits that are stored in the ROM. The cut links switch off the other transistors at that address, and give the off-pulses.

LINK CUT

POWER LINE

ADDRESS LINE 0 CLOSED

TRANSISTOR OFF

TRANSISTOR OFF

ADDRESS LINE 1 OPEN

LINK CUT

TRANSISTOR ON

DATA LINE ON

TRANSISTOR OFF

DATA LINE OFF

FLASH MEMORY

R AM chips (see p.331) are volatile: they must constantly be refreshed with a source of electric power in order to keep bits. Unless backed up with a battery, they lose their memory when the machine is switched off. As digital devices shrink and become portable, they require a compact form of non-volatile storage. A flash memory chip stores bits without constant power, yet can replace the stored bits with new bits at any time. It has a grid of special transistors that once switched on or off, remain so.

DIGITAL CASH

A bank stores your money as bits in its computer. You can now spend money in the form of bits. Instead of getting notes from a machine, you insert a cash card. Bits (in the form of on-off electric pulses) representing an amount of money are sent to your card and stored in a tiny flash chip in the card. As you spend, the stored amount is reduced by a terminal in the shop.

AMOUNT LEFT TO SPEND

LOADING CASH
Insert the cash card into a load machine and key in the amount you require. The machine loads the card with this amount.

SPENDING CASH
At the store, the sum you spend is keyed into a terminal. You insert the card, and this sum is deducted from the stored amount.

CHECKING CASH
A small card reader displays how much digital money remains stored in the card.

CARD CONTACTS
Contacts in the card connect the flash chip with contacts in the load machine, terminal, and reader in order to access the memory cells in the flash chip.

CARD MEMORY
A tiny flash chip is embedded in the plastic of the card beneath the contacts. Just as bank notes come and go from your wallet, the amount of money stored as bits in the chip increases and decreases. When this amount reaches zero, you can load the card with more digital money from a load machine.

DIGITAL CAMERA
Image bits are stored on a flash chip in the camera, and on separate memory cards containing flash chips (see p.326).

MOBILE PHONE
A flash chip in the phone stores personal telephone numbers that you key in and can then call at the press of a button.

CAR IMMOBILIZER
In the car key or car remote controller is a flash chip with the car's identity code. The car's computer also stores this number. The code goes to the computer, which controls the immobilizer so that the car starts only if the code is correct.

MAGNETIC STORAGE

Memory chips are unable to store the billions of bits that make up computer programs and data, and digital sounds and images. Instead, the bits are transformed from the on-off electric pulses produced by input units into magnetic form and are stored on magnetic disks and tapes. Bits that are no longer needed can be erased and new bits stored.

FLOPPY DISK

Inside the plastic sleeve is a flexible disk with a magnetic coating. Bits are recorded in concentric circular tracks divided into sectors, all numbered so that any set of bits can be quickly located. A read-write head in the disk drive (see p.283) moves in and out to access a particular track on the disk.

READ-WRITE HEAD

SECTOR

TRACK IN SECTOR

ROTATING DISK

FLEXIBLE MAGNETIC DISK

ACCESS
Inside the disk drive, windows open to allow the head access to the disk.

SLEEVE

HARD DISK

Floppy disks are used to carry programs and data from one computer to another, and are being superseded by CD-ROMs and file transfer by e-mail and the Internet (see p.351). Inside a computer, huge quantities of bits are stored in a hard disk drive. The drive contains several hard magnetic disks, sealed to exclude dust. The read-write heads are on arms that swivel back and forth across both surfaces of each disk.

READ-WRITE HEAD

HARD DISKS

ARMS

MAGNETIC BANDS

DISK

MAGNETIC COATING

CORE

COIL

PULSE

ONE BIT STORED
The read-write head contains a coil wound around an iron core. A bit is converted into a pair of pulses. The pulses pass through the coil, which magnetizes the disk's surface. Each pulse is stored as a band of magnetism.

FIRST BIT (1) SECOND BIT (0)

TWO BITS STORED
When a bit is stored, the first band always reverses the direction of magnetization of the previous band to indicate a new bit. The second band has the same direction if the bit is a 0, or the reverse direction if it is a 1.

THIRD BIT (1)

TRACK ON DISK

THREE BITS STORED
Three bits – 101 – have now been stored in six bands. The bands create a circular track on the surface of the disk. Some of the bits stored form a directory giving the names and locations of files.

FOURTH BIT (1)

FOUR BITS STORED
Four bits – 1011 – have now been stored. To retrieve the bits, the disk is spun past the head, inducing an electric signal in the coil to produce bits as pairs of electric pulses.

MAGNETIC STORAGE

SWIPE CARD

A credit card or a debit card has a stripe with a magnetic coating on which bits are stored and retrieved in the same way as a magnetic disk (see p.333). The bits contain the card number, card owner's name, and expiry date.

Swiping the card moves the magnetic stripe past a read head in the card reader.

MAGNETIC
STRIPE

DIGITAL TAPE

Bits are stored on magnetic tape in a digital tape drive. This works in the same way as a video recorder (see p.244). Digital sound recording, in which the bits come from a microphone and analog-digital converter, uses small DAT (digital audio tape) cassettes. DDS (digital data storage) uses digital tape to back up a computer's hard disk (see p.367). Digital video recorders also use tape to record the bits that form digital television programmes in the same way.

DAT AND DDS CASSETTES FIT
IN THE PALM OF A HAND

OPTICAL STORAGE

BAR CODE

The pattern of black bars and white spaces in a bar code on a product stores bits which form a code number for that product. Depending on its width, each black bar represents one or more binary 1s, and each white space one or more binary 0s. As the assistant passes the product over the bar-code reader, or holds the bar-code reader up to the product, a bright beam of light moves across the bar code. A detector captures the reflected light, which flashes off and on as the beam moves past the black bars and white spaces. In a similar way to a compact disc player (see p.336), the detector converts the light signal to an electric signal containing the bits in the form of on-off electric pulses. The code signal goes from the reader to a computer that uses the code number to identify the product and its price. The name and price then appear on a display and may be printed out (see p.368).

GUARD BAR

CENTRAL PATTERN

BOOK CODE

This bar code contains two groups of six decimal numerals separated by a fixed central 01010 pattern. At each end of the bar code is a start/stop 101 pattern called a guard bar.

1 1 0 0 1 1 0 1 0 0 1 1 1 0 1 0 0 1 0 0 0 1 0

1   5   8   GUARD BAR

SEVEN-BIT BAR CODE

In most bar codes, each of the decimal numerals from 0 to 9 consists of seven bits. These are arranged in four groups of alternate bars and spaces, each containing from one to four bits.

DIGITAL SOUND TRACK IS LOCATED BETWEEN SPROCKET HOLES

INFRA-RED SOURCE

LENS

PATTERN OF DOTS

DIGITAL SIGNAL FROM DETECTOR

STEREO ANALOG SOUND TRACK FOR CINEMAS WITHOUT DIGITAL EQUIPMENT

CCD DETECTOR

PROCESSOR

AMPLIFIERS

RIGHT SURROUND SPEAKERS

LEFT SURROUND SPEAKERS

SCREEN

SIX-CHANNEL SOUND

The sound bits, which come from analog microphone signals fed through an analog-digital converter, are stored on the edge of the film as small squares containing thousands of black-and-white dots. The film passes a source of infra-red rays, which shines through each square and a lens to project the passing patterns of dots on a CCD detector (see p.243). The detector changes the dot patterns into bits consisting of on-off electric pulses. A processor, amplifiers, and loudspeakers convert this digital signal into six channels of sound.

TO RIGHT SPEAKERS

TO BASS SPEAKER

TO CENTRE SPEAKER

TO LEFT SPEAKERS

COMPACT DISC PLAYER

Up to about 70 minutes of music can be recorded in digital form on a compact disc. On the shiny underside is a spiral track of bits in the form of a sequence of tiny pits. The track is thinner than a human hair and several kilometres long. The disc spins at speeds ranging from 500 revolutions per minute at the centre, where the track starts, to 200 revolutions per minute at the edge. This causes the track to pass at a constant speed over the read-out system that retrieves the bits and produces an electric stereo sound signal. This signal goes to an amplifier and a pair of loudspeakers or earphones to reproduce the music.

SPIRAL TRACK OF PITS

OPTICAL READ-OUT SYSTEM
A system of mirrors and lenses fires a laser beam at the pits on the spinning disc. The beam moves across from the centre to the edge. The light-sensitive photodiode (see p.272) detects the reflected beam and produces bits in the form of on-off electric pulses. These are converted by a digital-analog converter (see p.360) into a sound signal.

TRACK CODES

The sequence of pits in the track of a compact disc contains several kinds of codes. Left-hand and right-hand stereo sound codes are recorded alternately, and the sequence also contains codes that control the motor speed and give timings.

UNDERSIDE OF DISC

ONS AND OFFS

In optical storage, an on-bit may be a binary 0 and an off-bit a binary 1. If necessary, passing the bits through a NOT gate (see p.341) changes each on-bit back to an off-bit and vice-versa. It is called a NOT gate because it changes a bit that is on to a bit that is NOT on, and a bit that is off to a bit that is NOT off.

READING BINARY 1

The laser beam enters a pit in the track and is not reflected, so the photodiode produces no signal.

READING BINARY 0

The disc surface reflects the light beam to the photodiode, which produces an electric signal.

LENSES

DISC SURFACE

TRANSPARENT LAYER

PIT

LASER

SEMI-TRANSPARENT MIRROR

PHOTODIODE

CD-ROM

A CD-ROM is a compact disc that stores bits forming computer programs, sounds, and images, often used in multimedia presentations and computer games. The disc is played back in a high-speed CD-ROM drive connected to a computer, or in a home console connected to a TV set. The digital signal from the detector goes to the processor in the computer or console.

RECORDABLE CDs

When a master compact disc or CD-ROM is made, a laser fires a beam at the surface to burn in the sequence of pits. Copies are then pressed from this master disc. With a CD recording deck or CD writer linked to a computer, bits can be stored on blank discs. Instead of burning pits, the laser darkens the surface and creates a spiral track containing a sequence of dark marks. The detector in the read-out system reads the marks in the same way as pits. CD-R (CD Recordable) discs can be used only once. With CD-RW (CD Rewritable) discs, the dark marks can be erased and new bits stored.

THE SURFACE OF A CD-R DISC CONTAINS A GREEN DYE THAT DARKENS

SHINY GOLD BACKING LAYER

DATA AND MUSIC

Recordable and rewritable CDs can be used to store computer data and programs in large quantities, and to record music in digital form.

DARK MARKS IN TRACK

GROOVE IN DISC SURFACE GUIDES LASER BEAM

DIGITAL VIDEO DISC (DVD)

The thousands of images that make up a movie contain many billions of bits when converted to digital form. Using data compression (see p.330), a new kind of compact disc, called the digital video disc, can store all these bits so that it is possible to record a whole movie on one disc. To play the movie, the DVD player is connected to a television set. Because it is digital, the quality of the pictures and sound is high and DVD may replace the videotape.

A DVD drive can be connected to a computer. As each DVD placed in the drive can store as many bits as a complete hard disk drive, rewritable DVDs may supersede the hard disk. DVD also stands for "digital versatile disc".

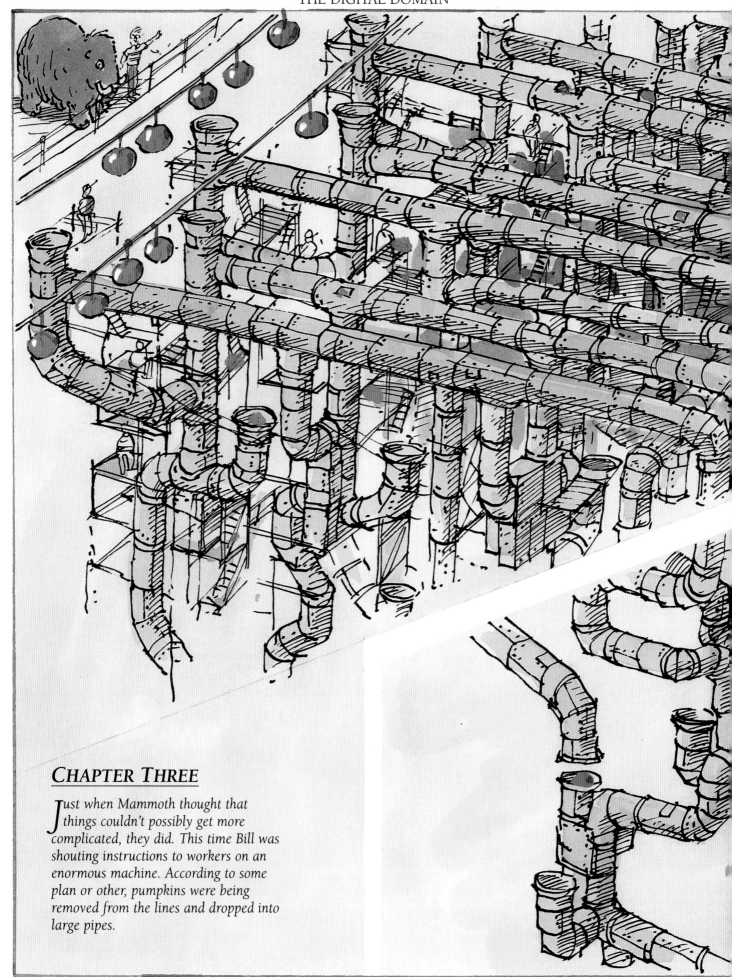

CHAPTER THREE

*J*ust when Mammoth thought that things couldn't possibly get more complicated, they did. This time Bill was shouting instructions to workers on an enormous machine. According to some plan or other, pumpkins were being removed from the lines and dropped into large pipes.

As circuitous as the pipe structure was and no matter how many pumpkins went in at the top, once again it was a combination of eight pumpkins and no-pumpkins that emerged at the bottom. These pumpkins, now much the worse for wear, slumped onto a sticky conveyor belt. When all eight spaces on the belt were accounted for, it started up and carried them away.

*B*ill explained to Mammoth that as the pumpkins travelled through the huge machine, they operated a series of spring-loaded gates. The opening and closing of these gates actually determined the precise pattern of pumpkins that would eventually emerge onto the conveyor belt. When they reached a couple of prototype gates in the test area, Bill sensed that his oversized companion was finally beginning to appreciate the ingenuity and technical sophistication of these contraptions. But then he realized that, in fact, it was their trunk-like geometry that had struck a familiar chord. For the first time in ages, Mammoth was feeling a little less alone.

PROCESSING BITS

*T*he mammoth now looks on as the bits representing its personal details arrive from the storage racks and are processed. The sequences of pumpkins drop into a vast and complex processing machine, where they approach gates which open to pass them or close to block them, so that new sequences of pumpkins emerge and continue on through the digital domain. The gates are worked by other combinations of pumpkins arriving from other racks.

Every digital machine and system contains a processor or CPU (central processing unit), which is a microchip containing thousands of miniature electronic gates called logic gates. Bits in the form of on-off electric pulses come from the memory and flash to the gates, which pass or block incoming bits so that new sets of bits emerge. These new bits are the result of the task set by the machine's program, and they pass back to the memory or forward to the next part of the digital machine.

LOGIC GATES

The processor in a digital machine or system is a type of miniature electronic brain housed in a powerful microchip. It receives two groups of bits from the machine's memory: program bits that direct the processor to carry out a task, and data bits that are processed to give a result. Every step consists of simple arithmetic performed electronically at great speed.

Inside the processor chip are a million or more tiny transistors (see p.343). These are connected to form thousands of logic gates, and the transistors inside them rapidly switch on and off to pass or block bits in order to perform binary arithmetic. The bits consist of on-off electric pulses with a high voltage (on or binary 1) or a zero or low voltage (off or binary 0).

PROCESSOR TRANSISTORS

A transistor is a sandwich of two types of semiconductor, n-type and p-type, with opposite electrical properties. It contains three pieces: the source, gate, and drain, arranged n-p-n or p-n-p. An electric current is fed to the source and a controlling bit (an on-pulse or off-pulse) goes to the gate. This may cause the electrical resistance of the gate to decrease so that the transistor switches on and passes the current. Alternatively, the resistance of the gate increases and the transistor switches off and blocks the current.

NOT GATE

Arithmetic occurs when a digital machine has to compare two numbers, as in clicking an icon with the mouse (see p.319). The processor subtracts one number from the other: if the result is zero, the numbers are the same. This kind of arithmetical action enables machines to make decisions. The NOT gate is the simplest of several kinds of logic gates performing arithmetic inside the processor. It changes an on-bit (binary 1) to an off-bit (binary 0) and vice-versa, and contains an NPN transistor fed with a low voltage and a PNP transistor fed with a high voltage. This is the real electronic version of the mechanical NOT gate encountered by the mammoth opposite. Other logic gates have more complex groups of transistors using two or more bits, but work in a similar way to pass either a high or low voltage.

MICROCHIP

Amicrochip or integrated circuit contains many thousands of electronic components squeezed into a thin sliver of silicon less than 1 cm (0.4 inch) square. These components are connected together to form devices such as logic gates (see p.341) and memory cells (see p.331).

The miniature components within a chip are not individually made and assembled. Instead, the components and all their connections are built up in layers of material in complex miniature patterns. These are made with masks produced by reducing large patterns photographically. These two pages illustrate the manufacture of one transistor component in a microchip.

SILICON CYLINDER

CHIP CHOP

A microchip is made mostly of *p*-type silicon (see p.271). A cylinder of silicon is first produced, and this is then sliced into wafers about 0.25 mm (0.01 inch) thick. Each wafer is treated to make several hundred microchips. The wafers are then tested and chopped up into individual chips. These are inspected under a microscope before being packaged.

MAKING A TRANSISTOR

1 FIRST MASKING

The silicon base is first coated with silicon dioxide, which does not conduct electricity, and then with a substance called photoresist. Shining ultraviolet light through a patterned mask hardens the photoresist. The unexposed parts remain soft.

2 FIRST ETCHING

A solvent dissolves away the soft unexposed layer of photoresist, revealing a part of the silicon dioxide. This is then chemically etched to reduce its thickness. The hardened photoresist is then dissolved to leave a ridge of dioxide.

3 SECOND MASKING

Layers of polysilicon, which conducts electricity, and photoresist are applied, and then a second masking operation is carried out.

4 SECOND ETCHING

The unexposed photoresist is dissolved, and then an etching treatment removes the polysilicon and silicon dioxide beneath it. This reveals two strips of p-type silicon.

5 DOPING

The hard photoresist is removed. The layers now undergo an operation called doping which transforms the newly revealed strips of p-type silicon into n-type silicon.

6 THIRD MASKING AND ETCHING

Layers of silicon dioxide and photoresist are added. Masking and etching creates holes through to the doped silicon and central polysilicon strip.

MICROCHIP

CONNECTORS
TO PINS

PINS

SILICON WAFER

WAFER WITH CHIPS

PACKAGE OF PINS
A finished microchip is dwarfed by
the connections needed to fit it into
a computer's circuit board. The chip
is set in a plastic base and connected
to two rows of pins which conduct
electric signals.

7 COMPLETING THE TRANSISTOR
The photoresist is dissolved, and a final masking stage adds three
strips of aluminium. These make electrical connections through the holes
and complete the transistor.

In this transistor, known as an MOS type, a high positive charge fed
to the gate attracts electrons in the p-type silicon base. Current flows
between the source and the drain, thereby switching the transistor on. A
low or zero charge at the gate stops electrons and turns the transistor off.

If the transistors in a chip were really this big, then
the whole chip would be the size of a city!

ALUMINIUM

ALUMINIUM

ALUMINIUM

SILICON DIOXIDE

POLYSILICON
GATE

SOURCE

DRAIN

N-TYPE SILICON

N-TYPE SILICON

ELECTRONS

P-TYPE SILICON

PROCESSOR

Inside every digital machine is a circuit board covered with microchips and other components all linked by electrical pathways called buses. It houses some of the basic units of the machine, such as memory units, and connects to external units like a keyboard. At the heart of the circuit board and connected to all units is the processor. Following software programs, the processor receives bits in the form of on-off electric pulses and processes them to produce a result, also in bits. The processor also controls the units so that they perform their actions at the right time and work together to carry out the required task.

SCREEN
This is an output unit that receives result bits from the processor and displays the result (see p.361).

PROCESSOR
The processor is a microchip also called the microprocessor or central processing unit (cpu). The speed at which the processor handles bits and controls a machine depends on its clock. This device puts out a timing signal at a rate measured in megahertz (MHz) that governs the speed.

ADDRESS BUS
Bits giving the address numbers of locations in the memory pass along this pathway and open locations in memory units for the processor to store and retrieve bits.

HARD DISK
This is the machine's main store for data bits and program bits (see p.333).

MODEM
This unit enables the processor to communicate with another machine and send or receive bits (see p.349).

TELEPHONE LINE CARRIES BITS

ROM
This memory unit holds permanent data and program bits required by the processor (see p.331).

RAM
This memory unit stores bits en route to and from the processor (see p.331).

CIRCUIT BOARD

DATA BUS
The processor fetches data bits and program bits, and sends out result bits, along this pathway.

BITS AND BUSES
The buses and processor handle bits in groups of 8, 16, 32, 64 etc. The more bits, the faster the machine.

CONTROL BUS
Bits forming control signals pass along this pathway between the processor and other units.

KEYBOARD
This is an input unit that produces data bits required by the processor (see p.317).

SOFTWARE

Every digital machine becomes little more than a useless chunk of processed sand and oil without software. This is the general name for the programs that instruct machines how to carry out tasks. They are called "software" to contrast with "hardware", the actual machinery. Written by programmers using computers, software consists of complex instruction codes in the form of bits. The programs are distributed in microchips inserted in machines, on floppy disks and CD-ROMs, and over the Internet (see p.350). Software may by inbuilt and give a machine one task, enabling a cash machine to pay out money and a digital camera to take pictures, for example. In a computer, the software is put on the hard disk and stored there. A computer can be given different programs and can carry out a huge range of tasks. These include word processing and desk-top publishing; playing games; recording music; drawing pictures; preparing financial statements; storing data.

Operating System

Every digital machine needs an operating system, which is the program that governs the basic way in which the machine works and enables you to use it. In a computer, this is a program such as Windows that makes the computer respond to the mouse. The operating system is stored on the hard disk so that it may be upgraded or improved when necessary.

ANGLE BUTTON
Click here to change the angle of the mammoth's trunk. A higher angle could make the mammoth squirt the water farther – but not always.

SQUIRT FORCE BUTTON
More force sends the water farther. But too much force could make the water miss the pumpkin patch altogether!

WATER BUTTON
Clicking here changes the amount of water that the mammoth sucks up and squirts out. Too little water will parch the pumpkins; too much will drown them.

COUNTDOWN BUTTON
This button controls the amount of time for each go. The computer counts down as you play, and stops play when the time reaches zero.

WEATHER BUTTON
Click here to control the amount of sunshine. Too much sun will dry out the patch; too little will not provide enough sunlight for rapid growth.

SCORE PANEL
This shows the biggest pumpkin's weight. The top figure is your score, and the lower figure the highest score.

TRUNK DIRECTION
Click on the mammoth to make the mammoth swivel its trunk.

SQUIRT BUTTON
Click here to make the mammoth squirt. The computer's processor stores all the chosen factors in the memory. Using mathematical formulas in the program, the processor calculates the path of the water and growth of the pumpkin hit. It then works out the display images so that you see the mammoth squirt the water and the pumpkin grow, and it updates the score.

PUMPKIN PATCH
The object of this game is to grow the biggest pumpkin in the time allowed. You get the mammoth to squirt water over the pumpkins. There are many factors to consider. There are the direction and angle of the trunk and the squirt force, so that the water will hit a promising pumpkin. The amount of water and the weather will also affect growth.

CHAPTER FOUR

Mammoth and Bill followed the belt into a large clearing in which eight ovens and eight chefs stood waiting.

"Hi, Bill." "Hi, Bill." "Hi, Bill." "Hi, Bill."

"Hi, Bill." "Hi, Bill." "Hi, Bill." "Hi, Bill."

When a pumpkin came to rest in front of a particular oven, the chef assigned to that oven would scoop it into a waiting pie crust.

Then he or she would light a fire in their oven and prepare to bake the pie. When a no-pumpkin arrived in front of an oven, that particular chef would do absolutely nothing. Since smoke was produced only by those ovens that were lit, a pattern of smoke and no-smoke was created that matched exactly the pumpkin/no-pumpkin pattern.

*B*ill admitted that in an earlier system they had simply launched the pumpkin patterns to distant locations, but complaints from various communities along the route, not to mention birdwatchers, had necessitated a redesign. What Bill didn't explain, because he enjoyed surprises, was that his workers had been using these smoke signals to gather information about the lifestyles and habitat of mammoths from a distant museum of natural history.

It didn't much matter what Bill was saying or not saying since Mammoth was far too busy snorting in as much warm pumpkin pie air as possible. To his great relief, the digital domain finally smelled of something other than metal, plastic, and wet laundry. A sudden "whistle-thud" "whistle-thud" told Bill that information was already coming back in response to his most recent smoke requests.

"Come on Mammoth," he shouted. "We're almost there."

Just around the corner from the ovens, a set of eight funnels and eight chutes had been set up to catch apples and no-apples, which were hurtling through the air. While Bill considered the apple rather low-tech and a little behind the times, he was clearly excited by the arrival of any information. To Mammoth's surprise and delight, the eight chutes ended above a tray of sweet-smelling chocolate syrup. After dropping through the funnels, the apples from each arriving sequence rolled down the chutes, shot through the gooey tray, and slid across a narrow strip of paper leaving a distinct chocolate smear. After a set of eight smears or no-smears had been made, the marked portion of the paper was yanked out of the way in order to record the next set.

SENDING BITS

The digital domain now reveals itself to be immense. Bits are no longer just patterns of pumpkins to be transported short distances. They are transformed into other kinds of bits that can fly swiftly through the air over huge distances to distant processors and memory stores. The bits return in different patterns carrying numbers that represent new kinds of information. These may include images and sounds, like those that the mammoth warily provided when it entered the digital domain.

Many digital systems involve communications in which bits are sent between machines, as in a fax machine sending a message to a distant fax and receiving a reply. Digital communications are revolutionizing telephone, radio, and TV, greatly improving sound and picture quality and offering more ways, often interactive, of using these services. Millions of computers can now communicate with each other in the worldwide Internet. Bits can arrive from anywhere, ready to proceed to the next step in the digital domain and – along with original home-grown bits – finally be put to use.

MODEM

Inside a computer, bits rush around at speeds of a million or more bits a second. To travel to another computer, the bits have to go along a telephone line. An ordinary telephone line carries low-frequency sound signals and cannot handle bits at this rate.

Unless you install a high-speed line, you need a modem to send and receive bits. The modem is an external or internal unit that connects the computer to a telephone socket, and from there into a network of links that can transfer bits quickly in several ways.

COMPUTER SENDS MESSAGE

MODEM CHANGES BITS TO SOUND SIGNAL

BITS GO TO MODEM

TELEPHONE LINE CARRIES SOUND SIGNAL

RADIO LINK
The sound signal is transmitted on a radio carrier wave in the same way as AM or FM broadcasting (see p.238).

BITS AND BEEPS

A modem works by converting the computer's fast digital on-off signal into a low-frequency sound signal. It splits up the bits into groups, and converts the groups into very short beeps of sound. One kind of beep carries a certain combination of on-bits and off-bits, another beep carries another combination, and so on. The sending modem puts all the beeps together to form a sound signal carrying all the bits, and the receiving modem changes the beeps back into bits.

RADIO WAVES

COMPUTER RECEIVES MESSAGE

MODEM

GLASS COATING   GLASS CORE   OUTER INSULATION   METAL CORE   OUTER INSULATION   METAL CORE

FIBRE-OPTIC CABLE
The radio wave is converted back into bits, which are sent as on-off flashes of infra-red laser light along a glass fibre-optic cable (see p.185).

SOUND SIGNAL
The bits are converted back into a sound signal, which travels along the metal core of a cable in the telephone line. The wavy line represents the beeps in the sound.

DIGITAL SIGNAL
The modem converts the sound signal back into a digital signal containing bits in the form of rapid on-off electric pulses. These bits go to the computer.

FREQUENCY 1   B   A   C   B   A   FREQUENCY 4

FREQUENCY 2   FREQUENCY 3   I   H   G   E   D   F   E   D

MULTIPLEXING
A communications link can carry many separate digital messages by multiplexing. The message bits are split up into small packets, and packets from different messages are interleaved, sent, and the messages are then reassembled on arrival. Several multiplexed signals can be sent at different frequencies over a link to increase its capacity even more.

FIBRE-OPTIC MULTIPLEXED SIGNALS
The glass core of this cable carries four light signals at different frequencies shown as different colours. Each signal is multiplexed and consists of interleaved eight-bit packets from three messages, so that the cable carries 12 messages; nine (A to I) are shown. Multiplexing enables a single link to carry thousands of messages at once.

HOME COMPUTER 1
*This user is sending
an e-mail message to
someone at Mammoth
Corporation.*

SERVICE PROVIDER
*Home users subscribe to a service
provider, which is a gateway to
the Internet and e-mail services.*

ROUTING COMPUTER

GOVERNMENT HOUSE
WEB SITE

GROUND STATION

ROUTING
COMPUTER

BACKBONE
A network of
routing computers – the
Internet backbone – links
organizations and service providers.
The routing computers decode
addresses to connect users with each
other and to sites throughout the
Internet. The links are
metal cables, fibre-
optic cables, or radio
links, possibly via
satellites (see
p.349).

UNDERSEA
CABLE

SERVICE PROVIDER
*The service provider
is an organization with
powerful computers that connect to
the Internet and store users' web sites.
A telephone line links each home
computer via its modem to the
service provider.*

BRIGHT LIGHT
WEB SITE

WEB SITE
Every web site has an Internet
address, which takes the form
http://www. mammoth.com/images.
This is a web site at Mammoth
Corporation showing images. http stands for
HyperText Transport Protocol, which enables you to use
the mouse to click on a word or image on the screen and
instantly jump to another part of the web site or to a different
web site. www is a code for the web site computer at
mammoth.com, the code for the commercial organization
Mammoth Corporation. Finally, the code word images takes
the user to the part of the web site containing pictures
to download or transfer from the web site.

BROWSER
To visit a web site, your
computer must have a browser.
This is a computer program
that enables you to use all the
facilities of the web site, such
as jumping from one part of
the site to another and
downloading material.

HOME COMPUTER 2
*This user first consults the
search engine to find out about
castles. The search engine provides the
web site address of Grimm Castle, and
the user jumps to the castle's web site.*

TEACHEM SCHOOL
WEB SITE

INTERNET AND E-MAIL

All computer users, at home and at work, can link into the global computer communications network known as the Internet. Bits flash to and fro between the computers to provide people with a huge variety of services. People can send each other messages by electronic mail or e-mail; they can visit web sites on the World Wide Web to obtain information, entertainment, commercial services, and software of all kinds; and they can take part in discussion groups and chat via the computer. Organizations have computers that link directly to the Internet. Home computers link to a service provider via a modem and a phone line or broadband cable.

E-MAIL (ELECTRONIC MAIL)

Every person has an e-mail address which takes the form of his or her name, the symbol @ (at), and a domain name, such as jsmith@ mammoth.com. The domain name contains the name of the person's service provider or organization followed by codes for the type of organization or provider and often its country, each separated by a dot. The domain name mammoth.com stands for Mammoth Corporation, which is a commercial organization (com). E-mail offers you more than a quick and easy way to send people written messages. It is possible to use e-mail to send computer data, such as word-processed documents and images.

SEARCH ENGINE

You can locate useful or interesting web sites by using a search engine. This is an organization with a web site containing a huge database of web site addresses. You key in a subject or a name that describes what you are seeking, and the search engine provides you with a list or selection of web site addresses that fit your enquiry. You then simply click on an address to jump to that web site.

COMMUNICATIONS
SATELLITE

GRIMM CASTLE
WEB SITE

GROUND STATION

ROUTING COMPUTER

ROUTING
COMPUTER

SERVICE
PROVIDER

SEAVIEW
HOTEL
WEB SITE

HOPE CHURCH
WEB SITE

MAMMOTH CORPORATION
This organization's powerful computers link up all its employees in an internal network and store its web site.

BUSINESS COMPUTER 1
The e-mail message arrives from home computer 1.

BUSINESS COMPUTER 2
This user is visiting the web site at Government House.

CASH MACHINE

A secure line connects a cash machine to the bank's central computer. Bits forming your PIN number and the amount requested go to the bank, which returns bits instructing the machine to pay out (see p.365).

FAX MACHINE

A fax machine contains a modem (see p.349), enabling it to send bits representing a document in coded form along a telephone line to another fax. The modem in this machine decodes the incoming telephone signal to receive the bits, and sends them to the fax machine's printer to print out the document (see p.358).

DIGITAL PHONE, RADIO, AND TELEVISION

A digital mobile phone transmits your voice as bits by radio to the base station (see p.236), and receives voice bits from the station. The phone also sends out a digital identification signal in order to connect to the nearest base station. In a similar way, sound or picture signals are transmitted as bits to the aerials of digital radio or television receivers or along cables. Using a digital-analog converter, the phone or receiver changes the bits back into sound or picture signals that go to the phone earpiece, the radio loudspeaker, or the television screen (see pp.360-1). A digital television receiver needs a set-top or inbuilt digital decoder to receive pictures.

SIGNAL 1 MOVES OUT IN CIRCLES FROM SATELLITE 1

GPS SATELLITE 1

GPS SATELLITE 2

SIGNAL 2

SIGNAL 3

GPS SATELLITE 3

PORTABLE NAVIGATOR

You can find out where you are, anywhere in the world, with a portable navigator. This device receives digital radio signals from satellites orbiting Earth. These are usually GPS (Global Positioning System) satellites. Each signal contains the exact time it left the satellite as well as the satellite's position. By working out how long the signals take to travel from the satellites to the navigator, the navigator can calculate its distance from each satellite. As a result, the navigator knows that it is located somewhere on a circle at its known distance from a satellite. The combination of the three satellite signals is enough for the navigator to work out its location. A fourth satellite signal gives the altitude of the navigator.

BOAT IS AT INTERSECTION OF THREE CIRCLES

ARROW INDICATES WAY TO GO

SHOWING THE WAY
The navigator's display can show the compass direction and distance of your destination. It can also give your exact position in latitude and longitude, or local map co-ordinates.

IN VIEW
At any time, four satellites are always in view from any point on Earth to fix a position.

CHAPTER FIVE

"Well, here we go," said Bill, coaxing the reluctant mammoth away from a pile of discarded chocolate-coated apples and into a large building where workers were fastening the last of the smeared strips together. They had created a single, large piece of paper, which they then stretched between two rollers.

Pressed into the floor in the centre of the space were four footprints, which to Mammoth's amazement precisely matched his own. No sooner had he placed his feet in them than two small orchestras complete with sheet music were rolled into position next to his ears. Mammoth was already beginning to feel a little claustrophobic, and when a large piece of machinery gently wrapped itself around his head, he let out an extraordinary wail.

At that very moment, the musicians began to play – or more accurately to recreate – almost identical trumpeting sounds. Then the paper began to roll past his eyes, which made the individual smears blur together, creating not only an amazing landscape but one which seemed to be in motion. When Mammoth turned his head to follow a particular sound, the scene shifted in exactly that direction. Endless clumps of swamp grass swayed gently in the breeze.

Most importantly, however, he thought he saw other mammoths – lots of them. He couldn't believe his tear-filled eyes. The years of loneliness were over. Solitary wandering would be a thing of the past. As the sounds grew louder and more wonderfully cacophonous, his head swung back and forth to take it all in. Feeling a pleasant dizziness, he stood still for a moment and noticed that one particularly beautiful mammoth was approaching him.

USING BITS

On its journey through the digital domain, the mammoth first saw personal details such as its dimensions, image, and sound changed into numbers. These were stored, then processed to produce new numbers, while yet more numbers arrived from elsewhere. The purpose of this number crunching now becomes clear as the bits representing the numbers are turned back into images and sounds so the mammoth can experience a virtual mammoth world. Aided by imperfect eyesight, and a little credulity, he sees and hears mammoths cavorting all around him.

The new friends are, in fact, near replicas of himself. The original bits giving the mammoth's details have been processed to produce bits that form images of a variety of mammoths in motion. The sound bits have undergone processing to provide a vocabulary of calls. From the mammoth museum have come bits representing a typical mammoth landscape, and bits that give information on mammoth lifestyles so that the virtual mammoths will move and call realistically.

But for us, the digital domain becomes an actual reality as the bits that have been made by an input unit of a digital machine, communicated to the machine, stored in its memory, and processed by its processor, are changed back into forms that we can understand and use. The bits become words, numbers, images, sounds, or movements in output units such as printers, screens, loudspeakers, simulators, and robots.

NUMBERS AT WORK

Thus do numbers serve us. Digital machines are changing the world and the ways in which we live because almost everything can be represented by a string of numbers. Once something is in numerical form, the numbers can be easily and swiftly changed to represent actions that are difficult or impossible to achieve by mechanical means. Digital machines not only outstrip and outperform their mechanical forebears. They inspire new kinds of things, new things to do, and new ways in which things are to work.

He was helplessly in love. She was wearing a bow in her hair and a name tag. He was at some kind of mammoth software convention. And then he remembered that mammoths didn't attend conventions! They flouted them. But she came closer and raised her trunk to kiss him. This was too good to be true. He decided to stop thinking. He closed his eyes and raised his trunk to return the caress. He tasted...chocolate. Chocolate? His eyes suddenly flew open. All he saw were smears.

Not the little smears, but big smears. The kind of smears you get when you drag a drooling trunk across a piece of chocolate-covered paper. He was stunned. Then he was furious. He shook the contraption from his head. The orchestras took cover where they could. By the time Mammoth calmed down, he was devastated. He felt cheated. Humiliated. It had all been some kind of trick. "Not a trick," said Bill somewhat defensively. "Progress."

DIRECT OUTPUT

Sequences of bits in the form of on-off electric pulses arrive at the output unit of a digital machine or system. If they are then arranged in a grid or array, bits representing an image or a character, such as a letter, form a pattern that reproduces the image or character. The bits go directly to a printer mechanism to be printed in this pattern. Bits representing characters also go directly to alphanumeric displays.

INK-JET PRINTER

Also known as a bubble-jet printer, this printer contains a print head that moves back and forth across the sheet of paper, which moves up after each pass. The print head fires tiny jets of ink onto the paper to produce rows of dots that build up into images and characters. Each on-pulse (binary 1) fires the print head to ink a dot; an off-pulse (binary 0) does not fire the head.

INCOMING BITS
(SEE P.352)

FAX MACHINE

A plain-paper fax machine contains an ink-jet or laser printer to print a copy of the document being sent to it. Some fax machines contain a thermal printer with a line of about 2,000 heating elements that prints rows of dots on a roll of heat-sensitive paper.

PRINT HEAD
The head contains an ink chamber, and vertical rows of very fine nozzles that fire jets of quick-drying ink at the paper.

INK-JET
NOZZLES

INK-JET NOZZLES
An enlarged view of the nozzles. Each one fires about 10,000 times a second

CABLE BRINGING BITS
TO PRINT HEAD

INSIDE AN INK-JET
An ink-jet printer works by forming bubbles in the ink, hence its other name of bubble-jet printer.

1 INK TUBE
Inside each nozzle of the print head is a tube containing a heating element. Ink is fed to it.

2 BUBBLE FORMS
A pulse of electricity heats up the element, instantly vapourizing some of the ink to form a bubble.

COLOUR PRINTER

Colour ink-jet printers contain four separate print heads that fire jets of yellow, magenta, cyan, and black inks at the paper. The coloured dots merge to form a full-colour picture (see pp.183 and 214). Three eight-bit colour numbers in the digital colour signal (see p.325) give the shade of each colour to be printed, and the print head fires a varying number of separate small dots. A light shade results from a few small dots spaced out, and a heavy shade from lots of close-spaced dots. A colour laser printer works in the same basic way, except that the paper makes four passes and the drum is fed with toner powder in the four different colours.

3 BUBBLE EXPANDS
The bubble grows rapidly as the heating continues, and begins to force some ink out of the tube.

4 TUBE FIRES
A jet of ink leaves the tube and the heating stops. The bubble collapses, sucking in more ink.

EYE TO EYE
A printed picture or document consists of a grid of rows of tiny dots printed one after another. From normal viewing distance, the dots merge together to form images and characters. This is a print of the eye scanned on page 323.

LASER PRINTER
The printing action of a laser printer is exactly the same as a photocopier (see p.260). The incoming on-off bits cause a laser or LED (see p.273) to fire rows of on-off flashes of light at the printing drum and build up dots in the image.

INCOMING BITS

LASER OR LED

LIGHT FLASHES

LENS

SPINNING MIRROR

FLASHES OF LIGHT SPREAD IN ROWS ACROSS ROTATING DRUM

PRINTING DRUM

ALPHANUMERIC DISPLAY
A simple display showing numbers, made up of the ten decimal numerals from 0 to 9, appears on many digital machines. These include the pocket calculator, digital watch, and the digital timer, thermometer, and scales shown on pages 319 and 321. Some machines, such as radio sets, also display letters of the alphabet. Each character (numeral or letter) is formed of several segments; numerals contain seven segments. On-off bits go directly to the segments in the display, and the on bits cause some of the segments to go dark. The resulting pattern of dark segments forms a number or letter.

DISPLAY

LIGHT SEGMENT

DARK SEGMENT

DECODED 7-BIT NUMBERS

DECODER

INCOMING 4-BIT NUMBERS

SEVEN-SEGMENT DISPLAY
The segments in an alphanumeric display work with liquid crystals (see pp.192-3). Natural light is either reflected from the display, or a light source is placed behind it. When an electric current goes to the segment, the liquid crystals inside it block the light so that the segment goes dark. Bits representing the characters to be displayed go to the display decoder. For numerals that have seven segments, these bits may be the four-bit binary equivalents of the decimal numerals to be displayed, so that 0011 arrives to become a 3, and 1001 arrives to become a 9. The decoder changes the four-bit numbers to seven-bit numbers, and each of the seven bits controls one of the segments. An on-bit (binary 1) causes a current to go to the segment and darken it; an off-bit (binary 0) stops the current and lightens the segment.

SIGNAL OUTPUT

DIGITAL-ANALOG CONVERTER (DAC)

Output units that produce sound through loudspeakers and earphones, as well as images on screens, do not work directly with bits. They require an analog electric signal with a varying voltage. The incoming digital sound and image signal, which consists of bits in the form of on-off electric pulses, first passes through a digital-analog converter. This is the reverse of the analog-digital converter that changes sound and light to bits when they enter the digital domain (see p.320).

THREE-BIT CONVERTER

This converts the three-bit digital signal 101 (on-off-on) into an analog signal of five volts. Three bits are shown for simplicity. In practice, DACs convert digital signals of 8, 16, or more bits.

5 VOLTS

CURRENT OF 5 VOLTS EMERGES FROM DAC

INSIDE A DAC

The incoming bits go to separate wires connected to transistor switches. These control an electric current going to resistors that reduce the voltage of the current to a half, a quarter, an eighth, and so on.

4 VOLTS

RESISTOR REDUCES VOLTAGE TO A HALF

0 VOLTS

RESISTOR REDUCES VOLTAGE TO A QUARTER

1 VOLT

TRANSISTOR 2 OFF

TRANSISTOR 3 ON

TRANSISTOR 1 ON

RESISTOR REDUCES VOLTAGE TO AN EIGHTH

8-VOLT CURRENT GOES TO ALL TRANSISTORS

1

0

1

FIRST BIT

SECOND BIT

THIRD BIT

DOUBLE, DOUBLE

Each resistor has double the value of the next resistor because each successive bit of a binary number represents one, two, four, and so on.

DIGITAL SOUND

Incoming sound bits, such as those that go to a digital phone, digital radio, and computer sound card, first pass through a digital-analog converter. The resulting analog sound signal is amplified so that it is strong enough to power a loudspeaker or earphone. A synthesizer receives a digital MIDI signal produced by an electric keyboard (see p.316), and decodes and converts this to give an analog signal that produces a musical note at a certain pitch and volume.

INCOMING DIGITAL SIGNAL

DIGITAL-ANALOG CONVERTER

SYNTHESIZER

LOUDSPEAKER

ANALOG SOUND SIGNAL

AMPLIFIED SIGNAL

AMPLIFIER

SOUND SELECTION

The kind of sound produced by the synthesizer can be selected by a set of bits in the incoming digital signal.

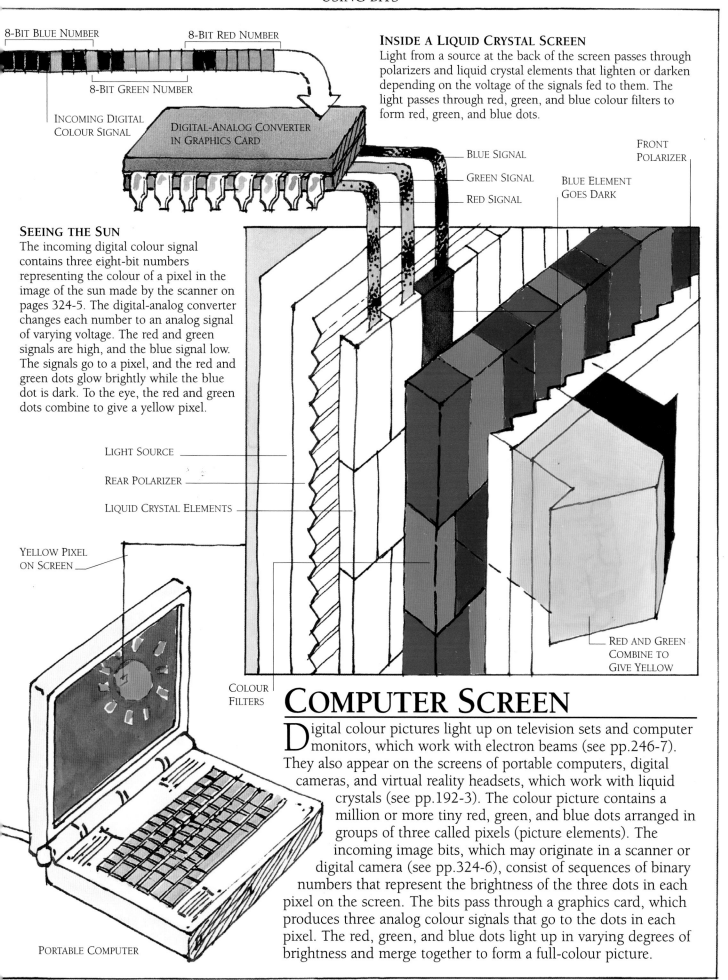

8-Bit Blue Number

8-Bit Red Number

8-Bit Green Number

Incoming Digital Colour Signal

Digital-Analog Converter in Graphics Card

INSIDE A LIQUID CRYSTAL SCREEN

Light from a source at the back of the screen passes through polarizers and liquid crystal elements that lighten or darken depending on the voltage of the signals fed to them. The light passes through red, green, and blue colour filters to form red, green, and blue dots.

Blue Signal

Green Signal

Red Signal

Front Polarizer

Blue Element Goes Dark

SEEING THE SUN

The incoming digital colour signal contains three eight-bit numbers representing the colour of a pixel in the image of the sun made by the scanner on pages 324-5. The digital-analog converter changes each number to an analog signal of varying voltage. The red and green signals are high, and the blue signal low. The signals go to a pixel, and the red and green dots glow brightly while the blue dot is dark. To the eye, the red and green dots combine to give a yellow pixel.

Light Source

Rear Polarizer

Liquid Crystal Elements

Yellow Pixel on Screen

Red and Green Combine to Give Yellow

Colour Filters

Portable Computer

COMPUTER SCREEN

Digital colour pictures light up on television sets and computer monitors, which work with electron beams (see pp.246-7). They also appear on the screens of portable computers, digital cameras, and virtual reality headsets, which work with liquid crystals (see pp.192-3). The colour picture contains a million or more tiny red, green, and blue dots arranged in groups of three called pixels (picture elements). The incoming image bits, which may originate in a scanner or digital camera (see pp.324-6), consist of sequences of binary numbers that represent the brightness of the three dots in each pixel on the screen. The bits pass through a graphics card, which produces three analog colour signals that go to the dots in each pixel. The red, green, and blue dots light up in varying degrees of brightness and merge together to form a full-colour picture.

VIRTUAL REALITY

The one way in which you can enter a digital domain is to put on a virtual reality headset. You find yourself in a world created by the computer. Objects are moving all around you and you can hear their sounds. As you move your head, the scene and sounds move too, just as if you were actually there and looking around, up, or down. In fact, you are looking at two small screens and listening to earphones. The computer connected to the headset is able to react to your movements because the headset contains a sensor that detects your head movements.

TRACKING SENSOR
A motion detector similar to that in an air bag (see p.292) produces an electric signal as you turn, raise, or lower your head. Virtual reality machines may also use detectors that track other movements, such as your hands.

EARPHONES
A pair of earphones (see p.229) produces stereophonic sounds that come from all angles.

—This is virtually nauseating.

SCREENS
Two liquid crystal screens (see p.361) display a pair of images, which are slightly different so that your brain combines them to create a three-dimensional scene.

COMPUTER CABLE
The computer processes incoming bits from the tracking sensor and returns output bits that control the image and sound output accordingly.

1 LOOKING AHEAD
You see a three-dimensional view of a kennel as the pair of screens display two images of the kennel.

2 LOOKING AROUND
You hear a dog barking in your left ear. As you turn your head towards it, the images shift to the right.

3 LOOKING LEFT
The dog appears, and the barking sound is now in front as sounds come from both earphones.

FLIGHT SIMULATOR

Virtual reality is a valuable way of training aircraft pilots. A flight simulator contains a mock-up of the aircraft flight deck. The pilot sits at the controls and through the windows sees a real airport and moving pictures of scenes that occur during take-off, flight, and landing. The pictures are generated by a powerful computer connected to the controls. As the pilot handles the controls, the computer processes the operations and sends output bits back to the simulator. These move the picture, vary the instrument displays, sound warnings, and tilt the flight deck exactly as if the aircraft were flying. The computer can switch to night landings or foggy weather, or conditions that require an emergency landing such as an engine failure. It can also record a "flight" and replay it so that the pilot and instructor can go back over the training exercise.

PROJECTORS
High-quality projectors throw adjacent sections of a wide, colour, computer-generated picture onto a curved screen that extends around the flight deck. Half of the screen can be seen here with two of the three projectors working.

CURVED MIRROR
The pilot looks through the windows of the flight deck at a wide curved mirror that extends around the windows. The mirror reflects the back-projected picture on the screen. This optical system makes the image appear to be a long way off. Half of the mirror is shown here.

CURVED SCREEN

INSTRUCTOR STATION
Behind the pilot, the instructor sits at the computer console, controlling the simulator's computer and assessing the performance of the pilot.

JACKS
Jacks beneath the simulator move in and out to tilt the simulator and mimic aircraft motion.

ROBOT

CONTROLLER

A powerful computer controls the actions of the robot. It calculates or remembers the various angles through which each of the joints must turn. It then sends control signals to the motors driving the joints. Sensors feed the angles of the joints back to the controller so that it knows when each joint has turned the required amount.

SHOULDER SWIVELS

WHOLE ARM ROTATES

The robot is the ultimate machine, able to carry out a wide range of physical tasks under its own control and with the potential to replicate almost every human action. For a brain, it has a computer that controls the movements of the robot's arms, legs or other appendages, sending output bits to electric or hydraulic motors that move the joints by precise amounts. The computer can be programmed with a particular set of movements that the robot can, if required, repeat exactly over and over again without ever wearying of its task. The robot is therefore an ideal machine for factory work, especially on assembly lines producing complicated machines such as cars. Some robots can handle parts, fitting them precisely in place, while other robots can hold and operate tools such as welding torches and paint sprayers. The robot may need a sense of touch, so that it does not apply too strong a grip and crush whatever it is handling. Its gripper or claw may therefore have pressure detectors that feed back information to the controlling computer. As computers develop, it is likely that robots will also gain a sense of vision with television cameras for eyes. A robot will scan an image of the scene before it, and be able to calculate the size and position of everything around it and thus move about and perform actions in much the same way as we do. As computers are now able to listen and talk to us, the day when the robot becomes an independent machine capable of interacting fully with people cannot be far off.

ELBOW BENDS

ANGLE SENSOR
In each joint is a slotted wheel like those in a computer mouse (see p.318). A light beam shines through the wheel to a detector, which gives an electric pulse every time a slot passes. The computer counts the pulses to sense the angle turned.

DETECTOR

SLOTS

LIGHT BEAM

FOREARM ROTATES

INDUSTRIAL ROBOT
This handling robot can perform complex actions because the various sections of the arm turn around six joints. These enable the robot's hand to move in all possible directions to any position within reach.

WRIST SWINGS UP AND DOWN

HAND ROTATES

GRIPPER CLOSES LIKE FINGERS TO SEIZE OBJECTS

TEACH PENDANT
This keyboard is connected to the robot controller. Six of the keys move each of the six joints. The operator "teaches" the robot an action by using the keys to move the robot's hand to each of a set of required positions. Each movement is then stored in the controller's memory so that the robot can repeat the action exactly.

CASH MACHINE
As you wait for a cash machine to pay out, the bank's central computer checks that your account has sufficient money and deducts the sum requested. It then sends output bits to the machine. These control a mechanism that picks up the correct number of bank notes from boxes of notes inside the machine. It then delivers them to the slot and motorized rollers feed the notes partly through the slot. The output bits also actuate rollers that return your card, and may print out and deliver a slip.

COMPUTER

This is the first of three common digital systems. These systems are made up of many input, memory, processing, communications, and output units linked together. A complete home computer system, given all the relevant software, is capable of a huge range of activities. Bits enter the computer from the mouse, keyboards, microphone, scanner, still camera, and video camera, which enables you to send live pictures over the Internet. Bits are stored in the various memory devices inside the computer's main box and tape back-up unit, and the modem sends and receives bits. Finally, bits go to the output units – the loudspeakers, screen and printer – as the computer performs a particular task.

DIGITAL VIDEO CAMERA

please wake up ... please wake up

MONITOR (SEE P.361)

LOUDSPEAKER (SEE P.360)

MOUSE (SEE P.318)

HARD DISK DRIVE (SEE P.333)

GRAPHICS CARD (SEE P.361)

RAM (SEE P.331)

FLOPPY DISK DRIVE (SEE P.333)

CD-ROM DRIVE (SEE P.337)

SOUND CARD (SEE P.322)

ROM (SEE P.331)

PROCESSOR (SEE P.344)

MICROPHONE (SEE P.322)

COMPUTER KEYBOARD (SEE P.317)

CIRCUIT BOARD (SEE P.344)

MAIN BOX

SCANNER
(SEE PP.324-5)

DIGITAL STILL
CAMERA (SEE P.326)

PRINTER
(SEE PP.358-9)

TAPE BACK-UP
UNIT (SEE P.334)

MODEM
(SEE P.349)

ELECTRIC KEYBOARD
(SEE P.316)

SUPERMARKET

Every time you make a purchase at a supermarket checkout, you come into contact with a huge digital system. The supermarket company uses a vast computer network built around the central computer at the head office. This communicates to a ring of depots in different locations. Each depot computer links in turn to a ring of individual stores. Each store contains an in-store computer that is connected to the computer in each checkout. The central computer is also linked to a network of bank computers.

IN-STORE COMPUTER
Digital signals pass to and from the central computer via the in-store computer. Every night, this updates each checkout computer with price changes and new products.

LINKS TO IN-STORE COMPUTER

CHECKOUT COMPUTER
Hard disk (see p.333) stores the name and price of thousands of products.

ALPHANUMERIC DISPLAY (SEE P.359) SHOWS PRICES, NAMES AND TOTAL BILL

SWIPE-CARD READER (SEE P.334) SENDS YOUR CARD NUMBER TO THE CENTRAL COMPUTER

KEYPAD (SEE P.316)

BAR-CODE READER (SEE P.334)

BAR CODE STORES PRODUCT NUMBER

CREDIT CARD OR DEBIT CARD

ELECTRONIC SCALES (SEE P.321) SEND WEIGHT OF PRODUCT TO CHECKOUT COMPUTER

CUSTOMER BUTTONS AUTHORIZE PAYMENT

INDIVIDUAL STORES

BANK

BANK

BANK

BANK

BANK NETWORK
Your payment goes to your bank, which sends the amount from your account to the supermarket account.

BANK

DEPOT

INDIVIDUAL STORE

SUPERMARKET'S BANK LINKS HEAD OFFICE TO BANK NETWORK

HEAD OFFICE
The central computer checks your card number, and sends a signal back to the checkout allowing purchase. It also collects details of all purchases for stock control and orders suppliers to send more stock to depots.

LINKS TO MORE DEPOTS

KEYBOARD (SEE P.317) MAY INPUT PRODUCT DETAILS

PRINTED RECEIPT
Printer (see p.358) prints out full receipt with the names and prices of all products purchased.

DEPOT
The depot computer receives instructions from the central computer to send more stock to stores.

INDIVIDUAL STORE

INDIVIDUAL STORE

INDIVIDUAL STORE

INDIVIDUAL STORE

AIRLINE

The whole process of making a flight connects you at several points to a large digital system. Your travel agent is one of several agents in a computer network. A routing computer connects the network of agents to a network of airline computers, which in turn link the check-in desks at airports. And, to handle payments, the agents and airlines are connected to the bank network. Computers, which may use the GPS navigation system (see pp.352-3), guide your aircraft, and your passport may undergo a computer check.

TRAVEL AGENT

TRAVEL AGENT

ROUTING COMPUTER LINKS ALL TRAVEL AGENTS TO CENTRAL RESERVATION COMPUTER

TRAVEL AGENT

CENTRAL RESERVATION COMPUTER
This obtains details of all available flights from airline computers, and sends details of passenger reservations back.

I'm sure you'll have a lovely trip.

BANK

BANK

BANK NETWORK

BANK

BANK

TRAVEL AGENT
You give an agent your destination and date of travel and the agent's computer first presents you with a choice of available flights. You then select the class of flight, special meals and other services, and the option to pay by cash or card. The computer then prints out a ticket containing your name and all the flight details.

DIGITAL TRAVEL
When you reserve a flight at a travel agent, the agent's computer gets details of all available flights from the airline computers. You may request special meals and services which, together with your personal details and the flight of your choice, are stored in the airline computer. When you check in at the airport, the desk computer contacts the airline computer to record your departure. It weighs your baggage and prints out bar-coded labels and your boarding pass. Your baggage, checked by bar-code readers, goes to the correct aircraft, which also receives special meals and instructions for special services required by passengers.

AIRLINE

AIRLINE

AIRLINE

CHECK-IN DESKS

CHECK-IN DESK PRINTER (SEE P.358)

BAR-CODED BAGGAGE LABEL

BOARDING PASS

SCREEN

KITCHEN
Notified by airline computer, the kitchen prepares and sends the required number of meals to each aircraft.

Vegetarian. Ha,ba,ha.

ELECTRONIC SCALES (SEE P.321)

PASSPORT

AIRPORT ENTRY CONTROL
A scanner with OCR (see p.323) reads passport details and contacts a central computer to check passengers for any bar on entry.

BAR CODE (SEE P.334) ON LABEL CONTAINS DESTINATION AND FLIGHT NUMBER

BAR-CODE READER

GATE CHECK-IN DESK

It's gone. Look for yourself!

Epilogue

While Mammoth had been impressed by much of the digital domain, there was also plenty about it that left him feeling uncomfortable. In the end, it was just too much, too big, too fast, and too unfamiliar. Mammoths, after all, had never really embraced the concept of progress and this one wasn't going to start now. In fact, as he left the digital domain, he had no intention of ever returning. Bill, smiling down from the top of the wall, knew differently. While it was true that the mammoth hadn't developed much of an appreciation for digital technology and all that it could complicate, he had developed a real taste for pumpkin pie and apples smeared in chocolate. These were a pleasant and entirely compatible replacement for swamp grass, which would soon be extinct. And Bill was the only supplier for miles and miles.

EUREKA!

THE INVENTION OF MACHINES

THE INCLINED PLANE

People have to eat to live and, necessity being ever the mother of invention, the very first machines to be invented were the tools used by prehistoric people in hunting and gathering their food. Stones crudely chipped to form tools date back about a million years, and stone axes and spearheads litter archaeological sites down to the dawn of civilization.

In cutting tools, the inclined plane became the first principle of technology to be put to work. On a larger scale, it may have enabled people to build at least one of the Seven Wonders of the World — the Great Pyramid. This was constructed in Egypt in 2600BC using high earth ramps to raise great stone blocks into position.

THE PLOUGH

The plough was invented in the Middle East in about 3500BC. At first, it was little more than a digging stick drawn by a person or an ox, but this primitive plough enabled people to dig deeper than before. Plants could put down stronger roots in ploughed soil, increasing crop yields and enabling farmers to produce a surplus of food. The plough thus freed some people from the necessity of growing their food.

LOCKS

Locks existed in ancient Egypt, and they made use of pins in the same way as the cylinder lock. The application of the inclined plane to the key, made by Linus Yale in the United States in 1848, is one of those fundamental inventions that long outlive their maker, and the cylinder lock is still often called a Yale lock. The lever lock dates from 1778 and was invented by a British engineer Robert Barron. The design resulted from a need to prevent burglars taking wax impressions inside locks and then making keys from them, and it too proved to be a fundamental advance.

THE ZIPPER

The zipper took quite a time to make its mark. It was invented by Whitcomb Judson in 1891, not in its present form as a clothes fastener, but as a device to do up boots. It did not take off until 1918, when the US Navy realized that Judson's invention would make an ideal fastener for flying suits. The name zipper, coined in 1926, clinched its success.

THE CAN OPENER

Methods of preserving food in sealed containers were invented in the early 1800s, at first using glass jars and then tin cans. The cans were ideal for transporting food, but opening them could be a problem. At first, a hammer and chisel — a crude use of the inclined plane — had to serve. Claw-like devices and levered blades were then devised to open cans, not without some

danger to the user. The safe and simple can openers that we have today were not invented until the 1930s, more than a century after the appearance of the tin can.

LEVERS

Levers also originated in ancient times in devices such as hoes, oars and slings. People realized intuitively that levers could aid their muscle power, but it took a genius to explain how levers work. The genius was the Ancient Greek scientist Archimedes (287-212BC), who first defined the principle of levers. He illustrated it with the famous adage "Give me a place to stand and I will move the Earth" — meaning that if he had a lever sufficiently long, he could shift the Earth by his own efforts.

The formulation of the principle of levers was a landmark in the development of science and technology. Archimedes' insight explained not only levers, because the same principle lies behind the inclined plane, gears and belts, pulleys and screws. Furthermore, Archimedes showed that by making observations and experiments, it was possible to deduce the basic principles that explain why things work.

WEIGHING MACHINES

The first device to make precise use of levers was invented long before Archimedes' time. This was the balance or scales used for weighing, which dates back from 3500BC. It may seem odd that a precision instrument was required so long ago: however, what had to be weighed was no ordinary material — it was gold. Gold dust was used as currency in the ancient civilizations of the Middle East, and amounts of it had to be weighed very precisely in order to assess their value.

KEYBOARD MACHINES

The piano was invented in Italy in 1709 by Bartolommeo Christofori, who sought a way of varying the volume of a keyboard by using levers to strike the strings with different amounts of force. His success is reflected in the instrument's name: the pianoforte or "soft-loud". The lever system was later improved to increase the response of the piano, resulting in the highly expressive instrument that affected the whole course of music.

The first practical typewriter was invented in the United States in 1867 by Christopher Scholes, and it was taken up by the Remington company. Unlike the piano, the typewriter gives little variety in performance and is consequently well on its way to obsolescence, ousted by computer printers capable of many kinds of typefaces and type sizes.

THE WHEEL AND AXLE

The development of mechanical power has its origins in the wheel and axle. The first machines to make use of this device may well have been the windlass and the winch. The Greek physician Hippocrates, who was born in 460BC, employed a windlass to stretch the limbs of his patients, a treatment uncomfortably like the rack of medieval torture chambers. Winches have been used to draw water from wells for many centuries.

THE WATERWHEEL AND WINDMILL

The waterwheel dates back to Greece in about 100BC, and it was developed by the Romans to power water mills grinding corn. The wheel had horizontal blades angled so that a stream of falling water could turn the wheel. Its advantage was that the vertical shaft of the wheel drove the horizontal grindstone directly. The bad news was that it required fast-flowing water and produced little power. The vertical waterwheel, first described by a Roman writer in about 15BC, is far more practical and it soon replaced the Greek wheel.

Rather like the first waterwheel, the first windmill was powered by a horizontal wheel bearing vertical sails. It was invented in Iran in about AD640. The vertical

windmill, also more practical, was invented in Europe in about 1170.

TURBINES

Modern turbines are a product of the Industrial Revolution, when the demand for power soared as factories developed. Engineers investigated blade design, seeking to maximize energy output. The Francis turbine, invented by James Francis in 1850 and now common in power stations, was literally a product of lateral thinking because Francis made the water flow inwards instead of outwards.

GEARS AND BELTS

Belts are simple devices, seen in the chains of buckets that lifted water in ancient times. The basic forms of gears were known by the first century AD. An extraordinary early application of gears is the Antikythera mechanism, a mechanical calendar made in Greece in about 100BC and recovered from a wreck sunk off the Greek island of Antikythera. This machine had 25 bronze gear wheels forming a complex train of gears that could move pointers to indicate the future positions of the Sun and Moon as well as the times when certain stars would rise or set.

CLOCKS

A rack-and-pinion gear was used in a water clock built by the Greek inventor Ctesibius in about 250BC. The water clock was an ancient device in which water dropped at a constant rate into a container, the level of the water indicating the time. Ctesibius improved it by having a float raise a rack that turned a pinion connected to a pointer on a drum. The pointer turned to indicate the time in the

same way as the hour hand of a mechanical clock.

The oldest surviving mechanical clocks date from the late 1300s. Gears transmitted the constant movement of a regulator to the hands or to a bell. A good regulator appeared only with the discovery of the pendulum in 1581 by the great Italian scientist Galileo, who timed a swinging chandelier with his pulse and realized that the time taken for each swing was always constant. Even so, it took nearly a century for the first pendulum clocks to appear.

THE EPICYCLIC GEAR

The sun-and-planet or epicyclic gear is of much more recent origin than other types. It was invented in 1781 by the great British engineer James Watt, who is best known for improving the steam engine. Watt needed a device to turn the reciprocating motion of the piston of his steam engine into rotary motion, but he could not use the crank because someone else had patent protection on it. Watt's alternative was the epicyclic gear, now found in salad spinners, automatic transmission and many other devices.

THE DIFFERENTIAL

This first appeared in the "south-pointing carriage" invented in China in the third century AD. The two-wheeled carriage was surmounted by a figure that always pointed south, no matter how the carriage turned as it moved. The figure was set to south, and then a differential driven by the wheels turned the figure in the opposite direction to the carriage so that it still pointed south.

Such a machine must have appeared magical to the people of the time. However, calculations show that the mechanism could not have been sufficiently precise for the figure to point south for long. Within 5km (3 miles) it could well have been pointing north instead!

CAMS AND CRANKS

Cams and cranks are old devices too – the cam appearing in the drop hammer and the crank in a winding handle. Their application in the sewing machine was developed during the early 1800s, the first successful sewing machine being produced in the United States by Isaac Singer in 1851. The four-stroke internal combustion engine, which similarly depends on the controlling movement of cams and cranks, was first put to use in the motor car by Karl Benz in 1885. These two machines are still with us in their basic form today, along with their inventors' names.

THE LIFT AND ESCALATOR

The lift is a relatively recent invention, the reason being that buildings had to reach quite a height before they became necessary. Although lifts are intended for public use, the very first lift had exactly the opposite purpose. It was built in 1743 at the Palace of Versailles for the French king Louis XV. Counterbalanced by weights and operated by hand, the lift carried the king in total privacy from one floor to another.

The modern safety lift is the invention of the American engineer Elisha Otis, who dramatically demonstrated its effectiveness in 1854. He ordered the rope of the lift carrying himself to be cut. The emergency braking system was automatically activated, and the lift did not fall.

Escalators date from the 1890s. The first models were basically moving belts and had no steps, so could only carry people up or down a gentle incline.

SCREWS

The screw is yet another machine associated with Archimedes, for the earliest known is the water-lifting auger know as Archimedes' screw. However, it may well have been invented before his time. The screw press, which contains the form of screw used in nuts and bolts, was first described by Hero of Alexandria.

Metal screws were used as a superior alternative to nails in 1556, when the German mining engineer Agricola described how to screw leather to wood to make durable bellows. The screwdriver however did not follow until 1780.

THE COMBINE HARVESTER

The combine harvester is the most important invention in farming since the plough, and a modern harvester makes use of several augers that work in exactly the same was as Archimedes' screw. The first combine harvester was built in 1835 by combining a horse-drawn reaper and a threshing machine. It took a century to develop the harvester into an effective self-powered machine.

PULLEYS

Simple cranes using single pulley wheels were invented some 3,000 years ago, and compound pulleys with several wheels date back to about the 400s BC. Archimedes is said to have invented a compound pulley that was able to haul a ship ashore. The shadoof, a counter-weighted lifting machine, is also of ancient origin.

THE MICROMETER

This important device based on the screw was invented in 1772 by James Watt. Watt's micrometer worked in much the same way as the modern micrometer, and was accurate to a fiftieth of a millimetre (one-thousandth of an inch).

ROTATING WHEELS

Ancient peoples could easily move heavy loads by rolling them on logs, and one would expect that the wheel developed in this way. But this is not the case. Unlike a roller, a wheel requires an axle on which to turn and so the potter's wheel was the first true wheel. It was invented in the Middle East in about 3500BC. From the potter's wheel, the wheel was soon developed for transport.

THE BICYCLE

The first bicycles were pushed along by the feet and not pedalled. They were novelties rather than a serious means of transport, and were known as hobby-horses. Kirkpatrick Macmillan, a blacksmith, invented the pedal-operated bicycle in Britain in 1839. Raising the feet from the ground to turn the pedals required the rider to make use of precession to balance.

GYROCOMPASS

The inherent stability or gyroscopic inertia of devices such as spinning tops has been known for centuries, but the development of the gyroscope in machines is more recent. Its most important application, the gyrocompass, was invented by Elmer Sperry and first demonstrated on an American ship in 1911.

SPRINGS

Springs are also of ancient origin, being used in primitive locks. Metal springs date from the 1500s, when leaf springs were invented to provide a primitive suspension for road carriages. Springs did not become common until two centuries later, when coil springs were invented.

SPRING BALANCE AND HAIRSPRING

The principle behind the spring balance – that the extension of a spring is proportional to the force acting on it – was discovered by the English scientist Robert Hooke in 1678 and it is known as Hooke's Law. Hooke also invented the spiral spring known as a hairspring, which is used as a regulator in mechanical watches and which made portable timepieces possible.

FRICTION

People have been making use of friction ever since they first set foot on the ground, and the first friction devices to pound grain into flour date back to the beginnings of civilization.

THE PARACHUTE

This was one of several inventions that were forecast by Leonardo da Vinci, who drew one in 1485. Understandably, neither Leonardo nor anyone else was very keen to try out the idea in practice. However, there was little need for parachutes until the first balloons took to the air three centuries later. The first parachute descent proper took place in 1797, when the French balloonist André Garnerin successfully dropped 680 metres (2,230 feet). Early parachutes were fashioned like huge parasols and similarly named, being proof against a *chute* or fall rather than the Sun.

DRILLING MACHINES

Drilling, which is basically pounding or grinding, is a surprisingly old activity. The Chinese drilled oil wells some hundreds of metres or yards deep as early as the third century BC. They dropped a metal drilling tool into the hole to break up the rock. The first modern oil well, drilled by Edwin Drake in Pennsylvania in 1859, was drilled in the same way.

BEARINGS

Devices to reduce friction are of ancient origin, the first being log rollers which were placed under an object that was to be moved. To work effectively a wheel needs bearings on its axle. These were invented in France and Germany in about 1000BC. The bearings were made of wood and then greased to improve speed and lengthen their life. Modern bearings date back to the late 1700s. They made the development of machines during the Industrial Revolution all the more effective.

FLOATING

The first form of transport to progress under its own power was the raft. In prehistoric times, people must have hitched rides on uprooted trees that happened to be floating down rivers. Rafts borne on ocean currents probably carried people across the world's oceans long before recorded history.

The earliest known hollow boats date back to about 8000 BC. These were canoes dug out of tree trunks, which were paddled through the water.

The principle of flotation, which explains how things float, was one of the many achievements of Archimedes, the great scientist who lived in Sicily (then a Greek colony) in the 200s BC. He is reputed to have made this discovery in his bath and then ran naked into the street shouting the inventor's classic cry of Eureka, which means "I have found it".

Although the principle that Archimedes put forward explained that an iron boat could float, nobody really believed this and all boats and ships were made of wood until just over two centuries ago. The development of the iron ship coincided with the development of a powerful steam engine, which drove paddle wheels in boats.

SUBMARINES

Travelling under the water and into the air can be risky ventures, and required intrepid pioneers. Understandably perhaps, the inventors of both the first submarine and balloon persuaded other people to try out their craft.

The first proper submarine took to the water in 1776 during the American War of Independence. It was an egg-shaped wooden vessel invented by the American engineer David Bushnell; it went into action (unsuccessfully) against a British warship. The *Turtle*, as it was called, was very much a forerunner of the modern submersible, having ballast tanks and propellers.

BALLOONS

The first balloon to carry passengers was a hot-air balloon invented by the Montgolfier brothers in France in 1783. It made its first flight in November of that year at Paris, and flew 8km (5 miles). A few days later the first gas-filled balloon took to the Parisian skies, piloted by its inventor Jacques Charles. It contained hydrogen, which also lifted the first airship into the air in 1852. This machine, which was steam-powered, was invented by the French engineer Henri Giffard.

SAILS AND PROPELLERS

Sails powered boats along the River Nile in Egypt as long ago as 4000BC. These were square sails, which could sail only before the wind. The triangular sail, which is able to sail into the wind, first appeared in about AD 300 in boats on the Arabian Sea.

The propeller was invented in 1836 by Francis Pettit Smith in Britain and John Ericsson in the United States. It first powered a sea-going ship, appropriately called the *Archimedes*, in 1839.

FLYING

The first people to fly were Chinese criminals lifted by large kites. The explorer Marco Polo reported the use of such kites for punishment in the 1200s, but kite flying was also used to look out over enemy territory. Then, five centuries later, balloons began to carry people aloft.

THE AEROFOIL

The principle behind the aerofoil — that increasing the velocity of a gas or liquid lowers its pressure — was discovered by the Swiss scientist Daniel Bernoulli in 1738, and the basic form of the winged aircraft was developed during the 1800s. Its design was due to the British engineer Sir George Cayley, who flew the first glider in 1849. This machine carried a child. Four years later, Cayley's coachman (against his will) became the first adult to fly a winged aircraft. On landing, he immediately gave Cayley notice!

POWERED FLIGHT

The invention of powered flight is indelibly associated with the Wright brothers, the American engineers who flew the first powered aeroplane at Kitty Hawk in North Carolina in 1903. Unlike all modern aircraft, the wings of the Wrights' flying machine did not have ailerons. This development occurred in 1908 in aircraft built by the British engineer Henry Farman.

instrument, he used the pressure of water to drive air into the pipes: the resulting music was ear-splitting.

PUMPS AND JETS

The water-lifting pump is another invention credited to Ctesibius. However, the slow development of pumps able to produce a continuous jet of water enabled the Great Fire to destroy much of London in 1666. The first proper fire engine did not appear until 1721. The pump was invented by the British engineer Richard Newsham. It was a reciprocating pump with two pistons

driven alternately up and down by hand. The fire engine was reputed to produce a jet of water nearly 50m (160 feet) high and to be strong enough to smash a window.

Portable fire extinguishers were developed in the nineteenth century, powered at first by compressed air and then by carbon dioxide.

HYDRAULICS AND PNEUMATICS

An understanding of pressure in both air and water came with the work of the French scientist Blaise Pascal. In the mid-1600s, he discovered the principle that governs the action of pressure on a surface. Pascal's

principle explains both hydraulics and pneumatics. One of its latest consequences is the hovercraft, which was invented in 1955 by the British engineer Christopher Cockerell. This machine began life as a pair of tin cans linked up to a vacuum cleaner, which demonstrated that an air cushion could produce sufficient pressure to support a hovercraft.

SUCTION MACHINES

The vacuum cleaner also began life in Britain, where it was invented by Hubert Booth in 1901. Again, a simple demonstration sufficed to prove its viability: Booth sucked air through a handkerchief to show how it could pick up dirt. However, a practical machine was developed in the United States in 1908 by William

Hoover, and it is his name that has always been associated with the vacuum cleaner. Its distant relative, the aqualung, is also firmly associated with its inventor, the French oceanographer Jacques Cousteau. The aqualung was developed during World War II, and Cousteau subsequently used it to pioneer exploration of the sea bed.

THE HELICOPTER

Like the Wrights' powered aeroplane, the development of the helicopter was contingent upon the invention of a light but powerful engine – the petrol engine. The very first helicopter, built by Paul Cornu, whirled unsteadily into the air in France in 1907. The development of a reliable helicopter took about thirty years.

THE HYDROFOIL

The first use of the principle of the aerofoil was not in air but in water. In Britain in 1861, Thomas Moy tested wings by fixing them beneath a boat and found that the wings raised the hull above the water. Thus the hydrofoil was born before the aeroplane. The production of a practical hydrofoil took place in Italy, where it was developed by Enrico Forlanini during the first decade of this century.

PRESSURE POWER

The achievements of Archimedes inspired generations of inventors and engineers. First was Ctesibius, who lived at Alexandria in Egypt at about the same time. Ctesibius was renowned for his self-powered devices, notably the first organ. Water was a convenient source of power and in this

THE FLUSH TOILET

The water closet, the first of many euphemisms (though more accurate than most) for the flush toilet, dates back to 1589, when it was invented by Sir John Harington, a British nobleman who was a godson of Queen Elizabeth I. The cistern in Harington's invention worked with a valve that released the flow of water. Harington recommended that it be flushed once or preferably twice a day.

Harington's important contribution to the history of technology was centuries ahead of its time, and the water closet did not attain its present form until the late 1800s. The use of a siphon, which does away with valves that can leak, dates from that period.

EXPLOITING HEAT

Harnessing heat was the first technological achievement to be made. The discovery of fire, which happened in China over half a million years ago, provided heat for cooking and warmth. Millennia were to pass before heat was to be turned to much more advanced uses such as smelting metals and providing motive power.

IRON AND STEEL MAKING

Iron making dates from 1500BC when the Hittites, in what is now Turkey, built furnaces to smelt iron ore with charcoal and so produce the metal itself. The process did not develop further until 1709, when the British iron maker Abraham Darby substituted coke for charcoal and added limestone. His furnace needed a powerful blast of air to burn the coke, but it could make iron in large quantities – a factor which helped to bring about the Industrial Revolution.

The large-scale production of steel from

iron made in blast furnaces did not follow until the 1850s, when the steel converter was invented independently by William Kelly in the United States and Henry Bessemer in Britain. Air was blown through the molten iron to form steel, a process leading to the use of oxygen today.

THE REFRIGERATOR AND VACUUM FLASK

Although preserving food by keeping it in an ice-filled pit is an art some 4,000 years old, the first machine capable of reducing temperatures was not built until 1851. James Harrison, an Australian printer, noticed when cleaning type with ether that the type became very cold as the ether evaporated. Using this idea, he built an ether refrigerator. However, it was not very successful, being unable to compete with ice imported all the way from America.

The first practical refrigerator, which used ammonia as the refrigerant, was made by the German scientist Karl von Linde

in 1876. He was able to produce liquid ox with it, but such a cold liquid was difficul to keep. James Dewar, a British scientist, developed the vacuum flask in 1892 to sto liquid oxygen, but it has since found far wider use in storing hot drinks.

STEAM POWER

The use of heat to provide motive power came in a brilliant invention by the Gree engineer Hero in the first century AD. He built the first steam engine, a little device spouted jets of steam and whirled aroun rather like a lawn sprinkler. Hero's engine was of no practical use and the steam engine vanished until the 1700s, whe was developed in Britain, notably by J Watt. The steam turbine was invented another Briton, Charles Parsons, in 188

PETROL, DIESEL AND JET ENGINES

The petrol engine followed the developme of oil drilling in the mid-1800s and also t invention of a four-stroke engine running on gas at about the same time. The first two-stroke engine was invented in 1878, b it was a petrol-powered four-stroke engin that came to power the horseless carriage A practical petrol engine was principally the work of the German engineer Gottlieb Daimler who developed it in 1883, fitting it first to a boat and then in 1885 to a bicycle. However, it was another German, Karl Benz, who built the first practical motor car in 1885.

The diesel engine was perfected by Rudolf Diesel in 1897, a year before the invention of the carburettor.

The petrol engine spurred the inventio of the aeroplane while the jet engine, bein cheaper and faster, has brought us mass worldwide air travel. The jet engine was invented by the British engineer Fran Whittle in 1930.

THERMOMETEI

The measuremen of temperature is associated with several famous names. The first thermometer was invented in 1593 by the great Italian scientis Galileo, who is better known for his discoveries astronomy. The instrumen used the expansion and

ntraction of a volume of gas, and was
ry inaccurate as well as bulky.
The first thermometer to use mercury
as invented by the German physicist
abriel Fahren ... heit in 1714, and he
so devised a ... temperature scale
at bears ... his name.

GUNPOWDER AND ROCKETS

Heat also became a source of power in
gunpowder, the first explosive, which
appeared in China about a thousand years
ago. Gunpowder had other uses too, and by
the 1200s, rockets fuelled by gunpowder
were being fired in China.

The first person to propose that rockets
be used for spaceflight was not an engineer,
but a Russian schoolteacher named
Konstantin Tsiolkovsky. At the turn
of this century, he realized that
rockets powered by liquid-fuel
engines working in several separate
stages would be required to provide
the immense power necessary to
carry people into space. However,
Tsiolkovsky was a visionary and did
not build rockets himself.

Liquid-fuel rocket engines were
pioneered by the American engineer Robert
Goddard, who first launched one in 1926.
The first space rocket was built by the
Russian engineer Sergei Korolev. It used
liquid fuel to launch the first satellite,
Sputnik 1, in October 1957, just a century
after Tsiolkovsky was born.

NUCLEAR POWER

The basis of nuclear power was discovered
in 1905 by the great German scientist
Albert Einstein. In his special theory of
relativity, Einstein explained that a little
mass could theoretically be converted into
a lot of energy.

Nuclear fission is the practical
application of Einstein's theory, and was
first achieved in the laboratory of the
Italian scientist Enrico Fermi in 1934.
Fermi did not realize at the time that
fission had in fact
occurred, and it was
not until 1939 that
other nuclear scientists
were able to confirm
that fission was

possible, and with it the release of
enormous amounts of energy. This
information was kept secret as World War II
loomed, and Fermi and the other scientists
went to the United States. There, at the
prompting of Einstein, a crash programme
to build a nuclear reactor went ahead in the
fear that Germany might build a fission
bomb first. Fermi constructed the first
experimental nuclear reactor in 1942.

The first atomic bomb was tested in the
United States in July 1945, shortly after the
defeat of Germany, and it was Japan that
suffered the first, and so far the only, use of
nuclear weapons. The hydrogen bomb was
first tested by the United States in 1952. The
first nuclear reactor to produce electricity
was built in Russia in 1954.

LIGHT AND IMAGES

People must have begun observing how light behaves thousands of years ago. They could see where it came from, and they could see that it was reflected by bright smooth surfaces and cast a shadow when something got in its way. The Greek philosopher Euclid was certainly familiar with the basic principles of optics around 300BC, and Alhazen, the famous Arab scholar, wrote an important treatise on the subject in the 900s AD. But no-one knew anything about the nature of light until 1666 when Isaac Newton discovered the colour spectrum and 1678 when the Dutchman Christiaan Huygens suggested that light is composed of waves. Until then, Newton's assertion that light is made up of particles or "corpuscles" was regarded as more convincing.

ELECTRIC LIGHTS

The American inventor Thomas Edison is usually credited with inventing the electric light. In reality, however, he was pipped at the post by a British competitor, Joseph Wilson Swan. Swan's filament lamp, not unlike Edison's, had been unveiled nearly a year before Edison's in December 1878. Incandescent lamps are relatively inefficient compared with fluorescent lamps, which give off little heat. Henri Becquerel, the discoverer of radioactivity, made the first

experiments with fluorescence in 1859, but it was not until 1934 that the American physicist Arthur H. Compton developed the first fluorescent lamp for general use in homes and offices.

MIRRORS

"Natural" mirrors made of polished obsidian (a natural glass) were in use in Turkey 7,500 years ago, but the earliest manufactured mirrors were highly polished copper, bronze and brass. Pliny the Elder mentions glass backed with tin or silver in the first century AD, but silvering did not come into widespread use until the Venetians found a way of doing it in the thirteenth century. A German chemist, Justus von Liebig, invented the modern silvering process in 1835. Modern applications of reflecting surfaces include the periscope and the endoscope. Periscopes were developed for use in submarines in France in 1854. The flexible endoscope using glass fibres with special coatings to reflect images round corners came into use in 1958.

LENSES

The Roman Emperor Nero (AD 37 -68) was one of the first people to use a lens (although he may not have realized it) when he watched performances in the arena through a fragment of emerald which just happened to be of the right shape to benefit his poor eyesight. Spherical lenses used as burning glasses were certainly known by the 900s, when Alhazen described how they work. The first lenses to come into general use were convex lenses in spectacles, sometime around 1287 in Italy. The zoom lens, giving a correctly focused image at a range of focal lengths, was developed for use in the movie industry in the 1930s.

TELESCOPES

Lenses had been in use for centuries before Hans Lippershey, a Dutch spectacle maker, happened upon the marvellous invention of the telescope. In 1608, he looked at a nearby church steeple through two lenses placed one in front of the other and found that it was magnified. The working telescopes that followed Lippershey's discovery all suffered from poor image quality caused by the refraction of light through the glass lenses. Isaac Newton solved this problem in 1668 by making a reflecting telescope that worked with mirrors rather than lenses. Binoculars are essentially two telescopes arranged side by side. They first appeared in a Paris opera house in 1823; although it is not known who invented them, they rapidly became popular for use both indoors and outside.

MICROSCOPES

Magnifying glasses have been used as long as convex spectacle lenses have existed, and they were developed into excellent single-lens microscopes by a Dutch merchant, Anton van Leeuwenhoek, in the mid-1600s. By using a tiny bead-like lens, he was able to obtain magnifications of up to 200 times.

The origin of the compound microscope, which has two lenses, is shrouded in some mystery. Another Dutch spectacle maker, Zacharias Janssen, has been credited with inventing the compound microscope in 1590. However, it seems unlikely that this would have preceded the discovery of the telescope, and Janssen's son is thought to have made up the story. Galileo is believed to have experimented with lenses for microscopy, but the biographers of the Dutch-born scientist Cornelius Drebbel insist that he built the first compound microscope in 1619. The first electron microscope was built over three centuries later in Germany in 1928.

LASER AND HOLOGRAMS

The first laser was built in 1960 by Theo Maiman of the Hughes Laboratory, USA. At the time it was scorned as the invention with no use. After this shaky start, the laser has become one of the most powerful and adaptable tools at our disposal. A phenomenon that may one day bring us totally realistic images – the hologram – depends for its existence on the laser. Dennis Gabor invented the hologram in 1947, but he could not put his idea into practice until he had a coherent light source, in other words a beam of light of a single wavelength. This the laser gave him.

PHOTOGRAPHY

Photography was invented when Joseph Niepce, a Frenchman, found a way of fixing an image created in a camera obscura ("dark room" or box), a device which had been used for many years previously as a drawing aid for artists. He took his first photograph in 1826. Niepce's young partner, Louis Daguerre, invented a new process in 1837. Eventually it reduced exposure times to under half a minute making portrait photography hugely popular. But modern photography is based on two breakthroughs made by the British inventor William Fox-Talbot in 1839; the negative-positive method of print-making, which allows many copies to be made of one exposure, and development of the latent image, leading ultimately to split-second exposure times. The first colour photograph — of a tartan ribbon — was made by the British physicist James Clerk Maxwell in 1861.

THE SLR CAMERA

Like all early cameras, the SLR was developed from the much older camera obscura. Thomas Sutton designed the first SLR camera in 1861. Large-format SLRs were popular from about 1900 to the 1930s. The Kine Exacta was the first 35mm camera to use the SLR method. It came out in 1936.

INSTANT PICTURES

The American inventor Edwin Land became so absorbed in his studies of polarized light and photography that he dropped out of his regular courses at Harvard University. It proved to have been the right decision, however, because in 1947 he succeeded in producing the world's first instant picture camera, the Polaroid. Colour pictures were introduced in 1963 and in 1972 a completely new design appeared, the SX-70. The SX-70 automatically ejected each photograph after exposure. It then developed as if by magic, without any need for peeling apart or timing. These had both been features of the original camera.

MOVING PICTURES

Two French brothers, Auguste and Louis Lumière, invented the first practical movie camera and projector in 1895. At the first showings of their films, people fainted in the audience as a train appeared to come steaming straight out of the screen into the auditorium. Despite this impressive demonstration of its power, the brothers remained strangely unaware of their invention's enormous potential. When someone offered them a large sum of money for it, Auguste thought he was doing the eager buyer a great favour when he rejected his offer. How wrong he was!

PRINTING

A basic form of printing was practised by the Romans in the third century. About the same time Egyptian clothmakers used figures cut in blocks of wood to put marks and patterns on textiles. Block printing of books developed in isolation in both Europe and China. The Chinese produced the first block-printed book in 868 and were also the first to invent movable type in 1041. Unlike blocks, these could be used in the printing of any book, not just one, and were the vital element in Gutenberg's invention four centuries later. The Chinese made type out of baked clay. It soon became clear that only metal type could withstand repeated use. These were first made in Korea in the early fifteenth century. The letterpress method of printing is still in use today.

PAPER

Before paper was invented, people wrote on anything they could lay their hands on: silk and bamboo in China, palm leaves in India, clay tablets in Babylon and wax tablets in Greece. Between 3000 and 2000BC the Egyptians started using papyrus, a type of sedge which they dried into strips and then glued together in two layers to form a sheet. Paper was invented in China by Tsai Lun in AD 105. In 751, the Arabs captured some Chinese papermakers at Samarkand and so the invention set out on its four-hundred-year journey to the West. Today paper is made chiefly from fibres produced by trees.

THE PRINTING PRESS

The printing press was invented by Johan Gutenberg in Germany about 1450. It was one of a number of elements in the printing process (including movable metal type) which Gutenberg was the first to perfect.

The press itself was adapted from existing screw presses used in trades like book binding and was so efficient that no significant changes were necessary until automation was introduced in the nineteenth century.

SOUND AND MUSIC

If archaeological discoveries are anything to go by, the first musical instruments were hollow bones used as whistles in prehistoric times. Pottery drums have been found dating back 6,000 years. After the drum came the lyre, a stringed instrument played 4,500 years ago in the ancient city of Ur; it later developed into the harp. Brass instruments have their beginning in hollowed animal horns used to sound fanfares and calls. Straight trumpets over 3,000 years old were found in Tutankhamun's tomb, but the modern valve trumpet dates only from 1801. Probably the first man to give his name to a musical instrument was Adolphe Sax, the inventor of the saxophone in 1846.

THE TAPE RECORDER

Danish telephone engineer, Valdemar Poulsen, invented magnetic recording in 1898. Strictly speaking, Poulsen's "telegraphone" was not a tape recorder as it used wire rather than tape. The American film producer Louis Blattner made the first tape recorder in 1920 and AEG of Berlin produced the first *plastic* tape recorder in 1935.

THE RECORD PLAYER

The problems of recording sound and playing it back were solved by one of the greatest inventors of all time, the American Thomas Edison. Using a tinfoil cylinder as his "record" he recorded and then reproduced the nursery rhyme *Mary Had a Little Lamb* on 6 December 1877. He called his invention a phonograph. Ten years later Émile Berliner, a German immigrant then living in Washington, invented the flat disc record player or gramophone.

TELECOMMUNICATIONS

Modern telecommunications have effectively solved the problem of sending messages rapidly over immense distances. Before the electronic age people had to use whatever methods their ingenuity could devise, such as flashing mirrors and smoke signals. The Greek historian Polybius is reported to have devised a system of alphabetical smoke signals in the 100s BC, but no Polybius Code is known today to rival the Morse Code, invented by the American Samuel Morse in 1838. Morse went on to construct the first electric telegraph, which carried his code over wires similar to telephone wires. In 1844, he sent the first message "What hath God wrought?"

THE TELEPHONE

During the great days of early sound engineering in the last century, inventors were often at a loss to think of things to say during their experiments and demonstrations. Alexander Graham Bell, however, had no difficulty when he used his newly invented telephone for the first time in 1876: "Mr Watson. Come at once. I want you" were his first words. He had spilt acid from a battery down his trousers and needed help from his assistant urgently. In inventing the telephone, Bell had also invented two important devices – the microphone and the loudspeaker.

RADIO

The introduction of the telegraph in 1844 solved the problem of sending messages using electricity. But the new machine had one big drawback: it depended on a physical wire link. Other scientists immediately began working on wire-less communications. A breakthrough came in 1888 when the German scientist Heinrich Hertz discovered the existence of radio waves. Seven years later, Guglielmo Marconi, the 21-year old son of a wealthy Italian landowner, made the first successful transmission using radio waves.

In 1901 he created an even bigger sensation when his radio sent a signal all the way across the Atlantic. Broadcasting began in 1906, when the Canadian inventor Reginald Fessenden first transmitted sound. However the invention of the electronic valve or tube in the same year by the American Lee de Forest was the major factor in the development of broadcasting.

TELEVISION

Considering that television is the most powerful tool of mass communication known to man, it was conceived in remarkably humble circumstances. John Logie Baird was a British amateur scientist who sold shoe polish and razor blades to finance his spare-time research. In 1925

after years of work he successfully transmitted the first television picture in his attic workshop, using a boy from the office downstairs as his subject. Because Baird's system was mechanical and gave low picture quality, it was only a matter of time before someone came along with a superior electronic product. That someone was Vladimir Zworykin, a Russian emigrant to America, who built the first electronic television in 1929. The world's first public broadcast was in 1936.

COMMUNICATIONS SATELLITES

The US government was responsible for developing the idea of communications satellites in the 1950s. In July 1962 the American Telephone and Telegraph Company launched Telstar, the first communications satellite to transmit telephone and television signals. It could only operate for a few hours each day, because its low orbit took it out of range of its transmitting and receiving stations for most of the time. Early Bird, launched in 1965, was the first satellite to solve this problem by keeping exact pace with the rotation of the Earth, maintaining an apparently stationary position.

RADIO TELESCOPE

The inventor of the radio telescope, and so of radio astronomy, was the amateur American astronomer Grote Reber. He built his first receiving dish in 1937, having heard about Karl Jansky's 1931 discovery that the Earth is constantly being bombarded with cosmic radio waves. Reber set out to focus these waves with his dish and thereby map where they came from. In 1942 he made the first radio map of the Milky Way galaxy.

SPACE PROBES

The first successful space probe was the Russian Luna 3, which sent back the first picture of the Moon's unseen far side in 1959. Probing the planets became a reality in December 1962 when the US spacecraft Mariner 2 reached Venus after a 290 million-kilometre (180 million-mile) journey lasting nearly four months.

ELECTRICITY

In about 600BC the Greek philosopher Thales noticed that amber rubbed with wool somehow acquires the power to attract light objects such as straw and feathers. Over 2,000 years later in 1600, William Gilbert, physician to Queen Elizabeth I, called this power electricity after the Greek word for amber. It was not until the 1700s that scientists began to learn more about the nature of electricity, and one of the pioneers in the field was the American statesman Benjamin Franklin, also an intrepid investigator. In 1752, Franklin daringly flew a kite in a thunderstorm to prove that lightning is electrical in nature. This famous experiment, in which he was lucky not to have been killed, led Franklin to invent the lightning conductor. Franklin also postulated that electricity consists of two varieties of "fluid", one positive and one negative. We now know that the fluid is a stream of negative electrons, which were discovered by the British scientist J.J. Thompson in 1897.

THE BATTERY

In 1780 an Italian anatomist, Luigi Galvani, noticed that the severed leg of a dead frog could be made to twitch when touched by pieces of metal. Galvani concluded rightly that electricity was producing the reaction, but it was another Italian, Alessandro Volta, who found that the electricity came not from the frog, as Galvani had thought, but from the metals. Eventually Volta found that copper and zinc together produce a strong charge and that if he built a pile of metal discs, alternately copper and zinc separated by pads soaked in salty water, he could produce a continuous electric current. Perfected in 1800, the Voltaic pile, as it is called, was the first electric battery. Since then, a great range of different types of battery has been developed.

THE PHOTOCOPIER

In the 1930s Chester Carlson was working for the patents department of a large electronics firm in New York. He was happy enough in his work except for one thing — the time and expense involved in getting patents copied. Eventually he became so frustrated that he decided to invent a whole new process himself. The result was the first xerographic copy, taken on 22 October 1938. Dispensing with the messy wet chemicals used in existing copiers, Carlson had invented a dry process based on the ability of an electrostatically charged plate to attract powder in the image of the original document. Several years later the rights to the process were acquired by a small family firm which later grew into the mighty Xerox corporation, making Chester Carlson a very wealthy man in the process.

MAGNETISM

Legend has it that the phenomenon of magnetism was first observed by a Greek shepherd called Magnes when he noticed that his iron-tipped crook picked up pieces of black rock lying around on the ground. This black rock was a kind of iron ore called magnetite. Queen Elizabeth I's physician, William Gilbert, was the first man to formulate some of the basic laws of magnetism and to speculate that the Earth itself is one big magnet. In 1644 René Descartes showed how magnetic fields could be made visible by scattering iron filings on a sheet of paper. Apart from the compass, however, no practical use for magnets was found until the invention of the electric motor — although Franz Anton Mesmer, the original mesmerizer, did manage to persuade eighteenth-century Parisians for a few years that magnetism was a cure for certain illnesses.

MAGNETS

The earliest magnets were made from naturally occurring magnetic rock called magnetite. Later when magnetite's directional properties were recognized, the name lodestone, meaning leading stone, was coined and it was used to make magnetic compasses. Magnets did not really come into their own until 1820 when the Danish physicist Hans Oersted made his sensational discovery of the link between magnetism and electricity. This event changed the course of human history by making possible the great electrical inventions of the nineteenth century such as the motor, the dynamo and, in the field of telecommunications, the telegraph.

ELECTROMAGNETS

The electromagnet was one of the discoveries made possible by Oersted's great discovery. Shortly after it was announced, a French scientist, André-Marie Ampère, proved that wires could be made to behave exactly like magnets when a current was passed through them and that the polarity of the magnetism depended on the direction of the current. So the electromagnet — a magnet whose field is produced by an electric current — was born. Later the American inventor Joseph Henry found that wrapping several layers of insulated wire round a big piece of iron produced a vastly increased magnetic field. In 1829 he built the first heavy-duty working electromagnet, capable of lifting one tonne.

MAGNETIC COMPASS

Chinese historians date the discovery of the magnetic compass to 2634BC. Whether or not this is true, the Chinese certainly seem to have been the first people to discover that magnetism could be useful in navigation, and by the third century AD magnetic compasses were in common use in the Far East. The Chinese were not noted navigators and it was left to the maritime nations of Europe to perfect the device. As with other inventions, the Arabs may have been responsible for transmitting the idea from East to West. By the eleventh century the Vikings were using compasses on their raids in northern Europe. More recent is a variation of the compass which measures the vertical angle that the Earth's magnetic field makes at its surface.

THE ELECTRIC MOTOR

In 1821, following Oersted's discovery the previous year, the British scientist Michael Faraday set out to show that just as a wire carrying electric current could cause a magnetized compass needle to move, so in reverse a magnet could cause a current-carrying wire to move. Suspending a piece of wire above a bowl of mercury in which he had fixed a magnet upright, Faraday connected the wire to a battery and sure enough it began to rotate. He had shown that electrical energy could be converted into mechanical energy, the principle behind the electric motor. The American scientist Joseph Henry built the first motor capable of work in 1830; by 1840 electric motors were powering machinery.

DOMESTIC ELECTRICITY SUPPLY

In the winter of 1880 a British industrialist, W.G. Armstrong, built a small hydroelectric station in the grounds of his country mansion in Northumberland to power its new electric lighting. It was the first domestic electricity supply anywhere in the world. The following winter the town council of Godalming in Surrey built the first power station to provide electric power for both private homes and public street-lighting. Take-up however was disappointingly slow and the station had to be closed a few years later. A few months later in January 1881 Thomas Edison's Electric Light Company installed a similar station at Holborn Viaduct in London. Unlike the Godalming scheme, this venture was highly popular and proved to be a roaring success.

SENSORS AND DETECTORS

Simple sensors triggered by movement have been in existence since ancient times. However, devices that can sense movement and then use this information to control machinery are more recent. Two important early examples were invented in the eighteenth century. The first was the windmill fantail, invented by Edmund Lee in 1745, which ensured that a windmill's sails always pointed into the wind. The second was James Watt's centrifugal governor, which ingeniously used centrifugal force to automatically regulate the speed of a steam engine.

THE SEISMOGRAPH

Historically, the Chinese have kept fuller records relating to earthquakes than any other country, so it is appropriate that they should also have produced the first seismograph. Invented by a mathematician, astronomer and geographer called Chang Heng (AD 78-139) it consisted of eight carefully balanced bronze balls arranged in a circle around a compass. Whenever the instrument picked up tremors from an earthquake, one of the balls would roll off, indicating which direction the vibrations had come from. The first seismograph to make use of currents produced by electromagnetism was invented by the Russian physicist Prince Boris Golitsyn in 1905.

X-RAYS

In 1895 Wilhelm Röntgen, head of the physics department at Würzburg University in Germany, was amazed to see chemicals glowing on the other side of his laboratory while conducting experiments using a cathode ray tube enclosed in a container. After investigating he found that the cathode ray tube was causing the glow, but not the cathode rays because they could not penetrate the container. Quite by chance he had discovered some completely unknown type of rays which he accordingly named X-rays. Before long he also discovered that photographic plates are sensitive to the rays even though the rays are invisible. This meant that it was possible to take photographs of objects not normally visible to the human eye, a discovery that revolutionized medical diagnosis. The X-ray measurement unit is named after him.

SONAR

In the early days of World War I, German U-boat submarines inflicted such heavy losses on Allied shipping that it became a matter of urgent priority to find some kind of effective submarine detection system. After experimenting with passive detectors, Paul Langevin, a French scientist, developed a much more sophisticated system using ultrasonic pulses generated by piezoelectricity. These found submarines even when their engines were not running by using echoes that bounced off their hulls to pinpoint each target's location.

RADAR

In 1935 the British Government asked a leading scientist, Robert Watson-Watt, about the possibility of producing a "death ray" to knock enemy aircraft out of the sky. Watt replied that the technology did not exist to produce a death ray, but that he could build a system that would give advance warning of an air attack. The details were written down on half a sheet of paper. Within the amazingly short space of a few months they had been developed into the world's first radar (RAdio Detection And Ranging) system. Within three years a whole network of radar stations protected the British coast and gave the RAF a decisive edge over the German air force in the Battle of Britain in 1940.

AUTOMATIC TRANSMISSION

Although automatic transmission is a sophisticated device, the first one was actually produced in 1896, not long after the first car. But it bore little resemblance to the first fully automatic transmission, the Hydramatic drive, invented in 1939 by American engineer Earl A. Thompson. Following Thompson's invention, automatic transmission became standard in American cars. The first model to be fitted with the new device was a 1940 Oldsmobile.

BINARY NUMBERS

The idea that number systems do not necessarily have to be based on 10 is not a recent one. Gottfried Leibniz, working in Germany in the 1600s, developed theories of binary numbers and logic. A century later the British mathematician George Boole devised a binary method of expressing logic that is used in logic gates in computers.

ELECTRIC KEYBOARDS

The first practical electric keyboard able to produce a range of sounds was an analog synthesizer invented by the American engineer Robert Moog in 1964. It used varying voltages for different notes. Digital keyboards did not appear until 1980. Other electronic musical instruments long preceded the synthesizer. The very first was the Telharmonium, a 200-tonne monster invented by Thaddeus Cahill in New York in 1906. It produced electric sound signals that travelled along telephone lines to listeners.

COMPUTERS

The first machine to process numbers was a mechanical calculator invented by the great French scientist Blaise Pascal in 1642 at the tender age of 19. Numbers were fed into the machine by turning dials, and the result appeared in a window. Inside, interlocking cogs tripped one another to calculate the result. Although it added and subtracted numbers with total accuracy, there was little need for such a machine at that time and it was a financial flop.

However, mechanical calculators did develop later to perform arithmetic for people. Unlike a computer, they could not store results and could not be given instructions to perform different tasks. The idea that such a machine could be built occurred to the British inventor Charles Babbage in 1833, a daring insight that has earned him the title of "father of the computer". Babbage designed such a machine, using complex arrangements of interlocking cogs and levers to process numbers in different ways and punched cards like those in automatic looms to give it instructions. It was said that the developed by the Dutch-based electronics giant Philips and Japan's Sony Corporation, and the first discs and CD player were introduced in Japan in 1982.

DIODES, TRANSISTORS AND MICROCHIPS

The ancestor of these miniature electronic devices was the electronic valve or vacuum tube, in which a beam of electrons carries a current through a vacuum between electrodes sealed in a glass tube. The diode (two-electrode) valve was invented by the British scientist John Ambrose Fleming in 1904, followed in America by Lee de Forest's three-electrode triode valve in 1906. They were crucial to the development of radio, television, and sound recording.

In 1948, three American scientists – William Shockley, John Bardeen and Walter Brattain – superseded the large and hot valve with small and cool-running devices made of semiconductors. These diodes and transistors were crucial in turn to the development of digital machines, which came about with the fabrication of several devices in a single piece of semiconductor – the integrated circuit. This was invented by the American Jack Kilby in 1958 and it led to the microchip, into which millions of components may be packed. The first microprocessor was produced in 1970.

INTERNET

The origins of the Internet go back to 1969 when the US Department of Defense set up a large network of military computers to make the country less vulnerable to enemy attack. Universities and research organizations then joined the network in order to exchange information, introducing electronic mail in the 1970s. The US military separated from the network in the 1980s, and in 1986 the routing computers of the Internet backbone were set up in the United States. Other

countries joined and companies began to connect up. The Internet has been growing ever since.

GPS

Like the Internet, the Global Positioning System began as a military project by the US Department of Defense. It was set up to enable US military units and weapons to get an exact fix of their position anywhere in the world at any time. The system was also made available for civilian use, though at less precision than military use. The 24 GPS satellites were placed in orbit by 1993, and the system became fully operational in 1995.

ROBOTS

The term robot, a Czech word meaning "labour", was first applied to automatic machines in the 1920s. However, robots that move themselves are much older than this. They reached the height of perfection in the clockwork automata of the 1700s, which performed complex actions for the amusement of their wealthy owners. One, for example, could write a whole sentence. These early robots were entirely driven by complex gears and levers. Robots have developed gradually as useful machines have become increasingly automatic in operation.

Analytical Engine, as it came to be called, would "weave algebraic patterns as the loom weaves flowers and leaves". Sadly, it was never built.

The electronic computer, like many inventions, was ushered in by the pressure of war. It was built on Babbage's principles but used speedy electronic valves (see below) instead of slow-moving cogs and levers. The first computer, called Colossus, was built in Britain in 1943 to break enemy codes, and may well have affected the outcome of World War II. Colossus was in fact only used for code-cracking. The first general-purpose computer was ENIAC, an American machine completed in 1946. It was hot and huge, containing 19,000 valves.

FAX MACHINES

Although fax machines have been in common use only since the 1980s, the very first device to transmit a copy of a document along a wire was patented in 1843. The British inventor Alexander Bain used a metal stylus to scan a document set in metal type. Every time it touched the raised edges of the letters, the stylus sent an electric signal along a wire to a moving pen which marked a paper so that a copy of the document appeared. The first picture was sent by fax in 1906. Arthur Korn, a German physicist, invented a photographic fax machine that scanned a picture using a light-sensitive photoelectric cell and reproduced it on photographic paper. This machine was used by newspapers to transmit copies of pictures throughout the 1900s. The first digital fax machine was made in the United States in 1974, and digital fax communications became common after today's digital standard was agreed in 1980.

COMPACT DISCS

Like many modern machines, the compact disc has no single inventor. It was jointly

TECHNICAL TERMS

A.C. See *ALTERNATING CURRENT*.

ACTION AND REACTION Two forces that act whenever an object is moved. The moving force is called the action, and the object pushes back with a force called the reaction. Action and reaction are always equally strong, and they always push in opposite directions. They also occur when a liquid or gas is made to move or when they themselves make an object move.

ADDITIVE COLOUR MIXING Combining light sources of the three primary colours of light (red, green, and blue) to produce all other colours.

AERIAL See *ANTENNA*.

AEROFOIL The curved surface of a wing that produces lift as the wing moves through the air.

ALTERNATING CURRENT (A.C.) Electric current in which the flow of current constantly reverses direction.

AMPÈRE (AMP) The unit of measurement for electric currents. A 1-amp current flows through a circuit if the resistance is 1 ohm and the voltage 1 volt.

AMPLITUDE The amount of energy in a ray or wave. It is equal to the change in energy (for example, pressure in a sound wave) that takes place as one complete wave passes.

ANALOG A kind of machine or system that works with, or produces, a quantity that may vary in level. A glass thermometer, in which the temperature is indicated by the level of a rising or falling column of liquid, is an analog device. Many analog machines and systems work with an electric signal that varies in voltage. The analog signal often represents the varying sound waves in speech or music, and the varying light rays in an image.

ANODE An electrode with a positive charge.

ANTENNA A part of a radio transmitter or receiver that sends out or picks up radio waves. Also called the aerial.

ARMATURE A part of an electric machine which moves in response to a current or signal, or which moves to produce a current or signal.

ATOMS The tiny particles of which the chemical elements that make up all substances are composed. An atom measures about a hundred-millionth of a centimetre (500-billionths of an inch) in size, and consists of a central nucleus surrounded by electrons.

AUGER A large screw that rotates inside a pipe to transport water or loose materials, or a screw that is used to drill holes.

AXLE The shaft on which a wheel turns. The axle may be fixed to the wheel so that the wheel turns when the axle rotates, or alternatively, the wheel may spin freely on the axle.

BALANCE A weighing machine, or the part of a mechanical watch that makes the watch keep time.

BINARY CODE A code used in digital machines that consists of sequences of bits making up binary numbers. The code represents data or programs.

BINARY NUMBER A number in the binary system, which contains only two digits or numerals, 0 and 1. From the right-hand end of the number, each successive digit signifies the presence (1) or absence (0) of 1, 2, 4, 8 and so on, doubling each time. The binary number 1101 indicates 1x8 + 1x4 + 0x2 + 1x1, which is equivalent to the decimal number 13.

BIT Short for binary digit. A digit or numeral in a binary number, written as 1 or 0. In a digital machine, bits take a physical form such as a sequence of on-off pulses of electric current in a wire or black bars and white spaces in a bar code. Sets of bits represent things such as numbers or amounts, words, sounds, and images.

BOOM The arm of a crane or excavator that raises the load.

BYTE A binary number containing eight bits. It represents decimal numbers from 0 (00000000) to 255 (11111111).

CAM A non-circular wheel which rotates in contact with a part called a follower. Together, the cam and follower are used to convert rotary motion into reciprocating motion.

CAPACITOR An electrical component that stores electric charge. Also called a condenser.

CARRIER WAVE A radio wave that is broadcast at a particular frequency or wavelength and which is modulated to carry a sound or picture signal.

CATHODE An electrode with a negative charge.

CCD Charge-coupled device. A row or array of tiny photodiodes that each produce an electric charge proportional to the intensity of light rays or infra-red rays falling on the CCD.

CELL A single device that produces electric current. A battery may contain several cells connected together, and a solar panel may contain several solar cells. Also a unit of memory that stores one bit of binary code.

CENTRIFUGAL A word applied to any rotating device or part which moves away from the centre of rotation.

CHIP See *MICROCHIP*.

CIRCUIT A source of electric current and a set of electrical devices or components that are connected together by wires so that current flows through them. A circuit board contains a printed metal pattern to conduct current to components fixed to the board.

CLOCK In a calculator or computer, a device that produces regular electric pulses which synchronize the operations of the components.

COG A toothed gear wheel or a tooth on such a wheel.

CONCAVE A word applied to a surface that curves inwards at the centre.

CONDENSER In heat, a device which cools a gas or vapour so that it changes into a liquid. In electricity, a component (also called a capacitor) that stores electric charge.

CONVEX A word applied to a surface that curves outwards at its centre.

COUNTERWEIGHT A weight that is fixed to one part of a machine to balance the weight of a load elsewhere in the machine.

CRANK A wheel or rotating shaft to which a pivoted connecting rod is attached. As the crank turns, the rod moves to and fro; alternatively, the rod's movement may turn the crank. In a car engine crankshaft, a number of cranks are linked together and turned by rods connected to the pistons.

A winding handle is also a form of crank.

DAMPER A part of a machine that absorbs vibration or prevents sudden movement. In a piano, the mechanism that stops the piano wires sounding.

DATA Information of any kind that can be fed into a computer or other digital machine, which stores and processes the data in the form of bits. Data mainly consists of numbers or amounts, words, sounds, and images.

D.C. See *DIRECT CURRENT*.

DENSITY The weight of any amount of a solid, liquid, or gas relative to its volume. Every pure substance has a particular density. Provided that two substances do not mix, the one with the lesser density will always float on top of the other. Wood floats on water because it has a lesser density than water.

DIFFRACTION The bending of rays or waves that occurs as they pass through an opening or around an edge. The angle of bending depends on the wavelength.

DIGIT A single numeral in a number, for example 2 or 7 in 27. The decimal number system uses ten different digits (0 to 9), the binary number system two different digits (0 and 1).

DIGITAL A kind of machine or system that works with or produces numbers. A digital thermometer measures the temperature and displays it as a number of degrees. Computers and many other digital machines and systems use numbers to represent things such as amounts, words, sounds, and images. The numbers are in binary code.

DIODE An electronic component through which current can flow in only one direction. A photodiode is sensitive to light or other rays, and a light-emitting diode (LED) emits light or other rays when a current flows through it.

DIRECT CURRENT (D.C.) Electric current that always flows in one direction.

DRAG The force with which air or water resists the motion of an object such as a car, boat, or aircraft. Drag is also called air resistance or water resistance.

ECCENTRIC A word applied to any object, often a wheel, that rotates about a point other than its centre. An eccentric pin is an off-centre projection on a wheel. It slides in a slot on an arm so that as the wheel rotates, it drives the arm to and fro.

EFFORT The force that is applied to a machine to produce an action.

ELASTICITY The ability of certain materials to regain their former shape and dimensions when forces cease to act on them.

ELECTRIC CHARGE The electrical property produced by the addition (negative charge) or removal (positive charge) of electrons. The charge on the electron is the fundamental unit of electricity.

ELECTRIC CURRENT The continual flow of electrons through a wire or other electrical conductor.

ELECTRIC FIELD The region around an electric charge. One field affects another so that a negative charge and positive charge attract each other, and two negative charges or two positive charges repel each other.

ELECTRIC SIGNAL A flow of electric current that causes a machine or system to operate in a particular way. A microphone produces an electrical signal that represents the sound waves entering it, and the sound signal goes to a loudspeaker to reproduce the sound. There are two kinds of electric signals. In an analog signal, the voltage varies in level and may have any value. In a digital signal, the voltage has only two levels – high and low or off – to represent the two digits in the sequence of bits that make up the signal.

ELECTRODE Part of an electrical device or machine that either produces electrons (cathode) or receives electrons (anode).

ELECTROLYTE A solution, paste, or molten substance that conducts electric current between electrodes.

ELECTROMAGNET A device that uses an electric current to produce a magnetic field.

ELECTROMAGNETIC WAVES The family of rays and waves that includes radio waves, microwaves, infra-red waves, light rays, ultraviolet rays, X-rays, and gamma rays. All consist of vibrating electric and magnetic fields and travel at 300,000 kilometres a second (186,000 miles per second) which is the speed of light. All the rays and waves differ only in their wavelength or frequency. Except for gamma rays, all electromagnetic waves are generated by accelerating electrons.

ELECTROMAGNETISM The relationship between electricity and magnetism; either can be used to produce the other.

ELECTRON The smallest particle in an atom. An electron is about 100,000 times smaller than an atom, and has a negative electric charge. Electrons surround the central nucleus of the atom. They may be freed from atoms to flow through a conductor in an electric current, or to move through a vacuum in an electron beam. Electrons also move to produce a charge of static electricity.

ELECTROSTATIC A word applied to a device that works by the production of an electric charge.

ELEMENT A substance containing only one kind of atom. Some elements, such as hydrogen, nitrogen, oxygen, and chlorine, are gases at normal temperatures. Others, such as iodine, sulphur, and most metals, including iron, aluminium, copper, silver, and gold, are solids. Only two, bromine and mercury, are liquids. Just over 100 elements are known, including several artificial elements such as plutonium. All other substances are compounds of two or more elements.

E-MAIL Electronic mail. A message that is sent from one computer to another. It may contain computer data, such as a document, sound or image, or computer programs.

ENERGY The capacity to do work. Every action that occurs requires energy and, except in nuclear reactions, converts one form of energy into another. Forms of energy include movement, heat, light and other electromagnetic waves, sound and electricity. There are also stored or potential forms of energy, such as chemical energy, that are available for conversion into other forms.

ESCAPEMENT The part of a mechanical clock or watch that connects the train of gear wheels, which moves the hands, to the pendulum or to the balance, which controls the hands' speed.

EVAPORATION The process by which a liquid turns into a vapour at a temperature below its boiling point. Evaporation occurs if the pressure of the vapour above the liquid is low enough for molecules to escape from the liquid into the vapour.

FIBRE OPTICS Devices that send images or light signals along glass fibres (optical fibres).

FILE A set of data for use by a computer. It may consist of a list, document, image, piece of music and so on. File transfer is the sending of files from one computer to another.

FISSION A nuclear reaction in which the nuclei of atoms split apart to produce energy.

FLUORESCENT A word often applied to something that glows with light. A fluorescent object, such as a screen, changes an invisible electron beam or ultraviolet rays into visible light.

FOCUS A point at which rays or waves meet. With lenses, a sharp image forms at the focus of the lens. The focus of a telescope is the position at which an image is produced.

FORCE The push or pull that makes something move, slows it down or stops it, or the pressure that something exerts on an object.

When a force acts on an object, it may be split into two smaller component forces acting at different angles. One of these component forces may move the object forwards in one direction, while the other component may support its weight or overcome a separate force acting in another direction.

FREQUENCY The rate at which waves of energy pass in sound waves and electromagnetic waves such as radio waves and light rays. Also the rate at which an alternating current changes direction, flowing forwards and then backwards. Frequency is measured in hertz (Hz), which is the number of waves or forward-backward cycles per second.

FRICTION A force that appears when a solid object rubs against another, or when it moves through a liquid or gas. Friction always opposes movement, and it disappears when movement ceases.

FULCRUM The pivot on which a device such as a lever is supported so that it can balance, tilt, or swing.

FUSION A nuclear reaction in which the nuclei of atoms combine to produce energy.

GAMMA RAYS Invisible high-energy electromagnetic waves with wavelengths shorter than about a hundred-billionth of a metre. Gamma rays are emitted by the nuclei of atoms.

GAS TURBINE A heat engine in which fuel burns to heat air and the hot air and waste gases drive a turbine. The jet engine is a gas turbine. Helicopters may have gas turbines in which the turbine drives the rotor.

GEAR Two toothed wheels that intermesh either directly or through a chain so that one wheel turns to drive the other. A screw called a worm or a toothed shaft called a rack may replace one of the wheels.

In a moving machine such as a car or bicycle, a gear is also a combination of gear wheels that produces a certain speed. Top gear gives a high speed, and low gear a slow speed.

GIGABYTE (GB) 1,073,741,824 bytes.

GRAVITY The force that gives everything weight and pulls objects towards the ground. The normal pressure of the air or water is caused by gravity.

HAIRSPRING A flat spring in which one end is fixed and the other end can move.

HARMONICS A set of accompanying waves that occurs with a main or fundamental wave. The frequencies of the harmonics are multiples of the frequency of the fundamental wave.

HEAT ENGINE An engine in which heat is converted into movement by the expansion of a gas, which is either steam or the products of burning a fuel. There are two main kinds: external and internal combustion engines. In an external combustion engine, the source of heat that raises the temperature of the gas is outside the engine, as in the boiler of a steam engine. In an internal combustion engine, fuel burns inside the engine. Petrol and diesel engines, jet engines and rocket engines are all internal combustion engines.

HEAT EXCHANGER A device in which heat is taken from a hot liquid or gas in order to warm a cool liquid or gas. Inside a heat exchanger, the pipes containing the hot fluid generally pass through the cool fluid.

HELICAL A word applied to any device in the shape of a helix, such as a coil spring or a corkscrew.

HOLE A space in an atom produced by the removal of an electron. As an electron comes from another atom to fill the hole, the hole "transfers" to the other atom.

HOLOGRAM An image formed by laser light that has depth like a real object, or the photographic film or plate that produces the image.

HOLOGRAPHY The production of holograms.

IMAGE A picture of an object or scene formed by an optical instrument. A real image can form on a screen or other surface. A virtual image can be seen only in a lens, mirror or other instrument, or a hologram. Images are recorded by photography, printing, video recording and holography, and can be stored in memory units.

INCLINED PLANE A sloping surface. An inclined plane can be used to alter the effort and distance involved in doing work, such as raising loads.

INDUCTION The production of magnetism or an electric current in a material by a magnetic field.

INERTIA The resistance of a moving object to a change in its speed or direction, and the resistance of a stationary object to being moved.

INFRA-RED RAYS Invisible electromagnetic waves with wavelengths longer than light rays and ranging from a millionth to a thousandth of a metre. They include heat rays.

INPUT UNIT The unit in a digital machine that originates the bits making up data and programs. It is often a keyboard or keypad.

INTERFERENCE The effects produced when two waves or rays meet. The combined wave has a different frequency or amplitude, giving colour effects in light, for example.

INTERNAL COMBUSTION ENGINE
See *HEAT ENGINE*.

ION An atom that has lost or gained one or more electrons and has an electric charge.

JACK A device that raises a heavy object a short distance, with reduced effort.

KILOBYTE (KB) 1024 bytes.

LASER A device that produces a narrow beam of very bright light or infra-red rays, in which all the waves have exactly the same frequency, are in phase and move exactly together. Laser stands for Light Amplification by Stimulated Emission of Radiation.

LED Light-emitting diode. A diode that emits a beam of light or infra-red rays when fed with an electric current.

LENS A device that bends light rays to form an image.

LEVER A rod that tilts about a pivot to produce a useful movement.

LIFT The upward force produced by an aircraft wing and helicopter rotor, and by the foils of a hydrofoil.

LIGHT RAYS Visible electromagnetic waves ranging from 4 to 8 ten-millionths of a metre in wavelength, and respectively from blue to red in colour.

LINEAR MOTION Movement in a straight line.

LOAD The weight of an object that is moved by a machine, or the resistance to movement that a machine has to overcome.

LOGIC GATE A miniature device within the processor of a digital machine that takes part in the processing of bits. It performs a certain logical operation. An OR gate, for example, opens to pass a bit if the first *or* second of two control bits is an on-bit (binary 1).

MAGNETIC FIELD The region around a magnet or an electric current that attracts or repels other magnets.

MAINS SUPPLY The supply of electricity to the home. It is alternating current at a voltage of about 240 volts and a frequency of 50 hertz.

MASS The amount of substance that an object possesses. Mass is not the same as weight, which is the force that gravity exerts on an object to pull it to the ground. A floating object loses weight, but its mass remains the same.

MEGABYTE (MB) 1,048,576 bytes.

MEMORY UNIT The unit in a digital machine or system that stores the bits making up data or programs.

MICROCHIP An electronic component containing many miniature circuits that can process or store digital electric signals. Also called a chip or integrated circuit.

MICROCOMPUTER A small computer that can be placed on a desk or carried about.

MICROWAVES Radio waves with very short wavelengths ranging from a millimetre to 30 centimetres.

MIRROR A smooth surface that reflects light rays striking it. A semi-silvered mirror partly reflects and partly passes light.

MODEM A device that connects a digital machine via the telephone network to another machine. It changes the outgoing digital signal into a sound signal that can be sent over a telephone line, and converts an incoming sound signal back into a digital signal. It does this by modulation and demodulation, and the name modem is short for modulator-demodulator.

MODERATOR A substance used in a nuclear reactor to slow the fast-moving neutrons produced by fission of uranium fuel. Fast-moving neutrons do not cause further fission, and must be slowed to promote fission in the fuel.

MODULATION Superimposing one kind of wave on another so that the first wave changes the second, often varying its amplitude (AM) or frequency (FM).

MOLECULES The minute particles of which all materials – solids, liquids, and gases – are composed. Each material has its own kind of molecules, which each consist of a particular combination of atoms. Water, for example, contains molecules each made of two hydrogen atoms fixed to an oxygen atom. In crystals, the atoms connect together in a regular network rather than forming separate molecules.

NEGATIVE In photography, an image in which the brightness is reversed so that black becomes white and vice-versa; in a colour negative, colours are reversed so that primary colours become secondary colours and vice-versa – blue becomes yellow, for example. In electricity, the charge on an electron is considered to be negative, so anything that stores or emits electrons is also negative. In waves, a minimum or opposite value of energy is considered to be negative.

N-TYPE SEMICONDUCTOR A kind of semiconductor that has been treated to produce electrons. It tends to lose these electrons and thus gain a positive charge.

NEUTRON One of two kinds of particles that make up the nucleus of an atom. The other kind is the proton. A neutron has almost the same mass as a proton but no electrical charge. All nuclei contain neutrons except the very lightest, which is the common form of hydrogen. Deuterium and tritium, which are the other forms or isotopes of hydrogen, do contain neutrons.

NUCLEUS (pl. NUCLEI) The central part of an atom, composed mainly of two smaller particles called protons and neutrons that are held together with great force. The nucleus is about 10,000 times smaller than the whole atom. It is surrounded by electrons.

OPTICAL FIBRE See *FIBRE OPTICS*.

OSCILLATOR A device that produces sound waves or an electric signal of regular frequency.

OUTPUT UNIT The unit in a digital machine that changes the bits making up data back into a form that we can use or understand, such as printed words, sounds, or images.

PAWL A pivoted arm that engages with the teeth of a ratchet.

PENDULUM A rod or cord with a heavy weight called a bob attached to the lower end. The pendulum pivots at the upper end and the bob swings to and fro. The time of each swing depends only on the length of the pendulum – not on the weight of the bob.

PINION The smaller of two gear wheels, or a gear wheel that drives or is driven by a toothed rack.

PIXEL Picture element. A tiny part of an image on a screen. The sharpness or resolution of the image depends on the number of pixels, often called dots, in the image.

PLANET WHEEL A gear wheel that moves around another gear wheel, the sun wheel, as it turns.

POSITIVE In photography, an image that looks like the original scene. In electricity, anything that receives electrons or from which electrons have been removed.

PRECESSION A movement of a rotating wheel in response to a force on its axle. Precession makes the wheel move at right angles to the direction of this force.

PRESSURE The force with which a liquid or a gas pushes against its container or any surface inside the liquid or gas. Units of pressure measure the force acting on a unit of surface area.

PRIMARY COLOUR A colour that cannot be formed by mixing other colours. All other colours can be made by combining two or three primary colours.

PRISM A glass block with flat sides in which light rays are reflected from the inner surfaces.

PROCESSOR The unit in a digital machine that processes data in accordance with the instructions of a program.

PROGRAM A set of instructions that causes a digital machine to perform a particular task. The instructions are in binary code.

PROPELLANT The liquid in a spray can or aerosol can which produces pressure that creates the spray, or the fuel of a rocket engine.

PROTON One of two kinds of particles that make up the nucleus of an atom. The other kind is the neutron. A proton has almost 2,000 times the mass of an electron and has a positive electric charge. The number of protons in the nucleus defines the identity of an element. Hydrogen, for example, has one proton per nucleus, while oxygen has eight.

P-TYPE SEMICONDUCTOR A kind of semiconductor that has been treated to produce holes (spaces for electrons). It tends to gain electrons and thus acquire a negative charge.

PULLEY A wheel over which a rope, chain or belt passes.

PULSE A short burst of electric current.

RACK A toothed shaft that intermeshes with a pinion.

RADIATION The electromagnetic rays that come from any source of heat, or the rays and streams of particles that come from nuclear reactions and radioactive materials. Heat rays are harmless (unless they burn), but nuclear radiation can be highly damaging to living cells.

RADIATOR The part of a car engine which removes heat from the cooling water that circulates through the engine; also a heater that warms a room by radiating (emitting) heat rays.

RADIOACTIVITY The production of radiation by materials containing atoms with unstable nuclei, such as nuclear fallout and the waste from nuclear reactors.

RADIO WAVES Invisible electromagnetic waves with wavelengths ranging from a millimetre to several kilometres. Radio waves used for radar have wavelengths of several millimetres or centimetres, shorter than the waves used for broadcasting sound radio and television.

RAM In mechanical machines, such as an excavator, a device that exerts a strong pushing or pulling force. In digital machines, random-access memory – a memory unit in which programs and data are held temporarily and can be changed.

RATCHET A device that allows movement in one direction but not in the other. A ratchet has a toothed shaft or wheel on which a pawl rests. The pawl is pivoted so that it can move over the teeth of the ratchet in one direction. If the pawl or ratchet moves in the reverse direction, the pawl engages the teeth of the ratchet to prevent movement. A pawl may also move to and fro to turn a ratchet wheel in one direction.

RAY An electromagnetic wave with a short wavelength.

REACTION The equal and opposing force that always accompanies the action of a force (see *ACTION AND REACTION*). Also, in chemistry, the process by which one or more substances change to become different substances. Chemical reactions often involve the production or consumption of heat. In chemical reactions, the atoms involved recombine in different configurations but do not themselves change. In nuclear reactions, the central nuclei of the atoms do change, producing new elements and emitting energy in the form of heat or radiation.

RECIPROCATING MOTION Movement in which an object moves repeatedly forwards and backwards.

REFLECTION The reversal of direction that occurs when a wave or ray bounces off a surface. Internal reflection occurs if light rays reflect from the inner surface of a transparent material.

REFRACTION The bending of a wave or ray that occurs as it passes from one medium or substance into another, for example from air into glass.

RESISTANCE In mechanical machines, a force that slows the movement of an object, such as air resistance and water resistance, and the resistance of a material to cutting or breaking. In electricity, the property of an object, measured in ohms, that obstructs the flow of electrons through it.

RESONANCE The production of vibrations or sound at a certain natural frequency in an object when it is struck by external vibrations or sound waves.

REVOLUTION One complete turn of a rotating object.

ROM Read-only memory. A memory unit in digital machines in which programs and data are stored permanently and cannot be changed.

ROTARY MOTION Movement in which an object spins around.

SCALE A set of units or an indicator marked with units for measuring. A weighing machine is also known as a scale or scales.

SCANNING The conversion of an image into a sequence of electric signals. Scanning splits up the image into a series of horizontal lines and converts the various levels of brightness and colours in each line into signals. Also the process in which a microchip in a keyboard or keypad continually sends a signal to all the keys to detect when one is pressed.

SCREW A shaft with a helical thread or groove that turns either to move itself, or to move an object or material surrounding it.

SECONDARY COLOUR A colour formed by mixing two primary colours.

SEMICONDUCTOR A substance, such as silicon, whose electrical properties can be precisely controlled to regulate the flow of electrons and handle electric signals.

SHAFT A bar or rod that moves or turns to transmit motion in a machine. Also a deep hole, as in a lift shaft.

SOFTWARE In general, the programs that make digital machines carry out tasks.

SOLAR CELL A device that converts light into electricity.

SOUND WAVE Waves of pressure that travel through air and other materials. At frequencies from about 20 hertz up to 20,000 hertz, we can hear these waves as sound.

SPEED The rate at which something moves. Also a combination of gear wheels.

SPROCKET A toothed wheel over which a chain passes.

STATIC ELECTRICITY Electric charge produced by the movement of electrons into or out of an object.

STEREOPHONIC SOUND Sound reproduced by two loudspeakers or earphones in which the sound sources, such as voices or instruments, are in different positions.

STEREOSCOPIC IMAGE An image with depth. This kind of image is formed by a pair of images of an object or scene seen separately by both eyes.

SUBTRACTIVE COLOUR MIXING Combining dyes or pigments of the three secondary colours of light (yellow, cyan, and magenta) to produce all other colours. These colours mix by absorbing primary colours from the light illuminating the dyes or pigments.

SUN WHEEL A gear wheel around which a planet wheel rotates.

SUPERCONDUCTIVITY The removal of electrical resistance in a conductor by cooling it. The conductor can then pass a very large electric current and generate a strong magnetic field.

SUPERSONIC Faster than the speed of sound, which is about 1200km/h (760mph) at sea level.

TENSION The force produced in a bar or a rope or string when it is stretched.

TERMINAL The part of an electric machine to which a wire is connected to take or supply electric current. Also an input unit or output unit at a distance from the central computer of a large digital system, such as a cash card terminal in a shop.

THREAD The helical groove around a screw or inside a nut.

THRUST A force that moves something forwards.

THRUSTER A propeller used for manoeuvring a ship or submersible; also a small rocket engine or gas jet used for manoeuvring a spacecraft.

TRANSFORMER A device that increases or decreases the voltage of an electric current.

TRANSISTOR An electronic component made of sections of n-type and p-type semiconductor that switches a current on or off, or amplifies the current. A controlling signal goes to the central section (the base or gate), which controls the flow of current through two outer sections (the emitter or source, and the collector or drain).

TURBINE A machine with blades that are turned by the movement of a liquid or gas such as air, steam, or water. The turbine may also turn to move the liquid or gas.

ULTRAVIOLET LIGHT Invisible electromagnetic waves with a wavelength less than that of light and ranging from 5 billionths to 4 ten-millionths of a metre.

VALVE A device that opens or closes to control the flow of a liquid or gas through a pipe. Valves often work one way and seal a container so that a liquid or gas can only enter it and not escape.

VAPOUR See *EVAPORATION*.

VOLTAGE The force, measured in volts, with which a source of electric current or charge moves electrons.

WATT The unit of power. One watt is produced when a current of one amp from a source of one volt flows for one second.

WAVE A flow of energy in which the level of energy regularly increases and decreases, like the height of a passing water wave. One complete wave is the amount of flow between one maximum of energy and the next. This distance is the wavelength.

WAVELENGTH See *WAVE*.

WEB SITE A set of pages (screen displays) of information stored in a computer that can be freely accessed by any other computer. Web sites contain information about people and organizations, and may offer services.

WEDGE A part of a machine with a sloping side that moves to exert force.

WEIGHT The force with which gravity pulls on an object.

WHEEL Any circular rotating part in a machine.

WHEEL AND AXLE A class of rotating machines or devices in which effort applied to one part produces a useful movement at another part.

WINCH A drum around which a rope is wound to pull, lift, or lower an object.

WORLD WIDE WEB The many different web sites that exist around the world.

WORM A screw that intermeshes with a gear wheel.

X-RAYS Invisible electromagnetic waves with wavelengths shorter than light and ranging from 5 billionths to 6 million-millionths of a metre.

INDEX

A

accelerometer, 293
action and reaction, 100, 101, 106, 118, 162
address bus, 344
aerial, television, 246
aerofoil, 100, 103, 106, 107, 114, 119, 378
aerosol, 138
Agricola, 376
aileron, 108, 109, 112-13
air: barometer, 134
flight, 106-18
floating, 104-5
pneumatic machines, 126-7
pressure, 120, 127, 379
suction, 130
air bag, 292-3
air cleaner, 262
air conditioner, 153
air hammer, 127
aircraft, 108-11
artificial horizon, 77
autopilot, 291, 293
flight, 106, 108-9
flight simulator, 363
history, 378
jet engine, 160-1, 380
jumpjet, 118
radar, 300-1
airline computer, 370-1
airliner, 111, 112-13
airport detector, 303
airship, 104
alarm systems, 277, 291, 295, 305
alcohol, breath tester, 294
Alhazen, 382
alphanumeric display, 359
alternating current, 267, 281
Ampère, André-Marie, 386
amplifier, 226-7, 228, 234, 235, 239
amplitude modulation (AM), 238, 239
analog-digital converter (ADC), 320, 322, 325
analog recording, 231, 232
anchor escapement, 42
aneroid barometer, 134
anti-roll bar, 81
aqualung, 131, 379
Archimedes, 374, 376, 378
Armstrong, W.G., 387
artificial horizon, 77
astronomy: radio telescope, 385
satellites, 249
space probes, 252-3
telescopes, 188-9, 250-1, 382
atom bomb, 168, 381
atoms, 150, 166, 167, 180, 194, 258
augers, 66-9
automatic door, 305
automatic machines, 257, 291, 389

B

automatic transmission, car, 306-9, 388
autopilot, 291, 293
axe, 14
axles, 30-3, 70, 375

Babbage, Charles, 388-9
baggage scanner, 297
Bain, Alexander, 389
Baird, John Logie, 385
balance, weighing machine, 19, 22, 24
ball bearings, 88
ball-point pen, 141
ballast tanks, 96, 97
balloon, 94, 105, 378
bar code, 329, 334
Bardeen, John, 389
barometer, 134
Barron, Robert, 374
Bartolommeo, Cristofori, 375
bathroom scales, 24
batteries, 259, 268-9, 386
beam scales, 22
bearings, 377
Becquerel, Henri, 382
Bell, Alexander Graham, 384
bell, electric, 278
belts, 36-7, 375
Benz, Karl, 376, 380
Berliner, Emile, 384
Bernoulli, Daniel, 378
Bessemer, Henry, 380
bevel gears, 37, 44, 45, 66
bicycle, 28-9, 38, 70, 377
Big Bang, 249
bimetal thermostat, 154
binary numbers, 315, 388
binoculars, 190, 382
bits: making, 315-26
processing, 340-5
sending, 348-53
storing, 329-37
using, 357-71
blast furnace, 148-9, 380
Blattner, Louis, 384
block and tackle, 57
boats, 94-5, 98-101, 103, 119, 378
body scanner, 304
bomb, nuclear, 168, 381
bookbinding, 216-17
Boole, George, 388
Booth, Hubert, 384
bottle opener, 22
Bourdon gauge, 134
bow thruster, 98
brace and bit, 32, 66
brakes: bicycle, 28-9
car, 86
hydraulic, 127, 128
power, 127
Brattain, Walter, 389
breath tester, 294
buoyancy, 96, 97, 104
burglar alarm, 277, 291, 305
burner, hot-air balloon, 105
burning, 146-7, 164
buses, computer, 344

C

Bushnell, David, 378
button battery, 268
byte, 330

Cahill, Thaddeus, 388
calculator, 388
calibrating plate, scales, 25
camcorder, 243
camera, 383
camcorder, 243
colour photography, 202-3
digital still camera, 326, 332
electronic flash, 180
film, 198-9
instant, 204, 383
lenses, 186
movie, 206, 383
single-lens reflex, 200-1, 383
television, 242
cams, 48-53, 376
can opener, 15, 374
candle, 180
canoe, 378
capacitor microphone, 224
capillary action, 141
carburettor, 140-1
Carlson, Chester, 386
carrier signal, radio, 238, 239, 240
cars: air bag, 292-3
automatic transmission, 306-9, 388
battery, 269
brakes, 86, 127, 128
carburettor, 140-1
clams and cranks, 49-51
clutch, 84-5
cooling system, 125, 152-3, 154
cruise control, 309
differential, 40, 45
electric horn, 279
engine, 156-7
gearbox, 308-9
ignition system, 288-9
immobilizer, 332
lubrication, 88
oil pump, 124
seat belt, 75
speedometer, 46
starter motor, 73
steering, 43, 129
suspension, 80-1
synchromesh, 85
temperature gauge, 270
thermostat, 154
tyre, 83
window winder, 39
windscreen wiper, 49
cash machine, 316, 332, 352, 365
Cassegrain focus, 188, 189, 251
Cassini space probe, 253
catalytic converter, 156, 157
cathode, 296
cathode ray tube, 388
Cayley, Sir George, 378
CCD (charge-coupled device),

243, 323, 325, 326
CD-ROM, 330, 337
centrifugal force, 71
centrifugal pump, 125
chain hoist, 56
chain reaction, nuclear fission, 166, 168
charge, electric, 258
Charles, Jacques, 378
chrominance signal, television, 242, 246
circuit, electric, 267
circuit breaker, 286
clocks, 42, 79, 265, 375
clutch, 84-5
COBE (Cosmic Background Explorer) satellite, 249
cochlea, 219
Cockerell, Christopher, 379
coil springs, 78, 80
coils: electromagnetism, 275, 276
transformers, 285
coin tester, 303
colours, 182-3
colour printer, 358
computer screen, 361
photography, 202-3
primary, 182-3, 202, 212
printing, 212-14
scanning, 212-13, 325
secondary, 183
television, 242, 246-7
combine harvester, 68-9, 376
combustion, 146-8, 164
combustion chamber, rocket engine, 163
communications: digital, 348-53
fax machines, 389
satellites, 248-9, 385
space probes, 252-3
telecommunications, 234-41, 384
telescopes, 250-1
commutator, 281
compact disc (CD), 329, 336-7, 389
comparator-register, 320
compass, 77, 276, 387
compressed air, 126-7
compression, sound waves, 218, 224, 227
compressor, 127, 152, 153
Compton, Arthur, 382
computer, 366-7, 388-9
airlines, 370-1
CD-ROM, 337
digital still camera, 326
digital video disc, 337
disk drive, 282-3
e-mail, 350-1
flight simulator, 363
Internet, 350-1, 389
keyboard, 317, 344
magnetic storage, 333-5
memory, 329-37, 342
microchip, 342-3
modem, 344, 349, 352
mouse, 318-19

ACKNOWLEDGMENTS

Research Robert Graham
Jacket Design Mark Richards
Senior Fulfilment Manager
Linda Berrisford
Index Hilary Bird

The editorial and design staff for
THE NEW WAY THINGS WORK
would like to extend their special
thanks to the following for their
help in the preparation of this
book: AS Fire and Rescue
Equipment Ltd; *Autocar*; Bayley
Ladders & Fire Equipment Ltd;
BMW; British National Space
Centre; Canon UK Ltd; Chubb
Alarms and Locks; Dolby; *The
Engineer*; Essex Police Camera
Enforcement Office; Fanuc
Robotics; Fox Talbot; Granada
Business Communications; Hanna
Instruments; IBM; Kodak;
Magellan Systems; Magner;
Mercedes-Benz (UK) Ltd; NASA;
NCR Limited; Nicam; Nova
Weigh; Philips Electronics UK Ltd;
Revere Transducers Europe; Road
Transport Department, Science
Museum, London; The Royal Bank
of Scotland plc; Royal Institute of
Navigation; Satellite Business
Systems Limited; Seiko U.K.
Limited; Sony; Jon Higgins at
Tesco; Neil Chinery at Thomas
Cook; TRW Automotive Occupant
Restraint Systems; Volvo; West
Midlands Police; Williams;
Xerox Limited.